DATE DUE

JAN 0 4 2010		

| Brodart Co. | Cat. # 55 137 001 | Printed in USA |

The USS *Ward*

The USS *Ward*

An Operational History of the Ship That Fired the First American Shot of World War II

RICHARD P. KLOBUCHAR

Forewords by
Kenneth C. Swedberg and Guy E. Thompson

McFarland & Company, Inc., Publishers
Jefferson, North Carolina, and London

LIBRARY OF CONGRESS CATALOGUING-IN-PUBLICATION DATA

Klobuchar, Richard P.
The USS Ward : an operational history of the ship that fired the first
American shot of World War II / Richard P. Klobuchar ; forewords
by Kenneth C. Swedberg and Guy E. Thompson.
p.   cm.
Includes bibliographical references and index.

ISBN 0-7864-2384-6 (illustrated case : 50# alkaline paper)

1. Ward (Destroyer)   2. World War, 1939–1945 — Naval operations,
American.   3. World War, 1939–1945 — Campaigns — Pacific Ocean.
I. Title.
D774.W24K66   2006   940.54'5973 — dc22   2005035204

British Library cataloguing data are available

On the cover: A lookout on the USS *Ward* (National Archives)

Manufactured in the United States of America

*McFarland & Company, Inc., Publishers
Box 611, Jefferson, North Carolina 28640
www.mcfarlandpub.com*

This book is dedicated to all those who served on the USS *Ward,* from its commissioning in 1918 to its final day in 1944. As a destroyer and as an APD this valiant ship, led by bold officers, repeatedly went into harm's way at a time when courage was desperately needed. The ship and its crew helped lead this country into a greatness that exists to this day. Those men, their deeds, and the *Ward* should never be forgotten.

Contents

Acknowledgments   ix
Foreword by Kenneth C. Swedberg   1
Foreword by Guy E. Thompson   3
Preface   5
Introduction   7
Poems by Orville S. Ethier   9

 1. A Fighting Ship Is Born   11
 2. Too Late for War   24
 3. A Ship and Crew Prepare for War   37
 4. *Ward* Goes to Sea   51
 5. First Shot of the War   66
 6. Assault from the Sky   86
 7. A Difficult December   97
 8. Liberty   107
 9. First Year at War   116
10. *Ward* Becomes an APD   133
11. In the South Pacific at Last   141
12. Amphibious Operations Begin   158
13. New Britain and New Guinea   174
14. Leyte   191
15. Destiny's Date Repeated   202
16. Epilogue   217

Appendices   235
Roster of Personnel   243
Chapter Notes   255
Bibliography   259
Index   263

Acknowledgments

When I first considered writing the history of a ship that was built in 1918 and sunk in 1944, I quickly discovered how daunting a task that would be. Sources of information regarding its World War I career, other than deck logs, were almost non-existent and, of course, no surviving crewmen were available.

Information about its World War II career was more readily available and some surviving crewmen could be located, but even that task was difficult. Except for Pearl Harbor, *Ward's* experiences were not followed closely, although she was in combat almost continuously during 1943 and 1944. Uncovering the details of those operations would be a challenge.

In addition, *Ward,* unlike many other World War II era warships, did not have an organization of all former crewmen. Thus, there were no crew rosters with current address listings and no nationwide reunions of former crewmen, items that would be invaluable to an author. Nevertheless, I pushed on.

Ward did have an organization of some former crewmen. This was comprised of members of the 47th Division Naval Reserve of St. Paul, Minnesota, who made up the bulk of the ship's first crew after its recommissioning in January 1941. A core of this group returned to St. Paul after the war and formed an organization, First Shot Naval Vets of St. Paul, which still exists and holds annual reunions.

I commenced my search for information on *Ward* there, not yet convinced that I should pursue a ship's history. After talking with several of the men individually and collectively, I discovered a story so compelling that I decided that I would attempt to put it into print for them. The book was thus born.

I am indebted to the First Shot Naval Vets of St. Paul for their assistance throughout the research process in providing organization rosters, open invitations to annual reunions and monthly breakfast meetings, and access to the organization's scrapbooks and other files, including photos. They also gave me rights to use material from their excellent pictorial book, USS Ward *Fires First Shot WW II.* As president of the First Shot Vets, Orville Ethier was custodian of the group's archives. His wife, Pat, a former librarian and member of the WAVES during World War II, was a storehouse of information on *Ward's* exploits and former crewmen.

I am also grateful to Ken and Donna Swedberg of the First Shot Vets. Ken, who took over as president when Orville died, was one of the founders. He and Donna provided considerable information and photographs and edited much of the manuscript. Ken also provided his impression of his days on *Ward* in the book's Foreword.

My thanks go out to those former crewmen of *Ward* who gave freely of their time to describe their experiences, either through face-to-face interviews, mailed questionnaires, or during various meetings or reunions. Collectively these permitted me to inject a human element into what would otherwise be simply a story of a ship. A list of these men is included in the bibliography.

I am especially indebted to Guy Thompson, former ensign and boat officer of *Ward*, who went on to a fine naval career following *Ward's* sinking. I leaned heavily on Guy for his recollections of *Ward's* final landings in the Philippines, her loss to a kamikaze, and many technical details of the ship's operations. I am also grateful to him for the use of several never-before-seen photographs, his review of the manuscript, and his excellent foreword.

I owe a debt of thanks to Will Lehner, one of the few crewmen to serve on the *Ward* for the entire period from her recommissioning in January 1941 to her loss in December 1944. Will freely gave of his time to review the manuscript and offered valuable suggestions.

My thanks also go out to Byron Baldwin, son of Lt. (jg) Russell Baldwin, James Morgan, son of David Morgan, for volunteering information and photographs of their fathers, both *Ward* crewmen; to Dorothy Hughes, for providing information and photos of her deceased husband, Fred, also a former crewman; and to Bernard Jungkind, Jr. for allowing use of several photographs taken by his father, an officer on *Ward* in 1944 and at the time of her sinking.

For historical data so critical to creating a ship's history, I am indebted to the many people responsible for maintaining our country's historical records. Foremost among these are the dedicated staffs of the National Archives and Records Administration's excellent facilities in Washington, D.C., and College Park, Maryland. They went "above and beyond" in their patience and assistance to ensure that I found the records and photographs I sought. I am also grateful to the staff of the Naval Historical Center in Washington, D.C., for assistance in obtaining information and photographs and to the staff of the Minnesota Historical Society for their assistance.

I am greatly indebted to operations director and chief pilot Terry Kerby, data department manager Rachel Shackelford and others at the Hawaii Undersea Research Laboratory of the National Oceanic and Atmospheric Administration at the University of Hawaii. Terry provided detailed background information and in-depth reports of the August 28, 2002, discovery of the midget sunk by *Ward* on December 7, 1941. Rachel assisted in providing underwater photos of the midget submarine and other photos and arranged for a review of parts of the manuscript. Their cooperation was also "above and beyond."

I am indebted to a number of individuals who assisted in the completion of the manuscript. Ken Hackler, a renowned historian on Pearl Harbor, provided many little-known details and sketches of *Ward's* encounter with the midget sub as well as information on the entire Pearl Harbor episode. He also reviewed portions of the manuscript. Tracy White, a noted *Ward* historian and owner of an excellent web site on the *Ward*, devoted considerable time to providing information not otherwise available to me. He also reviewed the entire manuscript and prepared a front cover design and several original sketches of the *Ward* used in the book.

I am grateful to Todd Mueller, a friend, who took time from his busy schedule to provide technical assistance on the intricacies of the word processor, scanning photos, and preparing the final manuscript. His continuing help was critical to completing this book.

My deep thanks to Ed Jackson, another friend and professional editor, who edited the manuscript and gave other valuable literary advice. His work was vital to the finished product. Maps and charts were prepared by Bill Timmerman, friend and former co-worker whose expertise in this area added a valuable ingredient to the book. Finally, my thanks go out to Marlene Horsman for her valuable assistance in the research phase of the book.

Preparation of this book was a rewarding experience. Everyone I approached for information or assistance was as eager as I to reveal the full story of *Ward,* and all gave freely of their time to that end. This book is the result of their collective efforts.

Foreword

By Kenneth C. Swedberg

On Wednesday, January 29, 1941, I was one of 82 naval reservists from St. Paul, Minnesota, who saw the USS *Ward* (DD-139) for the first time. She was tied up at a dock at the destroyer base at San Diego. We had expected to see a freshly painted, clean ship ready for sea duty. To our dismay, this was not the case.

Ward had just come from her 19-year sleep in "red lead row," the last of the many famous four-stackers removed from storage for recommissioning. Workmen were swarming over her and the St. Paul sailors quickly joined them. Below decks, our firemen turned to and cleaned up machinery, bilges, and berthing areas. Topside, our seamen faced the tedious task of scraping and chipping years of accumulated dirt, rust, and paint, and then repainting everything.

Ward was in terrible shape. She had been subjected to "midnight requisitions" for all the four-stackers reconditioned ahead of her and was missing much of her vital machinery and equipment. Being the last destroyer to be recommissioned, her crew had no other ships to "borrow" from. The navy was forced to provide the *Ward* with new motors, pumps, and other missing equipment. To our delight we now found ourselves receiving a ship that was in much better condition than most other four-stackers.

On February 6, after eight days of eating and living in off-ship housing, we finally moved aboard the *Ward*. On February 10 we put to sea for the first sea trials, and all ship systems functioned well. On February 28 we left the mainland to embark on a great adventure.

Our first experience at sea was almost a catastrophe as a major Pacific storm hit us just as we passed under the Golden Gate Bridge and followed us for days. Since the galley was topside our mess cooks literally risked their lives to bring food down to the crew compartments without being swept overboard. Despite temperatures in the firerooms reaching 124 degrees and 90 percent of the crew seasick, we somehow managed to survive the ordeal. On March 9 we reached Pearl Harbor and began our new life as sailors.

As with other small warships, most of the *Ward* crewmen knew each other by name. Men who stood watch or worked together were usually granted liberty as a group. They became close, bonded quickly, and had few secrets between them.

However, not all crewmen were close, even on a ship with a complement of only 125 men. The routine of daily watches prevented some men from associating with others. *Ward's* forward and after crew compartments were not connected below decks but separated by the boiler and engine rooms. Generally, the deck and bridge crews were berthed in the forward compartment while the boiler and engine room crew slept and ate in the after compartment. This made socializing even more difficult.

Thus, after we left the mainland it was not possible for me to know the happenings of every crewman, even some close friends with whom I had shared months of reserve duty in St. Paul. When I was asked to review this book I learned for the first time of some of the stories and experiences of shipmates I had known for many years. Except for this book, those stories would have remained hidden from me forever.

This book is a must-read for all *Ward* crewmen who will learn, as I did, of some of their shipmate's stories. It will also bring them up to date on the accomplishments of the *Ward* after they left the ship for other assignments. Every reader will discover the full story of the *Ward* in this exciting book.

Kenneth C. Swedberg
WT2c, USS *Ward* (DD-139/APD-16), 1941–1943
WT1c, USS *Salt Lake City* (CA-25), 1943–1945

Foreword

By Guy E. Thompson

When we picture USS *Ward*, whether as a destroyer or as an auxiliary personnel destroyer, in our mind's eye it should be more than a mass of steel, weapons, and engines. One ship's physical entity is much like that of any other ship of the same class. Yet, that entity no more defines the ship than a compilation of limbs and organs defines a human being. When we speak of a ship, it is of the ship's company that we really speak.

Ward was blessed with an extraordinary ship's company. Many started with a cohesion born of coming from the same naval reserve division, having the same hometown, and having known one another long before being torn from their homes and civilian lives. Although not all aboard the ship fit that category, a majority did. In the loneliness of war they were, in truth, among relatives. For them there was no anonymity.

Ward was further blessed in her commanding officers. She was particularly fortunate to have, during her most trying months, Frederick W. Lemly as commanding officer. While many men can wear the rank or be assigned to command, few have the art. Lemly was one of those who had honed that art to a fine degree. Sometimes there was loud complaining at his drill-happy ways. Still, equally fervent were the rejoicings when *Ward* served with distinction, as she did, without losing a single man to enemy action.

There are those who claim that *Ward* was a "lucky ship." While it is true that luck played a part, it is equally true that sound training and discipline brought the crew through many perilous events. The mass of steel, weapons, and machinery that was *Ward* achieved some noteworthy ends. But in each case it was the flesh and bones, the initiative and leadership, the spirit and élan which made the accomplishments possible.

From the leadership of Master Shipfitter J.T. Moroney came the record speed with which the ship was built. From the determination and courage of William W. Outerbridge came the decision to fire on the submarine while the nation was still at peace. From the skill of the gun crew came the success in hitting and sinking that submarine. From the leadership of Lemly came the long record of successful landings. From the highly trained state of all hands came the casualty-free loss of *Ward* from a kamikaze hit in Ormoc Bay, Leyte.

All of her accomplishments were those of men. One can say of those men, of that ship's company, of those whose spirit embodied the entity that was *Ward*, that supreme compliment of sailormen: They were man-o-warsmen.

Guy E. Thompson
Ensign USNR, Boat Officer, USS *Ward*, 1944
Lieutenant (jg) USN, Commanding Officer, USS *PCE* 897, 1946–1948

Preface

The hundreds of destroyers that served in the United States Navy during World War II fought gallantly, and 71 of them were lost in combat. They were so versatile that almost no naval operation was conducted without them. Yet, with only a few exceptions, the accomplishments of individual destroyers are not as easily remembered as are those of their larger companions, the battleships, aircraft carriers, and cruisers.

One destroyer that should be legendary in U.S. naval history is the USS *Ward*. This 23-year-old four-stacker, manned largely by a crew of naval reservists on their first tour of duty, gave the United States its first bright spot of World War II. It fired America's first shot of the war and sank a Japanese submarine an hour before the attack on Pearl Harbor began. Sinking an unidentified submarine while our country was still at peace exhibited a boldness that would become a trademark of *Ward's* officers and crew.

Ward's accomplishments did not end there, however. She fought for three more years, participating in almost a score of amphibious landings as a destroyer-transport. She carried thousands of troops to hostile shores and shot down at least nine enemy aircraft before she was sunk by a kamikaze.

Incredibly, her exploits have been virtually hidden for more than 60 years. With the discovery in 2002 of the submarine she sank at Pearl Harbor, it is finally time to reveal the full story of this gallant ship and her extraordinary achievements. This will be the first full-length book to do that.

Ward actually had three separate careers. Built in 1918, it was too late for World War I but did serve for three years before being placed in the reserve fleet. Reactivated in January 1941, *Ward* served two full years as a destroyer based at Pearl Harbor. After conversion to a destroyer-transport in January 1943, *Ward* served continuously in the island-hopping campaign of the South Pacific during 1943 and 1944.

Each of her careers is related chronologically. Chapters 1 and 2 describe her building and post-World War I duty; Chapters 3 to 9 detail her activation and service in 1941 and 1942, and Chapters 10 to 15 chronicle her last career, this time as a destroyer-transport. A final chapter describes the events occurring subsequent to World War II that kept the saga of the *Ward* alive for the past 61 years.

Telling the full story of a ship built 87 years ago and sunk 26 years later is an intimidating task. It required the examination of more than 4500 pages of archival reports containing the daily deck logs for the entire life of *Ward*, from its building to its sinking; war diary and action reports for every major naval engagement in which it participated; monthly muster rolls containing the ship's crew list; and various other naval documents. These provided the official and factual framework of *Ward's* life.

This was supplemented by scrutiny of 35 published sources providing additional information about *Ward's* activities, various newspaper accounts, scrapbooks and files of the organization of former *Ward* crewmen in Minnesota, and information from various governmental agencies in and outside the United States.

The final ingredient, the human side of *Ward's* career, required searching for, meeting, and interviewing every former *Ward* crewman who could be located, questioning several noted naval historians, and reviewing personal letters of several former *Ward* commanding officers.

Among the book's appendices is a complete roster of all officers and men who served on *Ward* from 1941 to 1944. Painstakingly compiled from deck logs and muster rolls, this may well be the only such ship's roster in existence. It is for the men on this roster that this book was written and it is my sincere hope that I have told their story well.

Introduction

This is the extraordinary tale of two ships with a common hull. Their collective lives spanned 26 years. Both ships received recognition for outstanding deeds performed under enemy fire. The destroyer USS *Ward* (DD-139) had the distinction of firing the first shot and sinking the first ship of America's war with Japan in 1941. *Ward* earned a battle star for this action at Pearl Harbor, which occurred while the two nations were still at peace.

After conversion to an attack transport in January 1943, *Ward,* now APD-16, participated in 16 amphibious landings in the South Pacific, many on hostile shores, and shot down a number of attacking aircraft. She earned eight more battle stars for these actions. She had just completed her sixteenth landing at Ormoc Bay in the Philippines in December 1944 when her luck finally ran out. A kamikaze bomber, one of three which dove at her simultaneously, crashed into her port side, starting fires which could not be extinguished. She had to be sunk by another U.S. ship.

The *Ward* was built in 1918, one of 267 similar ships designed to combat the German submarine menace. These destroyers were universally referred to as "four-pipers," "four-stackers," or "flush-deckers" for their distinctive appearance, having a flush deck and four evenly spaced smokestacks. Most of these joined the fleet too late to participate in the war for which they were constructed.

Following World War I, many of the earlier four-stackers were scrapped, but more than 200 of them were placed in the navy's reserve fleet in San Diego, Philadelphia, and other locations, awaiting a call for their services again.

For many of them that call came in 1940. When Japanese expansion in the Pacific in the late 1930s made a war more probable in that theater, it forced the United States to expand its fleet. In addition to accelerating new ship construction, the United States drew on its Reserve Fleet to quickly build up its destroyer force. From 1939 to 1941, the United States activated 80 four-stackers for immediate service. *Ward* was one of the 80 and was commissioned into the fleet on January 15, 1941.

No fighting ship was more steeped in irony during World War II than *Ward.* Her combat life lasted exactly three years to the day, beginning on December 7, 1941, and ending on December 7, 1944. Although she was strafed, bombed, shelled, and crashed by a kamikaze during her three years of fighting, she did not lose a single crewman or suffer any seriously wounded men as a result of hostile action. This outstanding feat may not have been matched by any other combat ship of any navy in World War II.

For 61 years, skeptics, including some high-ranking U.S. navy officers, expressed doubts over *Ward's* claims that it sank a Japanese midget submarine at Pearl Harbor an hour before the air raid on December 7, 1941. They were convinced that *Ward's* crew, like others that day, exaggerated the results of their actions. Through the years, surviving *Ward* crewmen told the story of their attack on the sub without benefit of corroborating evidence or facts, but convinced in their own minds of what they had seen and done.

On August 28, 2002, all doubt was erased. An underwater research vehicle of the Hawaii Undersea Research Lab discovered and photographed a midget submarine on the ocean floor in 1200 feet of water. The sub was found off the mouth of the Pearl Harbor channel near the location of *Ward's* encounter with a midget sub on December 7, 1941. The sub had a shell hole at the base of its conning tower, the exact spot at which *Ward's* gun crew said they hit it 61 years earlier. Now there could be no further doubt. The rest of the world was convinced of what *Ward's* crew had already known.

The Pearl Harbor episode, however, occupied only two hours of the combat life of *Ward*. For the following three years she gallantly carried the fight to the enemy on island after island, and with little fanfare.

Some crewmen remained on *Ward* for the entire war and experienced her final days. For these men, losing their home of almost four years was extremely painful. The bond between seamen and ship was especially strong on *Ward,* where many of the crew were activated as a unit and trained together even before the war began. It was instrumental in carrying this fighting ship and her crew throughout the South Pacific for three years without losing a man in combat.

For more than 60 years the real story of this gallant ship has largely remained buried in the archives and the hearts of the men who sailed her. With the discovery of the midget sub off Pearl Harbor, the world now knows what she did for two hours on December 7, 1941. It is finally time to reveal the entire story of the little ship with two faces and three lives. That story deserves to be told.

Poems by Orville S. Ethier*

Your Far Off Sons†

We, your far off Navy sons,
Know of your worries and your fears.
We realize we are the ones,
For whom you prayed throughout the years.

We only hope and also pray,
Your prayers are not in vain.
And on some not too distant day,
We will sail home to you again.

The APDs‡

Anchored in a moonlit bay,
Awaiting further orders,
Side by side, at ease they lay,
The fast transport destroyers.

Veterans of our global war,
They carry fighting Yanks.
Their troops are first to reach the shore
And face the yellow ranks.

Together with the LCIs
And the chubby LSTs,
They bask beneath the southern skies
And sail the tropic seas.

Whenever there's an isle to take,
The APDs are ready.
But Admiral, for heaven's sake,
Don't make their work so steady.

---

*Orville Ethier, 82, died on April 20, 2004, after contributing to the development of this book. †Orville S. Ethier, F2c, USS Ward, DD-139; written aboard the USS Ward at Pearl Harbor after the attack of December 7, 1941. ‡Orville S. Ethier, MM1/c, USS Ward, APD-16; written aboard the USS Ward in Purvis Bay, Solomon Islands, December 1943.

CHAPTER 1

A Fighting Ship Is Born

Even in the waning darkness of the approaching dawn, it was evident that the ship was on a mission. Men were barely visible at their watch stations on deck but all were giving full attention to their duties. Lookouts on the bridge peered intently through binoculars trying to penetrate the morning mist hanging low just above the rippling water surface. The ship showed no lights but it was common knowledge that it was out there.

Below deck, most of the crew was still in their bunks. Some sought the sleep that was so elusive in the oppressive heat of the interior of a ship that lacked air-conditioning. Others were manning their watch stations in the engine rooms, boiler rooms, or other spaces critical to keeping the ship moving and alert.

The ship was capable of reaching 28 knots if she was in a hurry, but on this mission she was doing only half of that. This was to ensure that her underwater detection gear would operate effectively. At 15 knots she could still cover her entire patrol area quickly enough to detect any ship attempting to evade, her whether it was on or below the water surface. On this mission she covered her area through a continuous series of figure eights several miles off the mouth of the channel entrance to the most important U.S. naval base in the Pacific Ocean.

Her mission was to allow no ship to enter the harbor unless she first identified it. If an unauthorized foreign ship attempted to enter the harbor, her standing orders were to prevent the ship from entering the harbor, by force if necessary. That included sinking it. She also kept all fishing boats, sight-seeing craft, and other civilian boats, large or small, out of the patrol area, again by force if needed.

Of particular interest to her were submarines. All U.S. submarines were ordered to enter or leave the harbor on the surface so they could be identified and escorted by another U.S. patrolling destroyer, to prevent being mistaken for a foreign submarine. Any submerged submarine detected within the patrol area was therefore assumed to be foreign and was attacked if it did not surface to be identified. The ship was authorized to use all of its weapons to accomplish this.

Such specific orders were common to ships on patrol during wartime. On this gray morning, however, this ship was not at war. Its country gave it wartime orders while it was still at peace, a measure of the importance of its mission.

The immensity of the responsibility for protecting America's principal Pacific naval base cannot be overstated. At any given time, the base held up to 100 of the country's most important combat ships, including three of its precious six aircraft carriers. The importance of the base can be seen by the protective ring of three airfields strategically located to provide a shield of airpower surrounding it. These included separate fields operated by the U.S. navy, marines, and army. Three additional airfields were located within 15 miles of the naval base.

The ship given the responsibility of guarding the harbor entrance this particular morn-

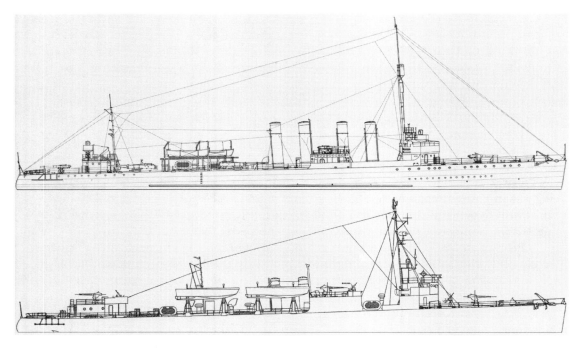

USS *Ward* in two different roles — *Top,* USS *Ward* as DD-139, 1918–1922, 1941–1942; *bottom,* USS *Ward* as APD-16, 1943–1944. (sketches by Tracy White)

ing and one-fourth of all the mornings was not the largest ship in the U.S. Navy, but was, in fact, one of its smaller ones, a destroyer. Destroyers were traditionally assigned missions such as harbor patrol because of their maneuverability and the array of anti-submarine weapons they carried. Prior to World War II, submarines were the primary threat to ships in or near a harbor.

The naval base this ship was guarding was the huge U.S. facility at Pearl Harbor on the island of Oahu in the Hawaiian Islands. Among the nearly 100 U.S. combat ships based at Pearl Harbor on this day were 10 destroyers, including some of the newest and largest in the U.S. fleet. The destroyer on sentry duty at this most important anchorage was not only one of the smaller ones at Pearl Harbor, but one of the oldest. It was USS *Ward* (DD-139), built in 1918 for use in World War I and already 23 years old.

The fact that it was a destroyer protecting larger ships inside the harbor was an intriguing twist in naval development. Destroyers had their origin in the 1870s, following Robert Whitehead's invention of the self-propelled torpedo. Whitehead, a British engineer working in Fiume, Austria, borrowed a concept from Commander Guiseppe Luppis, a retired Austrian naval officer in 1864.[1] After four years of development and tests, he took his torpedo to England for demonstrations before the Admiralty.[2] Eventually, they accepted the weapon for use in the British navy.

This single development completely revolutionized naval warfare in the latter part of the nineteenth century. Naval powers, led by Great Britain, scrambled to build boats to carry and launch this new weapon. It was not until 1877, however, that Great Britain built a craft to launch the Whitehead torpedo. The boat was the HMS *Lightening,* a 27-ton boat built by Thornycroft, capable of making 19 knots and carrying two torpedoes. It showed so much promise that the Admiralty quickly ordered 19 more of that design.[3]

A proliferation of small, fast torpedo boats quickly followed among the world's navies. These smallest of boats could now seriously threaten the largest of the dreadnaughts and battle-cruisers. Their quickness made them almost immune to the large, but slow and clumsy ships that stocked the navies of the naval powers. Torpedo boats proved so popular that, by 1883, most European navies had between 100 and 300 of these newest weapons. France, Britain's potential enemy, owned 220 of them. Germany had 143 and Russia, 152. Great Britain had built 186 of its own but realized that she was now being threatened by her own invention.[4]

The United States finally joined the race in 1890 with its first torpedo boat. This was the 105-ton *Cushing*, built by Herreshoff Manufacturing Company and which could make 23 knots. It was followed by 13 more in the next six years.[5] Although the U.S. torpedo boat performance was disappointing, it provided U.S. shipbuilders with valuable experience in small boat design and construction. This would be critically important within a few years when larger ships were needed in quantity in a short time.

Another race now began, one to develop a ship to combat the torpedo boat. The race culminated with Great Britain's design of a ship type it referred to as a "torpedo boat destroyer." The ship would be fast enough to match the speed of the torpedo boat and would carry sufficient rapid-firing, small-caliber guns to destroy them. Britain's very first torpedo boat destroyer, HMS *Havock,* commissioned in October 1893, was the world's first destroyer.[6]

The *Havock* could reach a speed of 26 knots, and carried one three-inch and three two-inch guns as well as three of its own torpedoes.[7] In tests, it showed that it could catch and destroy torpedo boats of current designs. Soon destroyers were integrated into fleets around the world.

Again, the United States was a late entry into the development of a new naval weapon. It officially joined the rest of the world on May 4, 1898, when Congress authorized a building program of 16 destroyers of four different designs. Three of these designs would be developed by private builders, the fourth by the U.S. Navy. The shortcomings in the earlier torpedo boat designs would now be addressed and corrected in the design of destroyers.[8]

The United States emerged from the war with Spain in 1898 with a new realization of the importance of destroyers. The Spanish fleet it battled off Santiago, Cuba, included two destroyers. Although both were sunk in the ensuing action, U.S. naval experts recognized that the destroyers, if used correctly, could have influenced the battle's outcome. The navy was ordered to accelerate its destroyer program.

The United States adopted some British design features, with modifications, and commenced building its first group of destroyers in 1899. This was the Bainbridge class of nine ships which was to be followed by seven more of similar design. Although the USS *Bainbridge* was to be the first ship of this class and given the hull number of DD-1, the USS *Decatur* (DD-5), was actually completed first. It had the honor of being the very first destroyer commissioned into the United States navy, joining the fleet on May 19, 1902. The *Bainbridge* itself was commissioned into the fleet on November 24, 1902.[9]

These 16 destroyers (DD-1 to DD-16) were quite modest in size at 250 feet in length and 420 tons in displacement. They carried two 3"/50 caliber guns, several smaller guns, two 18-inch torpedo tubes, and were manned by a crew of 75. With their 29-knot speed, they were capable of catching and destroying any torpedo boat in the world.[10] The Bainbridge ships were considered a "wet' ship and even moderate seas would spray over their decks. Nevertheless, these ships were arguably best of the pre-World War I destroyers.

The Bainbridge class of destroyers ushered the U.S. Navy into the Twentieth Century with a gigantic shove. Ironically, they were built for fighting but they never fired a shot in anger in World War I. They served a role more important than combat, however. As prototypes of the world's most versatile ships of the future, they served as testing beds for destroyer design, weaponry, propulsion systems, and other marine equipment. Their contributions were soon showing up in newer destroyer designs.

These initial 16 destroyers were all completed and commissioned into service by 1904. The navy continued to improve on them when Congress authorized five additional destroyers of the Smith class (DD-17 to DD-21) in 1906 and 1907 and 21 more of the Paulding class, (DD-22 to DD-42) in 1908 and 1910. These two classes were significantly larger than the Bainbridge designs, at 700 and 742 tons respectively.[11]

Major improvements were incorporated into the classes in propulsion, armaments, and other features. The Paulding class was the first U.S. destroyer design to include oil-fired rather than coal-fired boilers. These classes also saw the emergence of the destroyer as a legitimate fleet combat ship as both packed more and larger weapons. Both carried five 3"/50 caliber guns and three twin 18-inch torpedo tubes. All 26 were commissioned by 1912 and the fleet now boasted 42 destroyers.

Although U.S. destroyers were among the best in the world, efforts to improve them continued. Lessons learned from Smith and Paulding classes spawned the design of the next generation of destroyers. With the shadow of war hanging over Europe, the U.S. Navy sought to bring its destroyer fleet to a state of readiness with even newer concepts in ship design. The navy's General Board determined that the primary role of the destroyer in the future would be to protect the line of battleships with torpedoes and gunfire. Destroyers would therefore be required to match the battleships not only in speed but cruising range. Anti-submarine capability was not yet seen as a mission for destroyers and thus did not influence early destroyer designs.

Congress authorized eight ships of the new Cassin class (DD-43 to DD-50) on March 4, 1911, and six ships of the O'Brien class (DD-51 to DD-56) on March 4, 1913. These were the first of the "Thousand Tonners" which would be involved in combat in the war, which was sure to come. Eleven more destroyers of the Tucker and Sampson classes, authorized the following year (DD-57 to DD-67), completed this newest design grouping.[12]

The Thousand Tonners were impressive ships. They now carried four 4"/50 caliber guns as a main battery and eight 21-inch torpedo tubes in mounts of two. The additional fuel capacity, armament, and other features pushed the latest designs to 315 feet in length and 1100 tons displacement. Sixteen of these ships joined the fleet by 1916. Additional classes authorized in 1916 would carry twelve 21-inch torpedo tubes.

With the advent of war between Germany and the Allied powers in 1914, the Atlantic Ocean quickly became a deadly battleground between German submarines and British shipping. The inevitable occurred when the submarines sank ships carrying American passengers. Sinking of neutral ships, including American, rose steadily and could no longer be ignored. Finally, on April 6, 1917, despite the national sentiment towards isolationism, the United States declared war on Germany and the Central Powers.

In recognition of the threat that submarines posed, the U.S. Navy now declared that depth charges be added to a destroyer's weaponry. Initially two depth charge tracks were constructed on the ship's stern.[13] Later some destroyers were also fitted with one or more 'Y' gun depth charge projectors. Earlier destroyer designs did not include any underwater detection gear, however. "Fighting submarines" was now added to the role of destroyers.

The most urgent British need was assistance in combating submarines that threatened to isolate England and starve the country's island. By April 24, six U.S. destroyers were on their way to England, and within three months 28 more were dispatched. U.S. Admiral Sims overcame British reluctance and convinced the Admiralty to reinstate the convoy system, which they had earlier abandoned as being ineffective.[14]

Merchant ship losses began to decrease immediately as American destroyers were successful in damaging and driving off many submarines from the convoys. Technology still favored the submarines. It was difficult to locate submerged submarines, attack them, and confirm an actual submarine sinking. The intensity of the struggle increased and, on October 15, the USS *Cassin* took a torpedo in the stern. Quick efforts to save the ship were successful and it returned to a British port for repairs. On November 17, 1917, U.S. destroyers *Fanning* and *Nicholson* forced submarine *U-58* to the surface with depth charges, after which her own crew scuttled it.[15]

The submarines exacted revenge three weeks later when on December 6, the *U-53* sank the USS *Jacob Jones* in the English Channel. The destroyer sank in eight minutes with a loss of 64 crewmen. To the amazement of the survivors, the *U-53* surfaced after the sinking, gave them food and water, and radioed their location to Allied authorities. To verify their success, the submarine also took two of the crewmen with them as prisoners.[16]

Before World War I ended on November 11, 1918, a total of 80 U.S. destroyers, on duty in the Atlantic, had an extraordinary impact on the war. They escorted convoys carrying more than two million men to Europe without the loss of a single man or ship. In more than 300 encounters with submarines, they lost only the *Jacob Jones* while bringing security to the convoy system and convincing the British that the system was feasible. They developed techniques for locating and combating submarines that would be used again 20 years later. The versatility exhibited by U.S. destroyers in World War I would make these little ships the workhorse of future fleets.

During 1917 and 1918, U.S. shipyards had difficulty meeting the navy's demands for new destroyer construction as the Atlantic war increased in ferocity. The conventional design of the first 67 destroyers incorporating a raised forecastle was now replaced with a new flush deck design. In the new design, the entire deck from bow to stern would be at a single level, giving the ships greater longitudinal stiffness and strength. The design soon acquired several names by which they would be forever called — "flush deckers," "four stackers," or "four pipers."

The terms are not completely interchangeable, however, as some of the earlier designs had four stacks but not flush decks. Thus, all of the flush deckers had four stacks but not all of the four pipers had flush decks.

After some experimental design developments in the USS *Shaw*, six flush deck destroyers of the Caldwell class (DD-69 to DD-74) were authorized on March 15, 1915, to test various types of machinery and propulsion systems. These would be the guinea pigs for the mass production of destroyers for World War I that was soon to begin.[17]

Destroyer production began in earnest with the passage of the Naval Appropriations Act of 1916, which called for ..."the United States to have a navy second to none." Included in the authorization were 10 battleships, six battle-cruisers, 10 light cruisers, 72 submarines, 14 auxiliary ships, and 50 destroyers (DD-75 to DD-124) capable of operating with larger ships. Since cruisers were designed to achieve 35 knots, these destroyers were mandated to have a 35-knot maximum speed as well.[18]

An act of Congress of March 3, 1917, created a Naval Emergency Fund for "such additional torpedo boat destroyers ... as the President may direct." With this additional authority, the navy authorized eleven more destroyers. Thus, by the end of May 1917, contracts for 61 destroyers (DD-75 to DD-135) had been awarded. Later authorizations in 1917 and 1918 provided for 224 additional new destroyers (DD-136 to DD-359). This huge program would give the United States a formidable response to the German submarines if the war lasted long enough. Of these authorizations, all but six of the ships were actually constructed. Destroyers DD-200 to DD-205 were subsequently cancelled.[19]

The requirement for a 35-knot destroyer complicated the design. Designers calculated that achieving a 35-knot speed would require 50 percent more power than that needed to produce a 30-knot speed. In order to meet this requirement, 100 tons of additional equipment and other design changes would have to be made to the Caldwell class.

The first of the new generation of mass-produced flush deck destroyers would be USS *Wickes* and the first 111 built (DD-75 to DD-185) would carry the class name of Wickes. Two almost identical designs by Bath Iron Works and Bethlehem Steel were used. Difficulties arose with the premature deterioration of the Yarrow boilers in the Bethlehem ships, and use of this British boiler design was later discontinued. With an excess of old destroyers on hand in 1930, 60 destroyers built with Yarrow boilers were scrapped rather than replace their boilers.[20] They were replaced with 60 destroyers from the Reserve Fleet. Most shipyards, including the navy yard at Mare Island, California, used the Bath design. All 111 Wickes class ships were completed by the fall of 1919.

Before all Wickes class destroyers were completed, an updated design rolled off the drawing boards. This would be a new Clemson class of 156 ships incorporating a number of minor improvements to the Wickes class. A significant improvement was the 35 percent increase in fuel capacity, to allow for a greater range in order to operate with other fleet ships. The Clemsons were thus somewhat heavier than the Wickes ships. With the exception of nine ships, all Clemson class destroyers would be contracted for construction at private shipyards.

While the Wickes destroyers would prove to be a major improvement over the previous Caldwell class, they did, nevertheless, display several major faults in range, maneuverability, and forecastle design. Wickes ships had difficulty staying with the fleet on long cruises because of low fuel capacity. This was improved in the Clemson design but was not fully resolved for both classes until the 1920s. By that time the navy had developed a procedure for refueling destroyers from other ships while under way.

A narrow V-shaped stern caused the Wickes class ships to "squat," even at moderate speeds, giving them an exceptionally large turning radius. For a submarine hunter this was highly undesirable. Larger rudders installed on the Clemson class did little to address this problem. Their "wet" forward section was also an irritating feature for the crew and would not be solved until later designs incorporated a higher forecastle.

Building 285 new destroyers in a hurry would prove to be a greater hurdle than convincing Congress to authorize them. Besides the three navy shipbuilding yards at Charleston, South Carolina; Norfolk, Virginia; and Mare Island, California; only six private yards were capable of building destroyers. The private yards were already working to near capacity on merchant ships, battleships, battle-cruisers, and scout cruisers. Work on all of these was now suspended to give highest priority to the destroyer program.

Orders went out to the yards in May 1917, and the first 61 ships were laid down quickly. Of these, 58 were distributed among the private yards, two to Mare Island, and one to Charleston. In July 1917, the navy placed orders for 50 more destroyers from the private yards, with completion required by the end of 1918. Because the small Bath yard had no excess capacity remaining, her allotment of six of these latest 50 ships was given to the Mare Island Navy Yard instead. These destroyers would be DD-136 to DD-141. Of particular interest in that group is DD-139 which would become the USS *Ward*.

Despite the urgency of the destroyer building program, only 39 of the 111 Wickes destroyers would be commissioned before the end of World War I. Together with the pre-Wickes class destroyers constructed, this still gave the United States the largest destroyer fleet in the world. The shipyards continued to turn out destroyers after the war's end to fulfill their contracts. By building such a huge destroyer force, in addition to ships of other types in the 19 months that the United States participated in the war, U.S. shipyards gave the world a taste of what they would do 20 years later.

Of significance here was the group of six destroyers assigned to the United States Naval Shipyard at Mare Island. The yard was located on the western edge of the city of Vallejo and separated from the city by the mouth of the Napa River. The yard was approximately 30 miles northeast of San Francisco.

The shipyard was established in 1854 and became the first naval station on the U.S. west coast. The navy appointed Commodore David Farragut to be the yard's first commandant. Its mission was to maintain, overhaul, repair, re-supply, refuel, and service U.S. ships. New ship construction was, initially at least, of low priority.

Budget restraints kept the fledgling yard's accomplishments modest at first. It launched its first ship, the paddle-wheeled gunboat USS *Saginaw* in 1859, in time for the Civil War. Other ships took longer. The USS *Mohican* was begun in 1872 but not completed until 1885. Work commenced on the monitor USS *Monodock* in 1876 but it did not join the fleet until 1896. This pace, however, would change dramatically by 1914 and continue to accelerate throughout World War II.

At its peak in World War II, Mare Island Shipyard encompassed 4351 acres, contained 996 buildings, 20 ship berths, four dry-docks, two shipbuilding ways and all of the municipal services for the 46,000 yard workers. The yard was one of the largest navy facilities in the world. During its lifetime, the shipyard built 512 ships, from landing craft to battleships,[21] and repaired hundreds more. Among the ships built at Mare Island during the 1960s were 17 nuclear-powered submarines. After 142 years of service to the navy, the shipyard closed in 1996.

The urgency of building up the nation's naval forces during World War I spawned a rivalry between shipyards around the country and even between ship-fitters within the same shipyard. Some of the first flush deck destroyers were on the shipbuilding ways for almost a year before they were launched. This time frame gradually diminished as the construction crews became more proficient.

The three destroyers begun at Mare Island, just prior to laying of the keel of hull 139, averaged four and one-half months from keel-laying to launching and another five months from launching to commissioning, for a total construction period of nine and one-half months. This was a great improvement over previous ships.

Master Shipfitter J.T. Moroney was assigned to build hull number 139 for Mare Island. Moroney was known as Mare Island's famous "fighting Irishman" and had a reputation for being an aggressive individual and shipbuilder. After seeing the results achieved by other master shipfitters, Moroney vowed to launch hull 139 no more than 30 days after keel-laying, a feat never before accomplished!

His promise was met with disbelief from many, including the yard commandant. No one seriously believed that he could accomplish in 30 days what the previous three master ship-fitters at Mare Island had taken four and one-half months to complete. After much discussion, however, he was given the green light to attempt it. He wasted no time and laid the keel of hull 139 on Wednesday, May 15, 1918 at 7:30 A.M.[22] That action became a social event in Vallejo and was preceded by a parade, including a band, and a formal keel-laying ceremony. *Ward* was born.

Moroney had not made an idle boast and had made plans in advance to greatly accelerate the process of building a ship. He unveiled a prefabrication technique that would soon become the industry standard. Even before the keel was laid, he fabricated sections of the hull in the shop where equipment and workmen could be concentrated. He then transported the sections to the shipbuilding way, where they were quickly erected as a unit.

The *Ward* became the guinea pig for prefabrication techniques in the shipbuilding industry for generations to come. By shortening the time a ship is on the way, not only is the construction of that ship accelerated, but the way is cleared for construction of another ship, thus increasing the capacity of the shipyard.

Working around the clock, up to 18 gangs of riveters employed simultaneously saw to it that the hull was erected rapidly, quicker than any destroyer to date. Moroney exhorted the men to work hard every minute and erected large signs to keep a running tally of the number of days left to meet their goal. The gangs hammered in 16,000 rivets daily, the clamor continuing day and night. They would place 275,000 rivets in *Ward's* hull by the time it was launched.[23]

Master Shipfitter J.T. Moroney boasted that he would launch *Ward* in 30 days but set a record by launching it in 17½ days using a new pre-fabrication technique. The record still stands. (First Shot Navel Vets of St. Paul)

On-lookers marveled at the unbelievable rate at which the hull took shape and even yard workers were impressed. They had never seen anything like it. Darkness did not slow the pace at all, and work continued under illumination from banks of lights. Framing was erected by May 18 and deck plates were already being laid down on May 20. After deck plates were installed, progress accelerated as workers now had platforms on which to move about.

Miraculously, the hull was ready for launching at 8:30 P.M. on Saturday, June 1, only 17½ days after the keel was laid.[24] Moroney shattered his "unrealistic" prediction of 30 days to launching. He exceeded it by almost 13 days and broke the existing world's record by 9½ days. People everywhere shook their heads over his tremendous accomplishment.

This record-setting accomplishment was even more impressive than it seemed. Moroney had installed the ship's masts, crow's nest, motor launches, anchors, and other rigging before launching the ship. These were normally added after launching.

Top left: After only one day of around-the-clock work at the Mare Island Naval Shipyard, the *Ward* is taking shape as Moroney is determined to set a new standard in shipbuilding. *Top right:* By the fifth day the framing was completed and the deck plates were installed. Onlookers were stunned at the progress. *Bottom:* A bow-on view of *Ward* after 15 days and nights of work. The incredible pace set by Moroney had the *Ward* ready for launching in two more days. (National Archives)

The enormity of Moroney's achievement cannot be fully grasped without putting it into proper perspective. The remaining five destroyers, included in the same Mare Island contract with *Ward*, were launched in an average time of five months, twenty-six days. The launching time for all 13 other Wickes class destroyers built at Mare Island was eight months. The launching time for all 267 flush type destroyers was seven months.

In light of this, Moroney's feat of launching the *Ward* in 17½ days is even more remarkable. No other ship would come close to this and Moroney's record would stand forever. The *Ward's* reputation for extraordinary achievement, already begun, would continue throughout her career.

The record launching attracted thousands of visitors. The entire city of Vallejo, as well as residents of surrounding areas, turned out to celebrate the event. A carnival-like atmosphere prevailed as throngs of people filled the streets and hills near the navy yard. *Ward* was christened by Dorothy Hall Ward, the 11-year-old great-granddaughter of Commander James Harmon Ward, after whom the ship was named.[25]

At precisely 8:19 P.M. as thousands cheered, and with gangs of workmen riding her as tradition dictated, *Ward* majestically slid down the way and felt the sea for the first time. The crowd then moved into the downtown area of the city for festivities that included a parade, speeches, and a street dance. The celebration lasted past midnight. In the bay, the final stage of work on *Ward* was already beginning.

Ward was getting an excellent name, one steeped in naval tradition. Her namesake had a reputation for extraordinary accomplishments as a member of the United States Navy. Born in Hartford, Connecticut, in 1806, James Ward graduated from the military academy at Norwich, Vermont, at the age of 17. On March 23, 1823, just prior to graduation, he was

Afloat for the first time, *Ward* had just been launched at 7:22 P.M. on June 1, 1918. Moroney's prefabrication technique would revolutionize shipbuilding. (National Archives)

given an appointment to the U.S. Naval Academy then located at Philadelphia and graduated in 1827.

He spent the first years of his naval career sailing the Mediterranean aboard the USS *Constitution.* He was fascinated by the use of steam propulsion as it applied to ships and in 1828 took a year's leave of absence to study at Washington (now Trinity) College in Hartford, Connecticut. There he delved into steam engineering with a passion for knowledge.

Upon completion of his leave he went to sea, spending the next 15 years on various ships, devoting every spare moment to the study of naval history, tactics, and gunnery. Following sea duty, he spent several months lecturing on naval guns and gunnery. He later published his lectures as an "Elementary Course of Instruction on Ordnance and Gunnery for Midshipmen."

The navy took note of Ward's standing as one of its most knowledgeable and experienced officers by appointing him to be an instructor at the new naval school (now the Naval Academy) at Annapolis. There Ward taught gunnery, ordnance, and steam engineering. He was soon appointed to be the school's first Executive Officer. One of his first goals was to improve the reference library, and he requested the purchase of books on his subjects. His request was approved with the stipulation that the cost of books not exceed one hundred dollars.

In 1847 he left the school for active duty and was given command of the USS *Cumberland* during the Mexican War. Later, while commanding the USS *Jamestown* off the African coast, he wrote a *Manual of Naval Tactics,* which became a popular textbook at the Naval Academy. Another of his books, *Steam for the Millions* was also widely read.

Commander James Harmon Ward, first Union officer killed in the Civil War, is the namesake of the *Ward.* He was brilliant in steam engineering and naval tactics. (Naval Historical Center)

When the Civil War broke out, Ward was serving at the Brooklyn Navy Yard. He immediately turned his attention to seeking ways to use the navy against the Confederacy. Confederate forces were located in Virginia, just across the Potomac River from Washington D.C. To prevent these forces from attacking or blockading the nation's capital, Ward proposed a "flying flotilla" of ships to patrol the river. The navy accepted his recommendation and he was ordered to Washington D.C. Here he took command of the Potomac Flotilla, a group of three gunboats.

On May 26, 1861, this force engaged Confederate shore batteries in the first naval battle of the Civil War and emerged victorious. Ward's

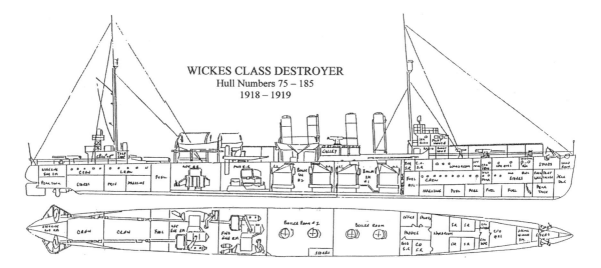

Sketches of the deck layout and outfitting of *Ward* as commissioned on July 24, 1918, at Mare Island. The sleekness of the design of Wickes class destroyers is evident. (Sketch prepared by John L. Dickey II, LCDR, USN [Ret.])

flotilla fought several more successful battles over the next four weeks. On June 27, Ward again encountered hostile shore batteries on Matthias Point, Virginia, 50 miles from Washington D.C.

During the skirmish a gunner operating a cannon on Ward's flagship, *Thomas Freeborn,* was felled by a Confederate rifle bullet. Seeing that, Ward instantly took the gunner's place. Ward, himself, was quickly hit in the chest by a sharpshooter. He died an hour later on the deck of his flagship. He was the first Union naval officer to die in the war. Ironically, Ward was the only Union fatality in this encounter. He was buried in Hartford, Connecticut, in a massive ceremony.

Ward was credited with developing naval tactics and gunnery standards that guided the U.S. Navy for decades. The men who would fight from the deck of hull number 139 would do so on a ship carrying the name of one of the greatest naval leaders of the Nineteenth Century. As an intellect and a leader, he was a giant.[26]

With the *Ward* formally launched in world record time, work continued at a hectic pace to complete her. Workmen swarmed over her as *Ward,* now afloat, was tied to a dock. Workers added the machinery, crew's quarters, torpedo tubes, deck facilities, and the profusion of equipment and rigging that transforms a hull into a fully operational destroyer.

At the beginning of July, *Ward* took on the appearance of a fighting ship. The last of her major components were installed by the third week of the month. Although much finishing work remained, the navy decided to formally commission the ship on July 18.[27] To celebrate the event, all 1700 of Mare Island's shipfitters paraded to the dock, preceded by a brass band, for *Ward's* third parade. The workers presented the crew with a new Victrola record player to commemorate the commissioning.[28]

It was an impressive ceremony on the ship's dock with the crew assembled on the after section of the ship. The commandant of the navy yard addressed the crowd, after which the ship's colors were hoisted to the mast for the first time. Commander Milton S. Davis, *Ward's* first commanding officer, read his official orders, spoke to the throng, and assumed command of the ship. His first order was to set the watches for *Ward's* first day as a ship of the U.S. Navy.[29]

Following the ceremony, the crowd marched back to downtown Vallejo for a celebration that lasted several hours. Over 6000 people joined in the festivities. *Ward's* record-setting construction became a rallying cry for the town's residents, who were disappointed to see the ship leave.

Ward was not yet ready to leave, however. Her accelerated building schedule had provided for completion of the hull, and installation of the boilers, engines, weapons, and most major machinery and equipment. However, many areas of the ship still had rigging and other support equipment that were unfinished. It would take about six more weeks to install all of these items.

The power plant installed in the Wickes class destroyers was impressive; it had two Parsons geared turbines developing 26,400 horsepower. Each was in turn divided into a high-pressure turbine for maximum speeds and a cruising turbine for economical speeds. These drove two three-bladed, high-pitched propellers that had shaft housings lined with lignum vitae, an extremely hard wood.[30] The power of *Ward's* engines was comparable to some contemporary battleships at Pearl Harbor in 1941, including the 29,000 ton *Nevada* and *Oklahoma*.

The ship also had to be fully provisioned. This involved bringing on board hundreds of individual items of supplies and food that would allow *Ward* to be self-sufficient for up to a month at a time. These ranged from ball peen hammers to 100-watt light bulbs, from rubber insulating tape to 10-amp fuses, and from burn ointment to canned peaches. Provisioning a new ship was a logistical nightmare which still remained to be done.

Most importantly, the ship and all of its many operating systems and machinery were still untested. A series of sea trials would be required to check out *Ward* and correct any deficiencies. The crew would also have to be checked out, but until the ship itself was free of defects its crew could not begin serious training. Much work remained before *Ward* could take its place in the world's fastest growing navy. This work began on July 19, 1918. *Ward* was now officially part of the U.S. Navy and eager to taste the sea. But it would have to wait a little longer.

CHAPTER 2

Too Late for War

July 19, 1918, dawned clear as *Ward* began six weeks of fitting out, tied to a dock at Mare Island Naval Yard. Workmen reported early and disappeared below deck. The ship continued to bring out a sense of urgency among all who worked on her. *Ward's* own crewmen were already at work at their respective stations checking out equipment, stowing gear, and orienting themselves to their new surroundings.

The crew numbered 125 men, to date, and more were expected to report in the next several weeks. Six officers were already on board and two more would join the ship shortly to fill out the roster. To allow workmen full freedom of movement, only a skeleton crew of *Ward's* complement would remain on board to oversee work in vital areas. The bulk of the crew was temporarily assigned ashore to one of the many barracks on the base.

During the week following the commissioning, the dock was a beehive of activity as a steady stream of trucks pulled up to *Ward*. They were provisioning the ship with everything a destroyer would need to keep its many systems and equipment operating and to keep up to 150 men fed for a month. The number of items was staggering and the volume of food was impressive. On July 24, six tons of food and food products were taken on board. While the exact ship's menus are not known, insight into the nature of the meals enjoyed by a destroyer's crew in 1918 can be gathered from the list of food items stowed on that very first provisioning of the ship. The list is shown below[1]:

Apples (dried)—100 lbs.
Apples (tinned)—216 lbs.
Apricots (tinned) 252 lbs.
Bacon (tinned)—288 lbs.
Beans (kidney)—100 lbs.
Beans (navy)—400 lbs.
Beans (lima)—100 lbs.
Beans (green)—171 lbs.
Beef (chipped)—144 lbs.
Beef (corned)—288 lbs.
Biscuits (hard)—300 lbs.
Butter (tinned)—400 lbs.
Butter (apple)—96 lbs.
Catsup—18 gals.
Citron—40 lbs.
Cheese—15 lbs.
Clams—72 lbs.
Cocoa—40 lbs.

Currents—80 lbs.
Vanilla—24 lbs.
Buckwheat—100 lbs.
Hominy—100 lbs.
Hops—25 lbs.
Jams—306 lbs.
Lard—120 lbs.
Sugar (powder)—96 lbs.
Syrup—16 gal.
Tea—40 lbs.
Vinegar—16 gal.
Lard substitute—120 lbs.
Macaroni—100 lbs.
Mackerel—200 lbs.
Milk (evap.)—576 lbs.
Mince Meat—100 lbs.
Mustard—25 lbs.
Oats—90 lbs.

Pepper (black)—24 lbs.
Pepper (chile)—25 lbs.
Pickles—114 lbs.
Pineapple—270 lbs.
Pork, Salt—200 lbs.
Powder, Baking—60 lbs.
Prunes (tinned)—425 lbs.
Pumpkin (tinned)—78 lbs.
Raisins—60 lbs.
Rice—200 lbs.
Salmon (tinned)—288 lbs.
Salt—200 lbs.
Sauerkraut—210 lbs.
Sausage -114 lbs.
Sardines—252 lbs.
Soda, baking—10 lbs.
Spices—25 lbs.
Sugar (gran.)—600 lbs.

Coffee — 300 lbs.	Oil (cotton seed) — 24 lbs.	Tapioca — 48 lbs.
Corn (tinned) — 180 lbs.	Peaches (evap.) — 100 lbs.	Tomatoes (tinned) — 756 lbs.
Corn meal — 100 lbs.	Peaches (tinned) — 270 lbs.	Worcester Sauce — 10 gal.
Corn starch — 40 lbs	Pears (tinned) — 261 lbs.	
Crackers, soda — 80 lbs.	Peas (tinned) — 180 lbs.	

The above is not a complete list of the ship's stores as it prepared to get under way but merely the first shipment Ward ever received. It would be supplemented with additional items in the following days. While the ship was tied to a dock, it received shipments of some foodstuffs every several days. Some interesting observations can be made from this first shipment.

Potatoes, the serviceman's staple, is missing. Except for corned beef and chipped beef, meat items are scarce. It is assumed that meat and potatoes, as well as eggs, bread, and rolls were included in later deliveries. The quantity of the sailors' favorite beverage, coffee, does not appear to be adequate for a crew of 150 men who will spend much of their time on lonely watches somewhere in the ship. Nevertheless, while *Ward's* crew would not be eating fancy meals, neither would they experience hunger. There was a sufficient variety of items for creative ship's cooks to keep the crew fed and satisfied.

On July 25, *Ward* took on two shipments of hand tools and electrical stores. For this, a tug pushed the ship to a dock adjacent to an electrical warehouse. *Ward* was not yet maneuvering under its own power. A week later it received a shipment consisting of hundreds of items, such as electric bulbs and globes, lubricating oil, grease, and gasoline. To the joy of the crewmen berthed on the ship, it also took on a modest supply of eggs, butter, lettuce, hamburgers, frankfurters, and bread.[2] The menus would now include some of the crew's favorite items.

Work continued briskly and on August 3, the base paymaster came aboard to give the crew the first of their monthly salaries. This ritual would become the center of much of the sailors' lives. Signs that *Ward* was nearing its sailing date were now unmistakable. Few workmen could be seen anywhere on the ship. On August 23, 61 crewmen who had been training and berthing ashore reported to the ship. On August 31, the final officer, Lt. Earl Pomeroy, reported and the officer ranks were filled. *Ward's* complement was now complete; her first crew included eight officers and 139 enlisted men. The ship was fully manned and ready for sea trials.[3]

A destroyer in 1918 was a montage of men with special skills. Forty-three different ranks were represented in the crew, Ordinary Seaman the most prevalent. By work area, the deck gang had 57 men, including 38 seamen and an assortment of gunner's mates, boatswain's mates, and quartermasters.[4] In general these men performed various deck functions and operated the deck equipment, including the boats, guns, torpedo tubes, and depth charges.

The 58 men of the engine room or 'black gang' operated the ship's engines, boilers, and other propulsion and below-deck equipment. They consisted of 18 machinist's mates, 22 firemen, and assorted watertenders and oilers. Special maintenance functions were performed by a group of 12 trade-type personnel, including electricians, carpenters, and shipfitters. A crew of nine cooks, stewards, and mess attendants handled cooking and mess duties.[5] The number and distribution of men on a destroyer would not change appreciably over the next 30 years.

On September 1, preparations were completed and *Ward* was ready for sea. The ship was fully manned, provisioned, and fueled and all workmen were removed. *Ward* would taste the sea air for the first time on the following day.

Ward was a graceful looking ship that embodied the latest designs in destroyer development. With an overall length of 314 feet- 4½ inches, a beam one-half inch short of 31 feet, and a displacement of close to 1100 tons, it was comparable to other destroyers in size.[6] Its shaft horsepower and maximum speed of more than 35 knots made it more powerful and faster than most of it contemporaries. Some observers, in noting the size of the power plant, claimed that the four-stackers were merely a tight-fitting shell built around two powerful Parsons turbine engines.

Ward's offensive punch lay in her main battery of four 4"/50 guns, her 12 21-inch torpedo tubes in four triple mounts, her stern depth charge racks, and Y-gun depth charge projectors. A single 3"/23 gun constituted her anti-aircraft defense.[7] In 1918 aircraft were not considered a threat to ships. Submarines were a threat, however, and *Ward* was equipped with a new but crude hydrophone apparatus to detect underwater sounds. Although not sophisticated enough to pinpoint the location of a submerged submarine, it could detect the presence of one in the vicinity.

Boiler Number Three was lighted off at 0400 on September 2, the crew was at their stations, and Commander Davis and his Executive Officer, Lt. Walter Reidel, were on the bridge.

At 0512 all lines were cast off and *Ward* (DD-139) moved slowly away from the dock. She was on her own power for the first time.[8] The ship cleared Mare Island harbor and increased speed to 15 knots, creating her first bow wave. She was moving briskly, but at 0620 a fuel pump failed. The ship anchored while the engine room crew repaired the pump. The repairs were quickly made and *Ward* was under way again at 15 knots. She anchored again an hour later off Sausalito, California, to check all operating systems.

Ward resumed her sea trials on September 3, including the firing of her four-inch guns and dropping of several depth charges. She topped off with stores, fuel, and ammunition of September 19 and prepared for her first extended sea trial. At 1725 on September 20, she cleared Mare Island and passed under the Golden Gate Bridge shortly after. For the next six days she ran speed trials at various speeds off the California coast.

She returned to Mare Island on September 27 to make repairs and adjustments to machinery. On October 20, following the repairs, she moved into one of Mare Island's dry-dock to have her hull bottom repainted. Two days later she moved out of dry-dock and took on stores and provisions. Her crew now realized that *Ward* was in a tight race against time to see if she would be able to get to the Atlantic and fight German submarines. This was the reason she had been built, but time was running out.

Training was continuous with drills and exercises held daily to test the ship, its equipment, and the crew. Every day the officers selected two or three from their menu of drills. They called unscheduled collision, fire, abandon ship, gun, torpedo attack, depth charge attack, fire and rescue, general quarters, and physical exercise drills and timed the response to each drill. Speed trials continued through October and November. On November 11, the crew learned that the war was over and *Ward* had missed it.

On December 8 during speed trials, *Ward* maintained a speed of 35.2 knots for a half-hour while turning out 28,000 horsepower, a remarkable achievement.[9] This was equivalent to a land speed of 37 miles per hour and clearly exceeded the navy's speed requirements. It proved that *Ward* would be capable of moving quickly if called upon to do so.

On December 9, *Ward* anchored off San Pedro Bay, California, and made last-minute preparations for its first long distance voyage. The crew learned that the ship would finally reach the Atlantic Ocean, but several months too late for combat with German submarines.

The Ward is under way with all four boilers on the line during the builder's trials in September 1918. Her bow wave and squat of her stern indicate she is doing about 25 knots. (National Historical Center)

A more sedate pose with only one boiler on line during builder's trials. Note the dazzle camouflage and hull number under the bridge wing. That would soon be moved to the bow. (National Historical Center)

The anticipation of a cruise that long was still exciting for a crew of a record-breaking ship which had not sailed very far off the California coast in three months.

Although *Ward* was an imposing looking ship and the recipient of the finest warship design of its time, its crew facilities were quite Spartan. The ship was not built for comfort, but for fighting. After the ship was crammed full of boilers, engines, fuel and water storage tanks, storage lockers for everything, guns, magazines, and gear of all kinds, it left precious little space for living quarters.

Small officers' staterooms were located forward, one deck down from the weather deck. Chief Petty Officers had a nearby communal quarters consisting of a mess table surrounded by bunks. Sanitary and shower facilities for officers and petty officers were located adjacent to their quarters.[10]

Enlisted men were crowded into two crew compartments, one forward, one aft. Each compartment was divided into two sub-compartments with individual bunks in tiers of two forward and three aft, and center mess tables. Each man had a personal foot locker stowed under the lower bunks. Fifty-four men were stuffed into the forward compartment and 48 in the aft compartment, which was used for eating, sleeping, and socializing.

The tables were bolted to the deck and contained wire racks beneath for storage of dishes. The crew's footlockers became the benches requiring that the lower bunks be raised for seating. Although the upper could remain in use during messing, it was usually raised as well.[11]

Sanitary facilities and showers for the crew were located in the after deck house on the weather deck. This was right above the after crew compartment and had direct access to the crew compartment. The route to these facilities from the forward crew compartment, however, required traversing almost the entire length of the ship.

At 0610 on December 10, *Ward* weighed anchor at San Pedro Bay and pointed its bow southward towards a warmer climate and a passage to the Atlantic. Moving briskly at 20 knots, the ship paralleled the Mexican coast for several days, keeping the lights of coastal towns visible to port. It anchored off Salina Cruz in the Gulf of Tehuantepec on the afternoon of December 14 to check over the ship after more than 100 hours of continuous steaming at 20 knots. The engines and other operating systems were functioning beautifully.

Ward left Salina Cruz the next morning and continued south at 20 knots, again following the Mexican coastline. At 1524 she passed Point Ocos near the Guatemala border, and at 2148 steamed past the Acajutla lighthouse on the El Salvador coast. Continuing at a steady pace and without any stops, the ship left Nicaragua and Costa Rica in her wake on December 16.

Finally, after a week of steaming, *Ward* arrived off the Pacific entrance to the Panama Canal at 0645 on December 17. The Canal was still relatively new, having been open to shipping only since 1914. An hour later, the ship picked up a Canal pilot and entered the Canal with the pilot conning the ship. By 0950 it moored to an oil dock and began refueling.[12]

At 1245 while refueling, a cry of "fire!" suddenly arose from the after engine room. Oil dripping on a hot engine had ignited and quickly spread to surrounding areas. Engineer room crewmen attacked the fire using the techniques they had learned in the many fire drills. They were soon joined by deck gangs as the flames reached the weather deck. As a protective measure, crewmen flooded the after magazine. Smoke and flames continued to rise out of the ship throughout the afternoon, but by 1855 the fire was extinguished and the ship secure again.

Although the fire had burned for six hours, the damage was surprisingly light and mostly superficial. Machinery and bulkheads were scorched below deck but no serious damage occurred. On the weather deck a small dory burned, a motor launch was damaged, and several boat falls and gear were destroyed. No crewmen suffered serious injury. The *Ward* was not only a fast ship, it was a lucky one as well. Miraculously the ship escaped what could have been a very damaging situation.

As soon as the fire was out, repairs and cleanup commenced immediately. Despite the damage, *Ward* continued with its plans to transit the Canal and cruise the Atlantic. The ship took on supplies as cleanup progressed and, at 1545 on December 18, blackened and battered a bit, *Ward* got under way. By 2015 it passed through all locks and dropped off the pilot. At 2055, *Ward* was under way at 20 knots again, this time in the Atlantic Ocean for the first time.

Her first port of call would be the U.S. naval base at Guantanamo Bay, Cuba. She anchored there at 1240 on December 19 and began taking on fuel. Commander Davis made a courtesy call on the Base Commandant as the ship refueled. Two hours later, after taking on 55,000 gallons of fuel oil, *Ward* departed, heading north at 25 knots. Again she was a ship in a hurry.

Ward continued north at 20 to 25 knots for 60 hours without making landfall. Finally, before dawn on December 22, lookouts spotted the lights of Hampton Roads, Virginia. It dropped anchor at 0310 after a non-stop voyage of 1300 miles from Guantanamo Bay. *Ward* remained there long enough to inspect the engines and other machinery and left 13 hours later for a short jaunt to the navy yard at Norfolk, Virginia.

At Norfolk, the crew continued their inspection of boilers, engines, and other operating systems and filled the fuel oil bunkers. The following day, all hands were given liberty in Norfolk since they would be under way again on the Christmas holiday. At 1730 on Christmas Eve, *Ward* weighed anchor and continued north for a port of call at the nation's largest city. The ship's crew spent Christmas Eve and Christmas Day steaming along the Atlantic coast at 20 knots. A tree that someone had picked up at Norfolk was quickly set up in the crew compartment and decorated with items that materialized out of nowhere. The crew would celebrate Christmas at sea.

Ward reached New York harbor on the 26th and anchored in the North River opposite 96th Street.[13] The crew was given liberty in New York, for most, their first visit to the big city. Walking the brightly lit and decorated streets of New York was a memorable experience for the men who had spent the past two months on the water. Most returned to the ship with prized souvenirs of their short visit. At 0850 on the 28th, *Ward* left New York and steamed north for her next port of call, the U.S. navy base at Newport, Rhode Island, where it moored late in the afternoon.

On December 29, *Ward* took on stores, fuel, and six torpedoes. She now had a full allotment of 12 torpedoes. Base personnel also repaired her radio compass, which had suddenly failed. With all systems again operating, the ship left Newport at 2350 for a return to Norfolk, Virginia, where she would undergo a complete inspection and take on new personnel.

Ward's crew spent a busy seven days at Norfolk taking on fuel and supplies, inspecting the entire ship and machinery, and making repairs. In recognition of the end of the war, base personnel removed the ship's depth charge racks and depth charges. The ship retained all of her guns and torpedo tubes, however.

In Norfolk, *Ward* experienced her first major change in personnel. Twenty-three crewmen were released from the service and 14 others were reassigned to other ships. They were replaced by new men who reported later in the week.[14] The crew received a welcome liberty which most used to celebrate the arrival of the New Year, as only sailors can.

With a full crew, *Ward* left Norfolk on January 7, 1919, and steamed north again to New York where she would join a flotilla of other ships for a series of maneuvers. It anchored there the following day. New York harbor was full of destroyers. The destroyers were preparing to leave for the Caribbean with *Ward* as their flagship, an honor for the ship. *Ward* joined the other ships in topping off with fuel and provisions for a lengthy voyage and they departed New York the morning of January 12, 1919.

Ward led a double column of two destroyer divisions out of New York at 18 knots. As Commander Davis looked aft from the bridge of *Ward*, he saw an imposing sight, one not seen often in peacetime. Lined up behind *Ward* were the destroyers *Mayrant, Patterson, Dent, Gamble, Dorsey, Breese,* and *Ludlow,* all four-stackers.[15]

As the ships steamed south, upon signals from *Ward*, the group assumed various combat cruising formations. Davis was not only proud to be a part of this force but even prouder to be given the opportunity to have his ship lead it. By themselves the destroyers were a formidable force, but if the United States was at war, these ships would be escorting a line of battleships on its way to meet an enemy fleet.

The formation reached Cuban waters on January 15 without an intermediate port of call and entered Guantanamo Bay at 1805. As flagship of the group, naval protocol allowed the *Ward* to be the first ship to refuel, so Davis took it immediately to the refueling dock, where it took three hours to fill *Ward's* fuel bunkers. The entire group refueled, resupplied and prepared for an extensive series of drills, exercises, and maneuvers south of Cuba.

The force departed Guantanamo Bay on January 18 and began a series of maneuvers, including gun and torpedo drills, that would last 28 days. They were interrupted only by several refueling stops at Caribbean ports. In between Division operations and firing drills, Davis held in-ship drills on *Ward* seeking perfection on his own ship. As flagship, all eyes were on *Ward* and Davis intended to set the standard. Finally, on February 15, the exhaustive maneuvers were concluded and *Ward* led the flotilla back to Guantanamo Bay for resupply.

Ward's stay in port was short and at 2040 on February 18, she led Destroyer Division 18 out on maneuvers again. Following her were destroyers *Thatcher, Crosby, Palmer, Delphy,* and *Buchanen.* Destroyer Divisions, 5 and 14, also participated in the maneuvers. Fifteen destroyers steaming in various combat formations provided a sight seldom seen in the Caribbean in the post-war period.

On February 26 the exercises took on a new and imposing look as several battleship squadrons arrived in the waters south of Cuba. They joined the destroyer divisions in joint cruising formations to practice the techniques of escorting battleship groups. The firepower represented by this combined force of combat ships was awesome. The battleships then acted as 'targets' for simulated torpedo attacks by entire destroyer divisions.

Some days of the maneuvers were devoted to gunnery target practice by individual ships over previously established target ranges. On one range the battleships competed against each other for accuracy with their 12-inch and 14-inch main batteries. On another range the destroyers used their four-inch guns while the battleships fired their secondary batteries. Maneuvers ended on April 8, and the destroyers returned to Guantanamo Bay on the following day.

Two days later Division 18 was on the move again, with *Ward* leading it north from Cuba. A four-day non-stop cruise ended in New York harbor. The division devoted the next two weeks to inspecting and repairing engines and machinery, and resupplying and refueling. Although the past three months had been extremely difficult on the men and equipment, both had come through it magnificently. The ship and crew had received vital training in many aspects of combat tactics and operations which had united them. *Ward* was now a fighting ship and capable of leading a division or flotilla of destroyers into combat.

While in New York, *Ward* received orders to participate in an historic operation in the Atlantic in May. On May 2, *Ward* led destroyers *Walker, Thatcher, Crosby,* and *Laub* out of New York harbor to Newport, Rhode Island, on the first leg of this new assignment. The entire division, along with 25 other destroyers, would have a major role in the impending operation.

The destroyers left Newport on May 4 and immediately encountered a dense fog that descended like a white blanket over each ship. Visibility was zero, and keeping station with the other ships now became extremely difficult and hazardous. *Ward* commenced sounding her fog whistle at two-minute intervals and directed her searchlight on the water surface directly astern of the ship. With all five destroyers duplicating these measures, the formation was able to continue slowly on course without incident. It broke out of the fog later in the day to the relief of all crews.[16]

As the fog thinned, a new and even deadlier hazard emerged as lookouts sighted icebergs ahead. The formation maneuvered around the icebergs and the ships continued, but with lookouts doubled. Had the icebergs been encountered earlier in the day, it could have been disastrous for the entire formation. The ships continued with extreme caution and reached Trepassey Bay, Newfoundland, on March 6, safely but with weary lookouts.

At Trepassey Bay the ships received information on the Atlantic operation. The U.S Navy intended to demonstrate that naval airpower was capable of reaching over long distances to extend its influence. It proposed to send a flight of four flying boats across the Atlantic in the first ever trans-Atlantic flight. This was a huge and perilous undertaking given the state of aviation in 1919. The four-engine flying boats would fly non-stop from Trepassey Bay to the Azores Islands. From there the aircraft would continue on to Lisbon, Portugal, to complete the Trans-Atlantic leg, and terminate the flight in Plymouth, England. The entire journey would be 4107 miles long with the main non-stop Atlantic leg covering 1200 miles of that distance.[17]

The aircraft to be used were new Curtiss NC bi-wing flying boats with a top wing span of 126 feet and a length of 68 feet. For this flight the aircraft would carry 1891 gallons of gasoline in ten fuel tanks. Their four 12-cylinder Liberty engines would normally push the aircraft at a modest speed of 77 mph but this would be reduced to 58 knots fully loaded. At a cost of $100,000 per aircraft, the navy was investing much in this flight. Three of the aircraft (NC-1, NC-2, NC-3) would carry a crew of five men while a fourth, NC-4, would carry six.[18]

With the primitive navigation equipment carried by the aircraft, reaching a fixed destination after flying nearly 20 hours and over 1200 miles of water would be extremely difficult and not likely to succeed without navigational assistance. The navy decided to station a line of ships along the entire route, from Cape Cod, Massachusetts, to Plymouth, England. Sixty-one ships, including five battleships, one cruiser, and 55 destroyers would be used. On the cross-Atlantic Newfoundland to Azores leg, 22 destroyers would be spaced at 60-mile intervals. The ships would provide continuous radio and visual signals and weather reports to the aircraft and hopefully lead them to the Azores.[19]

Ward left Trepassey Bay at 1813 on May 9, leading destroyers *Palmer, Walker, Thatcher,*

Crosby, and *Laub* to their positions. All, except for the *Laub*, had consecutively assigned stations in the line of destroyers. The *Laub* had another assignment on the operation. Steaming out of Newfoundland, *Ward's* division sighted icebergs again, but visibility was good and they easily avoided the huge bergs. *Ward* reached her designated location, Station 6, on May 13. She was now at latitude 44–33 north, longitude 46–32 west, approximately 250 miles southeast of Newfoundland. The other division destroyers occupied Stations 7 to 11.

Three flying boats, NC-1, NC-3, and NC-4, left Newfoundland in early evening of May 16. The fourth, NC-2, was used to provide parts for NC-1, which was damaged severely before it left New York. Only the three aircraft would now make the long and dangerous flight. On Station 6 *Ward* waited patiently for the aircraft to appear.

At 2200 on May 16, *Ward* made radio contact with NC-1 while it was still some distance away. At 2310 the ship turned on all lights, directed her searchlight straight up, began firing star shells, and commenced emitting a set of designated radio signals. Finally, at 2348, the crew heard the sound of aircraft engines to the northwest. Two minutes later they heard NC-1 pass directly over the ship. Unseen in the darkness, the aircraft continued southeast toward Station 7.[20]

Ward remained on station and continued her signals until midnight. She secured all signal lights at 0037 and left her station at 0055. She steamed directly for Trepassey Bay, arriving there at 0241 on May 17. Her mission was over, but the aircraft flew into history with mixed results.

After passing *Ward,* all three aircraft continued to follow the line of destroyers. As dawn broke and with less than 200 miles to the Azores, they flew into a dense fog. Unable to spot the line of ships and unsure of where they were, NC-1 landed on the water at 0810 to determine its position. Because of the fog, the crew was not aware that the sea was running with close to 20 foot swells, and the aircraft was damaged in the landing. Unable to take off again, the crew radioed SOS signals in the hope of being located by one of the destroyers.

Four of the destroyers did receive the signals and started a search for NC-1. Several hours later, to the relief of the five crewmen, a ship appeared in the fog. It was the Greek freighter *Ionia*, which had heard the SOS as well. Despite the heavy seas, the *Ionia* managed to pick up the men. Shortly, the U.S. destroyer *Gridley* arrived on the scene also and attempted to tow the aircraft to the Azores. The towline parted and NC-1 sank.

NC-3 was also lost in the fog and landed on the water at 0830 to determine its position. Rough seas damaged it and rendered it unable to fly as well. It was able to taxi, however, and headed in the direction that the crew felt would take it to the Azores. No ship was able to find it in the fog and high seas, and NC-3 was on its own. Despite the heavy seas, the aircraft held together and 52 hours later it taxied into Porta Delgado, Azores, to complete this portion of its incredible journey safely.[21]

Aircraft NC-4 navigated through the fog, landing safely in the Azores at 0920. Commander John Towers, who was the Squadron Leader and a member of the crew of ill-fated NC-3, was not able to complete the flight. After World War II, Towers would become Commander in Chief of the United States Pacific Fleet. After a layover of several days to refuel and repair, NC-4 left on May 20 to continue its mission as planned. With stops in Portugal and Spain, it successfully completed its flight by landing in Plymouth, England, on May 31. *Ward* had participated in the most significant aerial feat of its time.[22]

Her role in the trans-Atlantic over, the *Ward* returned to Newport, Rhode Island, on May 21. After a week layover to refuel and reprovision the ship, the *Ward* left Newport and returned to the Norfolk Navy Yard for an extended stay in port. She entered dry dock there for scraping and painting of her hull. Another five weeks were devoted to a complete inspection and servicing of all machinery, armament, magazines, and operating systems. Here two 3"/23-caliber anti-aircraft guns were added in recognition of the growing capabilities of airpower, something the *Ward* had just helped to prove.

New officers reported aboard and, except for Commander Davis, a complete turnover in officers took place. Lt. John Bates was promoted to be the ship's Executive Officer or second in command.

Ward emerged from Norfolk on July 18, ready to again face the rigors of the open sea. Leading Destroyer Division 18 again, she steamed south to return to the Pacific via the Panama Canal. She arrived at the Canal and passed through the locks on July 25. With *Boggs, Palmer, Thatcher,* and *Crosby* following her, she left Panama on July 29, bound for her home port of San Diego. They were accompanied by *Lamberton, Ramsay, Montgomery, Breese, Gamble,* and *Radford* of Destroyer Division 12, also on their return to San Diego.

The two divisions followed the Mexican coast, stopping in Acapulco on August 2 with a welcomed liberty for the crew. They dropped their anchors in San Diego on August 8 after an absence of eight months. After a brief stay to refuel and resupply, the division began four weeks of maneuvers off the California coast with in-ship drills held daily between

Ward is nested with destroyers to the right and left during a Panama Canal passage on July 24, 1919. It was returning to the Pacific after maneuvers. (National Archives)

division exercises. Ports of call at San Pedro, San Luis Obispo, Monterey, Eureka, and San Francisco allowed opportunities for reprovisioning and liberty. The division left San Francisco on September 2 and headed north at 16 knots to participate in another historic event.

On September 6, the division steamed into Portland harbor, where it anchored for six days. It completed the short jaunt to Seattle on September 13 to take part in a crucial presidential initiative. President Woodrow Wilson was in the midst of a lengthy nationwide tour to gain support for a peace treaty to end World War I and for U.S. membership in the newly created League of Nations. His tour took him to Seattle for another major speech. To call further attention to his mission, Wilson requested a gathering of the Pacific Fleet at Seattle.

The navy assembled an impressive armada for the President — 51 ships, including six battleships. It was the largest U.S. fleet ever amassed on the West Coast. The *Ward* led her division past the presidential entourage with signal flags flying and her crew "manning the rail." It was another great day in the career of the *Ward*.[23]

On September 16, Destroyer Division 18, with *Walker* now present, left Seattle and returned to San Diego, where it anchored on the 22nd. The destroyers now settled in for an extended stay as the navy was winding down its activities and attempting to live within a reduced budget. The division remained in San Diego for the remainder of 1919 and into 1920. On December 21, 1919, *Ward* experienced an infrequent "change in command" ceremony as Commander Davis was reassigned.

The several hundred destroyers hastily built from 1916 to 1919 could not be sustained as active ships by a navy forced to reduce its fleet size in peacetime. Many of the four-stackers would be placed in reserve for future use if the country ever needed them again. A reserve fleet of destroyers would be anchored at the Philadelphia Naval Yard and another at San Diego. Davis would be the commander of the San Diego Reserve Fleet. He chose to remain on board *Ward* and use the ship as his headquarters. *Ward's* Executive officer, Lt. John F. Bates, replaced Davis as the ship's new commanding officer.

Ward remained moored to the Santa Fe dock in San Diego through June 1920. The routine of the crew was broken only by daily inspections and drills. With the inactivity of the division, the ship's crews were now reduced in size and the excess men assigned to active ships. By May 1920 *Ward's* complement was down to 103. Then, Lt. Bates, himself, was reassigned, and on June 19, 1920, Lt. Charles J. Reno became the new commanding officer. Reno was replaced in July by Lt. (jg) T.P. Kane.

Ward had now been tethered to the dock for ten months and it appeared that she was destined to spend the rest of her life moored close to, but yet so far from, the sea that she was built to roam. The crew had long tired of drills and inspections. Finally, on July 16, the ship took on stores and fuel and prepared to leave the harbor. At 2010 she slipped her lines and left the dock.

Her cruise was a short one, however, just up the coast of California to Mare Island. There, the following day, she entered Dry Dock No. 2 where she would have her hull bottom scraped and two coats of rust preventative paint applied. Even in dry dock *Ward* made life challenging for her crew. During the hull work, a crewman fell 40 feet to the dry dock floor but was miraculously not seriously injured. *Ward*, her hull now protected against the ravages of saltwater corrosion, left Mare Island on July 27 and returned to San Diego.

Ward was now down to 46 crewmen, barely enough to get the ship under way, if required. In August she made several short jaunts outside San Diego harbor but returned after several hours. The ship was not finished with her career yet and continued to fight

Red Lead Row at the San Diego Destroyer Base, where *Ward* resided for close to 20 years. More than 60 destroyers can be seen. *Ward* is the ninth ship from the right in the middle of the three long rows of ships. (Naval Historical Center)

for survival. She was assigned to Destroyer Division 17 with destroyers *Boggs, Hamilton, Kennison,* and *Claxton.* In the next several months, even with a reduced crew, *Ward* and her division made several voyages up the coast to Los Angeles and San Francisco. *Ward* returned again to Mare Island on October 1, where Lt. W. J. Lorenz was appointed as her new commanding officer.

Ward remained at Mare Island for the remainder of 1920 and into 1921, still on the active roll but moored to a dock. Her crew size varied from 45 to 60. The men were now engaged in only those tasks required to keep the ship's equipment in operating condition in case there was a call for her services.

On occasion an officer found some creative work for the men. In April of 1921, *Ward's* crew was ordered to assist in the building of a baseball diamond at the Mare Island base.[24] The men welcomed this diversion from the daily inspections and drills that seemed to have little purpose now. In early July, 1921, *Ward* went into dry-dock again for a week at Mare Island for inspection and cleaning of her bottom.

Ward still wasn't through and took on fuel, ammunition, and supplies on July 13. After testing of her engines, *Ward* moved out on July 20, for the first time in ten months. Destroyer Division 17, now containing *Ward, Boggs, Hamilton, Kennison, Claxton,* and *Kilty,* steamed south from Mare Island in two sections at 15 knots. The division's cruise ended at San Diego, where it moored the following day. On July 21, *Ward* was officially placed on reserve status but not decommissioned, as many sources indicate. Except for a one-day voyage to

San Pedro on August 13, *Ward* remained at the San Diego naval base for the remainder of this phase of her active career.

Ward carried on with a reduced crew, who continued with daily inspections and drills. The drills, however, were now designed to keep idle men busy rather than to maintain critical skills. The crew was well aware that the *Ward* would soon be decommissioned without a crew at all. The ship, although inactive, continued to change its commanding officer at intervals. Lt. Lorenz was followed in turn by Lt. Francis Denebrink, Lt. H. A. Harrison, Ensign Carl J. Christopherson, Ensign Clyde A. Coggins, and Lt. Marcus L. Kurtz as commanding officers.

On June 5, 1922, *Ward's* life as an active and commissioned ship ended. At 1630, a letter to the crew from the Commander of Destroyer Divisions of the Pacific Fleet was read. The letter placed *Ward* out of commission.[25] Her 54-man crew was transferred to other ships, 45 to the destroyer *Boggs* and nine to the destroyer *Stoddert.* Her remaining three officers were also transferred, Lt. Kurtz to the *Boggs* and then to the destroyer *MacDonough,* and Ensigns Roenicke and Christopher to the destroyer *Hamilton.*

Later, tugs would push *Ward* into a line of decommissioned destroyers at the base where they would reside until and when they were again needed. Ultimately there would be more than 200 destroyers resting in reserve fleets, of which 67 would be keeping company with *Ward* in San Diego, moored side by side in what was referred to as "red lead row."

Given the state of technology in the 1920s, very little was done to preserve the ships while in the reserve fleet. Although pans of slaked lime were placed in the interior to reduce the effects of moisture, this accomplished little. Rust and corrosion would take their toll through the years but the ships would still be there, if needed.

Ward was built in world record time to fight German submarines in World War I. She took to the seas too late to accomplish that, but she would have a second opportunity to fulfill that destiny. It would be a different enemy in a different ocean in a different war and with a different crew. She would have a chance at glory that few combat ships ever have. But that was still in the future. Before that day arrived, *Ward* would have to languish for 19 years in "red lead row" at San Diego. *Ward's* day would come and she could wait for that.

CHAPTER 3

A Ship and Crew Prepare for War

The world was relatively peaceful for the first ten years of *Ward's* hiatus with the Reserve Fleet in San Diego. There was not a war or even a major conflict to be found anywhere. The seeds of war, however, had been planted on several continents and could easily bloom into open warfare if not checked by responsible nations.

In Europe, their defeat by the Allies and the extremely harsh terms of the Treaty of Versailles enraged the Germans. They were disarmed, burdened with huge reparations, and stripped of their colonies. They were further devastated by colossal economic chaos, which gripped their nation for six years. The worldwide depression of the early 1930s slowed Germany's recovery, extending the hardship of the German people even further.

This spawned the rise of fascism, the Nazi Party, and the emergence of Adolph Hitler as a major force in German politics. He fanned the flames of nationalism and was named Chancellor in January 1933. Using this position as a stepping stone, he seized absolute power two months later. *Ward* had now been in reserve for 11 years when this occurred and, except for periodic pumping of her bilges, she was free of any activity.

In total defiance of the Versailles Treaty, Hitler began to arm Germany and in 1936 German troops marched into the Rhineland, a demilitarized zone between France and Germany. The seeds of war were now close to germinating. In March 1938 Hitler sent his troops into Austria. Six months later, they occupied the Sudetenland in Czechoslovakia and by March 1939, took over the remainder of Czechoslovakia.

The seeds finally sprouted in Europe on September 1, 1939, when Germany unleashed a blitzkrieg invasion of Poland. War officially broke out two days later as Great Britain and France declared war on Germany. *Ward* had now been in the reserve fleet for 17 years and her time was rapidly approaching.

In Asia, a similar militaristic movement was occurring. Japan's burgeoning population, its lack of natural resources, and global depression caused it to look beyond her borders for a solution to her problems. It made its first major aggressive move in September 1931 when it marched into resource-rich Manchuria and took it over as a province. Japan continued to re-arm through the 1930s and in 1937 openly invaded China. War had now officially come to the continent of Asia and *Ward* was another step closer to the battles she was built to fight.

That war came close to breaking out on December 12, 1937, when Japanese aircraft attacked U.S. vessels on the Yangtze River while attempting to evacuate American nationals from danger. Three steamers were damaged and the gunboat USS *Panay* was sunk with loss of life.[1] Although the Japanese government apologized for the incident and agreed to pay reparations, this act was clearly a harbinger of things to come.

Still seeking critically needed resources, Japan moved into French Indochina in

September 1940. In an effort to pressure her into withdrawing, the United States now banned the sale of aircraft, aviation fuel, scrap metals, and other strategic war-making materials to Japan. In July 1941, following Japan's complete occupation of Indo-China, the United States, Great Britain, and the Netherlands froze all Japanese assets. This cut off most of Japan's imports from these three countries, including the most crucial, oil.

With only a year's supply of oil on hand, Japan was now forced to make a momentous decision upon which the future of their empire would depend. That decision would take them down a path to peace or to war with the western powers. *Ward* had now been in the reserve Fleet for 18 years, but the U.S. Navy was finally beginning to stir.

After almost 20 years of relative calm in the world and an isolationist mood gripping the United States, the U.S. Navy had been reduced to levels below that of other naval powers. Its most modern battleship was built in 1921 and it had not constructed a destroyer in 12 years. World events of the late 1930s finally forced the U.S to begin to quickly enlarge its naval capabilities and attempt to catch the rest of the world.

On July 19, 1940, Congress passed the Two Ocean Naval Expansion Act, which provided for the construction of 218 new combat ships, including 18 aircraft carriers, 11 battleships, 6 battle-cruisers, 27 cruisers, 115 destroyers, and 43 submarines.[2] Although Japan would still hold a numerical advantage in combat ships for another two years, soon the U.S. shipbuilding industry would change the balance of power forever.

With a time lag of more than a year between authorization and completion of destroyers, the United States looked for a more rapid way to build up its destroyer force. Great Britain also faced a shortage of destroyers, one similar to the one it had faced in World War I, which threatened its very existence. A German submarine blockade was again slowly strangling the British Isles. Desperate for convoy escorts, the British urgently requested destroyers from the United States. The several hundred World War I four-stackers in the Reserve Fleet were the only ships available in 1940, and in September of that year, the two countries completed a trade which would prove extremely beneficial to the U.S. and life-saving to Great Britain.

The United States turned over 50 of its reserve fleet destroyers in exchange for 99-year leases for U.S. bases on British territories in Newfoundland and six Caribbean colonies. The bases would be instrumental in protecting sea lanes in the western Atlantic and U.S eastern seaboard. The destroyers would be crucial in keeping Britain supplied with food and war materials. They may have saved the British Empire from falling.

The U.S. drew on the same source, its Reserve Fleet, to quickly enlarge its destroyer force. From 1939 to 1941 it activated 80 more four-stackers for immediate service with its own navy.[3] The very last of these to be activated was *Ward*. Tugs moved it from its mooring location in one of the lines of destroyers in "red lead row" at the San Diego naval base. After gathering rust for almost 19 years awaiting a call for its services, it was finally moving. Its first move was a short one, merely taking it to one of the many docks at the same naval base.

Here a cadre of workers swarmed over her. They would clean the effects of years of weathering, refurbish her, and bring her to a fighting condition again. The work would not take long and she would soon be ready for a second tour of duty, one that would be much more exciting than the first. This time she would fight, but before she could do that, she would need a crew. That effort was already under way in Saint Paul, Minnesota.

Following World War I, budget cuts had forced the U.S. to drastically cut its active military. Military planners foresaw the need to maintain a force of experienced men to supplement the active navy in case of national emergency. They established a naval reserve with units scattered in major cities around the country. These units, designated as divisions, were empowered to recruit and train young men in the various occupations of a navy combat ship. The divisions also included men who had already served a hitch in the navy and elected to remain in the reserves on stand-by call. A typical tour of duty for new reservists was three years followed by one year in the active navy.

In Minnesota the reserve unit was located in the state's capital, St. Paul. Its headquarters was an armory, a building at the Minnesota Boat Club on the Mississippi River. The armory was situated under the Wabasha Street bridge on the shore of Raspberry Island, now called Harriet Island. The armory was the home of the 47th and 48th Divisions of the 11th Naval Battalion, 9th Naval District, from the 1920s to the early 1940s.

Each division numbered fewer than 100 men, the 47th Division meeting for several hours every Monday evening, and the 48th Division meeting on Tuesdays. Initially the 47th Division consisted entirely of "deck" ratings while the 48th Division included only the engineering-rated men. In the late 1930s the navy recognized that when reservists would be called to active duty, it would undoubtedly be to take over an entire reactivated ship. To facilitate this, the divisions were reorganized to include both deck and engineering personnel. Thus each of the two divisions could now be reactivated as a unit and assigned to a single ship.

Training consisted of instruction in basic seamanship, navy regulations, tying knots, manual of arms, first aid, fire fighting, rowing, signaling, Morse code, and basics of small arms. It also included several of the sailors "favorite" duties, such as scrubbing decks and polishing brass. Opportunities for hands-on instruction on the water were provided by several training vessels.

One, a 75-foot patrol boat, USS *Ramsey* was assigned to the 11th Battalion. Kept at Raspberry Island, it became the private navy of the St. Paul Naval Reserve. The *Ramsey* spent most of her early career in the Gulf of Mexico as U.S. Cruiser 225, chasing rum runners who were attempting to bring liquor illegally into the country. When the need for her services there disappeared, the navy brought her to Minnesota for use as a reservist training vessel. The St. Paul unit renamed her in honor of Minnesota's pioneer governor, Alexander Ramsey.[4]

Ramsey was manned by a crew of two officers and nine men but for training exercises would carry a large contingent of men. It offered a variety of on-water training and took reservists to various ports of call on the St. Croix and Mississippi Rivers. On one warm summer weekend, *Ramsey* took a group of reservists up the St. Croix to visit the city of Stillwater's annual Lumberjack Festival. In white uniforms the men walked the streets, taking in the sights and activities, much like any sailor on liberty.

On another summer day in 1940, the reservists took the boat down the Mississippi to a secluded area near Castle Rock, Wisconsin. After anchoring the boat, the crew, under the watchful eye of Lieutenant Hartwell Doughty, a tough taskmaster, engaged in small arms target practice. They were using the standard military issue 0.45 caliber pistol and their targets were all the old cans and bottles the crew could round up in the brush around the sandbar. It was hot, so Doughty took off his shirt but kept his undershirt on.

With Doughty observing intently, Dick Thill, 17 and a new reservist, squeezed off several rounds hoping to get close to one of the targets to impress Doughty. One of Thill's hot ejected casings flew through the air and down inside Doughty's undershirt causing him to yelp in surprise and discomfort. Thill related later, "I tried to look apologetic but I also had to bite my lip to keep from laughing out loud."[5]

Without doubt, the highlight of the reservists' training was the annual two-week cruise on the Great Lakes. The navy maintained a fleet of gunboats for regular navy trainees at the Great Lakes Naval Training Station north of Chicago and for the 9th Naval Reserve District. The Reserve District made these boats available to all naval reserve divisions in the upper Midwest.

Most of the boats were already old and not initially intended to serve as active gunboats. Tight budgets after World War I, however, did not include new gunboats for reserve training. Through the post-war years, a number of boats served the reservists, only to be replaced by "newer" boats as they became available. The boats were based at various ports including Chicago and Detroit. From 1938 to 1941, this fleet included the gunboats *Dubuque*, *Paducah*, *Sacramento*, *Wilmette*, and *Wilmington*, among others.

Although at least four gunboats were normally available, the 47th Division in St. Paul used only two of them from 1938 through 1940. *Paducah* was used on the cruises in 1938 and 1940, while *Wilmington* was used in 1939.[6] Both were old and nearing the end of their service life in the late 1930s.

USS *Wilmington* was built in 1895 in Newport News, Virginia. At 252 feet long and 1571 tons in displacement, it was actually larger than *Ward*. Its normal crew size was 212. To facilitate training of destroyer crews, it was equipped with eight 4"/50 caliber guns, the same guns carried by all U.S. destroyers. It was usually moored at the foot of Randolph Street in Chicago.[7]

The USS *Wilmington,* a 1571-ton gunboat built in 1895, took the 47th Division reservists on their summer cruise on the Great Lakes in 1939. (Naval Historical Center)

Wilmington participated in the blockading of Cuba during the Spanish-American War, spent the next 21 years in the Pacific, and returned to the U.S. in 1923. It was then based on the Great Lakes to provide training to regular navy and naval reserve personnel of the 9th Naval District. It was there that St. Paul's 47th Division reservists met this well traveled ship and spent two weeks aboard her on the 1939 summer cruise.

With the outbreak of World War II, *Wilmington* was again needed on the combat rolls and left the Great Lakes. After a year on active duty escorting Atlantic convoys, it was replaced by newer escort vessels. It spent the remainder of the war in New Orleans training gun crews for the large numbers of merchant ships now being mass-produced by U.S. shipyards, all of which contained at least one gun for defense against submarines.

The ship on which most of *Ward* crewmen received their training was the gunboat USS *Paducah.* It was built in Morris Heights, New York, in 1904 and served in the Caribbean until the U.S. declaration of war in 1917. During the war, *Paducah* was based at Gibralter and provided escort to Allied convoys to African and Mediterranean ports. In 1922 it was assigned to the Great Lakes as a training ship. It was moored at various locations including Duluth, Minnesota, and Chicago, Illinois.

In early 1941, it moved to Chesapeake Bay on the Atlantic coast, where it also provided training to merchant ship gun crews. After a 41-year life the venerable lady was finally decommissioned in 1945 and sold the following year.

Paducah, at 200 feet in length and 1084 tons in displacement, was considerably smaller

The USS *Paducah,* a 1084 ton gunboat built in 1904, carried the St. Paul reservists on the summer training cruises of 1938 and 1940. Most of the 47th Division men had at least one cruise on her. (Naval Historical Center)

than *Wilmington.* With a raked bow it looked more like a yacht than a gunboat. In 1904 it was capable of a modest 13 knots and manned by a crew of 184. Initially, its main battery consisted of four 4"/50 caliber guns although as a training ship, like *Wilmington,* it carried a single 4" gun. Originally a coal burner, *Paducah* had later been converted to burn fuel oil.[8]

With a lifetime of service already behind her and older than the men walking her decks, *Paducah* was still useful in the 1930s. She was destined to meet the future crew of *Ward* and play a role in their historic achievement.

In 1938, the nucleus of *Ward's* first crew in almost 20 years began to form in St. Paul. Young men were drawn to the naval reserve for a variety of reasons. Some, like Gordon Hultman and Walter Campion, felt a personal need to serve their country. For many others, the effects of the Depression that still gripped the nation were a major factor in their decision. With the scarcity of jobs, the future for young men finishing high school looked bleak at best.

This prompted Ray Nolde and others to join the reserve with the intent of serving a stint in the regular navy following the Reserve. Nolde, 24, had spent some time working for the Civilian Conservation Corps (CCC), the massive federal government work program of the 1930s. But for Nolde this was only a short-term solution; he was looking for more.

Don Pepin, Ed Mrozek, and Maurice Hurley joined for the extra money that reserve service put in their pocket. A naval reservist was paid seventy cents a meeting in 1938 which was same rate of pay that a regular navy seaman received. As one reservist put it, "that was pretty good money then." Don Pepin summed it up in practical terms: "We had reached the age, 17, where we began noticing girls, and it was nice to have a little pocket money."

Ed Zechmann joined the reserve because he was interested in seeing some of the world beyond the city limits of St. Paul. He thought the navy way of traveling would be a great experience. Frank Hajdu joined because of a recruiting ad in the local paper.

Some like Russell Reetz, Bob Ball, and Jack Peick joined because the United States was introducing the military draft in October 1940 to build up its army, and, if they had to be in the military, preferred navy service.

Bob Ball had another reason to avoid the army. He was attending Hamline University in St. Paul and had only one more semester left to get his degree. Getting drafted into the army would have prevented that, but joining the naval reserve allowed him to remain in St. Paul while he served.

Many of the reservists joined because they had a prior interest in the navy. Dick Thill, John Merthan, Will Lehner, Ed Bukrey, Orv Ethier, Tom Nadeau, and Ken Swedberg were in this group. Nadeau wanted to join the regular navy but was told by the recruiter that he would have to wait six months. He didn't want to wait so he joined the naval reserve that would accept him immediately.

"I always enjoyed the water, especially lakes that I couldn't see across, and the Atlantic and Pacific would fit that bill," admitted Ed Bukrey. He, Ed Mrozak, and Don Pepin, all students at St. Paul Johnson High School, joined the Reserve together.

Dick Thill even wrote a paper about the navy while in high school, complete with pictures. "I got an A on it," he quipped, "one of the few I ever got in high school." Thill had one of the more interesting tales about joining the Reserve. Because of his interest in the navy, he wanted to have his own white sailor's hat. He asked his father, who worked at Northern States Power Company, to ask a fellow worker who was a navy lieutenant where Dick could get such a hat. "Hell," said the lieutenant, "tell your son to join the naval reserve and he'll get the whole damn uniform." Dick took that advice and he soon had his uniform, hat and all.

Thill was only 16 when he joined the reserves in 1940, one of the youngest in the 47th Division. Most were 17 or 18 years of age and still in high school. A few were older. Bob Ball was 22; Ken Pfaff was 23; and Ray Nolde, Russell Reetz, and several others were 24.

The core of what would some day become the first crew of the *Ward* began assembling in 1938 when the 47th Division received a large influx of enlistees. By late 1940, much of the future crew of *Ward* had now mustered in St. Paul and the Division was nearing full strength at just fewer than 100 men. Training continued year around at the Raspberry Island armory. In the summer of each year the 47th and 48th Divisions took part in their major training effort of the year, the two-week Great Lakes cruise.

On a warm July evening in 1938, the St. Paul Reservists packed their sea bags and gathered at the Union Depot railroad station. At 9:45 P.M. the contingent left on a sleeper train for Chicago, where they would board *Paducah* at Navy Pier. This scene would be repeated in 1939 and 1940. In some years the crew took a train to Duluth to pick up the ship, and rode the train back from Chicago.

Men like Don Pepin, who joined the Reserve early in 1938, and Gust Mondo, who joined in 1937, made three summer cruises. Others like John Merthan, Jack Peick, or Russell Reetz, who joined late in 1940, did not attend any cruise. They would have been on the 1941 cruise but by that time they had been activated into the regular navy and were already in the Pacific. These men would be forced to acquire their sea training on the job.

In Chicago the St. Paul reservists boarded *Paducah* to begin a working adventure. For most, it would be their first time on a large body of water. Even leaving the pier was an adventure of sorts for Ed Bukrey. He was watching a young lady waving goodbye to her boy friend on *Paducah.* In her exuberance, she waved so enthusiastically that her underpants dropped down to her ankles. All crewmen who saw this unexpected sight, Bukrey included, gave her a hearty and lusty cheer.[9]

As soon as *Paducah* left the pier, the men were introduced to life on a ship at sea. They were given duties commensurate with their rating. Men with Seaman ratings were introduced to the various features of the deck and stood watches such as lookout, bridge steering, torpedo, gun, or depth charge watch. Those with Watertender, Fireman, or Machinist Mate ratings went below for orientation on the operation of the engines, boilers, or other equipment. Men with Quartermaster rating became involved in laying out the course for the cruise.

Like typical navy combat ships, watches were four hours on duty and eight hours off. One of Ed Bukrey's least favorite duties was striking the ship's bell every 30 minutes while on messenger watch. In describing that duty he said wryly, "After one watch I never wanted to hear a bell again."

Orv Ethier enjoyed the variety of experience the cruise offered. On the 1939 cruise he was a member of one of the gun crews, and on the 1940 cruise he was a member of one of the boat crews. *Paducah* carried several whaleboats, which were used to take men ashore for liberty if the ship could not tie at a dock and to carry messages to Coast Guard Stations whenever *Paducah* passed one of these facilities.

Not all of the personnel on the ship were reservists. At critical positions in the engine room, regular navy crewmen operated the equipment and served as instructors.

Everything was totally new to Dick Thill. He had joined the reserve only a month before the 1940 cruise. His only exposure to the navy was the several reserve meetings he attended before the cruise. On *Paducah* he was a yeoman striker, or trainee, so he quickly delved into the maze of reports and clerical duties found on a navy ship.

Service aboard *Paducah* was a learning experience around the clock. The men quickly learned that life aboard a combat ship would be a major change from their routines in St. Paul. For Gordon Hultman the new learning experience began on the very first evening, when he was introduced to the hammock. After what seemed like hours, and probably was, he was finally able to achieve a shaky, perilous equilibrium in the monster. He spent a restless night attempting to sleep without moving a muscle. He was abruptly awakened with a resounding whack on the rear end. The boatswain's mate, rousing the crew with a paddle, was Hultman's welcome to a new day in the seaborne navy of 1940.

The welcome was extended to the entire crew on the first day when they were mustered on deck. They were given a quick refresher course in some of the basic disciplines of life at sea, including swabbing the deck, polishing brass, repairing nets, chipping rust and old paint, and applying new paint. They would become veterans at these chores, especially swabbing, before the cruise was over. The wooden deck was scrubbed every morning.

Lake Michigan soon revealed itself to be a vastly different body of water than the Mississippi River or the lakes of St. Paul, where the reservists had grown their sea legs. Fortunately for the crew, they were spared the ferocity of terrible storms for which the Great Lakes were noted and which had littered the lake bottoms with wrecks over the years. However, they were still treated to the Great Lakes version of foul weather and learned that even a 200-foot ship rolled heavily in a brisk wind.

However bad the weather on Lake Michigan could be, the weather on Lake Superior was even worse. The east-west orientation of the lake allowed the prevailing westerly winds a long sweep down the length of the lake. These winds piled up waves higher than the crew had ever seen before and made the mere task of walking on deck an exciting adventure at times.

On the 1940 cruise, a new menace appeared when the crew awakened to fog. On one occasion *Paducah* was enveloped in a dense gray blanket for three days. Before the advent of radar, a ship's best protection from collision in fog was its foghorn. The *Paducah* blew hers continuously, day and night, until visibility improved. To a number of crewmen who had strung hammocks on the weather deck, attempting to sleep in zero-visibility fog with a fog horn blaring was extremely unsettling.

An uninhabited island in Lake Michigan provided an opportunity for live firing exercises with *Paducah's* lone four-inch gun. Gun crews alternated firing at a target set up on the island. This was vastly more exciting that the dummy drills the crews usually practiced. Ed Bukrey served as "hot shell man" on his crew, an operation he claimed to have mastered. On December 7, 1941, Bukrey would be a member of another gun crew on another ship, the *Ward,* that would make an historic hit on a more meaningful target.

Will Lehner also put this experience to good use later. As a loader on the *Ward's* Number 4 three-inch gun in 1943 and 1944, he helped to fight off many Japanese aircraft during the ship's frequent battles. Orv Ethier, who would be in *Ward's* boiler room on December 7, 1941, could also serve on a four-inch gun crew, if needed, because of training he received firing at that deserted island in Lake Michigan.

Paducah carried several oar-powered longboats, which served as lifeboats but which were also used in exercises. A crew armed with bayoneted rifles and puttee leggings manned the boats for a simulated landing on an adjacent shore. Upon reaching the shore, the crew would disembark, stretch their legs, and board the longboat for a return to *Paducah*.

Dick Thill recalled the exercise well. "There I was," chuckled Dick, "sixteen years old, weighing only 132 pounds, and attempting to manipulate an oar about 15 feet long and as big around as my legs. God, I could barely lift it. But I rowed."

On the 1939 cruise, one of the young seamen had the starboard lookout watch on a dark night. He noticed a bright light just over the horizon and thought he better report it to the Officer of the Deck. The officer acknowledged the report and moved on. He returned shortly and asked the seaman, "Where is the light now? Is it any bigger?" When the seaman pointed out that the light was getting bigger, the officer wryly remarked, "It should. That's the moon coming up."[10]

The cruise usually provided one and sometimes two shore liberties. Favorite ports of call for the crew were the twin cities of Marinette, Wisconsin, and Menominee, Michigan; Green Bay, Wisconsin; and the scenic Apostle Islands on the north shore of Wisconsin. Here the men were given an afternoon or evening of liberty to do what they wanted. It was a welcome respite from the routine of working and learning.

Tragedy struck the ship on the 1940 cruise. One of the crew who would occasionally sleep-walk slept on deck next to his brother. One dark night he simply walked over the side. He was seen by one of the lookouts, who raised the alarm. The ship stopped immediately and both longboats were launched at about 0300. Another naval training ship was in the vicinity and assisted in the search. The boats searched for an hour as searchlights plied the surrounding area, but the search was unsuccessful. The sailor was a reservist from Ohio, not one of the St. Paul members. His brother was shaken terribly by the incident and was sent home the following day.[11]

Will Lehner, on one of the boat crews, recalled the incident. "Rowing those big boats in total darkness on the big lake was a scary experience." Ken Swedberg also recalled the incident. He was moved by the amount of effort expended by the navy to locate the missing man, who was an entry-level sailor. He would discover soon that looking after sailors in peril was common procedure in the navy.

In 1940, the two weeks passed quickly and the reservists returned to St. Paul more aware now of what the sea-going navy was all about. It whetted their appetite and, to a man, they were already looking forward to the next cruise. It would come much sooner than they realized. In October 1940 the navy informed the 47th Division that it would be activated in January 1941. The men were advised to put their affairs in order before then.

For most men, the news was no surprise. Europe was already at war and the United States was gradually being drawn into active conflict in the Atlantic convoys. In the Pacific, the U.S. fleet was being expanded to counter the Japanese threat. It seemed likely to the men that the 47th Division would be called up soon. Walter Campion's reaction was typical, "I knew it was coming, because problems with Germany and Japan were becoming serious. I felt excited about being activated. It's what I wanted."

Preparing for activation was not difficult for most of the men. Most were single and did not hold permanent jobs. They were all young; most, under 19. Some were still in high school. Dick Thill was still a junior in St. Paul Humboldt High School when he learned of the activation. He had to tell his principal that he must leave school in January to go on active duty. Thill thought it was exciting, but his parents were quite upset that he could not finish high school.

Following the notification of the impending activation, training at the reserve armory in the last several months of 1940 continued on a more serious tone. The men now realized that they would soon be going to sea for real and for an extended time, not merely two weeks. They were excited but knew that they could be caught up in a shooting war that made the future uncertain at best. To most of them, going to sea would be an adventure, probably the greatest adventure of their lives. Without exception, they all looked forward to it. For now, combat seemed too far away to be a concern.

The St. Paul reservists celebrated Christmas 1940 at home, the last Christmas they would share with their families for five years. This one took on a special meaning for them.

Each reservist received a letter from the navy on January 21, 1941, confirming their activation and ordering them to report with a full sea bag for transfer to an active unit. The die was now cast for them. They were issued additional clothing to bring their sea bag up to date. In 1940 the navy was still furnishing all clothes for servicemen. Later, the navy provided clothing allowances and the men bought their own clothes.

With preparations complete, the 47th Division boarded a train at the Union Depot in St. Paul at 1100 on January 23, 1941. It was 20 degrees below zero as the men began their journey to San Diego, California. The temperature would be about 100 degrees higher when they arrived. Waving goodbye to their family, friends, and the City of St. Paul, the men, now on active duty, began an adventure beyond their wildest imagination. It would be almost two years before they would return.

For most of the men, even the train ride was a new experience. Many had never been on a train before and most had never left the Upper Midwest. For all, the trip to San Diego would be their longest to date. The train's first stop was Omaha, Nebraska, where they picked up a dining car. There the men were given meal tickets, which allowed them to eat in the dining car with civilian passengers and order right off the menu. "This was an unexpected treat," remarked Gordon Hultman. "The food was excellent."

Most of the sleeping compartments were taken by civilians, leaving fewer remaining compartments for sailors. A few men, such as Ken Swedberg, had their own berth. Others had to share a berth. Dick Thill remembers that officers looked for skinny guys to pair up with. "I was pretty thin then," laughed Thill. "They paired me up with Harold Flanagan who was also skinny. It was probably unethical and maybe even illegal, but at least we got a decent night's sleep."

Everyone else had to sleep sitting up in the wooden seats they sat in all day. Orv Ethier was one of those without a sleeping berth. "We didn't mind it," chuckled Ethier. "We were all young yet and this was still a new experience for us."

At North Platte, Nebraska, the train stopped to change engines at the big Union Pacific yard there. While the men waited for the switch to be completed, a group of women came out to the train passing out coffee, cookies, and doughnuts. This was another unexpected treat.

The St. Paul contingent was experiencing the beginning of what would later become one of the most famous servicemen's hospitality centers in the country, the North Platte Canteen. During World War II, this organization, housed in the Union Pacific Depot, met every train passing through the city. During the ten-minute stop, volunteers rushed to the train with free refreshments, cigarettes, and magazines. The volunteers were not only from North Platte but from small towns in Nebraska, Colorado, and Kansas. They met up to 20 trains and welcomed and fed up to 5000 servicemen daily. This canteen welcomed more than 6 million servicemen in this fashion during the war. The St. Paul men remember that train stop to this day.

The train's next stop was a four-hour layover in Colorado Springs. Most of the men used the time to walk around the downtown area of this scenic city set in the mountains, which most of the men had never seen. What left a lasting impression on Dick Thill were the drinking fountains situated on the corners of each block downtown. "Imagine that," said Thill, "drinking fountains. I'd never seen that before."

When the train passed through Royal Gorge, the noted tourist attraction west of Colorado Springs, it stopped below the bridge 1000 feet above them. Everyone got off the train to view the famous bridge they could barely see directly above. The men were thoroughly enjoying the trip. Walter Campion was intrigued by the magnificent scenery from the flatlands of Nebraska to the white-tipped mountains of Colorado, the likes of which he'd never seen in Minnesota.

The inevitable card games quickly sprung up. Lieutenant Hartwell Doughty, who commanded the 47th Division in St. Paul, was still in command and was traveling with the group. A strict disciplinarian, Doughty reminded the men that gambling for money on the train was absolutely prohibited. Nevertheless, poker games could be found in every car, with money at stake. The men laid their coins on the table as any group of men on their way to war would do. Someone was always designated to watch for officers. When one entered the car, the alert was given, and match sticks quickly appeared out of nowhere to replace the coins.

John Merthan was one of the players, if only for a short time. While in high school, John had purchased a 1930 Ford Model A for $50 he raised himself. John was proud of the car, but when he was activated, he sold it to a friend for $45. He took the entire $45 with him to San Diego to use as spending money until he got paid.

Although he did not know how to play poker, others were "kind" enough to teach him. The predictable happened. John lost the entire $45 before the train was half way to San Diego. He didn't have a nickel left when he reached the base and had to wait for payday to go to town with the others on liberty. "The officers looking for gambling on the train didn't bother me," laughed Merthan. "I was out of the game pretty quickly."

Dick Thill did not play poker either. He simply had no money. Seamen only made $21 a month, $10.50 on the 5th and 20th of each month, and he started sending half of that home early.

Days were uncomfortably warm on the train, but nights were cold in the unheated railroad cars. Walt Campion would slip on his wool "watch" cap after the sun went down. He misplaced his cap one night and searched the entire car, seat by seat. He never did locate his cap but he found a sleeping puppy that someone smuggled on the train. "I let him sleep," said Walt. I wasn't warm but at least the puppy was."

A day after leaving Colorado Springs, the train passed through Salt Lake City and made a several-hour-long stop. There was only time for a visit to the Mormon Tabernacle and most of the crew went. The train then continued to California, stopping in Los Angeles before reaching San Diego.

The men loved California. The warm temperature appealed to them. So did the scenery. As the train moved through one orchard, the men were able to reach out the car windows and pick oranges right off the trees. This was another unexpected treat. The five-day trip was almost over and was an enjoyable experience for a group of sailors from Minnesota on their way to a war half-way around the world.

As the train pulled into San Diego on January 28, the men wondered what lay ahead for them in the great adventure they had chosen for themselves. What ship would they draw? Would it be a new one or a carry-over from World War I from the reserve fleet? How big would it be? Would it have many guns? These questions would quickly be answered.

The men were taken from the depot directly to the destroyer base at the sprawling naval base. Here they were assigned bunks in a large wooden barracks. This would be their home for the next week. It was here that the men learned that their ship would be a 1050-ton World War I destroyer, USS *Ward* (DD-139). Restoration of *Ward* was already under way at berth F of the destroyer base. Workmen were occupying its sleeping compartments and the 47th Division would have to wait until they left before taking over their own compartments.

The navy had earlier moved *Ward* out of "red lead row," where it had resided since 1922 in the reserve fleet. At berth F a full restoration was under way to make *Ward* ready for sea again. It was the last Reserve Fleet destroyer to be activated and thus had been used as a floating supply depot for all ships activated before her. Restoration crews on other ships used the time-honored military technique of "midnight requisitions" to obtain difficult-to-locate parts and equipment. They simply stole them from *Ward* rather than look for a warehouse with 23-year-old parts.

Soon *Ward* was missing bunks, deck plates, radio and other communication equipment, gun sights, engine room parts, pumps, and countless other items. It was in this condition that the ship was moved to berth for restoration. *Ward's* condition actually worked to the ship's benefit. Missing items now had to be replaced with new equipment purchased on an emergency basis. When *Ward* would go to sea, she would now be in better condition than most of her sister ships.

At berth F, crews of welders, electricians, carpenters, and ship fitters from the navy yard, as well as regular navy crewmen, swarmed over the ship attempting to create a fighting ship out of a derelict. On January 15, although the ship was still three weeks from completion, it was in condition to be recommissioned into the United States Navy.

At 1130, with a temporary crew on hand, the commanding officer of the destroyer base placed *Ward* into commission. The colors were raised, Lt. Commander Hunter Wood read his orders to take command as the ship's captain, and watches were set. Present at the ceremony were three officers, 50 enlisted men assigned to the crew, and 64 men temporarily assigned to the ship until the reservists from St. Paul could report.[12] In St. Paul, the reservists were still a week away from leaving for San Diego. After the commissioning ceremony, work on the ship continued, and stores and provisions were taken on daily.

At 1400 on January 29, the 47th Division from St. Paul with two officers and 80 enlisted men reported to *Ward* for the first time. In addition to Lt. Doughty, the St. Paul contingent included Ensign Donald Haynie. Ensign Theodore Grefe, not from St. Paul, also became part of Ward's first crew. Haynie would be the ship's Assistant Engineering Officer, while Grefe was assigned the position of Assistant Gunnery Officer.[13]

This was the first look at their new home. The deck was cluttered with loose rigging, stores, provisions, construction equipment, and workers engaged in a variety of restoration tasks. Don Pepin turned to a crewmate and remarked, "We're not going to sea in that are we?" Twelve days later they would do just that.

Many of the St. Paul crew were taken to *Ward* daily to assist in the work. They spent days chipping and wire-brushing barnacles, old paint, and 19 years of rust, repainting, and loading provisions. At 1600 they were returned to their barracks and, if they didn't have duty, they were given a liberty pass.

Sailors on liberty in San Diego with very little money in their pockets have to be creative in their pursuit of recreation. Some searched for fun amid the bright lights of downtown. Others went swimming. Ed Bukrey, an avid golfer, discovered Balboa Park and golfed there. Ken Swedberg and Scotty Fenton were ice skaters and skated often on the neighborhood rinks of St. Paul. After searching around they discovered an indoor ice rink in San Diego that rented skates, and visited when they could. Swedberg was flabbergasted to think that San Diego would have an indoor ice arena. Many stayed on base at night, usually because of the lack of ready cash. One sailor brought his guitar along and usually started a songfest every night.

Life in the barracks was very informal; men were allowed to lounge around in shorts and T-shirts. The men considered the food to be quite acceptable. There was actually little to gripe about, but Ed Bukrey found something. He thought the barracks were too hot during the day and too cold at night.

On February 6, workmen finally left the crew's quarters on the *Ward,* making it available for the legitimate ship's crew. The reservists moved en mass from the barracks to the ship to take up occupancy on their own ship. *Ward* and her crew were finally united. Some of the original 50-man commissioning crew were reassigned off the ship, leaving a crew of 39 experienced men and the 80 men of the 47th Division from St. Paul to man *Ward* as her first crew since 1922.

The men continued to work on the ship but could now simply go below deck to crawl into their own bunk instead of making the trip back to the barracks. On February 8, Seaman 2c William Griep, playing football on the dock alongside *Ward,* broke an ankle while kicking the football. He was taken to the naval hospital in San Diego and there joined several others who had injured themselves in accidents on the ship.

The men were assigned to either the forward or after crew compartments depending on their rating. The deck gangs were berthed in the forward compartment while the engine and fire room crews, or black gangs, took the after compartment. When the war broke out, the fallacy of this berthing arrangement was recognized. A torpedo hit in the aft section could wipe out most of the engineering division leaving few to run the ship. A hit in the forward section could have the same effect on the deck division. Beginning early in 1942, the gangs would be intermixed so that half of the deck and engineering forces were assigned to either end of the ship.

The bunks were actually steel tube framing with a sheet of canvas tied within that frame. Bunks were two or three units high and lined both sides of the compartments. Each man also had a personal locker in which he kept his clothes and other effects. Like most features on the ship, the selection of bunks followed a pecking order. First-class ratings were given the lower bunks; second-and third-class rated men had the uppers.[14]

By February 9, work on *Ward* was nearly completed and the ship's oil bunkers filled. At 0930 on the 10th, two boilers were lit off and steam pressure began building. Two tugs pushed her away from the dock and *Ward* was on her way for her trial run, her first movement under her own power in 19 years.

She cleared San Diego harbor and spent the day conducting a variety of maneuvers at various speeds to check out her propulsion, steering, and other vital systems. She returned to the dock at 1623 with no significant problem encountered. *Ward* was one step closer to going to war. For the St. Paul crew, it had been their first experience on a combat ship.

At 1103 on February 13, *Ward* went out on trials again and returned at 1620 with no major problems uncovered. At the dock the ship took on stores daily, getting closer to the day it would be ready to join the active navy. Seamen Griep, along with Seaman Lombardi, who was hospitalized for a high fever, returned from the base hospital. The crew was whole again.

On February 24 *Ward* left San Diego for a run to Mare Island, the place of her birth in 1918. On the relatively short cruise the crew calibrated the radio direction finder and the degaussing equipment. The first noteworthy problem occurred when a clogged fuel oil strainer required shutting down the forward fireroom. The ship stopped at sea while crews lit off the after boilers and waited for steam pressure to build.

At 1247 on February 26, the reservists received another thrill as *Ward* passed under the Golden Gate Bridge. For most of the crew, it was their first glimpse of the national landmark. They would all see it again within a few days under somewhat different circumstances. *Ward* docked at Mare Island at 1529, not far from the building way where she had been built in 1918.

Ward now proceeded with the final major preparation prior to joining the fleet—acquiring armaments. Dock handlers and crewmen swarmed over the ship, loading hundreds of ordnance items, including torpedoes, depth charges, cartridges for firing the "Y-gun" depth charge thrower, three-and four-inch dummy and live ammunition, 0.30 and 0.45 caliber small arms ammunition, star shells for illumination, Very pistol guns and cartridges, and a variety of percussion caps, fuses, and spare parts for all weapons. *Ward* could now fight if called upon. On February 27, *Ward* topped off her fuel bunkers for the final time, taking on 23,000 gallons of fuel oil.[15] *Ward* was now ready to leave. Tomorrow *Ward* would begin her longest journey to date.

The St. Paul reservists and the rest of *Ward's* crew were about to embark on a great adventure, one that would include an unimaginable experience, eternal fame for the ship and crew, and a place forever in the naval history of the United States, They did not know what lay ahead of them, but they would discover that in due time. Their destination: Pearl Harbor.

CHAPTER 4

Ward Goes to Sea

A dark gray overcast day greeted early risers on *Ward* on Friday, February 28, not the kind of day they would have liked for the beginning of a long awaited cruise to Hawaii. They still preferred this to the weather they knew their friends back in Minnesota were experiencing. The skies even looked sinister but they had seen threatening skies before in their short stay in California.

Ward was moored alongside USS *Bridge,* a 5207-ton stores ship at the Mare Island Navy Yard. One boiler, Number 4, was in use to supply auxiliary power to the ship while in port. After a 0745 muster call at quarters, the crew completed final preparations for getting under way. The St. Paul reservists were looking forward to finally being out of sight of land. This was the reason many of them joined the reserve — a sea voyage to a distant land. They were about to embark on their first such cruise and it was the topic of conversation all over the ship. To the older hands on the ship, this was just another cruise; they had been on many before.

At 1300 *Ward* pulled away slowly from *Bridge.* A Mare Island pilot familiar with the tricky tides and currents in Mare Island Harbor and San Pablo Bay was on the bridge giving instructions to the helmsman. Soon the engine room throttles were giving 171 revolutions per minute on the two screws pushing the ship at a comfortable 15 knots. The docks and buildings gradually grew smaller and then disappeared as Ward left them in the distance.

The harbor pilot disembarked at 1338 and *Ward* continued through San Pablo Bay with the captain conning the ship. It passed famous Alcatraz Island to port at 1538 and steamed under the Golden Gate Bridge 13 minutes later. At 1628 it passed the main channel buoy and cleared the San Francisco entrance channel.[1] *Ward* was now free of the mainland and on its way to Pearl.

Then all hell broke loose! As soon as *Ward* passed under the Golden Gate Bridge most of the crew would have returned to Mare Island if the choice was theirs to make. All of a sudden they were in a different world, a savage one. Their welcome to the Pacific was in the form of dark gray to black dangerous-looking skies; rough, rolling seas; and a northeast wind that was still gathering strength as they left the harbor. The wind quickly increased in ferocity, driving a pelting rain before it and piling up huge waves. It howled through the ship's rigging with a shriek that added to the terror of being on deck.

The ship pitched and rolled, sometimes in several directions simultaneously. By 1702 the ship was taking such a pounding that the captain ordered the speed reduced to eight knots. As darkness fell, the crew realized that they were in the grip of a major Pacific storm. Winds were now clocked at 50 miles per hour, howling even louder as they lashed the ship. Waves swept across the deck and visibility was almost zero.

Many in the crew were now concerned with the ship's ability to ride out such a storm. The St. Paul men had never been on the ocean and had never been in a major storm on water before. Having both events occur simultaneously was not something they had anticipated.

The new day brought no change in the weather or sea. The gale force winds were still driving in from the northeast creating huge waves. The ship still pitched and rolled heavily. The seas to the west looked ugly and mountainous, and no place for a ship of only 1100 tons. During the night the captain changed course, deciding not to follow the path of the storm on a direct line for Hawaii. Instead, he headed southeast following the coast at eight knots and keeping within sight of land.

Finally at 0628 on March 1, the captain felt that the ship could navigate safely in the open sea and changed course to steam directly for Hawaii. Throughout the day *Ward* plowed into heavy seas with the wind at her stern. With steering difficult at eight knots, the captain increased speed to ten knots, allowing the ship to answer her helm better. He soon decreased it again because of the heavy pitching, which was punishing both ship and crew. With a following wind, *Ward* would be traveling with the storm for days, not a comforting thought to the officers and men.

The pitching and rolling made most activity on the ship impossible. Safety lines were rigged on deck from bow to stern for those who absolutely had to be on deck. Even so, John Merthan was almost lost when a large wave knocked him off the safety line. He was barely able to grab a torpedo tube before going over the side.

Below deck it was impossible to stand up and most men not on duty simply lay in their bunks. Two-thirds of the crew were sick, but Merthan and Will Lehner were not among them. Some of the crew did not get out of his bunk for days. Merthan was not affected. He was able to eat whatever the ship's cook fixed, which was not much. Cooking was almost impossible. The crew lived for days on soup, sandwiches, oranges and coffee. Merthan even scrounged cold hot dogs when he could.

Lehner, one of the mess cooks even though he held a fireman's rating, watched the ship roll from side to side. "I was concerned that on one of those rolls, the ship wouldn't come back and just roll right over," he recalled. "I really didn't think the ship would make it." He had to bring chow down to the crew's quarters from the galley but, because few men were eating, he did not have much to do. Lehner learned later that the storm they sailed through was one of the roughest Pacific storms in years. Gene Heiberger had dreams about the storm for years after. He heard that the ship had rolled up to 48 degrees.

Ken Pfaff had the closest call of all the crewmen. He was on deck watching the parade of men throwing up over the side. This finally made him throw up and as he leaned over, a wave hit him hard. "It felt like someone whacked me with a plank," he recalled. "My feet left the deck and I was going over the side. All of a sudden I felt a hand tug at my belt and pull me back. I never saw who it was and to this day I don't who or what it was that saved my life."

Ward was a sturdy ship, however. The crew of J. T. Moroney had not only built *Ward* in record time in 1918, they had also built it well. In 1941 *Ward* was still the same basic ship that Moroney had built. It still had an over-all length of 314'-4½" and a beam of 30'-11½". The original Normand boilers and Parsons geared turbines still propelled the two three-bladed screws.

Its weaponry in 1941 was the same as it had been in 1918, with one exception. Its main battery of four 4"/50 caliber guns was still its principal threat, and it retained the two 0.50-

caliber machine guns for anti-aircraft defense. Its 12 torpedo tubes, depth charge racks and Y-gun were those it had carried in 1918. However, one of the two 3"/23 caliber anti-aircraft guns it carried in 1918 was removed, leaving only the one immediately aft of the forward 4"/50 gun.[2]

The two-month restoration following her activation from the reserve fleet primarily removed dirt, grime, and rust that had accumulated over the past 19 years at anchor. It also included servicing of all equipment and replacement of missing equipment which, in this case, was a good share of her equipment. Some of it, such as radio and other electronics, was removed and updated.

Otherwise, the *Ward* which was being buffeted by wind, rain, and waves, on March 1, 1941 was the same ship launched in June 1918. The passage of time did have its affect on the ship, however, and it could no longer make 35 knots. Its top speed was now 25 knots but the engine room crew could coax several additional knots from the tired engines for short periods of time.

It was a mixed crew that manned *Ward* on its story voyage to Hawaii. The crew numbered seven officers and 119 enlisted men. Of the officers, only two, Lt. Commander Hunter Wood, the captain; and Lt. Hilary Rowe, the Engineering Officer; were regular navy men. The remaining five — Lt. Doughty, and Ensigns Goepner, Haynie, Grefe, and Andrews — were all reservists called to active duty and assigned to *Ward*.[3]

The enlisted men came from three sources — regular navy, fleet reserves, and naval reservists. The core of the crew was the cadre of 25 regular navy personnel and 14 fleet reservists. These men filled the critical positions in the engine room, boiler or fire room, and deck crew as well as specialist positions such as ship's cook, pharmacist's mates, machinist's mates, electrician's mates and the various senior positions of "chief" throughout the ship.[4] Because the rapid expansion of the navy outgrew the navy's ability to staff new ships entirely with regular full-time navy personnel, *Ward* was allocated 25 experienced regulars reassigned from other ships, usually destroyers.

Regular navy personnel were augmented by a small number of fleet reserves. These were men who had already served one or more hitches in the navy, but chose to stay on reserve status upon completion of their regular service. Although now reservists, they were experienced in some field and could bring that knowledge and maturity to any crew they joined.

The bulk of the enlisted men came from the 47th Division Naval Reserve unit from St. Paul. Most of the men in this group of men had anywhere from three months to three years of training in the unit, including summer cruises, but were otherwise inexperienced in destroyer service. They had never participated in a formal navy "boot camp" and much of their training would be "on the job." A few of the 47th Division group were fleet reserves, however, having previously served in the navy. They brought some much needed experience to the division.

Collectively the mix of regular navy men, experienced fleet reservists, and younger and enthusiastic reservists from a single area gave *Ward* an excellent crew chemistry. This would soon transform the group into a tightly knit and efficient unit.

Ward maintained her direct course for Hawaii throughout the next several days with no abatement in the conditions. The storm continued to move westerly along with the ship's progress. On March 3, while attempting to eat breakfast, the ship's pitching threw Seaman Frank Fratto into a bunk, knocking him unconscious. Two other men were injured later in the day when one of the ship's violent lurches flung them to the deck in the Chief Petty Officer's quarters.[5]

Fire room personnel had a difficult time standing up to attend the boilers. They would periodically shut down two burners for maintenance and light the remaining two. This required removal of the burner tips for cleaning and immersion in a bucket of solvent until used at the next switch in burners. The buckets kept sliding across the deck plates with the rolling of the ship, overturning several times and dumping solvent all over the fire room. Eventually the watertenders devised a safer method of storing the burner tips.

Dave Morgan, a watertender, suffered from chronic sea sickness for the first day or two of every cruise, and this would plague him for his entire career. He would trade watches with another black-gang member and tie himself to a catwalk in the engine room. This particular storm was tough on him. After the war ended, Ken Swedberg claimed that Morgan still owed him several watches.

On March 5, heavy rains returned and, although seas were still heavy, *Ward* was able to increase speed to 12 knots. At 2313 on March 8, after eight days in the throes of the wild vicious storm, lookouts sighted their destination, the Makapuu Point light on the southeast tip of Oahu, 28 miles away. At 0305 on March 9, the lookouts sighted the Diamond Head light and the unmistakable outline of Oahu's most famous landmark. *Ward* was practically in port, but not quite.

An hour out of Pearl Harbor, *Ward's* engines stopped when they lost all suction. The ship lay to in sight of the coast while boilers 1 and 2 were shut down, boilers 3 and 4 lit, steam pressure raised, and repairs made. The ship was under way again at 0805 and entered the Pearl Harbor entrance channel at 0910. It stopped briefly to pick up a harbor pilot and proceeded into the harbor. It moored alongside the destroyer *Schley* at berth X-5 at 1010 and shut down the engines.

The harrowing journey was over, a journey some crewmen felt they would never survive. The St. Paul reservists had received their initial baptism of fire in the perils of Pacific Ocean weather. It was the latest in a continuing series of adventures, one they would have preferred to avoid.

Although other crew members had been to Pearl Harbor, only a few of the St. Paul reservists had seen it before. As they scanned their surroundings, they were amazed at the scene. Ships of every size and type lay at anchor all over the harbor. More than 70 ships were in port, including several battleships moored along Ford Island. They had not seen any battleships at either San Diego or Mare Island and were astounded by their size.

Pearl Harbor had been a U.S. naval base since early in the Twentieth Century but it was largely undeveloped until the 1930s. When other world naval powers began to make major increases in their naval forces, the United States was reluctantly forced to follow suit. Since an expanded Pacific Fleet required a naval base capable of accommodating it, enlargement of Pearl Harbor paralleled the expansion of the fleet.

New and larger facilities were needed, not only to provide safe anchorage for the many types of ships in the fleet, but to refuel, re-supply, maintain, and repair them as well. Fuel-tank farms, to store the millions of gallons of fuel oil used to power the ships, were an essential component of a major base. Several such farms were built within the confines of the base. Housing and related support services, such as a naval hospital and recreational facilities for the many thousands of naval personnel a fleet carried, were also an integral part of a base. These began to spring up adjacent to the harbor.

Since a modern fleet carried several hundred aircraft, similar facilities were required for these as well. The U.S Army had constructed an airfield, Luke Field, on Ford Island in the middle of Pearl Harbor in 1918 along with hangars and a variety of administrative buildings.

In 1923 Congress authorized construction of a naval seaplane base which was soon built on the southeastern tip of Ford Island. The two services operated jointly from Ford Island into the late 1930s, when the increasing naval presence caused over-crowding. The army constructed a large new facility, Hickam Field, adjacent to the harbor and moved its operations there in 1939. This left Ford Island exclusively to the navy.[6]

A new naval air station, complete with modern steel hangars, repair and maintenance shops, gasoline storage tanks, barracks, and administrative buildings was needed and constructed concurrently with the harbor facilities. By 1940 Pearl Harbor had developed into a modern naval base capable of accommodating a large fleet with its aircraft.

By June 1940, the importance of the base had changed dramatically. Because of the rapidly deteriorating political and military situation in the Pacific, the U.S. needed major combat ships closer to any potential threat. The nation's primary Pacific Fleet base at San Diego was simply too far from the areas of tension, such as the Philippines and Dutch East Indies, to permit U.S. naval units to respond quickly enough.

The United States also owned isolated but strategic Pacific territories, including Guam, Midway and Wake Islands to protect. To accomplish this, President Roosevelt ordered the navy to move its Pacific Fleet from San Diego to Pearl Harbor.[7]

Pearl Harbor was an excellent fleet anchorage although it was somewhat small for the number of ships and aircraft it had to accommodate. The harbor resembled a flattened doughnut with a flattened hole in the middle. That hole was Ford Island, upon which the Pearl Harbor Naval Air Station was built.

When the Pacific Fleet moved to Pearl Harbor, it brought with it four large aircraft carriers, each carrying about 75 planes. When the aircraft carriers were about to enter the harbor, they flew off their planes, which then landed on Ford Island. Here they would be serviced, overhauled, and repaired if necessary while the carriers remained in port. When the carriers left port, the aircraft took off from Ford Island and landed aboard the carriers at sea. It was an ideal arrangement.

Pearl Harbor was an inland body of water connected to the sea by a short channel. The channel gave the harbor some degree of protection but it was also the harbor's greatest liability. If a ship sank in the channel, it could bottle up the entire harbor for months. Potential enemies were well aware of this weakness.

The harbor provided various types of ship's moorings. Large concrete mooring quays along both sides of Ford Island were designated for capital ships. Battleships were moored side by side at the quays along the east side of the island; aircraft carriers, when in port, on the west side. The southeast sector of the harbor contained maintenance, repair, and supply warehouses plus three dry-docks and was designated as the "navy yard." The various finger piers in this sector could dock approximately 30 ships for servicing, maintenance, or repair. The dry-docks could each accommodate one or more ships needing hull servicing or repair.

A submarine base, adjacent to the navy yard, could handle more than a dozen submarines for servicing. Scattered around the harbor were designated mooring berths where up to six ships could moor side by side in nests. More than 50 ships could be moored in this fashion. For much of 1941, *Ward* would moor at a berth designated X-5 north of Ford Island. Although Pearl Harbor was, in fact, a small harbor, on most days it provided an anchorage for close to 100 ships. If necessary, it could hold more.

By March 24, *Ward* was restored to pre-storm condition. All repairs were completed, supplies and fuel replenished, and the ship ready to take her place as a fully operational destroyer with the United States Pacific Fleet.

Ward was assigned to Destroyer Division 80 of the Hawaiian Sea Frontier along with destroyers *Allen, Chew,* and *Schley.*[8] These were all four-stackers of the same vintage as *Ward.* This division's principal mission was to patrol a two-mile by two-mile area of the mouth of the Pearl Harbor entrance channel. This mission was officially referred to as "Inner Harbor Patrol" but was also called the "offshore patrol," "restricted area patrol," "prohibited area patrol," or "defensive area patrol." All of these terms described the same mission, which was to prevent unidentified or hostile vessels from entering or operating within this zone.

Given the political situation in the Pacific in 1941, the greatest threat at the harbor mouth was likely to be enemy submarines. The large volume of ship traffic entering or leaving the harbor, all of which would be traveling at a relatively slow speed, made the harbor entrance area a very vulnerable zone for Pacific Fleet ships. A hostile nation would undoubtedly station submarines off the harbor entrance to attack U.S. combat ships and possibly sink one in the channel itself.

Since the harbor and entrance channel were dredged to a depth of only 45 feet, fleet-sized enemy submarines would not be able to enter the harbor submerged without being seen. The nets at the harbor entrance were, therefore, not intended to keep submarines out. Instead, they were designed to prevent submarines outside the harbor from firing torpedoes into the harbor.[9]

Inner Harbor Patrol destroyers were thus responsible for locating submerged submarines and forcing them to the surface to be identified and escorted from the harbor mouth. Since all U.S. submarines entering or leaving the harbor were required to travel on the surface, for identification purposes, all submerged submarines in the harbor approach were assumed to be foreign.

The patrol destroyers were also responsible for identifying all surface craft in the restricted zone and either escorting them out of the area or holding them until a U.S. Coast Guard Cutter could be dispatched from Honolulu harbor to take the unauthorized craft into the harbor to be impounded. Thus, no fishing vessels, sight-seeing boats, or tourist crafts were permitted in the restricted area for any reason.

On all of these missions, patrol destroyers were authorized to use force if necessary. In the case of fishing vessels or tourist craft, a verbal warning was given, followed by a shot across the bow if the warning went unheeded. If submarines were encountered, gunshots or depth charges with the intent to force them to surface would be used. Later, the patrol destroyers were given the authority to sink unidentified submarines in the restricted area.

The harbor entrance protection was considered so vital that a separate level of supervision was established to oversee the forces assigned to it. Protecting the harbor entrance area was the responsibility of Commander John Wooley, whose Inshore Patrol Command included not only the four destroyers of Destroyer Division 80 but three Coast Guard Cutters, USS *Taney,* USS *Tiger,* and USS *Reliance,* and four small minesweepers, USS *Cockatoo,* USS *Condor,* USS *Crossbill,* and USS *Reedbird.*[10]

The Coast Guard Cutters had the traditional responsibility of patrolling the coastline to prevent illegal entry of people or goods. With a possible war pending, the cutters were also charged with seeking out and preventing acts of espionage.

In November 1941 the three cutters were taken over by the navy, equipped with underwater sound detectors, and ordered to assist in locating submarines in the Restricted Area off the Pearl Harbor mouth. Much of their time was devoted to checking out the many sampans fishing offshore but whenever they passed through the Restricted Area they searched with sonar. The Coast Guard had a number of smaller boats in Oahu also, all based at Honolulu Harbor.

The *Taney* was an imposing cutter and, in most respects, was more than the equal of *Ward* in anti-submarine capability. Built in 1936, at 327 feet in length, 41-foot beam, and 2216-ton displacement, it was a much larger ship than the *Ward*. It carried three five-inch and three three-inch guns. Cutters' *Reliance* and *Tiger* were much smaller, at 125 feet in length and 220 tons displacement. They carried a single three-inch gun.[11]

Included in the inner harbor patrol was a daily sweep for submarine-laid mines by two of the four minesweepers assigned to this mission. Sweeping usually commenced about 0200 in the morning before ship traffic became heavy. It was completed by 0630.

In addition to the Inner Harbor Patrol, a second line of destroyers, referred to as the "outer harbor patrol," guarded the approaches to Pearl and Honolulu harbors. This line was manned by several destroyers spaced along an arc five to ten miles from the harbor mouth. These had the responsibility of identifying approaching ships, and escorting U.S. naval or merchant vessels into or out of the harbor. Destroyer Division 80 would be assigned to this line in 1942, but in 1941 the outer harbor patrol was assigned to other destroyer divisions.

Ward left her berth at 0845 on Monday, March 24, and cleared the harbor by 0950 in her first working assignment outside the harbor. She had to calibrate her magnetic compass and had to be outside the harbor to accomplish this. In the evening *Allen* and *Chew* joined *Ward* in an exercise in formation-keeping as they cruised around the southeast tip of Oahu.

The destroyers returned to the harbor at 0900 the following morning. It was not a long or important cruise but it was the first opportunity for *Ward* to work with her division mates and begin learning to be part of a larger force. The crew felt good when they finally tied up in the navy yard. They now had a purpose for being and a role in the navy.

Ward's crew witnessed a magnificent sight on the morning of March 26. Six battleships, *Idaho, Mississippi, Nevada, Arizona, Pennsylvania,* and *West Virginia* left their anchorage along Ford Island. One by one, they steamed majestically past *Ward* on their way to a fleet exercise. Several hours later, *Ward,* with all four boilers on line, left the harbor on her maiden voyage to the island of Maui southeast of Oahu.

The crew, aware of Maui's reputation as perhaps the most scenic of the Hawaiian Islands, eagerly looked forward to the cruise and a possible visit to the island. However, this was only a training cruise for the purpose of calibrating her radio direction finder and other equipment. She would steam to Maui at 15 knots, turn about, and return. She reached Maalaea Bay the following morning and lay to for several hours. The crew peered longingly at the island which, they agreed, was surely an island paradise. They would have to wait for another visit to set foot on the island.

Allen was also in Maalaea Bay on a similar mission, and at 0915 the two ships left together. They practiced station-keeping as *Ward* completed her equipment calibration on the return trip to Pearl Harbor. Once in the harbor, they moored at berth X-5. For the next 21 months she would spend much of her harbor time moored here alongside the old cruiser *Baltimore* with her division mates.

Men of *Ward* soon discovered that crews of combat ships were dynamic and not static in their composition. The makeup of *Ward's* crew began to change almost as soon as she reached Pearl Harbor on March 9. *Ward* received a new Ensign on March 10, and temporarily assigned six men to machine gun school on March 17. Seaman Robert Gorman left the ship to attend sonar school in San Diego. CEM Denis Mahan, CRM Buckner Harris, and S2c Gordon Hueffmeier were transferred to other ships on March 24. SC3c Peter Fritzham was transferred off the ship for purposes of medical discharge on April 6.

At the same time, *Ward* received new men. F1c Wilfred Smorowski reported from USS *California,* while GM1c Leo Jankowski and CEM Ernest Daniels transferred in from other ships. This turnover would continue throughout 1941 as men left for other assignments and were replaced, usually by men from the regular navy or fleet reserves. By mid-1941, 10% of the original crew was new and by the first week in December, the turnover was 22%.

At 2107 on April 7, *Ward* relieved *Chew* on harbor patrol, her first assignment to the mission for which she was brought to Pearl Harbor. This same mission would, eight months later bring her combat and fame. This first patrol was a short one, lasting only one day. It was long enough, however, to orient her crew to the procedures of guarding the harbor entrance. Her next assignment to patrol on April 12 lasted three days.

On April 15, *Ward* joined *Allen* and *Schley* in one of the more exciting exercises, live gunnery practice. With the tug *Sonoma* towing wooden targets 120 miles southeast of Oahu, the three destroyers fired live shells using all four main battery guns. *Ward* crewmen not involved in the operation of the guns were detached to *Allen,* some to observe the results of *Ward's* fire; others to repair the targets for further use.

On April 28 *Ward* conducted a two-hour test run at full speed in which she averaged 26.8 knots. This confirmed that the ship had lost 8 knots in her top speed after sitting idle in the reserve fleet for almost 20 years. Nevertheless, she was still capable of speeds adequate for her role as a patrol destroyer.[12]

Whether *Ward* was at sea, moored at some berth, or sitting on blocks in dry-dock, there were some constants. One was the need for inspection of critical areas of the ship. Some were held daily, some weekly, and others less frequently. Every day, without exception, the ship's magazines and samples of her powder were inspected. Every week the sprinkling system in her magazines was tested to ensure that they could be flooded quickly if necessary.

A ship's magazines were its Achilles heel. A fire or explosion in a magazine could sink a ship almost instantaneously. In 1941, several of the world's largest warships were destroyed by fires in their magazines. The British battleship *HMS Hood,* pride of the British fleet, sank in less than a minute when a shell from the German battleship *Bismarck* started a fire that caused an explosion in her magazine. Only three of her 1500-man crew survived.

On December 7, the U.S. battleship *Arizona* would be destroyed seconds after a Japanese bomb started a fire in her forward magazine causing a catastrophic explosion. The blast snuffed out the lives of more than 1100 of the *Arizona's* crew in an instant.

Ward's crew discovered that days moored in the harbor were not idle times for them. The officers kept them busy on a variety of activities, especially those which could not easily be undertaken while at sea. With the boilers and engines shut down, the black gang inspected, removed, and serviced critical parts of the propulsion systems, such as the burner tips, boilers, fuel oil pumps, feed-water pumps, shaft bearings, lubrication systems, fresh water evaporators, and various other pumps. On the weather deck, seamen swabbed the deck, polished brass, and cleaned rigging.

The crew was mustered daily and checked for absences. The ship received some food or other supplies almost every day while in port. One of the ship's whaleboats made runs to the receiving dock at Merry's Point across the harbor to pick up provisions, mail, or men returning to the ship.

Mess cooks met the returning boat to unload provisions. All food was inspected immediately by an officer and the Chief Pharmacist's Mate to verify quantity and quality of the items received. The mess cooks then placed the items in storage. The ship used about 60 loaves of bread daily and received this amount every day from their designated vendor, Love Biscuit and Bread Company of Honolulu. Just prior to leaving the harbor on exercises when replenishment was usually not possible, the ship took on several hundred loaves.

If *Ward* was on patrol just outside the harbor, the whaleboat still made runs into the harbor for mail or supplies. The several-mile trip was not difficult unless the sea was rough. The food supplies often included a treat for the crew, 25 pies or 20 cakes, enough for a piece of dessert for all hands.

The mess cooks were kept particularly busy on some supply runs. On an April day, the whaleboats delivered 1220 pounds of potatoes alone, plus 700 pounds of assorted vegetables from the principal vegetable vendor, Chun Chong Company of Honolulu. On another day they received 1000 pounds of potatoes and 1600 pounds of fruits and vegetables. Stowing almost a ton and a half of food was a chore for the galley crew. Will Lehner, one of the mess cooks, often wondered what it must be like to be a mess cook on a battleship where provisions for 1500 men had to be received and stored almost daily.

Drills continued whether the ship was in port or at sea. The heavy seas and rolling ship prohibited drills on the voyage from the West Coast, but the captain commenced them on March 14. They became part of the ship's routine for the remainder of her career. On any given day, the crew could be called to a drill for air raid, general quarters, darken ship, fire, pointing and training for gun crews, abandon ship, whale boat crews, towing, searchlight, fire and rescue, collision; or gun, torpedo, or depth charge. In addition to the drills, the ship conducted actual live firing exercises of guns, torpedoes, or depth charges.

On a typical day, the captain would call for as many as five consecutive drills involving the entire ship's complement. The drills were designed to increase the crew's efficiency in reacting to various simulated occurrences, usually emergencies. Through repetition, the crew acquired the ability to react immediately to the call of any drill, report to their designated station, and take whatever action was required.

The drills acquired the desired results even though the men realized they were only drills. The fire response crews were eventually able to mobilize at the fire hose, unreel it, and spray water on a simulated fire within one minute and ten seconds after the call for the drill. In her three-year life, *Ward* would, at some time, be required to respond for real in almost every drill scenario that the crew practiced.

Ward spent her first full week on inner harbor patrol from May 3 to 10. Much of her non-patrol time was spent on anti-submarine exercises with her division mates. The submarine *Cuttlefish* joined them in realistic exercises on May 26 by simulating an enemy sub attempting to enter Pearl Harbor. By proceeding at agreed-upon depths, the Cuttlefish provided *Ward's* sonar operators with live training on what submerged submarines sounded like at various depths. *Ward* would put that training to actual use seven months later.

On June 2 *Ward* and *Schley* conducted tactical maneuvers near Maui and moored in Kahuli Harbor upon completion of the exercises. The long anticipated day for *Ward's* crew had arrived. They would finally get a liberty on Maui. Many visited a well-known volcano; others toured the island or searched for their favorite refreshment. Upon returning to the ship they all agreed that if there was an island more scenic than Maui, they would have to see it to believe it.

The destroyers remained at Maui for three days, conducting whale boat drills in the surf of Maui's north coast before they left. On the return to Pearl Harbor, the *Schley* simulated a breakdown so that *Ward* could tow her at 10 knots for an hour. On their return, *Ward* observed a rare glimpse at a British man-of-war when the British cruiser *Liverpool* entered Pearl Harbor and moored for several days. As the Ward's crew looked over the stranger they threw out guesses as to the ship's destination. Most believed it was on its way to Australia.

Ward went into Dry Dock No. 1 for five days in July. She had her screws, rudder, and all underwater fittings inspected and repaired. A complete scraping and repainting of her hull followed and *Ward* emerged with a clean bottom. The ship spent the remainder of the summer on patrols and trips to the other Hawaiian Islands on exercises with *Allen, Chew, or Schley.*

A memorable trip was to the big island of Hawaii with *Chew* on July 21. The two ships moored side by side at Dock No. 1 at Hilo on July 22. This was *Ward's* first port of call on the island, and the crew made the most of every minute of liberty. For some it would be their only visit to the scenic city.

In small groups they spent a day sight-seeing and souvenir-hunting. In order to maximize the use of their time, they pooled their resources and rented cars to tour the island. They allowed enough time, however, to sample the beverages on the island. *Ward* left the island on the 24th with an abundant collection of stories.

The four destroyers now settled into a routine of full seven-day assignments on inner harbor patrol, one assignment per month. The remaining three weeks would be spent in port or at sea on maneuvers.

The USS *Chew* (hull no. 106) and *Ward* take a break from harbor entrance patrol to visit Hilo, Hawaii, on July 22, 1941, mooring at the Sugar Dock. (Naval Historical Center)

On August 2 while on patrol, the *Ward* observed yet another strange man-of-war steaming into Pearl Harbor. It was the large British battleship HMS *Warspite* on a voyage to British South Pacific bases. It made a two-day refueling and liberty stop before pressing on to her destination.

Exercises were now becoming more realistic and intense. On August 6 *Ward* engaged in serious night training with *Schley* with each being the simulated enemy of the other. The two stalked each other in the dark, seeking to discover her adversary before she was discovered herself. When they located the "enemy," they illuminated it with searchlights and simulated firing from their main battery.

The ships would separate and stalk each other again, this time to simulate firing of torpedoes and retiring behind a smoke screen. During this exercise, *Ward* simulated damage to her bridge and shifted to local control for firing of torpedoes.

Ward made a run to Kailua on the west coast of Hawaii Island on September 2 to drop off a construction party and materials. Her whale boats took the men and supplies ashore and no other crewmen set foot on the island. *Ward* would have frequent errand runs similar to this one.

While on week-long harbor patrol on September 12, *Ward's* crew observed another unfamiliar ship's silhouette several miles away. It was the Free French large destroyer, *LeTriomphant* entering nearby Honolulu Harbor. The ship was visiting several French colonies and making a liberty call at Honolulu, much to the delight of her crew.

Ward continued to prepare for war in earnest. On September 15, she joined *Allen, Schley,* and coast guard cutter *Taney* in intensive daytime and night exercises for four days off Oahu. The first two days consisted of simulated gun and torpedo attacks on each other. On the third day the ships fired actual torpedoes with the explosives removed. *Taney* did not have torpedo tubes and acted at the target ship as well as retrieving the dummy torpedoes.

On the final day, the U.S. submarine *Pompano* joined the exercises, serving as a submerged target. The destroyers tracked her by sonar and made simulated depth charge attacks. A week later *Allen, Schley,* and *Ward* conducted live gunnery practice on towed targets. *Ward* was gradually honing her skills for a war, if it came.

On October 8, Doctors Root and Parker of the Navy Yard dispensary came aboard the *Ward* to administer the sailor's worst nightmare, shots. All officers and men, with no exceptions, lined up and received malaria and typhoid shots amid a background of grumbling.

War clouds darkened over the Pacific as October passed. Although the crew was not privy to all the navy's dispatches, they followed political events closely. They were well aware that Japan was likely to make some move within months somewhere in the Pacific. The crew understood the reasons for intensified exercises.

On October 17, *Ward* acted as a target ship for Pearl Harbor-based PT boats. The patrol boats tracked *Ward* at night to deliver simulated torpedo attacks. The following day *Ward* made another two-hour, full-power run to check her maximum speed. This time it was down to 24.1 knots. The almost continuous operation since January was taking its toll on the ship and turbines.

The deteriorating political situation now caused a change in *Ward's* patrol status. Until now, the ship conducted patrols after dark with her navigation and other deck lights burning. Orders were received requiring that all ships be darkened and no lights visible after dark.

This order affected a popular after-dark crew activity. On a warm moonlit night, a group of crewmen would usually gather on deck, swap tales, and enjoy the evening. One man always brought his guitar so the gang could have a songfest before retiring. The new orders still allowed the songfests, but they now had to be conducted in the dark, with smoking prohibited.

Following the full-power run, *Ward* returned to berth number 6 in the navy yard for six days. Almost all of *Ward's* time in the harbor was spent at either berth number 6 at the dock or berth X-5 in open water north of Ford Island. She would moor in the navy yard if she needed any maintenance, servicing, or repair. Otherwise she moored at X-5 next to the old cruiser *Baltimore.* All of the repair facilities, including huge cranes, construction materials, and skilled workers were concentrated in the navy yard.

While moored in the navy yard, *Ward* still needed vital services to keep the ship operating. These were available at every dock in the navy yard including dry-docks. At berth 6 *Ward* received fresh water, electricity, and steam for the ship's systems. As soon as *Ward* moored to a dock, connections were made quickly and *Ward* drew on these services immediately.

When moored somewhere in the harbor or at another port, these connections were not available. Instead, *Ward* would keep one of her four boilers operating to provide power for the ship's systems. One of the harbor's water barges moored alongside the ship to fill *Ward's* fresh water tanks, an operation which took nearly an hour. Delivery of personnel, supplies, mail, and other items was accomplished by small boats, usually the *Ward's* own whale boats.

On October 29 *Ward* received another officer as Ensign Richard Farwell reported on board as the Assistant Engineering Officer. Farwell, also a reservist, would remain with the ship for the remainder of her life and would earn the respect of the crew as a very capable officer. He would also become the ship's last commanding officer.

Ward was on patrol off the harbor entrance when Farwell reported for duty. Dressed in a new white uniform, Farwell had to ride several miles in *Ward's* whaleboat in a choppy sea to reach the ship. He was soaked when he finally climbed aboard to be greeted by Lt. Doughty in khaki trousers and a white tee shirt. Farwell had just been introduced to the "dungaree navy."[13]

In November, training became still more intense as Japan's conservative government was replaced by a hawkish faction led by General Hideki Tojo. As Tojo assumed the position of Premier the road to war was now completely open in Japan. Calls by the United States for Japan to end its occupation of China and French Indo-China were quickly rejected. With the Allied embargoes of strategic materials, including oil, now threatening to strangle Japan's economy and military machine, the two nations were clearly on a path to war.

The *Ward's* crew followed these events closely as 1941 was coming to an end. Orv Ethier spoke for many when he commented, "We knew that the Japanese would do something in the Pacific but we thought that it would be in the Philippines, New Guinea, Borneo, Malaya, or some other place in the Southwest Pacific. We never thought they would attack Hawaii. It was simply too far away." Top U.S. military leaders harbored identical thoughts.

On November 6, *Ward* began two days of intensive battle exercises with *Chew* in which the ships made practice runs at each other. Simulating battle damage to her bridge and loss of steering control, *Ward* shifted steering control to the after steering station and continued the exercise. The exercise covered various scenarios that *Ward* could encounter in battle, each one providing essential training that would later be used for real.

On November 10, *Ward* and *Chew* cruised to the village of Kaunakakai on Molokai

Island. The village was holding an Armistice Day parade and asked the navy to provide a unit of sailors to march in the parade. *Ward* and *Chew* were selected. Conducting exercises on the way, the destroyers reached Kaunakakai in mid-afternoon.

At 0830 the following morning, a detachment from each ship left for the parade. *Ward's* contribution was one officer and 26 men in full whites and carrying rifles. Years later, Dick Thill, one of the 26 men, was still amused by it. "We had to march a mile from the dock to town," he chuckled. "Then the parade route was only a block long so we actually had to march two miles just to march that one block in the parade."

Despite the long march to get to town, Orv Ethier enjoyed the day. After the parade the crew was invited to a luau in the village and had a huge Hawaiian meal before they marched the mile back to the ship. The destroyers remained in Kuanakakai until midnight before leaving for Pearl Harbor, conducting gunnery exercises on the return trip.

November 18 was just another day to Ward and her crew. The ship was on inner harbor patrol and experienced nothing unusual. Motor Torpedo Boat Squadron Number 1 emerged from the harbor and spent a half-hour on an exercise with *Ward* before they reentered the harbor. Except for routine ship arrivals and departures, nothing occurred to highlight this particular day.

Several thousand miles away, a boat that *Ward* would encounter soon was having anything but a routine day. It, along with four others like her, left Kure Harbor, Japan, on a long journey that would take it to the very gates of Pearl Harbor. Its two-man crew was confident but concerned about the dangerous mission they had been given. Their concern was justified. They had only two weeks before they would meet the *Ward,* and only two weeks to live.

Two *Ward* crewmen were lost temporarily on November 24, one by accident, one by illness. TM2c Lyle Winter suffered severe lacerations on his left hand and a compound fracture of the little finger when he caught his hand between two depth charges. Five hours later F2c Fred "Fritz" Phenning was diagnosed with acute appendicitis and transferred to the new hospital ship *Solace* (AH-5) moored nearby in the harbor. For some unexplained reason, this ailment was quite common on combat ships in the 1940s. Having a naval hospital and hospital ship within the harbor undoubtedly saved the lives of some of those stricken with it.

November 26 was also an easy day for *Ward* at berth 6 in the navy yard. No drills or exercises were scheduled and the harbor in general was quiet. Two thousand miles away at Hitokappu Bay in the Kurile Islands north of Japan, thousands of sailors of another navy were experiencing a much busier day. They were part of a large task force which included six large aircraft carriers carrying 441 planes. The task force slowly left the Kuriles on its way to Hawaii and would come within 200 miles of the harbor that on November 26 was so tranquil.[14] Two hundred miles was close enough for their purpose, which was not a peaceful one.

Another event occurred on November 26 which would directly affect *Ward* and history. The 14th Naval District Headquarters at Pearl Harbor received a message from Washington, D.C. indicating that negotiations with Japan were very delicate and that Japan could take military action somewhere in the Pacific at any time. As a result of this message, subsequently referred to as the "war warning message," the fleet was placed on alert. The harbor patrol destroyers were now authorized to fire upon and sink any unauthorized submarines found in the "restricted zone."

On December 3, *Ward* took on 37,000 gallons of fuel oil and provisions and got under way at 1723 for her next round at inner harbor patrol. The following morning the captain decided to work off any rust that had settled on the crew in the previous 11 days in the harbor. He called for five consecutive drills within an hour and a half.

At 1633 on December 4, a visitor reported on board while on patrol. It was not just any visitor, however. It was the incoming captain, Lt. William Outerbridge, who would replace Hunter Wood as the commanding officer on December 5. Outerbridge decided to report a day early to observe the ship and crew before officially assuming command.[15]

The *Ward* was relieved on harbor patrol by *Chew* 20 minutes later and returned to the harbor at berth X-5. It was scheduled to remain there a week while Outerbridge oriented himself to the ship and crew. This was his first command and he could put the week to good use before taking the ship out for the first time.

On December 5, Captain Wood put the men through general quarters, fire, collision, and abandon ship drills in the morning to demonstrate to Outerbridge the efficiency of the crew. Two minutes after the final drill, Outerbridge inspected the upper and lower decks, followed by an inspection of the crew at quarters. At 1130, he read his orders to the assembled officers and officially assumed command of *Ward*.

Although the ship was 23 years old and obsolete in many ways, Outerbridge was proud of his first command already. The crew was efficient and knew how to run a destroyer. He had no worries there.

Outerbridge had been born in the British crown colony of Hong Kong in 1906, the son of a British sea captain and a U.S. Army nurse from Ohio. When he was seven his father died and his mother took him back to Middleport, Ohio, where he attended school. He entered the U.S. Naval Academy in 1923, graduating in 1927.

Following that, he served for 13 years on the battleship *California*, four destroyers, a supply ship, and the heavy cruiser *Augusta*. In 1940 he was assigned to the new destroyer *Cummings* as Executive Officer. He was rewarded for his excellent service by his promotion to commanding officer of *Ward*.[16]

By 1855 on December 5, Captain Wood had collected his personal effects, paid his respects to the officers and crew, and had a final discussion with Outerbridge. Then, with mixed feelings, he left the *Ward* for the last time.

Ward would hear of Hunter Wood again. He left *Ward* to take command of a newer destroyer, USS *Smith*. On October 26, 1942, *Smith* was escorting a U.S. task force during the battle of the Santa Cruz Islands, one of the many naval battles fought around the strategic island of Guadalcanal. During a Japanese air attack, *Smith* was deliberately crashed by a torpedo bomber in the forward superstructure. The torpedo exploded, killing 57 men, wounding 12, and converting the entire forecastle into an instant inferno.

Despite the flames, carnage, and deaths on his ship, Wood ordered the crew to keep firing at the planes and fighting the fires while he kept the *Smith* in its assigned position to escort the carrier *Enterprise*. When the flames threatened to completely engulf *Smith*, Wood tucked *Smith's* bow in the wake of the battleship *South Dakota* to use the spray in fighting the fire. *Smith* was credited with shooting down six of the aircraft, all while on fire, with a third of her crew dead or injured.[17]

After the battle, when the Task Force commander signaled his commendation to Wood for a job well done, Wood remarked to his officers, "I was embarrassed that I could not acknowledge the tribute." *Smith's* signal flags and lights were all destroyed in the explosion and fire. Ironically, while *Smith* and Wood both survived the kamikaze attack on his ship, the ship he left on December 5 would be struck by a kamikaze three years after he departed.

The results would be much different, however. Wood completed an excellent career, retiring as Rear Admiral.

Outerbridge began what he expected to be a full week of getting to know the ship and its crew. These plans abruptly changed the following morning when the harbor patrol destroyer *Chew* reported having engine problems. *Ward* was ordered to relieve her immediately. Outerbridge's learning would have to be "on the job." *Ward* was under way at 0628 and relieved the *Chew* at 0720 on its new captain's first full day as commanding officer.

December 6 was uneventful and Outerbridge was thankful for that. He was silently hoping for at least several more uneventful days. The following day was Sunday and the fleet was already in the harbor. These factors usually produced quiet days outside the harbor and there was no reason he could think of that would make tomorrow an exception.

Outerbridge wanted to be close to the bridge on his first night at sea, but *Ward* lacked a captain's sea cabin that was a fixture on most modern destroyers. Improvising, he set up a cot in the nearby chart room, which would have to be his sea cabin.

His cot sat right next to the sonar indicator, which emitted a continuous pinging sound when it was operating. From his experience on the *Cummings,* Outerbridge was accustomed to loud sonar sets and would be able to sleep through the noise.

As he lay on his cot, thoughts of the ship spun through his mind. Finally, fatigue took over and he dropped off to sleep. His sleep would be short, however, and the following day would be long and stressful. Others had already decided that Sunday would not be a quiet day at Pearl Harbor. Many men would not even see the day's first light.

CHAPTER 5

First Shot of the War

When Outerbridge finally dropped off to sleep, hundreds of miles north of Oahu a huge Japanese naval task force silently approached the island. They were about to execute a master plan for disabling the United States Pacific Fleet at anchor in Pearl Harbor. Although Outerbridge had many things on his mind as he lay on his cot, an attack on the Pacific Fleet by Japanese naval forces was not one of them.

Like his crew, he was aware of Japanese troop and ship movements into Southeast Asia. But every indicator suggested that if the Japanese begin hostilities, it would come in the form of a surprise attack on the Philippines, Malaya, New Guinea, or the oil-rich Dutch East Indies.

Every one of those locations contained not only the critical resources that Japan desired but held a strategic position from which control over Southeast Asia could be maintained. They were also within easy reach of Japanese air and naval forces with little standing in their way.

Since destroyer captains were not privy to the exchange of messages between the Japanese and American governments, Outerbridge could not know how critical the negotiations between the two nations had become. Those at the highest level of the U.S. government recognized that war was now imminent and could break out at any moment. Outerbridge, however, not having this information, slept peacefully.

Why would Japan send a huge armada thousands of miles across the Pacific to attack the fleet of the world's greatest industrial power when other Asian territories were what it coveted? Behind that question lay the cause of four years of global conflict that would change the face of the world forever.

It would also explain why *Ward* would have its place forever etched in history by the following morning.

Although Japanese strategic planning was, by its very nature, overly complex, the events that brought its fleet to Oahu's doorstep are easier to understand. Since the beginning of the Twentieth Century, Japanese leaders, concerned about their shortage of land and natural resources, looked beyond their borders for the implements to be a great and self-sufficient power.

Japan's quest for space and resources was unmasked when it invaded Manchuria in 1931 and China in 1937. After France surrendered to Germany in 1940, Japan continued her march southward by occupying portions of French Indochina. In the midst of these moves Japan withdrew from naval limitation negotiations in 1936.[1] It was now free to continue the expansion of its navy, which would soon rival those of Great Britain and the United States in size and exceed them in certain technologies.

In 1940, to slow down Japan's military machine, the United Sates and other western nations imposed an embargo on strategic materials, including rubber, tin, steel, and scrap

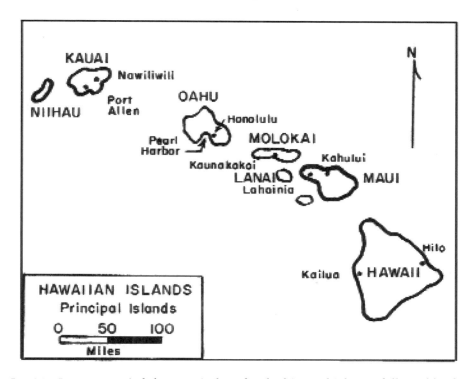

iron. In 1941, Japan occupied the remainder of Indochina, which was followed by freezing of all Japanese assets in the west and adding oil to the list of embargoed materials. Without these materials Japan's military, especially its oil-hungry navy, would be idle within a year. In July 1941 the United States demanded that Japan withdraw its troops from China and Indochina in exchange for lifting of the embargo.[2]

Japan's next moves were predictable. Its forces were now at the threshold of Asia's greatest sources of natural resources and it was left with two options. It could withdraw as demanded and lose face around the world, or continue south and seize the resources it needed to remain a strong military power. Japan's new military-led government decided to occupy British Malaya, the Dutch East Indies and other territories necessary to establish a defensive perimeter in the Pacific. This, it felt, would make Japan impregnable.[3]

Only one military force in the Pacific was capable of interfering with Japan's occupation plans if it chose to, the United States Pacific Fleet based at Pearl Harbor in the Hawaiian Islands. Japan's leaders thus directed Admiral Isoruku Yamamoto to implement the plan he had developed to disable that fleet in a surprise attack. This would allow Japan's occupation of the targeted areas to proceed unhindered.

Yamamoto's plan provided for a massive air attack by aircraft from Japan's six largest aircraft carriers. The attack would occur on a Sunday morning, when the U.S. Fleet would be in port. The aircraft, consisting of approximately 350 fighters, dive bombers and torpedo bombers, were to sink or disable all battleships and aircraft carriers in Pearl Harbor and destroy all aircraft on Oahu's six airfields.

As a surprise weapon, Yamamoto approved the inclusion of five two-man midget submarines in the plan. These would be carried to Pearl Harbor on the deck of five large submarines and launched in the darkness ten miles from the harbor entrance before the Japanese air armada reached Oahu.

Their mission was to enter the approach channel, await the commencement of the air attack, proceed into the harbor itself, and fire their two torpedoes at any major ship still afloat after the air raid. They were then to exit the harbor in the resulting confusion and rendezvous with their mother submarines for the return to Japan.[4]

The Japanese plan was brilliant in its daring but overly complex, as most of their naval plans in World War II would be. It would need a very favorable set of circumstances and extremely good luck to succeed. Fortunately for the Japanese, they encountered these circumstances and were blessed with the luck they needed.

Their fleet was able to cross the Pacific undetected and reach its designated aircraft launching just before dawn on December 7. That was their first stroke of luck, as they were under orders to return to Japan if they were discovered before December 6. Had they been discovered there would have been no attack and the history of the entire world would not have changed so dramatically.

The most flawed element of the Japanese plan was that it was ill conceived. The attack on Pearl Harbor was totally unnecessary; Japan could have achieved its goals in Southeast Asia without it. Japan did not have to deliberately attack the world's greatest industrial power and the only naval power in the Pacific that could destroy them.

Japan's decision to attack Pearl Harbor exposed a lack of understanding of the true balance of naval power in the Pacific and an ignorance of American politics. On December 7, Japan already held a numerical superiority in the Pacific in every major class of ships.[5] Any overall numerical superiority the United States held was due to its Atlantic Fleet. But with the threat to U.S. shipping posed by German submarines and surface ships in 1941, significant numbers of the Atlantic Fleet were not likely to be transferred to the Pacific and overcome Japanese superiority there.

Because it had been preparing for a naval war for many years, the Japanese navy also enjoyed technical superiority over the U.S. fleet in a number of critical areas. Their night combat techniques, huge 24-inch "long lance" torpedoes, and use of destroyers were clearly superior to those of the U.S. in 1941.

It was not likely that the U.S. would send its Pacific Fleet to oppose Japanese landings in Malaya or the Dutch Indies. The isolationist mood that swept the United States in the late 1930s would not have permitted the United States to intervene to stop Japanese moves in the Pacific *unless it was first attacked by the Japanese.*[6]

Even though the very survival of America's closest friend and ally, Great Britain, was at stake in 1940 and 1941, the U.S. did not intervene directly against Germany. Even the sinking of several U.S. destroyers by German submarines was not a great enough provocation to drag the United States into the war. Although the opponent was different in the Pacific in 1941, the issue was the same. Should the United States intercede militarily against a country with which it was not at war?

With the answer to that question being "no" in Europe when England itself was threatened, the answer could hardly have been "yes" months later in the Pacific when the threat was to some remote colonies of England and the Netherlands, valuable as they may have been.

There has never been any evidence to suggest that the U.S. would have contested Japanese occupation of Malaya or the East Indies and initiated open warfare in the process. Although President Roosevelt personally favored intervention opposing a Japanese move against these territories, Congress, not the President, would have the last word. Despite Yamamoto's knowledge of the United States from his several years of experience as naval attaché at the embassy in Washington, Japanese planners never understood this point. Japan thus initiated a war it did not have to fight.

Japan already held the position it sought in 1941. It held a numerical superiority in fleet size in the Pacific, and an isolationist political climate prevailed in the United States. It could move without fear of open intervention from the U.S. Contrarily, attacking Pearl Harbor would not ensure their victory; it would, instead, guarantee their defeat. But that still lay ahead.

Off the mouth of the Pearl Harbor entrance on the morning of December 7, *Ward* was on station on inner harbor patrol. It had been on patrol since 0720 on December 6, replacing the destroyer *Chew*, which had experienced engine problems. *Ward*, with two of her four burners lit, was patrolling at 15 knots as usual on her "easy circle eight" pattern in a two-mile square "restricted zone." It was a warm, clear night and an uneventful one. The only ship to pass through the harbor mouth was the destroyer *Litchfield*, another four-stack destroyer one year younger than *Ward*. It exited the harbor at 2304.

At 0200 minesweepers *Crossbill* and *Condor* emerged from the harbor entrance to conduct the morning minesweeping operation. As they did, the net tender *YNG-17* closed the torpedo net behind them. *Ward's* Officer of the Deck noted their presence, glanced to the bridge lookouts and reminded them, "Keep your eye on them." Lacking radar, tracking of other ships in close proximity had to be done visually and was difficult in the dead of night.

At 0342, as the minesweepers were well into their operation, Ensign Russell McCloy, *Condor's* Officer of the Deck, sighted a suspicious object in the water about 150 feet away. He asked Quartermaster 2c R.C. Uttrick what he thought the object was. After watching it for several minutes Uttrick replied, "That's a periscope sir, but there's not supposed to be any submarines in this close."[7]

The Minesweeper *Condor* sounded the first alert of submarines outside Pearl Harbor. It summoned the *Ward* at 0342, but the search turned up nothing. (National Archives)

Helmsman R.B. Chavez could not see the periscope in the dim light but could see it's fluorescent wake on a collision course with them and veered sharply to starboard. At the same moment the submarine turned to port, now heading west.

Condor was a small 88-ton, 83-foot long minesweeper not equipped to fight submarines. Its only weapon was a 0.30 caliber machine gun. The ship's skipper, Ensign Monroe Hubbell decided that it was time to get help. At 0400 he sent a blinker signal to *Ward*, "HAVE SIGHTED SUBMERGED SUBMARINE ON A WESTERLY COURSE, SPEED NINE KNOTS."[8] *Ward* responded by radio, "ONE MOMENT. PLEASE STAND BY."

The wording of this message probably saved the life of the submarine and its crew. It indicated that the sub was on a westerly course when it was, instead, simply making a temporarily evasive maneuver to the west. This would lead *Ward* to search the wrong area.

Lt. (jg) Oscar Goepner, who had just come on duty as Officer of the Deck, acted quickly. He had been conducting inner harbor patrol for eight months and had never received a message like this unless it was part of a drill. This message mentioned nothing about a drill and he treated it as a legitimate communication. It was also a chilling one fraught with numerous possibilities and dangers.

Goepner ordered Ensign Louis Platt to awaken the captain. Platt did so and Outerbridge

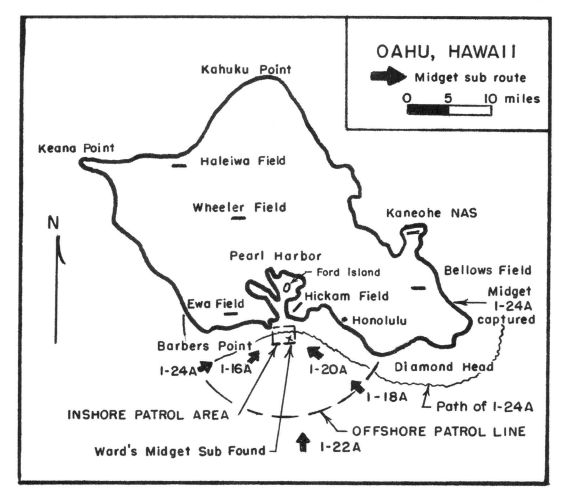

arose immediately, rushing to the bridge in his pajamas. Goepner quickly briefed him on the situation. Although this was only his third day on *Ward*, Outerbridge, aware of the international situation, instantaneously recognized the potential danger created by an enemy submarine just outside the harbor entrance.

He assumed that that the *Condor* did, in fact, sight a periscope and at 0408 ordered Executive Officer Hartwell Doughty, who had just arrived on the bridge, to sound General Quarters.

Below deck *Ward's* crew jumped to their feet, many of them grumbling. Will Lehner ran up to his battle station on the starboard side aft. He was an ammunition handler for the Number Four gun, passing four-inch shells coming up from the after magazine. On his way to his battle station, he said to no one in particular, "What the hell kind of a skipper have we got now to call a General Quarters drill at 0345 on a Sunday morning? Boy, this guy's going to be a tough one."

Russ Reetz had just come off his watch at 0345 in the fire room. The fire room was unusually hot that night and he came up on deck to cool off before he went to bed. His battle station was midships damage control, where he manned a phone directly to the bridge to report battle damage. He was practically at his battle station when the call to General Quarters came.

Ken Swedberg had just reported to his duty station in the Number 1 fire room, where he had the 0400 to 0800 watch. When General Quarters sounded, his relief man reported to the fire room and Swedberg ran to his battle station on the main deck forward. He was the gunner on the three-inch anti-aircraft gun there. The gun was manned entirely by fire room personnel. He was a newcomer to the weapon and had just received his first training on it the previous day.

Outerbridge ordered *Ward* to close on the *Condor*. At 15 knots, *Ward* was approaching the minesweeper within a few minutes. All bridge personnel and deck hands were searching the black water attempting to find whatever it was that the *Condor* spotted. Because of *Condor's* minesweeping gear, which trailed behind it, *Ward* could not approach the little ship too closely. Fouling a minesweeper's gear on a new captain's third day would have been embarrassing.

Outerbridge was a bit puzzled over *Condor's* report that the sub was moving westerly since a sub attempting to approach the harbor entrance should be on a northerly course. Nevertheless, *Ward* slowed to 10 knots and immediately commenced a sonar search to the west.

Finding no underwater contact, Outerbridge ordered *Ward* to completely circle the *Condor,* continually searching the dark waters with her sonar. A half hour passed with no underwater contact or visual sighting of a submarine. Outerbridge then radioed to *Condor* at 0415, "WHAT WAS THE APPROXIMATE DISTANCE AND COURSE OF THE SUBMARINE YOU SIGHTED?"

Condor replied at 0420, "THE COURSE WAS ABOUT WHAT WE WERE STEERING AT THE TIME, 020 MAGNETIC, AND ABOUT 1000 YARDS FROM THE ENTRANCE, APPARENTLY HEADED FOR THE ENTRANCE."[9]

Ward was now some distance from the entrance and headed back toward the harbor. Outerbridge was still not sure where the sub was when it was sighted by *Condor* and followed up with another message at 0426. "DO YOU HAVE ANY ADDITIONAL INFORMATION ON THE SUB?"[10] *Condor's* reply came quickly, "NO ADDITIONAL INFORMATION."

Still looking for something substantial, Outerbridge made one more attempt for some details. "WHEN WAS THE LAST TIME APPROXIMATELY THAT YOU SAW THE SUBMARINE?" he radioed to *Condor*.[11] "APPROXIMATE TIME 0350 AND HE WAS APPARENTLY HEADED FOR THE ENTRANCE," replied *Condor*.

At 0435 Outerbridge told his radio operator to thank *Condor* for the information and request that they notify *Ward* if they have any more information. *Condor* had unknowingly given *Ward* conflicting information. Its first message to *Ward* gave the sub's course "when last seen" as westerly. Its later message gave the sub's course when first seen as 020 or directly toward the harbor entrance. *Ward* had spent almost a half-hour searching to the west when, in fact, the sub was by then back on its original track to the harbor.

Outerbridge continued the search until 0443 and, when he saw no further sign or evidence of the sub, he ordered the ship secured from General Quarters. As he stood on the bridge reviewing the events of the previous hour, he now was not sure that the *Condor* had really seen a submarine. Nothing confirmed their sighting. The *Ward* circled *Condor* and found no evidence at all. Buoys often broke loose from their mooring and were a common sight near the harbor entrance. *Condor* may have seen one in the dark.

Condor did not report the sighting to naval headquarters so Outerbridge chose not to as well. Had he reported the sighting by *Condor,* headquarters would have asked for confirmation and he had just spent an hour unsuccessfully looking for that confirmation. Had *Ward,* itself, seen the periscope, Outerbridge would have reported it.

One of the shore radio stations that was supposed to monitor radio traffic between *Condor* and *Ward* did not pick them up and therefore could not pass them along either. One of the officers at the station, Ensign Oliver Underkoffer, the Communications Watch Officer, was in another room and did not hear the radio traffic. His assistant, Ensign Gordon Kennedy, was in a coding room. Both were nearing the end of a 24-hour shift. Thus, no one at headquarters was aware that a minesweeper had claimed to have seen a submarine at 0345. An opportunity to mitigate what was about to occur at Pearl Harbor was lost.

Ward itself seeing this submarine at 0342 would have set up an interesting problem. Outerbridge would have reported it and headquarters would have requested confirmation. *Ward's* various crewmen on watch would have provided that confirmation. Headquarters may have wanted to wait until the identity of the sub could be determined. However, Outerbridge's actions of several hours later indicate that he would not have waited and, instead, followed standing orders to attack. *Ward* may have sunk a submarine a full four hours before the air attack which was to follow.

Four hours of advance warning of hostile activity at the harbor entrance would not have been sufficient to prevent the events of the day from occurring. However, it would have allowed enough time to disperse aircraft and ships and save hundreds of lives. With that much advance warning, it is interesting to speculate what steps the military leaders would have taken.

After the final exchange of signals, quiet was restored to *Ward* and the *Condor*. Outerbridge and the crew, except for those on watch, went back to sleep. Events would later prove that, in all probability, *Condor* had seen a submarine at 0345, one of five Japanese subs launched earlier in the morning.

Only one of the ten crewmen of the five midget subs would survive the approaching battle. Kazuo Sakamaki, captain of the midget launched by submarine I-24, was captured when his sub ran aground on the north side of Oahu on the morning of December 8. The submarine sighted by *Condor* was not his but was one of the remaining four.

When Outerbridge crawled back into his chart room cot at about 0500, the five midget subs were still converging at the harbor entrance. Hours earlier, on a clear night with the moon almost full, the two-man crews slipped through the small hatch into the cramped confines of their sub. They could see the colored lights of Honolulu and could even pick out the lighted towers of the Royal Hawaiian Hotel on Waikiki Beach.

The ten men who were attempting the dangerous mission in the midget subs had been subjected to a difficult and demanding training with the subs since April. On November 16 they were addressed by Vice Admiral Shimizu, who read their orders to them: "You are directed to take positions of readiness for war with the United States of America. The day to open hostilities is December 8 at daybreak. Orders to open fire will be issued by the General Staff before the time of the attack. Under no circumstances are you to take action unless ordered."[12]

The midget crewmen were stunned at what they had just heard. They were frightened at what lay ahead of them but then swelled with pride as they realized that they would be participating in the first day of war with the United States. What an honor to be given such a great responsibility. They vowed as a group to succeed in the important mission.

Now, after a journey across the Pacific to the gates of Pearl Harbor, they were ready to begin their greatest day. Before leaving the mother submarine, all ten men prepared for the mission in a similar manner. After packing their belongings they washed, sprinkled themselves with perfume, and wrote a letter to their family. They inserted a sliver of a finger nail and hair clippings before they sealed the letter. This was the traditional ritual for a Samurai warrior before a battle.

When the crews were ready, the hatches were closed and the mother submarines slowly submerged. They released four huge clamps that held the midgets to the deck of the mother sub just aft of their conning tower. The midget sub crews started their electric motors and began their fateful journey toward the harbor entrance on their own power.

These small submarines were one of many weapons the Japanese carefully kept secret for this day. Developed in the early 1930s, the craft were 80 feet long, six feet in diameter, and displaced 46 tons. Each carried two 18-inch diameter torpedoes and was propelled by a 600 horsepower electric motor.

These motors would drive the subs at 23 knots on the surface and 19 knots submerged. The subs' greatest weakness was their extremely short range. Their limited battery provided a range of only 15 miles at full speed but would propel the subs 80 miles if the speed were kept to 2 knots.[13]

Unlike conventional submarines, their batteries could not be charged at sea nor did they carry diesel engines. Once launched their life expectancy was short, unless recovered by their mother submarine.

They were not designed to be used against defended harbors but Admiral Yamamoto allowed their use at Pearl Harbor. He insisted, however, that provisions be made to recover the crews. Although they were not considered suicide vessels, realistically there was little chance for their crew's survival on this mission, given the harbor defenses and the distance they would have to travel to get to the harbor and return to be picked up.

I-16 was the first mother sub to launch its midget, getting it off at midnight. I-22 followed with her launching at 0116. I-18 released hers at 0215. I-20 and I-24 completed their launchings at 0251 and 0333 respectively.[14] I-24's midget launched late because of a non-functioning gyro compass. With the midgets successfully on their way, the five mother subs headed for the designated rendezvous point west of the island of Lanai. There they would pick up any midgets able to return after their mission.

The ten submariners were all extremely dedicated individuals, raised in an environment of poverty and strict discipline. Their mission would require men of that kind of background.

The skipper of I-16's midget was Masaji Yokoyama, whose father died when Masaji was only six, leaving his mother to raise 13 children.[15] His crewman, Warrant Officer Sadamu Uyeda, was born of poor but hard working parents in a small mountain hamlet. The commander of I-18's midget, Lt. Commander Shigemi Furuno, was subjected to harsh discipline at home and quickly learned the importance of obedience. His crewman, Shigenori Yokoyama, had a reputation for never giving up in the face of adversity.

Commanding I-20's midget sub was Ensign Akira Hiro-o. His crewman was Petty Officer 2nd Class Yoshio Katayama. At 22, Hiro-o was the youngest of the ten midget crewmen. Born in 1919, his life had been shaped by his parents, both school teachers. He had perfect school attendance his entire life. Although physically short, with constant exercise and drills he became superior to his classmates in physical tests. His crewman, Petty Officer Yoshio Katayama was born of a poor farm family in Gojo.

The midget of I-22 was piloted by Lieutenant Naoji Iwasa, the oldest of the ten submariners, at 26, who had been raised on a farm by hard-working parents. His crewman was Naokichi Sasaki, orphaned at the age of six and raised by relatives. I-24's midget was commanded by Kazuo Sakamaki, known as the "peace boy" because he was born a week after the 1918 Armistice. His crewman, Petty Officer Kiyoshi Inagaki, was the quiet one of the group, known for his attention to detail.

At 0600 a midget commander, making a periscope observation, spotted the supply ship *Antares* approaching the harbor. *Antares* was returning from a run to Canton and Palmyra Islands southwest of Oahu after delivering supplies and a contingent of construction workers. She was towing a 500-ton barge and traveling at nine knots. Her captain, Commander Laurence Grannis, had not left the bridge for four hours and was eager to get ashore and relax. He was also nervous about crew rumors that a submarine had been following them through the night. *Ward* had also seen *Antares* and had exchanged radio signals with her at 0605. *Ward* was also keeping an eye on the *Antares.*

The midget commander immediately saw *Antares* as the solution to the problem of how to get into the harbor. *Antares* would be his key to open the nets at the harbor entrance. When the nets opened to let in *Antares,* he would follow closely in her wake.

Unknown to him, he did not have to worry about how to get through the net. When the net was opened to let in *Condor* and *Crossbill* at 0458, it remained open for almost four hours, contrary to standing orders.[16] *Condor* passed through the net at 0508 and *Crossbill* went through 24 minutes later. The gate to the harbor was already wide open. One midget submarine already discovered this and successfully entered the harbor.

Commander Grannis had radioed ahead for a tug to come out of the harbor and take the barge off his hands. He could not tow the barge through the narrow channel and into the confined harbor. A tug could easily push it into the harbor. The tug would also deliver a harbor pilot who could navigate *Antares* through the tricky channel. The fleet tug *Keosanqua,* designated to meet *Antares,* left her berth at 0600. When *Antares* reached the harbor entrance, however, *Keosanqua* had still not appeared. Grannis ordered *Antares* to circle outside the harbor as it awaited the tug.

A magnificent dawn was breaking at 0627 and by 0630 *Keosanqua* still had not showed up. *Ward* was heading west-southwest on its patrol circuit and passed *Antares,* 1000 yards seaward of her, heading east. At that moment a lookout on *Antares* noticed an object 1500

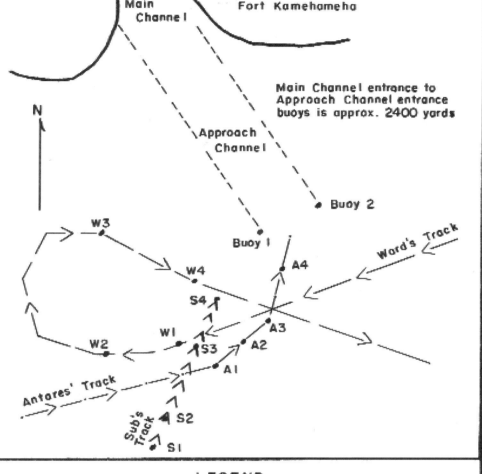

USS WARD MOVEMENTS PRIOR TO FIRING ON MIDGET SUB
December 7, 1941

Main Channel

Fort Kamehameha

Main Channel entrance to
Approach Channel entrance
buoys is approx. 2400 yards

N

Approach
Channel

Buoy 2

Ward's Track

W3

Buoy 1

A4

W4

S4

Ward's Track

W1

A3

W2

S3

A2

A1

Antares' Track

S2

Sub's Track

S1

LEGEND

Ward's Track → — → >
Sub's Track > > > > > > >
Antares' Track → —.— > —.—→ —.

W1 Ward first sights Midget sub which is at position S1. Antares is now at position A1

W2 Ward's OOD orders Ward to come about for a better look. Sub is at S2, Antares is at position A2

W3 Captain Outerbridge arrives on the bridge and orders ship to GQ, speed increased to 20 knots, and course change to 125 degrees. Sub is at S3, Antares is at A3

W4 Ward changes course to 110 degrees and No. I gun fires. Sub is at S4, Antares is at position A4 yards off the ship's starboard quarter. He immediately told Grannis but neither the captain nor the lookout was sure what the object was. They both thought that it resembled a submarine's conning tower, however. Grannis immediately signaled *Ward* alerting the destroyer to the presence of the object.

Events were occurring rapidly now and, simultaneous with *Antares'* signal, bridge messenger Ambrose Domagall on *Ward* also sighted the object behind *Antares. Ward's* helmsman Herbert Raubig saw it as well. He looked over to Quartermaster Howard Gearin and said, "Put a glass on that thing, Howie."[17] Gearin had the 0400 to 0800 watch and had been on the bridge for almost three hours.

Gearin reported the object to Lt.(jg) Oscar Goepner, Officer of the Deck, who peered at the object now about a mile away. None of the three men could identify it but Goepner thought that it looked like a buoy. He told Gearin, "Keep an eye on that thing." Gearin, watching the object intently since it was first sighted, then called out to Goepner, "Sir, it looks like a conning tower." Both agreed that they had never seen an object like that. Everyone on the bridge now agreed that the object was moving, something that buoys usually did not do. Goepner ordered *Ward* to come about so they could give the object a better look.

This patch of water now became even more crowded when PBY patrol plane 14-P-1, on routine patrol out of Kaneohe Naval Air Station, suddenly flew over and started circling. The pilot, Ensign William Tanner, sighted the object and assumed that it was an American submarine in distress since it was submerged in the restricted area. Goepner, staring intently at it, was now convinced that it was, indeed, a submarine's conning tower. At 0637 he called out. "Captain, come on the bridge!"

Outerbridge awoke immediately and noted two items of significance as Goepner called. First, he was somewhat taken aback by the tone in which Goepner addressed him. He assumed that on his third day as commanding officer he would have been addressed in a more courteous manner. He did, however, note the sense of urgency in Goepner's voice and quickly threw on a blue and white kimono over his pajamas, He hurried from the chart room to the bridge wearing a World War I type helmet and tied his kimono as he walked. As he stepped onto the bridge, he looked over at Goepner and asked, "What do we have, Mr. Goepner?" Goepner gave the captain a quick report on the sighting.

One look by Outerbridge took in the entire scene—*Antares,* the barge, and the object between them. The object was moving. Outerbridge reminded himself that he had never before seen a buoy move through the water at five knots. It was obviously a submarine. It could not be anything else. But whose submarine was it?

"That is not a buoy, Mr. Goepner. It is a submarine following *Antares,*" Outerbridge remarked when he put his binoculars down. As everyone on the bridge turned their eyes back to the submarine, the PBY made another low pass at it and two small objects fell from the aircraft. As these dropped into the water they emitted a white smoke. Tanner, still believing that it was a U.S. submarine, dropped two smoke bombs to mark its position.[18]

Executive Officer Lt. Hartwell Doughty now arrived on the bridge on a run and asked, "What's up, Captain?" After Outerbridge pointed out the conning tower, Doughty responded, "What are you going to do?" Outerbridge's answer was quick, "We are going to shoot as soon as we are ready. All engines full ahead." With that he said firmly, "Sound General Quarters, Mr. Goepner."

As the men on the bridge ran to their battle stations, the ship's speakers blared the ominous announcement, "GENERAL QUARTERS! GENERAL QUARTERS! ALL HANDS

MAN YOUR BATTLE STATIONS! MAN ALL GUNS! PREPARE DEPTH CHARGES! PRE-PARE TO RAM!

It was now 0640. For the second time in little more than two and a half hours, *Ward* went to General Quarters. Domogall heard the captain's order before it went out to the rest of the ship. He immediately left the bridge and rushed to his battle station on the galley deck, donning his own helmet as he ran. He was a loader on the Number Three gun there. When the rest of the gun crew arrived he was waiting for them with a shell in his arms.

Things were now happening fast on the bridge. *Antares* sent a message by blinker light that the object behind her seemed to be following her. *Ward's* officers had already reached that same conclusion. Outerbridge ordered that the message be acknowledged.

The clanging of the General Quarters bell again aroused the crew from an uneasy sleep. Some felt that the General Quarters call at 0408 was only a drill and this was another one. Don Pepin raced to his battle station still adjusting his clothes as he ran. He was a lookout on the starboard wing of the bridge. From there he was able to witness and confirm the entire action that followed.

Russ Reetz ran to his battle station again at midships damage control. He, too saw the entire action. Dick Thill, one of the ship's cooks, was on duty in the galley. Although he thought this latest call was also a drill, he immediately dropped his pots and pans and went to his battle station. He was the sight-setter on the Number Two four-inch gun on the port side of the galley deck. The approaching action would occur on the ship's starboard side so Thill had a bird's eye view of what took place.

Sidney Noble heard the General Quarters call and climbed out of his bunk immediately. He threw on his dungaree trousers and his shirt, which he left unbuttoned. He did not bother with sox but put on shoes right over his bare feet. He closed and dogged the hatch to his sleeping compartment and hurried to his battle station on deck. There he noticed the strange object. It appeared to him to be a mine that had broken loose.

Will Lehner was grumbling as he made his way to his battle station near the Number Four gun aft. He told his crewmates, "We're going to have to straighten this guy out," without really knowing how one straightens out the captain of a destroyer. The first thing he noticed when he was topside was the strange object behind *Antares*. He would also witness the entire action.

Orv Ethier was on his way to his duty station in the forward fire room when the call to General Quarters came. He saw the object but thought that it was one of the many buoys that broke loose from time to time.

Walter Campion was on watch on the bridge and witnessed the initial sighting and the conversations that followed. At the call to General Quarters he left the bridge to go to his battle station on the torpedo tubes. When it was apparent that the torpedo tubes would not be used, he was ordered aft to help on the depth charge racks. There he would see action.

Yeoman Gerald Pearl responded to the General Quarters call by hurrying to his battle station which was the range finder on deck. Once there, the object was pointed out to him and he immediately took a range on it. It was 660 yards away. The range soon dropped to fewer than 600 yards, at which point the range finder would not give readings. Ranges would now have to be estimated.

With the captain's order for full speed, *Ward's* stern dug in and a frothy wake quickly appeared behind her as it gathered speed on a course of 125 degrees directly at the sub. Gun crews were assembling and the bridge crews, with helmets on, awaited the captain's next order.

Outerbridge watched with satisfaction as the gun crews ran to their stations. "These crews are good," he thought to himself. "No need to worry about them." As he observed Number One gun, the crew was already training it on the sub. Forward of Number One gun, Gunner's Mate Louis Gerner had closed the hatch to the anchor engine and began running to his battle station with his head down. Outerbridge leaned out over the bridge rail and yelled, "Look out, sailor!" Gerner looked up just in time to see the barrel of Number One gun and avoid getting it across his skull. With a sheepish grin, Gerner waved to the captain to acknowledge his concern.

Outerbridge's next order came quickly. "Load all guns!" he yelled. *Ward* was headed directly at the sub with its deck beginning to vibrate as speed built up rapidly to 20 knots, its maximum speed on only two boilers. Number 1 boiler room was not on line. Since the ship's bow was pointed directly at the sub, he momentarily considered ramming it. He quickly concluded that this would only mess up the *Ward's* bow and there was no need for that yet.

Outerbridge decided instead to pass between the barge and the sub which now trailed the barge. To do this, *Ward* had to change its angle of attack. With confidence now that his mind was made up, he ordered, "Come left 15 degrees." "Coming left, sir," replied Raubig.

As *Ward's* thin bow swung to port, Outerbridge spoke once more. "Rudder amidships." "Rudder amidships," responded Raubig as he straightened out the helm. *Ward* was now settled in on a course of 110 degrees.[19] Outerbridge was pleased with the setup the course change had provided. Before, only his bow gun could bear on the sub. Now, both his Number One and Number Three guns could bear quickly. The Number Four gun aft could also bear as *Ward* passed the sub. Yes, he liked the setup now.

As *Ward* closed the distance to the sub, more of its details could be seen. About six feet of the conning tower were now exposed and occasionally the crewmen could see the shape of the cylindrical hull. Some men thought it was covered with rust. Gearin saw barnacles and seaweed on the conning tower. No one could see any markings of nationality on it anywhere. The sub had given no indication that it had seen the *Ward*, so far.

Outerbridge could not understand how the sub's captain could miss seeing a destroyer throwing up a huge bow wave less than 1000 yards away. Soon it would make no difference if the sub spotted them anyway.

In the last moments before Outerbridge had to give the fateful order that everyone on deck was now anticipating, conflicting thoughts ran through his mind. He had the sub dead to rights. It could not escape now and standing orders allowed him to shoot. If this was a U.S. sub unable to surface, however, he could set a record for losing a command less than 24 hours after receiving it. If it was a foreign sub on innocent passage, he could possibly start a war. No, his decision was the correct one. He had no choice.

The range closed quickly to 500 yards, then 400 yards, and then to 300 yards. The sub still had not seen *Ward*. Men on *Ward's* bridge glanced at Outerbridge wondering what he was going to do. When the range was 200 yards and still closing he removed all doubt. "Commence firing!" he yelled, and his place in history was sealed.

By the time *Ward's* guns crews responded to the order to fire, the sub was less than 150 yards from Outerbridge. The sub commander had apparently been so intent on following *Antares'* barge that he committed the cardinal sin of submarine commanders— not checking all around the sub periodically. Had he done this he would have immediately seen *Ward* approaching on the sub's port side with a bone in her teeth.

He had assumed that *Antares* was going directly into the harbor and was undoubtedly

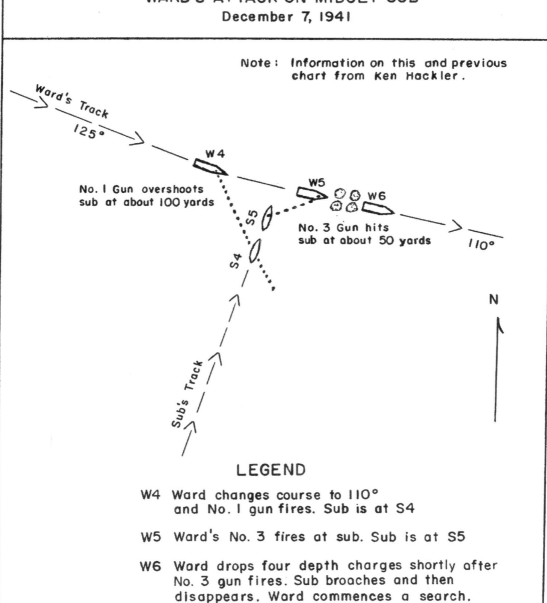

WARD'S ATTACK ON MIDGET SUB
December 7, 1941

Note : Information on this and previous chart from Ken Hackler.

Ward's Track

125°

W4

No. I Gun overshoots sub at about 100 yards

W5

W6

No. 3 Gun hits sub at about 50 yards

110°

S5

S4

N

Sub's Track

LEGEND

W4 Ward changes course to 110° and No. I gun fires. Sub is at S4

W5 Ward's No. 3 fires at sub. Sub is at S5

W6 Ward drops four depth charges shortly after No. 3 gun fires. Sub broaches and then disappears. Ward commences a search.

confused by its swing to the east as it circled. He also may have had trouble with the sub's depth control and was not aware that part of the sub's conning tower was exposed. Nevertheless, he was positive that *Antares* would be inside the harbor within 30 minutes and so would he. He was surely excited that he was now very close to succeeding in his mission.

Except for the depth control, his submarine had functioned very well. He probably heard a sharp sound close by followed by a faint slap on the water's surface as *Ward* fired its first shot. If he said anything aloud, those were his last words on earth.

As soon as Outerbridge's order to commence firing was given, it was relayed by Lt. Goepner to Panagiotes Dionisopoulis, the fire control talker on the flying bridge just above the navigation bridge where Outerbridge stood. Dionisopoulis in turn relayed the order by phone to the crews of all four main battery guns.

The crew of a 4"/50 caliber-gun is rather large, consisting of nine men, each with a specific function. The gun captain relayed the orders from the bridge and directed the crew's actions. The sight setter, receiving information on the target from the gunnery officer on the bridge through headphones, put the target range and deflection into the gun's sighting mechanism. He would adjust the fire controls located on the left side of the gun. Four loaders brought live shells to the gun, loaded them into the breech, and closed it. One of them, designated as the "hot shell man," threw the spent shell casing over the side after firing. The gunner's mate was trained to get the gun back into operation if any problem occurred.

The gun's "trainer" sat in the seat on the right side of the gun barrel and controlled the horizontal movement of the gun using a wheel in front of him. He kept the vertical crosshair on the target. The "pointer" sat in the seat to the left of the gun and controlled the vertical movement of the gun with a similar wheel in front of him, keeping the horizontal crosshair on the target.

The pointer also fired the gun electrically with a mechanism located at his position. If the ship lost power to the gun, the gun captain would fire the gun manually by pulling a lanyard.

The "caliber" used in the gun's designation referred to the relationship between the gun's barrel length and its bore diameter. Thus *Ward's* main battery guns, at 50 caliber, all had a barrel length of 50 times the barrel bore diameter of four inches, or 16½ feet.

On Number One gun, gun captain Anthony Ort's crew was ready, but they were having some difficulty. When the trainer attempted to place the crosshairs on the sub's conning tower, Ort discovered that *Ward* was too close to the sub to use the gun sights. He simply had the trainer sight over the top of the barrel until it pointed at the sub, similar to a youngster aiming a shotgun. He kept the gun sighted that way until the order to fire.

The pointer on Number One gun pressed the firing switch and *Ward's* first shot, fired in anger, sped toward the sub. The sharp crack announced the firing to the entire ship and to *Antares* as well. Just beyond the midget's conning tower a small geyser erupted as the shell passed over the conning tower and smacked the water surface. A clean miss!

It was now 0645. Getting off a shot only five minutes after going to General Quarters was an amazing feat. All of the General Quarters drills of the past months proved their worth. The gun crew removed the spent shell casing and rammed another live shell into the breech, ready for a second shot. By now, however, the *Ward's* speed had taken it past the sub and Number One gun could no longer bear on the conning tower.

The crews of Number Two and Number Three guns, located on top of the galley deck house, watched the action intently. Number Two gun was on the port side and could not engage the sub, which was on *Ward's* starboard side. Number Three gun on the starboard side would be the next gun to bear and was already prepared.

Earlier Karl Lasch, the gun's sight setter, on the phones, reported the gun "manned and ready." In return he received information on the target. The four loaders, Domagall, Dan Gruenning, John Peick, and Harold Flanagan, had loaded the gun and were awaiting further orders. Flanagan was the "hot shell man."

In the air, Tanner, the PBY pilot, was also watching *Ward's* actions closely and still had doubts about the sub's nationality. When he saw the *Ward* fire the first shot, he put his doubts aside. He swooped low over the water and dropped two depth charges. They threw up two columns of water as they exploded, drenching the bow of *Ward* as it approached.[20] The explosions did not affect the sub and it continued following the barge. Tanner radioed a report back to Kaneohe on his actions.

On the *Ward's* bridge Lt. Goepner saw the shell kick up water beyond the sub and swore loud enough for everyone on the bridge to hear. Outerbridge recognized that Number One gun could no longer bear on the sub and shifted his gaze to Number Three gun. He watched the crew as they trained on the sub, now dropping behind *Ward*.

The bearing to the conning tower was changing rapidly but the trainer, Ray Nolde, kept the crosshairs on it all the way. Outerbridge knew that Number Three gun would fire in a matter of seconds and glanced once more at the sub. It was still moving like it was totally unaware of *Ward*.

Gun Captain Russell Knapp of Number Three gun realized that they would get only one shot before his gun could no longer bear. At 20 knots the sub would quickly pass from their view. Had the *Ward* been doing 10 or 15 knots, they would have had time for two or three shots. They would have to make the first shot count.

Like many others in the crew, Knapp had been stunned twice in the past several minutes, first by the order to load the guns and then by the order to fire. He was about to order his crew to fire on someone's submarine with live ammunition. All other drills had stopped short of firing or, if the guns were fired, they were aimed at a wooden target. This was a real sub with live men in it.

He quickly dismissed those thoughts as both Scotty Fenton and Ray Nolde were zeroed in on the sub's conning tower. The range to it was now down to 50 yards. Knapp had to shoot now or lose his only chance. "Fire!" he yelled. He had fired only 30 seconds after Number One gun had fired, but it seemed like minutes.

Once more the solitude of the Sunday morning was shattered by the sharp crack of the four-inch gun. All eyes were on the conning tower as the sound of the gun firing reached 80 sets of ears on *Ward's* deck.

"It's a hit, a clean hit!" someone yelled. It, indeed, was a hit, a perfect shot. The shell hit the conning tower right where it joined the hull and right at the water line. Considering that the speed of *Ward* was opening the range and changing the bearing with every split second, it was a fantastic shot.

Water began pouring into the sub immediately. The impact of the shell hitting the conning tower heeled the sub over to port and exposed the shell hole to the *Ward's* crew. Everyone on deck saw it. Then the sub straightened up and kept moving forward again but submerging as *Ward* passed it.

Outerbridge's heart skipped a couple of beats as he saw the shell hit. He was convinced that the sub was finished even though he had heard no shell explosion. He decided to make sure. "Drop depth charges, pattern of four," he yelled to Goepner. Goepner relayed the command and four sharp blasts of the ship's whistle sounded as the signal to the depth charge crew to drop four depth charges.

Ward was now almost completely past the midget and the sub was approaching the destroyer's boiling wake. On the stern depth charge racks, Chief Torpedo Man Bill Maskeawitcz had earlier set the depth at 100 feet on the depth charge pistols. When the charges reached that depth, water pressure would activate the pressure-sensitive pistols, which would explode the 300-pound depth charges.

As *Ward's* stern approached the sub's track, Maskeawitcz could clearly see the sub's

The crew of No. 3 gun that sank the midget sub on December 7, 1941. From left are: Ambrose Domogall, Ed Bukrey, Russell Knapp, Ray Nolde (seated), Clarence Fenton (seated), Karl Lasch, Jack Peick, Don Gruening, and Harold flanagan. Fenton, as the gun's trainer, fired the killing shot. (Naval Historical Center)

dark green, cigar-shaped hull covered with rust. He saw no walks, guns, or other equipment on its deck. The sub was still awash as Maskeawitcz rolled the first depth charge off the stern right into the path of the sub. He then dropped three more in quick succession.

As the depth charges settled down to their exploding depth, the sub's forward motion seemed to take it directly into the pattern he had just dropped. His heart was also pounding. He knew the sub could be right over the charges when they exploded. Moments later the sea erupted four times, hurling huge waterspouts in the air. The explosions lifted the sub out of the water momentarily and surrounded it with a violent turbulence before it settled beneath the surface.

Maskeawitcz uttered a cry of jubilation as the eruptions subsided. "That sub doesn't have a chance," he thought. "It waded right into them." The entire depth charge crew displayed smiles of confidence as the sub disappeared for good. It would be 61 years before it would be seen again.

It was 0647, only seven minutes after the call to General Quarters. Unbelievably, within the span of a mere seven minutes, a crew of 125 men was unexpectedly called to General Quarters; they had rushed to their battle stations, loaded and trained their weapons, fired shells from two different guns, and dropped four depth charges on an unidentified submarine. This was an utterly fantastic achievement for any ship, especially one manned by reservists.

As the echo of the last depth charge was subsiding, everyone on deck, including the officers on the bridge, stood glued to their spots as if waiting for something else to happen. Nothing did. As calm returned to the water surface, Outerbridge ordered *Ward* to reverse her course and begin a sonar sweep of the area to locate the sub again.[21] The search was fruitless. The sub must have gone straight to the bottom, 1220 feet down.

He asked several men on the bridge "What did you see?" in an attempt to confirm what he had seen himself. The responses were the same. Everyone had seen the first shell hit beyond the sub, the second shell hit near the base of the conning tower, the sub heal over temporarily, and move directly into the path of the depth charges. All agreed that the explosions lifted the sub, after which it disappeared.

The crews of Number One and Number Three guns saw the same thing. Dick Thill, Frank Hajdu, and Gordon Hultman of Number Two gun had also had a good view of the action. Thill swore that he could see the cigar shape of the sub's hull as *Ward* thundered on by it.

Ken Swedberg, Ed Zechmannn, Maurice Hurley, and others manning the three-inch anti-aircraft gun forward, had ring-side seats for the entire attack. *Ward* passed so close to the sub that for a moment they thought that Outerbridge intended to ram it.

The nine midget crewmen who perished in the attack. Kazuo Sakamaki was omitted from the photo for allowing himself to be captured. From the left they are: Yoshio Katayama, Naokichi Sasaki, Shigenori Yokoyama, Masaji Yokoyama, Naoji Iwasa, Shigemi Furuna, Akira Hoir-o, Sadamu Ueda, and Kioshi Inagaki. (Naval Historical Center)

John Tido and William Scholtes on Number Four gun, on the after deck house, heard the shots fired by Number One and Three guns and awaited their chance to shoot. It never came. They had a good look at the sub, however, just 25 yards away from the ship just as the depth charges exploded. The feeling of everyone was unanimous. They had hit the sub and sunk it.

The crew all agreed on another critical point. The shell that hit the conning tower *did not explode.* That is what Outerbridge noticed immediately. Shells, like torpedoes, must travel a minimum distance before they arm themselves, and until they travel that distance they cannot explode. *Ward* was so close to the sub when Number Three gun fired that its shell did not have time to arm itself before it hit the conning tower. Thus, it did not explode but, instead, punched a hole in the conning tower. Incredibly, *Ward* sank the sub with a shell that did not explode![22]

The shell did not pass completely through the conning but hit the controls inside. The hole caused the sub to take in water as it dropped beneath the surface. Since the sub's interior was a single compartment, it did not have the kind of watertight integrity larger submarines had. Any hole in the sub's outer skin would flood the entire sub and cause it to sink. *Ward's* Number Three gun did just that.

The shell that hit the sub did more than punch a hole in the conning tower. The positioning of the sub's controls was such that when the sub's captain was manning the periscope, his upper body was at the level of the base of the conning tower. Since the captain was certainly at the periscope, the shell would have hit him in the head or shoulders. That shell thus caused the first death in the undeclared war between the United States and Japan. The sub's crewman would have drowned, as the sub filled with water, and become the war's second casualty.

Crewmen on deck of *Antares* watching the encounter realized that a submarine had been involved and that the *Ward* had just sunk it. They

Ward's leaders during and after Pearl Harbor off the ship together, from left, Lt. Com. William Outerbridge, CO, Lt. Oscar Goepner, Gunnery Officer, and Lt. Hartwell Doughty, XO. (First Shot Naval Vets of St. Paul)

Lt. Com. Outerbridge receiving the Navy Cross from Admiral Chester Nimitz for meritorious actions in sinking the submarine on December 7, 1941. (National Archives)

immediately relayed the exciting news to those below deck. Tug *Keosanqua,* now only a mile away from the barge it was to pick up, heard the shell fire and saw the depth charge explosions but could not see the small conning tower. They assumed that the activity was merely an unusual Sunday morning anti-submarine exercise.

As Outerbridge swept the still swirling water with his binoculars, he was confident that the submarine he had just sunk was Japanese. As the Executive Officer of the destroyer *Cummings* on China Station, he had been told that the Japanese had small submarines like the one that *Ward* just encountered.

Others were not so confident. Lt. Goepner still had fears that the submarine might have been American and that the sinking may have been a big mistake. Tanner, after reporting the incident to his base, continued his patrol but was dreading receiving a report in return that he had attacked a friendly submarine.

Other events within the next hour would clarify this issue to everyone's satisfaction. Nevertheless, Outerbridge reflected on what had just occurred in the seven minute span as he peered out at the now peaceful sea around him. "Secure all guns, secure all depth charges!" he ordered, as if to put a finish to the event.

It was difficult for him to believe that so much had transpired since he had assumed command of *Ward* only two short days before. He wondered what else could possibly happen on what was supposed to be a quiet day. He would soon have the answer to that question. *Ward's* day had just begun. It would be the longest day that Outerbridge and *Ward* would ever experience together.

CHAPTER 6	

Assault from the Sky

It had been several minutes since the submarine disappeared beneath the now calm waters outside the channel entrance. Crewmen all over *Ward* continued to scan the water for debris or a trace of the sub to confirm that it had been destroyed.

Some men thought they had spotted floating oil patches but that was not possible. Although the men did not know it, midget submarines did not have diesel engines and thus did not carry fuel oil. Their sole source of power for both surface and submerged cruising was their battery pack. If the sub resurfaced, *Ward* was ready for it with loaded weapons.

As Outerbridge waited for another report from the sonar operator, he decided to check out a sampan only 500 yards away that had entered the restricted zone. All fishing boat operators knew of the restricted area but some liked to crowd its limits. He ordered Doughty to head for the vessel.

As the *Ward* closed on the sampan, Outerbridge mulled over the message he would send to the 14th Naval District Headquarters at Pearl Harbor. He did not have many details yet so the message would have to be brief. At 0651 he had his radio operator, Maurice Gatewood, send an initial contact report in the clear, "WE HAVE DROPPED DEPTH CHARGES ON SUB OPERATING IN DEFENSIVE SEA AREA."[1]

As soon as the message was away he realized that it left itself open to misinterpretation. It was not clear from the message that he had even seen a sub. All headquarters would know for certain was that *Ward* had dropped depth charges. He knew that depth charges were sometimes dropped on sound contacts that were not submarines. Headquarters was aware of this as well and needed to be told that a submarine was actually sighted. No, he needed a stronger message, one that would trigger an immediate reaction.

At 0653 he sent a follow-up message, also in the clear, "WE HAVE ATTACKED, FIRED UPON, DEPTH BOMBED, AND SANK SUBMARINE OPERATING IN DEFENSIVE SEA AREA."[2] That, thought Outerbridge, should get a reaction from headquarters. When no confirmation of the message was received, Outerbridge quickly sent a third message, "DID YOU GET LAST MESSAGE?" Confirmation followed immediately.

That taken care of, and with no further sound or visual sighting of the submarine made after the depth charging, he decided to stop the sampan. As soon as *Ward* pointed her bow at the fishing boat, it turned to the west as if it was attempting to flee. Outerbridge could clearly see the number 248 on her stern. This identified her as the *Ebesu Maru No. 2*, a 34-foot boat owned by the Hawaii Suisan Kaisha Fishing Company.[3] It usually carried a crew of three, all Japanese.

Outerbridge's officers now informed him that this boat had been seen in the restricted area before and warned several times. The warnings apparently went unheeded. Outerbridge decided that it was time to take stronger measures with the sampan and would have it taken into Honolulu Harbor under guard this time.

The race was an unequal one and *Ward* quickly overtook the fishing boat. Using a bullhorn, he ordered the sampan to stop. When it continued on the same course, Outerbridge turned to a gunner's mate standing by with a loaded rifle and yelled, "Put a couple of shots over its bow."

Several loud cracks punctuated the order to halt and brought an immediate response. The vessel stopped and a crewman, undoubtedly the captain, rushed on deck waving a white flag. Attempts by several of *Ward's* officers to explain the restricted area boundaries revealed that no one in the sampan's crew could speak English.

Dick Thill, still at his battle station on Number Two Gun, thought this whole episode was very strange. Here was a fishing boat manned by an all-Japanese crew in an area where *Ward* had just sunk a submarine, undoubtedly also Japanese. "That can't be a coincidence," he thought, "someone should look into that."

Outerbridge also thought the incident strange, especially the white flag. Using sign language he ordered the sampan to return to Honolulu Harbor and began to escort her until a coast guard cutter could take it off his hands.

The U.S. Coast Guard maintained a fleet of three cutters plus smaller vessels at Honolulu, all assigned to harbor patrol. One of their responsibilities was to bring impounded vessels into the harbor for inspection. *Ward* now signaled her captain's request to headquarters, "WE HAVE INTERCEPTED A SAMPAN IN THE RESTRICTED AREA. PLEASE SEND A COAST GUARD CUTTER TO RELIEVE US OF SAMPAN."[4]

The headquarters radio operator did not read this message clearly and asked *Ward* to repeat it. They did. *Ward* moved slowly toward Honolulu harbor with the sampan as it awaited the cutter.

Just to the west of the harbor entrance, the Coast Guard Cutter *Tiger,* a 125-foot craft, was on routine patrol checking sampans along the west coast of Oahu. Hearing *Ward's* two messages regarding the sub, *Tiger's* radioman called Captain Mazonni to the bridge. Mazonni decided to steam south to assist the *Ward* if she needed help.

Rounding Barber's Point, the *Tiger's* rudimentary sonar gear picked up an underwater echo. Not certain what it was, Mazonni decided to follow it as it moved slowly easterly toward the harbor entrance.

Unknown to Mazonni, the contact he was following was a midget sub launched earlier in the morning. The sub was attempting to maneuver to the harbor entrance and enter when it could. Although it had used periscope observations, the midget commander was unaware that the *Tiger* was coming on the scene.

Ward had just picked up another sonar contact at 0703 and was following that contact. With the knowledge that there had been one sub outside the harbor, Outerbridge had to assume that there may be another. He had already decided that *Ward* would attack every sound contact it picked up. He ordered Goepner to drop depth charges on this latest contact and again the bridge whistle blared, twice this time.

Maskewitcz rolled two charges over the stern at 0705 and the sea erupted once more. As soon as the water surface stopped boiling the sonar operator reported that it had contact with the object again. Outerbridge ordered another attack. *Ward* made another run over the contact and dropped two more depth charges from the stern racks plus one from the depth charge projector. Three new underwater explosions were followed by huge geysers that threw tons of water in the air.

Following the trail of *Ward's* radio messages of 0651 and 0653, advising headquarters of the attack and sinking of the sub, is a study in frustration. Both messages were received by Ensign Oliver Underkoffer, the Communications Watch Officer at the radio receiving station at Barbers Point.

The first message surprised Underkoffer, but the second one suggested to him that something serious was occurring. He immediately showed it to the duty officer, Lt. (jg) Albert Kilhefner. He, in turn, forwarded the messages to the Chief of Staff at 14th Naval District Headquarters, Captain John Earle. As could be expected, Earle's response to Kilhefner was to request confirmation from *Ward*.[5]

At 0712, the messages were forwarded to Lt. Commander Harold Kaminski, in charge of the harbor's boom and net defenses. Kaminski considered the sightings to be legitimate and determined that he would pursue it. This was a noble decision considering that he had already been on duty for 24 hours and was exhausted.

He immediately began calling headquarters staff officers and reached the assistant to the Fleet Duty Officer, Commander Vincent Murphy, who was dressing. After a discussion with his own assistant, Murphy attempted to call Kaminski back to learn what actions he had taken so far. Kaminski's line was, of course, busy and more time was lost.

Meanwhile, Kaminski, on his own initiative, contacted the "ready" destroyer *Monaghan* and ordered it to get under way immediately and report to the *Ward* in the restricted area.[6] He sent a copy of this order to *Ward* so that Outerbridge would know that *Monaghan* was coming. One destroyer in the harbor was kept in a "ready" status at all times to respond to emergency situations. Ready status meant that her boilers were lit off and the ship was capable of getting under way in less than an hour.

Considerable time was lost in coding and decoding radio messages regarding *Ward's* attack, and it was not until 0751 that Kaminski's order was received on the *Monaghan's* bridge. She made immediate preparations to join *Ward*. Other events soon overtook *Monaghan,* however, and she was not able to clear the harbor until much later.

In a day filled with ironies, *Monaghan* did get involved with a midget submarine, but not outside the harbor with *Ward*. She sighted one inside the harbor at 0839 during the height of the first air attack as she was just getting in motion. In a scene of utter pandemonium, with ships burning all over the harbor, bombs still dropping, and Japanese aircraft strafing at will, a naval battle began *inside the harbor.*

Ships on the west side of Ford Island sighted the sub before *Monaghan* did and began shooting at its exposed conning tower. When *Monaghan* also sighted it, her skipper, Lt. Com. William Burford, ordered her guns to fire as well and headed directly at the sub. The midget now sighted *Monaghan* and fired one of its torpedoes at it. The torpedo just missed *Monaghan* astern, and a few moments later the bow of the *Monaghan* sliced into the sub, spinning it around and sending it to the bottom of the channel. For good measure, *Monaghan* also dropped a depth charge set at 30 feet that lifted the sub out of the water.[7]

True to its orders, *Monaghan* left the harbor after its battle with the sub. By that time, however, *Ward's* encounter with a midget sub outside the harbor was no longer the major issue for *Ward, Monaghan,* or anyone else.

Kaminski, continuing to burn up the telephone lines before 0800, next called Captain Earle. From his earlier conversation with Underkoffer, Earle was not convinced that a submarine was really involved or that shots had been fired. Kaminski's calls were thought by Earle to indicate that if there was a shooting incident, it was between *Ward* and something else.

The midget sub that penetrated Pearl Harbor on December 7, 1941, was shelled, depth charged, and rammed by destroyer *Monaghan*. It was recovered two weeks later and buried in a new pier at the sub base under construction at the submarine base. It is identical to the sub that *Ward* sank outside the harbor. (Naval Historical Center)

Earle did agree to take the incident higher in the chain of command and called Admiral Bloch, Chief of the 14th Naval District, who was of the opinion that the report was probably a mistake. He wanted a more detailed report on the incident before he could act on it and he ordered Earle to get one. Bloch was not overly concerned about the incident and concluded that even if it was a hostile submarine, *Ward* could deal with it handily.

While Kaminski continued to call attention to what he felt was a critical situation, he was receiving some help. Tanner's radio report from his PBY now was generating telephone calls also. Many staff officers at 14th naval District Headquarters felt that something must have happened at the harbor entrance if both a destroyer and a patrol plane reported it.

It was not until Assistant Fleet Duty Officer Murphy took it upon himself to call Admiral of the Pacific Fleet, Husband Kimmel, just before 0800, that the incident went to the very top. During one of these telephone conversations, an aide rushed in to tell Admiral Kimmel that Pearl Harbor was being attacked by Japanese aircraft.[8]

The issue was now moot. The hour's advance warning that *Ward* had given higher authorities, with her reports on sinking of the submarine, had been squandered. It was now obvious that her report was valid and her actions appropriate.

All of these phone conversations and discussions were, of course, unknown to *Ward*. For all she knew, her reports had generated important decisions and stirred headquarters into mobilizing forces all over the island. That was someone else's concern, however. Outerbridge was simply looking for a lull in what had been non-stop activity on *Ward* since 0342.

In the past four hours, he had called the ship to General Quarters twice, searched for a reported submarine, fired on and depth-charged another submarine, depth-charged a third submarine, stopped a suspicious sampan, turned it over to the Coast Guard vessel CG-400, and sent a stream of radio messages to headquarters on all of these incidents.

By 0740, the harbor entrance was calm again and it was hard to believe that all of this had really happened. *Keosanqua* had finally met *Antares* and was now proceeding toward the harbor entrance with *Antares'* barge. *Antares,* free of her tow, was also making its way toward the harbor to undergo the mandatory customs inspection.

The Coast Guard vessel CG-400 was now escorting the reluctant sampan 248 into Honolulu harbor at a leisurely pace. Coast Guard cutter *Tiger* continued to follow the underwater object it had encountered near Barber's Point. It lost contact with it several times but regained it again, always closer to the channel entrance.

Ward, finally free of these interruptions, resumed its patrol, making "easy circle eights" in the restricted area. Outerbridge kept the crew at General Quarters, maintaining the crew at gun positions on deck. Ashore, the only action generated by *Ward's* radio messages was the order by Kaminski to destroyer *Monaghan* to get under way and report to *Ward.*

At 0754 lookouts on *Ward* sighted several squadrons of unidentified aircraft flying past Barber's Point headed for Pearl Harbor. They flew directly over the *Tiger,* now near the entrance channel. Several strafed her and dropped small bombs. All missed, but *Tiger* became the first U.S. ship to be fired upon by one minute. The red "meat balls" were clearly visible on the aircraft and *Tiger* thus became the first U.S. ship to know the identity of the attackers.[9]

Minutes later *Tiger* could see the destruction occurring in the harbor and decided that this was not the place to be. She made a quick U-turn at the channel entrance, and was almost rammed by the destroyer *Helm* in doing so.

Within minutes crewmen on *Ward* could see angry black bursts over the harbor several miles away. Among the bursts, they could pick out individual aircraft and now they were able to see swarms of aircraft zooming and diving.

Will Lehner, like many others, thought it was an unusual but realistic Sunday exercise by army planes. "Then," he said, "I saw a lot of black smoke rising from the harbor. That told me that this was not an exercise. We had not received any word about an attack on the harbor so this was very puzzling."

Outerbridge's first thought was that the planes were from the aircraft carrier *Enterprise,* expected to return to Pearl Harbor about 0800. He remarked to others on the bridge, "Those must be Halsey's planes. They always put on a show when they return to the harbor." Someone else suggested to Outerbridge that the explosions might be coming from the new road being blasted out of the rock near the harbor.

As everyone on *Ward's* deck continued to observe the drama taking place over the harbor, a tremendous pillar of black smoke rose above the harbor in a strange mushroom-shaped cloud.

Russ Reetz knew that something big had just been hit. "I was sure that the oil tanks around the harbor were burning because the smoke was that black," said Reetz. It was not oil tanks but the battleship *Arizona* that was burning, but neither Reetz nor anyone else in the crew knew it.

Ward continued to patrol but all eyes were now on the harbor. The entire harbor area was now covered by a thick blanket of black smoke, individual columns extending skyward. The crew had still received no word on what was occurring in the harbor.

At about 0815 the mystery was solved. Two aircraft came barreling out of the harbor after making several strafing passes there. They had just finished a pass that took them over the entrance channel and were accelerating to gain altitude for another pass. Ahead of them they noticed a single destroyer guarding the harbor entrance. The number of stacks identified the ship to the pilots as a World War I vintage destroyer practically devoid of anti-aircraft weapons.

Each plane had a bomb left under its wing, of adequate size for a ship that small. They agreed that this ship should feel the wrath of the Japanese empire just as the ships in the harbor had already felt it. The two aircraft dove wing tip to wing tip at the destroyer now just starting to turn hard to avoid them. As they reached their release point, the two bombs separated from the aircraft and arched toward *Ward*.

On the bridge, Outerbridge, warned by lookouts of the approaching planes, ordered *Ward* into a series of sharp maneuvers to present a more difficult target. The aircraft dove straight at the ship, dropped their bombs and passed directly over *Ward* as they reached again for altitude.

Ward's two 0.50 caliber machine guns fired briefly during the pass, adding their sharp staccato to the noisy background. On the ship's bow, the engine room crew was manning the 3"/23-caliber gun, the only true anti-aircraft gun *Ward* had. *Ward's* main batteries could not be elevated to fire at aircraft. The 0.50 caliber machine guns were old and used water to cool the barrel. Salt from the salt water used as a coolant plugged the cooling apparatus causing frequent jamming. Both machine guns jammed after firing only a few bursts at the aircraft.[10]

The three-inch gun had a barrel less than six feet in length and was extremely inaccurate. It was not reliable for use against aircraft and now used primarily for firing star shells for illuminating a target. This "balloon buster," as its crew called it, was used in World War I against German dirigibles, hence its unique nick-name.

Ken Swedberg had just been assigned to the three-inch gun the previous day. He was given a walk-through with the gun crew then but had never fired the gun. Now, Ken and the rest of the gun crew, all from the boiler room, would finally get to fire it.

F1c Kenneth Swedberg. (Ken Swedberg)

Dave Morgan, a sergeant on the St. Paul Police Department before he enlisted, was the "talker" on the gun crew and was in contact by headphones with the bridge. Tom Nadeau was the "hot shell" man while Maurice Hurley and Bob and Ed Zechmann made up the rest of the crew.

Dave Morgan received the order to "fire" and relayed it to Swedberg. Ken pulled the trigger but nothing happened. The crew removed the shell, loaded another, and Swedberg fired again. This one misfired also.[11] Before the crew could reload another shell, the aircraft were out of range. The ammunition was as old as *Ward*.

The bombs straddled *Ward*, one exploding on either side of the ship. The explosions shook the ship and lifted the stern completely out of the water, exposing her screws. They also sprayed deadly shrapnel over her deck which could have killed any crewman in their path.

WT1c Dave Morgan. (James Morgan)

In describing the attack years later, Orv Ethier said, "If those bombs had been much closer, I wouldn't have lived to tell about it." Russ Reetz, at his damage control station on deck, had a good look at one of the aircraft as it passed over *Ward*. "It was so close that I could see the white scarf around the pilot's neck that floated in the slip stream. He was grinning as he looked down at us."

Russ noticed one other feature on the aircraft, the red meatball insignia on the wing and fuselage. This was the first confirmation *Ward* had that it was the Japanese who were attacking Pearl Harbor.[12]

Ward's crew was stunned and Outerbridge was shocked, but not surprised. He now realized that the island was under a general attack by Japan. He was one of the few people on Oahu who knew that it was being attacked, not only by aircraft but by submarines as well. He was now aware that war had come to the Pacific and the ship that had become his first command two days earlier was smack in the middle of it.

F2c Orv Ethier. (Pat Ethier)

About fifteen minutes earlier, two Zeros made a strafing pass at *Antares.* The first indication *Antares* crew had were the rows of splinters suddenly flying from the wooden hatch covers. Machine gun bullets were stitching deadly patterns all over *Antares'* deck. Some penetrated the lower deck area of the ship and scattered the engine room gang that had just come off watch and were preparing to have breakfast. When another fighter dove low on the ship, Commander Grannis yelled to a nearby mess attendant, "Throw a spud at him."[13]

As the two aircraft zoomed over *Ward,* they were chased by anti-aircraft bursts. The fire was not coming from *Ward,* however. The source of the fire was revealed with a glance at the harbor entrance. There, a destroyer was racing out of the harbor at close to 30 knots with black smoke pouring out of her funnels indicating that all of her boilers were on line. More important to *Ward,* the destroyer was firing at the aircraft with every gun she had.

It was not *Monaghan,* however. The *Monaghan* was still in the harbor. It was *Helm,* a new 1500-ton destroyer carrying a five-inch, dual-purpose main battery and anti-aircraft guns.

The appearance of *Helm* was a pure coincidence. It had been scheduled for routine deperming in West Loch and had just passed through the West Loch entrance at 0759 when aircraft appeared over the harbor. Several flew low over *Helm's* bow and strafed her. Her forward machine guns were still packed in cosmoline and could not fire immediately. Gunner's Mates cleared off the grease in world record time and soon had these guns operating.

Helm backed out of West Loch and began firing with all remaining guns, including her main battery. A port side machine gun knocked down a Zero which crashed into a grove of trees near Hickam Field.[14] By 0813 *Helm* passed the torpedo nets and four minutes later she had emerged from the channel firing at aircraft as well as at a midget sub she had just sighted. It was the same sub that had been attempting to enter the harbor an hour earlier.

Ward was glad to see *Helm* coming out. This would now give her some anti-aircraft protection that she could not give herself. After seeing *Helm* spitting fire from all guns, the two aircraft left *Ward* to find easier targets.

Orv Ethier had been on deck drawing drinking water for the fire room crew when the aerial attack began. Nothing made sense to him until the two aircraft flew by straddling *Ward* with bombs. He ran back to the fire room immediately to tell the black gang that they were in a shooting war with Japan.

As *Ward* kept patrolling, lookouts kept an eye out for additional submarines. They kept the other eye on the sky over the harbor which was now covered with black smoke rising from burning buildings, aircraft, and ships. At 0840 *Ward* picked up another sonar contact. She dropped two depth charges but saw no visible evidence of a sub. *Ward* and *Helms* were the only two ships outside the harbor and both were searching for submarines as well as aircraft.

Just before 0900 crewmen spotted an aircraft approaching *Ward.* As they watched it, the plane was on a course that would take it directly over the ship. On the three-inch gun, Swedberg watched it intently as crewmen all around him were yelling "Shoot, shoot, dammit!" When the gun was pointing almost straight up, Swedberg looked at Morgan and pleaded, "Permission to fire?"

He swore that he saw Morgan nod his head so he fired. This time the gun functioned properly and sent a three-inch shell toward the aircraft. The gun was located just forward of the bridge and rocked the bridge and everyone on it as it fired.[15]

Outerbridge, thinking a bomb hit *Ward,* dropped to the deck. He rose sheepishly after learning that it was his own three-inch gun firing. Apparently the bridge had not given the order to fire so everyone was surprised by the concussion. Fortunately, Swedberg's shot missed the aircraft. It was a B-17 attempting to land at nearby Hickam Field, a straggler from the squadron of 12 such bombers from the mainland which had arrived during the air raid.

At 0901 a stream of destroyers charged out of the harbor. They had been ordered to form a patrol line to hunt for submarines outside the harbor. The Coast Guard cutter *Tiger* emerged first, followed quickly by *Henley, Dale, Monaghan, Blue, Patterson, Ralph Talbot, Phelps, Farragut, Aylwin,* and others.[16]

Ward crewmen were ecstatic over the array of power spewing forth from the harbor entrance. Until *Helms* had come out earlier, *Ward* was a sitting duck as the only destroyer outside the harbor, and without anti-aircraft protection. Every one of the destroyers that now joined them was a modern ship with adequate anti-aircraft weapons. The destroyers formed a ring around Oahu's south shore and immediately began sonar sweeping for subs.

Later, the destroyer *Cummings* came boiling out of the harbor as well. Several days earlier, Outerbridge had been the Executive officer on *Cummings* and was well respected by her officers. In spite of the seriousness of the day, *Cummings'* commanding officer, G. D. Cooper, thought that a bit of levity was needed to lighten up the situation. As *Cummings* steamed past *Ward* with a bone in her teeth, she sent a blinker signal to Outerbridge, "NEVER MIND OLD BOY. YOU SIT THERE ON YOUR ASS. WE'LL GO AFTER THE JAP FLEET." The message had the desired effect and *Ward's* bridge personnel got a chuckle but did not respond.[17]

After the bombing attack began, mysterious explosions began appearing around *Ward*. Lookouts could see no aircraft above them and the explosions were too numerous to be torpedoes hitting underwater reefs. Outerbridge finally realized what was causing them.

There were now close to 100 five-inch guns on ships in the harbor firing at aircraft. In the excitement, some gun crews had forgotten to set the fuses properly and the shells, falling back, were exploding on contact with the land or water. Outerbridge now had another threat to worry about. During the raid, more than 30 five-inch shells exploded in downtown Honolulu, causing some of the 68 civilian deaths in the attack.[18] Initially it was thought that the Japanese were bombing Honolulu, but that was not the case.

The destroyers were picking up sonar echoes that in normal times would have been ignored. Now, every echo was the recipient of several depth charges and *Ward* treated every echo in this fashion. She dropped depth charges at 0840, 1020, and 1031. In the latter instance, she was in the midst of a sharp turn to port when she dropped three charges. The concussion rocked the ship, jamming the rudder at hard left. [19]

For three minutes crewmen worked feverishly to clear the rudder while the ship circled sharply. They finally straightened it out and *Ward* continued her patrol. At 1127 she picked up another solid echo and dropped a pattern of four depth charges. Oil rose to the surface but *Ward* did not stop to investigate.

At 1147 she dropped another pattern of four charges on a contact but none of them exploded. Even her depth charges were old. *Ward* was now running low on depth charges and requested permission from Headquarters to return to the ammunition depot in West Loch to replenish her supply. She was given permission to return as soon as *Chew* relieved her.

Chew was ordered out immediately, and on her way down the channel she picked up a contact and dropped two depth charges, only one of which exploded. At 1245 *Chew* was on station and *Ward* sped back to the harbor, zig-zagging all the way.

As *Ward* slowed at the West Loch entrance, the crew could now see some of the devastation in the harbor created by the Japanese attack. Several ships were sitting on the harbor bottom, others were completely capsized. Many were still burning. The *Arizona* was still a roaring inferno.

There was much cursing on *Ward's* deck as the crew, with grim determination burned into their faces, vowed to extract revenge for what the Japanese did to their fleet with a sneak attack.

At 1340 *Ward* moored alongside the ammunition dock in West Loch and began loading depth charges ten minutes later. By 1650 her crew had stowed 47 of the ash-can-shaped charges in her ammunition locker and cast off. At 1742 she rendezvoused with *Allen* outside the harbor to take on 14 of *Allen's* crew to relieve some of *Ward's* men.[20] With few exceptions, her crew had been at General Quarters continuously for 14 hours, much of that time in actual combat situations. Three minutes later *Ward* relieved *Chew* and was again responsible for inner harbor patrol.

Darkness soon settled over the restricted area and *Ward*. Her crew was still on constant alert but had not picked up any sonar contacts for almost four hours. Inside the harbor, it was relatively quiet but hardly calm. The entire harbor area was a gigantic powder keg waiting to be set off. Everyone from generals and admirals to privates and seamen expected some type of major attack or even invasion by no later than dawn. If the attack did not come that night it would surely come the following morning. Men on every ship and in every gun emplacement rested or slept alongside their weapons. Anything could set them off and at 2110, something did.

The aircraft carrier *Enterprise,* returning from delivering a squadron of fighter planes to Wake Island, had sent a formation of scout bombers escorted by six Wildcat fighters on a search for the Japanese fleet earlier in the day. Finding no enemy fleet, the aircraft returned to *Enterprise.* It was now dusk and a carrier landing in the fading light was considered too risky to attempt. Admiral Halsey refused to turn on the carrier's deck lights because of the threat of Japanese submarines in the vicinity. The fighters were therefore ordered to fly directly to Ford Island and land there.

The fighter's flight leader, Lt. Fritz Hebel, radioed ahead to Ford Island to alert them that he was bringing in a flight after dark and to give everyone his estimated time of arrival. At 2100, as the flight was near Ford Island, the control tower ordered Hebel to turn on his landing lights and proceed to land.

As the aircraft passed low over the harbor, someone on the *Pennsylvania* still in drydock, began firing at them. As if by signal, every ship in the harbor and every gun on Ford Island opened up simultaneously. The hysteria over an anticipated Japanese invasion overcame reason and a deadly barrage of bullets and shells reached out for the six fighters. Four of the aircraft were hit immediately and crashed in the harbor. [21]

Ensign Daniels turned off his landing lights and snuck in safely on Ford Island. Lt. Hebel escaped the fire, turned off his landing lights and headed for Wheeler Field only minutes away. As he lined up for a landing there, nervous gunners, who had not been expecting friendly planes, opened up on him.

This time the fire was accurate and he was hit repeatedly. He crashed in a nearby cane field, dying instantly.[22] Anti-aircraft fire had improved as the day progressed and it knocked down five of the six planes it encountered. Tragically, the aircraft were friendly.

On *Ward,* those men not on watch tried to catch some sleep but sleep was difficult. Most men slept on deck next to their guns, and with life jackets on. If a torpedo crashed into the ship they did not want to be caught below in a bunk in the dark compartments.

The barrage at 2110 lit up the harbor and was clearly visible on *Ward*. Anyone asleep awoke immediately. No one knew what caused the barrage but rumors flew about the expected Japanese follow-up attack or invasion. Outerbridge was taking no chances and immediately called the ship to General Quarters again. With all guns manned, *Ward* was again ready for whatever would come. To the crewmen, it seemed that the day would never end. Some hoped for daylight to arrive but others felt that dawn would bring a Japanese invasion fleet.

Within a few minutes the firing over the harbor ceased and aircraft could no longer be seen or heard. An uneasy calm again returned to the harbor. When Outerbridge was convinced that there would be no further action, he secured *Ward* from General Quarters. The crew tried to sleep again at their gun stations but few actually slept. The remainder of *Ward's* night was quiet, interrupted only when the destroyer *Litchfield* (DD-336) escorted the submarine *Thresher* through the restricted area and into the harbor.

At dawn *Ward* went to General Quarters again to prepare for whatever daylight would bring. This was a dangerous period for everyone on Oahu. If the Japanese were to invade the island, this is when it would occur. The entire island was now on alert and all ships were at General Quarters. At 0618 *Ward* picked up another sonar echo and dropped four depth charges. She picked up another at 0645 and dropped two more. Following this, Outerbridge secured from General Quarters and resumed patrolling.

The incredible day and night was finally over. What had begun as a routine Sunday morning more than 24 hours before had turned into a nightmare. *Ward* had been in action against Japanese submarines and aircraft, and bombed and strafed. Although she suffered no casualties she had seen the horrors of war up close.

On the morning of December 8, her crew was ready for whatever came. They all suffered from lack of sleep but they could deal with that. The biggest worry was what the next 24 hours would bring.

CHAPTER 7

A Difficult December

Ward was no longer the innocent 23-year-old destroyer manned largely by former reservists. True, the crew was only one day older by their biological clocks, but the surprise attack and its aftermath transformed the ship instantaneously into an 1100-ton fighting warship manned by young men who, overnight, had been welded into a crew with serious and deadly resolve.

It was a different ship and a mature crew that greeted the dawn on December 8. The ship had waited since 1918 for a chance to fight, and her day had finally come. She demonstrated to all that, although built for another war, she was a fighter. She also proved that she had a captain who was a bold and aggressive leader, who would not hesitate to confront the enemy. Most importantly, she had a crew who would follow him into battle anywhere, like seasoned veterans.

Ward was already beginning to acquire a reputation for being a fighter whenever she went into harm's way, a reputation that would follow her for her entire career. Although her captain had been in command of a combat ship for only three days, his willingness to act decisively in a difficult situation had already earned his crew's respect. This usually took much longer for new commanding officers. It also earned the recognition of the navy hierarchy. William Outerbridge was awarded the prestigious Navy Cross for his bold actions on the morning of December 7.[1]

Every action by the crew was now put into the perspective of a deadly war, where everyone depended on each other for the survival. The safety of the ship and crew was now of primary importance but no greater than the ship's responsibility to the other ships around her and for completing the missions she was given. The *Ward* was now a man-of-war, not a big one, but one that could hurt the enemy. She had already proven that, and the Japanese would feel her wrath many more times over the next three years.

On December 8, *Ward* continued her inner harbor patrol, ready to react to any situation within a moment's notice. She continued being aggressive in her response to sonar contacts, and at 1349 dropped four depth charges on a contact. At 1648, *Ward* witnessed the big carrier *Enterprise* enter the harbor. It was her aircraft that had precipitated the "friendly fire" incident the previous night. She was accompanied by other units of the Pacific Fleet that had been at sea during the attack.

To the relief of thousands of military personnel in Hawaii, including the crew of *Ward*, December 8 passed uneventfully. No further attacks or invasion materialized, and aerial patrols showed no Japanese forces near the island. Except for several sonar contacts, *Ward's* day was quiet.

Outerbridge called the ship to General Quarters for an hour at 0530 on December 9, a practice that would continue as long as *Ward* was in a war zone. At 0745 *Ward* dropped four depth charges on another sonar contact, none of which exploded. Outerbridge was fuming. Headquarters would hear about this when *Ward* returned to port.

After a patrolling aircraft dropped a smoke bomb on an apparent submarine it spotted, *Ward* raced to the spot and dropped six more charges at 1158. It made three other contacts on the 9th, dropping depth charges on one of them. No evidence of an actual submarine surfaced after any of the attacks.

Ward was not alone in attacking suspicious contacts. Other destroyers on outer harbor patrol also attacked any contacts their sonar gear picked up, and Coast Guard cutter *Taney* was doing the same outside Honolulu Harbor.

There were, in fact, a number of Japanese submarines in Hawaiian waters on both December 8 and 9. The five large mother submarines, I-16, I-18, I-20, I-22, and I-24, that carried the midget subs to Hawaii surfaced at the designated rendezvous near Lanai on the evening of the 7th and again on the evening of the 8th. When it was evident that none of the midgets were returning, the mother subs left Hawaii.[2]

I-69, another large submarine, loitered about four miles outside the harbor on the evening of December 7 and all day on December 8. This sub was almost discovered as it lost its trim several times and surfaced by accident. Miraculously it was not seen by *Ward* or any other ship.[3]

Enterprise stayed in the harbor a mere 13 hours, only long enough to refuel and resupply. Admiral Halsey had no intention of being caught in the confined harbor if the Japanese attacked again. The carrier left with a destroyer escort at 0540 on December 9. Halsey's resolve at seeing the devastation within the harbor caused by the sneak attack was clearly evident as he told as aide, "Before we're through with them, the Japanese language will be spoken only in hell."[4]

The following day, Halsey got his first revenge. One of the *Enterprise* aircraft caught the Japanese submarine I-70 on the surface northeast of Oahu and destroyed it with a single well-placed bomb. The revenge was even sweeter for the pilot of the *Enterprise* plane, Lt. Clarence Dickinson.

On the morning of December 7, Dickinson was one of 18 scout bombers from the *Enterprise* that flew into Pearl Harbor during the height of the attack. Zeros attacked Dickinson's plane killing his rear seat gunner. Dickinson had to bail out before his aircraft crashed. On December 10, Dickinson was flying with a new rear gunner when he bombed and sank the I-70 with all 121 men on board lost.[5]

Wednesday, December 10, brought no relief from the submarine contacts. *Ward* dropped four to six depth charges on every sonar contact she picked up. As with all previous attacks, she observed no evidence of a sub after the explosions.

Ward now had company in the restricted area. Since the 7th, headquarters assigned a second ship to provide even tighter coverage against submarines. Coast Guard Cutter *Taney* joined *Ward* for the first several days, with *Chew* replacing *Taney* on the 12th.

On Thursday, December 11, *Ward* was relieved on inner harbor patrol by the minelayer *Ramsay* and returned to Pearl Harbor to refuel. This was the first time the ship had been in the inner harbor since the attack. It was a sobering experience for the entire crew.

Oil and debris still covered the entire harbor. Fires were now extinguished on all of the damaged ships but smoke continued to rise from the twisted and blackened hull of the *Arizona*. *Utah* was completely capsized. The old minelayer *Oglala* and battleship *Oklahoma* lay on their sides with their superstructures jammed into the harbor mud.

Battleships *West Virginia* and *California* were sitting on the harbor bottom with their decks awash. Battleship *Nevada,* battered and burned, was beached on Waipio Point with a huge hole in her bow. In the dry-docks, the wreckage of the destroyers *Cassin, Shaw,* and *Downes* lay, burned badly and barely recognizable.

The most demoralizing sight was the lifeless, smoldering shell of the battleship *Arizona* with its deck just above water, its mainmast canted forward, and its steel upper works twisted by heat and explosions. It was now known that most of the Arizona's crew died when the ship's magazine exploded and many of them still lay entombed in their bunks in the sunken hull. The image of the once-great battleship on the harbor bottom was burned indelibly into the memories of *Ward's* sailors.

The enormity of the attack now hit home to the men of *Ward.* Nothing needed to be said after seeing the carnage left by the Japanese. The evidence of their treachery lay all over the harbor. Nine ships had been sunk, including four of the eight battleships of the Pacific Fleet: *California, West Virginia, Oklahoma,* and *Arizona.* Ten more ships, including battleships *Nevada, Tennessee, Maryland,* and *Pennsylvania* were damaged to some extent. Except for three, all ships were repaired and rejoined the fleet later in the war, most in 1942.

The Japanese also destroyed 171 aircraft, killed 2340 servicemen, and wounded 1143 others. As Outerbridge stared at the sunken and damaged ships, he observed something else. He saw the huge repair yards, the dry-docks, the immense fuel storage tank farms, the vast ammunition depot, and the important submarine base. These facilities were largely untouched and were already bustling with activity. It would take awhile to completely restore the fleet, but Pearl Harbor was already on its way to recovery.

Ward began fueling immediately after mooring at berth M-2. Fifteen minutes later she received on board ten men who had been in the boiler room of the former battleship, now target ship, *Utah,* when it was torpedoed and capsized on December 7.[6] Nine had managed to reach the main deck and dive over the side. One could not reach the main deck and had to crawl through a porthole to escape before the ship turned over.

All ten men were ordered out of the boiler room by Chief Watertender Peter Tomich, a 48-year-old native of Bosnia-Herzogovina. Tomich, recognizing that *Utah* was about to capsize, knew that the men had only minutes to escape from the boiler room before they would be trapped in it forever. He was also painfully aware that the boilers could not simply be abandoned. Unless they were shut down properly, they would explode when the water hit them and undoubtedly kill everyone on that part of the ship.

Someone had to stay behind to close valves, set gauges, and release steam pressure to prevent an explosion. He considered this his responsibility as Chief Watertender even though he, himself, would not have time to escape after securing the boilers. For giving up his life so that others on the ship could live, Tomich was later posthumously awarded the Congressional Medal of Honor, the nation's highest award.[7]

Because of Tomich's actions, the ten *Utah* men would live to fight again. And *Utah's* men were, indeed, fighters. On the afternoon of December 7, several hundred wet *Utah* sailors were gathered on the *Argonne* awaiting assignments to other ships that needed men. When 55 of them were selected to join several destroyers that were approaching the *Argonne,* some did not wait for a launch. They dove off the *Argonne* and swam to their new ships.[8]

The ten men who joined *Ward* also represented *Utah* well. They were eager to take a crack at a Japanese submarine, warship, or aircraft and *Ward* gave them a chance to do that. Decades later, Ken Swedberg recalled the resolve that the *Utah* sailors brought to the *Ward.* "These men wanted to fight now," said Swedberg and described an incident involving one of them.

Shortly after the *Utah* men joined *Ward,* an officer noticed one of the *Utah* survivors on deck without a life jacket and ordered him to put one on. The sailor refused and was taken to the captain for discipline. When asked by Outerbridge to explain his actions, the sailor told him that he was alive only because he was able to crawl through one of *Utah's* portholes. He explained that he could not have made it through the porthole with a life jacket on and had felt a phobia about wearing a life jacket ever since.

Outerbridge put his hand on the sailor's shoulder, looked him in the eye, and said, "Son, as long as you are on board my ship you will not have to wear a life jacket unless you want to."[9] The sailor discovered that Outerbridge could be a tiger when necessary but also had a human side that earned the respect of everyone who sailed with him. With the additional *Utah* men, Outerbridge now released the 14 men from the *Allen* who joined the *Ward* temporarily on December 9.

As soon as refueling and personnel transfers were completed, *Ward* got in motion again at 1410 to resume her station at inner harbor patrol. Outerbridge was anxious to leave the confines of the harbor. He felt safer outside the harbor where the *Ward* had room to maneuver.

Ward relieved the destroyer *Ramsay* outside the harbor and picked up a sonar contact 17 minutes later, dropping four depth charges. At 1543 she had another contact and dropped six more depth charges. This time the explosions brought some oil to the surface but none of the other debris that usually signaled a submarine sinking.

Action continued when at 1637 a navy Catalina patrol plane spotted what it believed to be a submerged submarine a mile from *Ward.* It dropped two smoke bombs to mark the location for *Ward.* Outerbridge headed for the smoke and quickly picked up an underwater contact. After reaching the area, *Ward* waited as the Catalina dropped two depth charges and then charged in dropping six of her own. Again, oil surfaced but without any other debris. Outerbridge was puzzled by this phenomenon but had no choice but to continue attacking every contact.

At 1920, pinging on the sonar gear heralded another contact and *Ward* raced in with a pattern of six more depth charges. The crew had been at their General Quarters station almost continuously for the past five hours and was looking for a respite.

Ward had now dropped 83 depth charges in 17 separate attacks on submerged objects in the five days since hostilities had begun. No one knew how many of these contacts were actual submarines and how many were underwater wildlife, debris, or reefs. Although other destroyers also made depth charge attacks during this period, *Ward,* because of her position as guardian of the restricted zone, was the leader in reducing the ammunition depot's supply of depth charges.

In half of the attacks, no visible results were obtained. In eight of the incidents, oil slicks rose to the surface either just before or just after the attack. The logical assumption was that the source of the oil was a damaged submarine. Several large Japanese submarines were in the area of Hawaii and were attacked with depth charges, but post-war records confirm that none were sunk or damaged other than I-70 on December 10.

Submarine commanders were known to deliberately release fuel oil to deceive attackers into believing a submarine had sunk. This was usually done after a prolonged depth charging, however. No depth charge attacks outside the Pearl Harbor channel were prolonged and the source of the oil slicks remains a mystery to this day.

The success of the anti-submarine efforts in the five days following the attack was not completely known until much later. Besides the five midget submarines, the Japanese employed 30 fleet-sized submarines in the Pearl Harbor operation. Only 12 of these were stationed close enough to Pearl Harbor to be engaged by destroyers guarding the harbor entrance. In addition to the five mother subs, the Japanese stationed a line of seven submarines 15 miles off the harbor.[10]

Although U.S. air and naval units did not sink any of the 12 Japanese subs outside the harbor, their liberal use of depth charges on the slightest provocation may have kept any submarines at a safe distance from the channel entrance. During this critical period when ships were transiting the harbor with regularity, not a single U.S. ship was torpedoed by any of the 30 submarines surrounding Oahu.

Anti-submarine efforts were successful against the midget subs, however. It was not known during the attack how many midgets were employed but it was obvious that more than one was involved. There were simply too many sightings and attacks for a single midget. It took weeks to sift through all of the sighting reports and official ship's action reports before an accurate summary of the midget's activities could be developed.

All five of the midgets launched by Japanese mother subs were destroyed in some fashion by U.S. forces. One of unknown identity was sunk by *Ward* by gunfire and depth charges several miles off the harbor entrance at 0650 on December 7. Another unknown midget successfully entered the harbor and was then shelled, rammed, and depth charged by destroyer *Monaghan* northwest of Ford Island at 0844. It was later buried in a landfill for expansion of the Pearl Harbor submarine base.

A third was sunk by unknown causes, possibly one of the many depth charge attacks just outside Pearl Harbor on December 7. Its assailant is unknown and could have been any one of the ships that attacked sonar contacts, including *Ward*. It was discovered in 1960 by U.S. Navy divers in Keehi Lagoon near the harbor mouth. Because its torpedoes were still on board, the bow section including the torpedoes was unbolted and disposed of in deep water. The remainder of the sub was returned to Japan, which now displays the restored sub at its Maritime Self-Defense Force School at Eta Jima, its Naval Academy.[11]

Because this sub still contained its torpedoes, it was probably sunk early on the morning of the 7th. After sinking its first sub, *Ward* made four more depth charge attacks on that morning. One of these could easily have been on this midget. *Ward* may have thus disposed of not one, but two of the five midgets attempting to enter the harbor.

I-24A was first depth-charged and then shelled by the *Helm.* As a result of the damage sustained in these attacks and several groundings on submerged reefs, it was unable to maneuver, and drifted aimlessly around the island. It finally grounded on the morning of December 8 in Waimanalo Bay near Bellows Field. Its commanding officer was captured but his crewmen drowned.[12]

I-16A radioed a message to Tokyo on the evening of the 7th that it carried out its attack successfully.[13] It later sent a second message but was never heard from again. No one has been able to determine whether it transmitted the messages from inside or outside the harbor. No trace of the sub was ever found. Because of its very short range, it could not have traveled far from the harbor. It undoubtedly will be found some day, clearing up one of the remaining mysteries concerning this sub.

Ward continued on patrol on December 12 accompanied by the destroyer *Chew. Ward* made additional sonar contacts but Outerbridge considered them questionable and decided not to drop any depth charges. The contacts were still stressful for the crew, which was called to General Quarters for every contact.

At 0735 on the 13th, lookouts spotted a body floating in the patrol area. *Ward* did not pick up the body but identified it as that of a Japanese pilot, on the basis of the flight cloth-ing. It was probably a pilot from one of the aircraft shot down six days earlier. *Ward* radioed headquarters, which dispatched a PT boat to meet *Ward* and take the body ashore for intel-ligence inspection and burial. The boat reached *Ward* at 0915 and was then directed to the body.[14]

Now that long-range, aerial reconnaissance had been organized and was running on a continuing basis, it was possible to confirm that no Japanese naval units were within striking distance of Oahu. The submarine menace was therefore considered the principal threat to Pearl Harbor and given top priority. Destroyers were now on patrol around the entire island and several formed a cordon line between Diamond Head and Barber's Point further out from the Restricted Area. As a further step, ships were entering or leaving the harbor in groups with destroyer escort.

At 1705 on December 13, *Ward's* crew was treated to another grand sight. The aircraft carrier *Lexington*, escorted by three heavy cruisers and five destroyers, approached the island. They were returning from Midway Island, where *Lexington* delivered a squadron of scout bombers. The formation was nearly at the harbor entrance when it was suddenly ordered to steam south at full speed because of suspected Japanese submarines off the har-bor entrance.

After two hours, the ships were recalled and they returned to the harbor at 25 knots. Just as the carrier was approaching the channel entrance again, a submarine was spotted two miles east of the entrance. Destroyers raced for the spot at flank speed, forcing the sub to dive, and dropped a barrage of depth charges. The 33,000-ton *Lexington*, pushed a huge bow wave before it hastily entered the channel, safe from any lurking submarines.

By December 14, *Ward* had been at war for a week and was settling into the routine of a wartime destroyer. The ship was called to General Quarters just before the dawn's first light every morning, a favorite time for submarine commanders to attack. Every sonar contact was investigated, many of which were depth charged. Lookouts were kept alert and the ship was darkened at dusk.

Lookouts spotted a second body floating in the Restricted Area at 0958 on the 14th and *Ward* investigated it. It was also a Japanese pilot, now in the water a week. *Ward* arranged for a boat to pick up the pilot and continued patrolling.[15]

At 1440 *Lexington*, with a cruiser and destroyer escort, steamed past *Ward* out to sea, a majestic sight for the destroyer's crew. Like *Enterprise*, *Lexington* was considered too valu-able to be bottled up in the harbor. It was safest in the open sea despite the threat of sub-marines.

After nine days of almost continuous patrolling at the harbor entrance, including being bombed and strafed, and attacking and sinking at least one submarine, *Ward* was relieved at 0745 on December 15 by converted minelayer *Montgomery*. After taking on fuel, *Ward* moored at her usual spot at berth X-5. Before the crew could have any shore leave, they had work to be done. In the afternoon an ammunition barge came alongside with 30 depth charges and a shipment of small arms which had to be stowed. Other supplies fol-lowed. The respite lasted exactly one day, and *Ward* weighed anchor the following morn-ing to relieve *Montgomery*.

Unknown to U.S. military authorities, Pearl Harbor had an unwelcome visitor earlier in the morning of the 16th. Japanese submarine I-7 carrying a float plane in a watertight compartment on her deck, surfaced at dawn 40 miles south of Pearl Harbor. It lowered the aircraft to the water and launched it. The aircraft then made a high altitude reconnaissance flight over the harbor. The pilot photographed the entire harbor and flew back to I-7 without being detected. Upon landing, the boat's crew did not take the time to recover and stow the aircraft in the hangar for fear of being discovered. Instead, they shot holes in the plane's floats to sink it quickly, submerged, and stole away with the valuable photos.[16]

Ward again picked up sonar contacts on the evening of the 16th. Making two runs, she dropped a pattern of four depth charges each time. On the second run the explosions brought up a huge air bubble and some oil. Outerbridge waited for the disturbance to subside and made a slow speed pass over the spot. Again they lost the contact and whatever had caused the initial contact was no longer there.

On the 17th, a patrolling aircraft sighted a shadow beneath the surface four miles south of the entrance, dropped a smoke bomb to mark the location, and summoned *Ward*. The destroyer raced to the spot at flank speed and dropped two patterns of four depth charges. No evidence of a sub was found nor any further sonar contact regained, and *Ward* returned to her patrol area.

At 2002 *Ward* had a positive and solid sonar contact at 1500 yards. She charged ahead at close to 25 knots, slowing to 15 knots as they approached the area of the contact. Ten seconds later the depth charge crew rolled four pairs of ash cans over the stern at four-second intervals. The charges were alternately set for 50 and 100 feet. The seventh charge threw up a double column of water, higher than the others. Like so many other attacks, although everything looking promising, no debris was raised by the explosions and contact could not be regained.

On Friday, December 19, converted minesweeper *Long,* a former four-stacker, relieved *Ward* so it could return to the harbor for refueling. It also picked up 40 depth charges at West Loch. At 1805, while moored at berth X-5, a boat returned crewman F3c John Merthan, who reported for duty.

Merthan had spent an interesting several weeks on shore and had not been on the

F3c Russell Reetz (left), and F3c John Merthan. (John R. Merthan)

Ward at the time of the attack. He had been transferred to the naval hospital at Pearl Harbor a week prior to the attack for medical treatment. His treatment was completed on Friday, December 5, and he could have been discharged from the hospital then. Although he held a Fireman's rating, Merthan's real interest was medicine and he intended to request training as a Pharmacist's Mate soon.

Because of this interest, doctors at the hospital allowed Merthan to stay a few extra days. In return, he assisted in looking after patients. On December 6 he moved out of the hospital and into a lanai overlooking the channel entrance. "It was a beautiful setting and I was enjoying myself there," Merthan said later. Then it all changed.

The following morning he had just finished his duties on the second floor and was chatting with a Chief off the heavy cruiser *Louisville* when a plane with red meatballs on the wing flew right over the hospital. Merthan yelled, "Jesus, that's Japanese!" They both ran outside and saw aircraft all over the harbor.

A car drove up and a sailor emerged holding his stomach, his uniform already drenched in blood. Merthan and the Chief both dove behind a pillar as a plane dove directly at them. Machine gun bullets stitched a pattern in the ground several feet in front of them but missed them both.

Merthan ran back into the hospital, where he knew his services would soon be needed. Within minutes men with burns were coming in by the score. The group included both the dead and the dying and he was soon ordered to help carry the dead outside to make room for newly arriving wounded.

He spent the remainder of the day carrying out dead sailors and laying them side by side on the lawn. Before long the line stretched a block long and in the middle of the line were two Japanese pilots. He had no idea how they got into the hospital. Merthan's voice quivered as he described the ordeal. "The worst part of this was seeing all of the burned bodies, some burned to a crisp and unrecognizable. There were also bags with nothing but body parts in them. It was awful," he said somberly. "Then we had to load the bodies into trucks for a mass burial somewhere. I can still see us loading all the dead and burned bodies into the trucks. I'll never get that out of my mind."

When night came he was ordered to join a squad of marines guarding the shore just beyond the hospital. "It was a scary night and everyone was shooting at shadows," he recalled.

On the 8th, Merthan, who ran one of *Ward's* whaleboats, was ordered to run one of *West Virginia's* boats and take a group of officers around the harbor to check on each ship. Ships were still burning and bodies still floating in the oil-covered water. As they moved past the *Oklahoma,* Merthan could see men cutting holes in the ship's hull to free sailors trapped in the capsized battleship.

In the afternoon he was given a rifle and bandoleer of ammunition and, with another sailor, ordered to guard the gate to one of the fuel oil tank farms adjacent to the harbor. He was told to shoot anyone attempting to enter the tank farm without authorization. He spent the remainder of the day and evening at that post.

Although he missed out on *Ward's* battle with the subs, Merthan was strafed by a Japanese fighter, spent hours carrying dead bodies out of the hospital and loading them on trucks, spent a night with marines expecting an invasion, guided a boat full of officers around the harbor, and guarded a tank farm with orders to shoot. It was a difficult and stressful two days for an 18-year-old *Ward* crewman who had merely been a patient at the hospital.[17]

Several other *Ward* crewmen were also in the Pearl Harbor Naval Hospital prior to the attack. Two, Robert Ball and Donald Gruening, both St. Paul reservists, were sent to the hospital on November 28. Ball had infected toenails; Gruening had an unspecified condition.

Ball spent a week there soaking his feet to reduce the infection before surgery. On December 5, the doctors gave him a 48-hour pass to visit his uncle who lived on Oahu. Ball took a taxi to his uncle's home in the country near Diamond Head. He was preparing to go to services at the nearby Methodist church with his uncle on the morning of the 7th when he heard a radio announcement describing the attack. All servicemen were instructed to report to their ship or base immediately.[18]

Realizing that he could not catch up with *Ward* on patrol, Ball decided to report to the hospital. He thumbed a ride with two native islanders who worked in the shipyard. On the drive through Honolulu the group could see aircraft over the harbor and dense smoke rising over the harbor and nearby Hickam Field. Just as they reached the base, a bomb landed close to the car showering them with dirt and debris.

At the hospital he helped carry incoming patients, put on plaster casts, and other tasks ordered by the doctors. He continued working there for two weeks until his toes were ready for surgery and doctors could spare time for him. On December 31, he finally had the infected toenails removed. He returned to *Ward* on January 5, but never forgot the difficult days at the hospital following the attack.

Ward was on harbor patrol on December 20, when at 1651 she witnessed a stirring sight. Battleships *Maryland, Tennessee,* and *Pennsylvania* all left the harbor together. All three had suffered minor bomb damage on the 7th but had been repaired quickly at Pearl Harbor's repair yard. They were now en route to the mainland for permanent repairs and modernization at West Coast shipyards.

The first convoy to reach Hawaii after the attack approached the harbor on the afternoon of December 21. It was a small convoy of only three freighters escorted by destroyers and a light cruiser. However it was the first of a steady flow of convoys that would, in a matter of months, transform Oahu into a gigantic warehouse of war-making materials. Some ships would not even unload but simply refuel and continue on to another South Pacific island base. Those supplies would stock the beginning of the long road to Japan. The three freighters entered Honolulu Harbor while the cruiser continued the short distance to Pearl Harbor, passing through the restricted zone.

Ward returned to the harbor on the 23rd where it would remain for three days, moored to a dock at berth 6. There the crew would spend a quiet Christmas Eve and Day. For many it would be their first Christmas away from home. The crew had a short liberty but liberties were now much different from those before the attack. The crew had to be back at the ship every night and Honolulu was blacked out after dark. Celebrating a holiday was difficult for men who had seen the horrors of war brought to Oahu less than three weeks earlier.

It was almost a relief, on the 26th, when *Ward* was ordered out on harbor patrol again. She plied the waters outside the harbor until the end of December. The crew spent New Year's Eve on a darkened ship outside a darkened harbor. As they sat on deck on a warm evening, some gathered around the guitarist in the crew. They sang their favorite songs of home as they stared across the water toward a city with no lights showing but still celebrating the arrival of a new year.

Many wondered aloud what their family and friends were doing on what was surely a frigid night in St. Paul. Some talked about friends on other ships in Pearl Harbor, friends that they had not seen since the attack. They did not know if their friends were even still alive. Others simply recalled the events of the past three weeks, the horrors they had witnessed, and the once proud ships now sitting on the bottom of the harbor.

They discussed the war news from around the Pacific. It was not good. Wake Island and Guam had fallen. The Philippines and Malaya had been invaded and the Allies were retreating everywhere. The men pondered whether the New Year would bring more of the same or if the United States would be able to stem the advance.

Closer to home, they wondered whether a Japanese invasion of the Hawaiian Islands would come and if so, how *Ward* would fare. The approaching New Year held many questions for a group of young men far from home on a 23-year-old ship that had already been brushed by a war that was going to get much bigger soon. The answers to those questions would determine if the men would live or die. The men slept an uneasy sleep awaiting 1942.

For William Outerbridge, December had been a difficult month. He had joined *Ward* for what he thought would be a leisurely time to take command of his first ship and, instead, leaped into a war. He had to make challenging decisions and did so boldly. His men would always respect him for that. Now with a recent promotion to Lieutenant Commander he, too, was awaiting the New Year wondering what lay ahead for himself, his ship, and his country.

CHAPTER 8

Liberty

Since the founding of the United States Navy, the most cherished times of any sailor's naval career are those days spent on liberty. Whether the liberty lasts only a portion of a day, overnight, or an entire weekend, it is an event that occupies a sailor's thoughts all out of proportion to the duration of the liberty.

Sailors in the 1940s were no different. They anticipated its arrival for days or even weeks, planning their activities carefully and marshalling their meager resources. Long after the liberty was over, they rehashed their movements, relating the highlights to anyone who would listen. It became something of an obsession to many sailors; they learned to measure time and accomplishments in terms of their liberties.

Regardless of a sailor's personality, a liberty was a little oasis in what were otherwise tiring, boring, stressful, and even dangerous periods on board their ship. It was an escape from a closed environment and provided sailors with an interval in their lives when they were allowed to act for themselves without the layers of supervision making decisions for them.

Ward's crew encountered the full range of activities provided by liberties during the ship's lifetime. At times the crew had a full 72 hours of freedom in what was probably the ideal liberty port in the world in 1941. At other times, the crew had nothing to look forward to on liberty but four hours on the sand of a hot Pacific island base with two cans of warm beer as their refreshment and entertainment. Even then, liberty served a purpose by giving them respite from the regimented routine of shipboard life.

Cities throughout the world are rated by sailors of seafaring nations as "good" or "lousy" liberty ports by the variety of excitement they offer to visiting sailors. During *Ward's* first career following her commissioning in 1918, her crew had liberty in a number of exciting ports, all in the western hemisphere. These included San Diego, San Francisco, Seattle, Acapulco, the Canal Zone, several Cuban ports, Norfolk, and New York City. It can be assumed that *Ward's* crew took full advantage of these facilities and hospitality, at least to the extent that a sailor's pay at that time permitted.

By 1941, when *Ward's* second tour of duty began, little had changed for U.S sailors on liberty. They still sought the same pleasures as their predecessors had in 1918: change of scenery, relief from the routine of shipboard life, excitement, and those delights that sailors could not find on their ship. At the top of this list were liquid refreshment and female companionship.

Sailors in 1941 still rated liberty ports based on the port's excitement and hospitality toward sailors. The biggest change over the previous 25 years was created by the new role of the U.S. Navy. The expanding mission of the navy following World War I was dramatic in despite the general mood of isolationism that gripped the country.

The various territories the U.S. now owned around the world were developing rapidly. In addition, World War I revealed that the U.S. must have a navy capable of extending its influence around the globe. It was now the navy's policy to display that influence by "showing the flag" in ports worldwide. The list of liberty ports available to sailors now became an international one. Ports rarely seen by U.S. ships previously had now become the sites of frequent visits. Word quickly spread throughout the navy where the exciting liberty ports were.

Some ports in the United States continued to be favorites among sailors of any country. San Diego, San Francisco, New York, and Boston still held attraction for sailors on the town. But even these cities lacked the mystique of a foreign port where cultural differences were welcomed by visiting sailors. By the late 1930s, liberty ports in the Atlantic and the Mediterranean now included the likes of Barcelona, Lisbon, Naples, Alexandria, Capetown, Rio de Janeiro, Montevideo, and Buenos Aires.

In the Pacific, they included Shanghai, Singapore, Sydney, Melbourne, Hong Kong, Manila, Surabaya and other Dutch East Indies ports. Other lesser known but attractive and enticing ports were available as well.

If sailors prepared a list of the most desirable features of a liberty port in 1941, Honolulu, Hawaii would contain all of them. It was a picturesque island far away from home, blessed with an ideal climate, and provided countless opportunities for recreation, friendly people, and cultural differences. Because much of the city's economy was supported by the military, sailors were welcome on the island.

Ward would find herself in a different part of the Pacific with totally contrasting conditions later in the war. On March 10, 1941, however, her crew found themselves stationed on an island that was as close to a paradise as a sailor could find. They would take advantage of that on their first liberty.

Ward's patrol assignment during 1941 also worked in the crew's favor. With only one week out of four on scheduled inner harbor patrol duty, the ship had at least one week per month, and usually more, in some port. Like other ships at Pearl, *Ward's* officers were liberal in granting liberty in peacetime. Crewmen were given liberty by divisions or watches so that part of the crew capable of operating the ship was always on board.

Liberty was usually granted in three forms. Day liberty allowed the men a portion of a given day off and had a firm expiration time. Overnight liberty allowed the men a night off the ship and expired at 0800 the following morning. Weekend or 72-hour liberty provided an entire weekend off the ship and expired at 0800 on Monday morning. On rare occasions, longer liberties were authorized. On average, *Ward's* crew had two or three liberties per month.

Liberty on *Ward* began with all sailors having liberty displaying their liberty passes before leaving the ship. One of the ship's whaleboats served as the boat taking the liberty party to Merry's Point, the designated pier for all trips to and from ships in Pearl Harbor. Orv Ethier, a Fireman 1c whose normal duty station was tending the Number One boiler, also doubled as an engineer on a motor whaleboat. Unless he was on duty or was in the liberty party himself, he ran the liberty boat and was the last to see the expectant faces of those about to enjoy time off the ship.[1]

In 1941 *Ward's* crew was relatively young, many still in their teens. They had not yet acquired the techniques and habits that regular navy veterans were noted for on liberty. Some never would acquire those habits. Although still under the legal drinking age, they could usually find places in Honolulu where even underage sailors were allowed to purchase beer. The younger men drank beer in moderation, usually only one or two bottles, and generally stayed out of trouble.

For many of *Ward's* crew, liberty began at the Army-Navy YMCA on Hotel Street in downtown Honolulu. This was the collection point for buses and taxis from all of the military posts on the island. Men using these conveyances from Pearl Harbor were always dropped off at the YMCA. If a sailor had only a day liberty, he usually picked up a bus at the Y that would get him back to the base by midnight. Liberty boats from the various ships in the harbor congregated there and sailors had to find their own ship's boat.

A sailor with an overnight or weekend liberty would look first for accommodations at the YMCA. It was the most popular lodging on liberty and often the only one they could afford. The few hotels on the island were priced beyond the sailor's means until the military took them over after the war began.

If individual rooms were available at the YMCA, sailors would share a room with a crewmate to reduce expenses. If the fleet was in port, indi-

Bmkr2c Bernard Kinderman, left, and TM3c Ed Mrozak on liberty in Honolulu. (First Shot Naval Vets of St. Paul)

vidual rooms were usually filled, but the Y filled their large ballroom with numbered cots. These were available for 25 cents a night in 1941 and *Ward's* men could usually find sleeping space there.[2]

Soon after December 7, the military took over the Royal Hawaiian Hotel on Waikiki beach and made it available for 25 cents to submariners and naval airmen coming off sea duty. If space was available, destroyer men were permitted to stay there as well.

The YMCA offered many amenities besides sleeping facilities. It served tasty meals and the men usually ate breakfast there before leaving for the activities of the day. Besides the pool and gymnasium, the Y had weight rooms with exercise equipment and a variety of game opportunities. Lockers were available for storage of personal possessions and changes of clothes.

For many crewmen such as Walt Campion, Ed Bukrey, and Ray Nolde, the YMCA itself was their favorite hangout. Ed enjoyed the swimming pool but usually looked for a pick-up basketball or billiards game also. Many crewmen rented box cameras at the Y for 25 cents so they could participate in one of the sailor's favorite pastimes—taking pictures to send home. With a purchased roll of film, they could record the sights of the island on their liberty. These filled many family scrapbooks.

Although sailors could not afford to stay at the Royal Hawaiian Hotel in 1941, they still visited it. "It was a real fancy place," recalled Ken Swedberg. "We used to walk around the lobby and take in all the sights. Movie stars stayed there on their vacation and we'd occasionally see one."

Like most of the thousands of men on liberty on Oahu, *Ward* crewmen did not have much money to squander. They were required to send a portion of their pay home every month leaving them even less for liberties. What remained had to be spent wisely to stretch it out to the next payday.

The barest of a sailor's pleasures—cigarettes and beer—were affordable. A bottle of beer cost only 20 cents at most taverns or bars. Underage sailors would be refused a drink at some places but they were allowed to purchase it at others. They frequented only those bars that would serve them if they were looking for a drink. At 24, Ray Nolde was one of the few St. Paul reservists who could buy a drink anywhere.

Most *Ward* crewmen spent their first several liberties seeking out the attractions that made Oahu famous. Waikiki beach was at the top of the list. As Don Pepin put it, "We loved to walk the beach where we could see more girls in bathing suits than we ever saw before in one place." Sometimes the men, themselves, went swimming at the beach.

Dick Thill was disappointed the first time he visited Waikiki. "I really thought there would be hula girls all over the beach," he laughed, "but the beach was no different than those in St. Paul, just bigger."

At that time the only two hotels on Waikiki were the Moana and the Royal Hawaiian. Across the street, on Kalakaua Boulevard, was an excellent steakhouse where the men would visit when they wanted a first-class meal. The Outrigger Canoe Club, an exclusive private club, was also at Waikiki. The men could only observe this club from the outside, however. The Ward sailors would usually stop for a beer at the outdoor beer garden at the Moana when they were at Waikiki. They enjoyed relaxing there while observing the beach and the mob of vacationers using it.

Sightseeing on Oahu was an extremely popular liberty activity for sailors from any ship. Four or five of them would pool their resources and rent a taxi for a tour

S2c Don Pepin, left, and GM3c Ed Buckrey. (Don Pepin)

of the island. Every sailor on the *Ward* did this at least once; some, many times. A popular stop was the Pali, a scenic overlook on Highway 61 which threaded its way through the Koolau mountain range between Honolulu and Kailua. The view from the Pali was breathtaking.[3]

Some sailors, like Kenny Pfaff, cut their sight-seeing costs by pooling resources and buying their own cheap automobile. By storing it in Honolulu it was available to any of the group on liberty.[4]

Other favorite spots that lured the sailors included the Diamond Head volcano, the Dole Pineapple plantation, coconut groves, and the island's north coast surfing beaches. A taxi tour took about four hours and cost four dollars.

Orv Ethier had his own idea of entertainment on liberty. He enjoyed riding horses back home and rode often. He found a riding stable near Diamond Head and would spend hours riding around the scenic spot on a rented horse.

One of the pleasures that attracted Don Pepin's attention were the banana planta-

SC3c Dick Thill. (Dick Thill)

tions. He would often buy a whole bag of bananas to munch on. "We didn't get bananas on the ship very often so they were a treat," chuckled Pepin. "Besides, a whole bag only cost five cents." His mistake was that he usually ate the entire bagful. "You haven't been sick until you've been sick on bananas," he laughed.

Russ Reetz and others simply enjoyed walking around downtown Honolulu starting from the YMCA. Eventually they'd take a bus to Waikiki and on occasion take in a movie at the brand new Waikiki Theater or visit Hugo Hatties, a favorite watering hole just off the beach.

There was always something interesting to see on Hotel Street, the street on which the YMCA was located. Reetz was intrigued by the many Orientals openly smoking opium pipes. The street was the heart of a rather notorious area, well known for its many pleasure parlors.

One of the most frequented was the Black Cat Café, right across the street from the YMCA. Every sailor visited the Black Cat Café at some time while in Pearl Harbor, if only to be able to brag about being there. It offered food, drink, and all the other pleasures sailors on liberty craved.

The Black Cat was not alone in offering these amenities. In a five-block area near the YMCA bordered by Bretania, Hotel, River, and Fort streets was Honolulu's busiest and most popular commercial district between 1940 and 1944. No fewer than 20 restaurants and bars were congregated in this compact area most politely referred to as Honolulu's red light district. The New Senator Hotel, Wo Fats Restaurant, Ritz, Bronx Bungalow, Pacific, and

Service Hotel were but a few of the establishments catering to servicemen's needs, whatever they may be.[5]

The most basic of their needs could be obtained for the price of three dollars. These services were highly regulated by the Honolulu Police as well as the military to keep these activities confined to this area, where they could be controlled, and to prevent the outbreak of venereal disease. Even in daylight hours during World War II, the sidewalks in this area would be a sea of white with sailors lined up on the sidewalk in front of the more popular bars.

Many of the ship's crews based at Pearl Harbor had a favorite bar or tavern where they would congregate on liberty, a spot where they would be assured of seeing friendly faces when they wanted a bottle of beer. *West Virginia's* crew liked the Wo Fat restaurant. *Ward* did not have a ship-wide favorite, probably because of the large number of underage sailors in her crew. Some of the crew, however, did make the Riverside Tavern on Canal Street their home away from home.[6]

When the fleet was in port, most bars and taverns were filled. Most would use a bouncer on the sidewalk to keep sailors from entering until a table was vacant. At other times men could simply walk in. As Ken Swedberg put it, "We did have our favorite bars but drinking was not a favorite sport of *Ward's* crew; sight-seeing was."[7]

Some of the men were intrigued by football on Oahu and attended games there. A semi-pro league existed on the island offering a first-rate brand of football. Ensign Grefe of *Ward* had played football at Purdue on the mainland and was a tremendous athlete. He played for one of the local teams and drew many of *Ward's* crew to the game when his team was playing.

Some of the crew were roller skaters and eventually found a rink in Honolulu where they often skated. On Sunday mornings, most of the crew on weekend liberty found a church of their denomination.

Whether the men were taking a tour or walking along the beach, they usually went on liberty with close friends, often those with whom they shared the same shipboard duty. Orv Ethier usually went with Scotty Fenton and Howie Gearin while Dick Thill could often be found with Harold Flanagan and Carrol Schmitt. Thill and Schmitt attended school together in St. Paul from the first grade on. Don Pepin traveled with Jack Peick, Ed Mrozak, and Ed Bukery on liberty. The three joined the reserves together in 1938 and stayed together.

Russ Reetz and John Merthan often went on liberty together although Merthan also traveled with friends from other ships. Will Lehner, Tom Nadeau, and Ken Swedberg usually chummed together as did Maurice Hurley, Harold Harris, and brothers Ed and Bob Zechman.

Some men, like Pfaff, Lehner and Swedberg, preferred to wear civilian clothes on liberty so as not to attract undue attention. They had their mothers ship them some "civvies" and rented a locker downtown to store them. Their first stop on liberty was to their locker, where they changed clothes. Then they looked like any other tourists on the street rather than sailors.

Swedberg also owned a hand-tailored dress blue uniform with full bell bottoms. The uniform was actually closer to black than blue in color and looked exquisite. He was proud of the uniform and bragged, "They were all wool, fine textured and looked sharp," he recalled. "That was my dress blue uniform all through the war."

Lehner and Swedberg often worked out on the exercise equipment at the YMCA and then took a swim in the big pool there. After that they were ready for a few beers at their favorite watering hole.

Bob Ball and Ken Pfaff traveled together and enjoyed the same activities as others. As Ball described it, "We had a few beers here and there and had fun downtown but we never stood in line." He was referring to the long line of sailors outside the houses in the red light district.

Ball had a unique place to visit on his liberties. He had a great-aunt living on Oahu and married to a native islander. Her husband was a big man, six feet, three inches tall, and 300 pounds, with a beautiful tenor voice. A territorial policeman by profession, he was also a professional musician on the side. He had his own orchestra that performed all over the island. Several of his nieces danced the hula with the orchestra, making the group a family affair.

He and Ball's great-aunt lived in a scenic valley near Diamond Head, where Ball would visit on liberties. Ball would often follow the orchestra on their engagements and engage in a family social event while enjoying the music.[8]

F1c Ken Swedberg, left, and F2c Will Lehner. (Ken Swedberg)

Sailors could enjoy some of the pleasures of a liberty without leaving the naval base. In 1940, with the movement of the Pacific Fleet to Pearl Harbor, the navy felt that a center was needed right on the base to provide thousands of new sailors with nearby recreational opportunities. It constructed a new recreational center to fill this need. Previously, the men had had to obtain transportation to downtown Honolulu for even the most basic liberty activities. A sailor was also more apt to find trouble in Honolulu than on the base itself.

At the center, named Bloch Arena, sailors could play cards, billiards or other games; bowl, take in a dance or concert by one of the ships' bands, see a movie or boxing match, and drink beer or eat. It was close enough to allow sailors to visit when *Ward* was tied up in the navy yard. The one attraction of downtown Honolulu missing at Bloch Arena was intimate female companionship. For that the men had to leave the base.

Another oasis for the men on the base was a refreshment stand near the docks in the navy yard. It was rather simply built, consisting of a corrugated tin roof extending over a concrete slab. Appropriately enough, it was named the "Tin Roof" and operated by the navy.

It contained a serving counter and table and benches. Its menu consisted mainly of sandwiches, ice cream, and beverages including beer. Sailors coming off a watch on their ship could easily walk to the Tin Roof for a snack or a nickel beer.[9] Russ Reetz remembered the place well. "A bunch of us would come off the 1200 to 1600 watch and walk over there for a bottle of beer. We'd go back to the ship for supper and then return to the Tin Roof for another beer."

For those who did not drink beer, a popular stop for those who wanted a quick refreshment was a Coke machine right on the dock. Eventually Bloch Arena replaced the Tin Roof. It will be fondly remembered, however, by those who shared a beer there.

Liberties were not restricted to Oahu Island. Throughout 1941 and 1942, *Ward* made many cruises to other islands in the Hawaiian group. In 1941 the cruises were part of the crew's training and ship's exercises. In 1942 the trips were almost exclusively for escort purposes. In both years *Ward* had opportunities to lay over in the port of call, sometimes for several days at a time. The crew was granted liberty during these visits although overnight liberties on the outlying islands were rare.

Captain Hunter Wood had considerable discretion to determine the length of stay in port during 1941, and liberties were common. In 1942, *Ward's* schedule was dictated by the timetables of the ships she was escorting as well as other demands of a destroyer assigned to guard duty at the entrance to Pearl Harbor. Liberties in 1942 were thus less frequent and usually shorter in duration.

When visiting other Hawaiian Islands the crew took every opportunity to get off the ship, even for half a day. With limited facilities in the smaller villages, these islands did not offer the activities sailors found on Oahu. However, the islands were unbelievably scenic, considerably less congested, and contained unique attractions of their own. This made them highly sought liberty calls to the men of *Ward*.

Because of their reputation as tourist attractions, Wailuku and Kahului on Maui were favorite liberty ports. *Ward's* crew also looked forward to any visit to Hilo or Kailua, Hawaii, Kaunakakai, Molokai, Port Allen and Kauai as well.

Most of the liberty time on these islands was spent sight-seeing by whatever transportation the creative sailors could arrange. Orv Ethier recalled a liberty at Hilo. "We went up the mountain in an old vehicle that resembled an armored truck. It had a lot of seats in the back and took us to see the volcano near the middle of the island. It was a fantastic sight but we weren't sure that the truck would get us back to Hilo."

Sometimes the crew would take their swimming suits ashore with them. On the islands they found beaches as beautiful as Waikiki but without any crowds. Eventually the men located a restaurant and sampled the island's delicacies and beverages. Dick Thill remembers his introduction to Sake on the island of Kauai in 1942. He purchased a bottle for 50 cents and proceeded to work on it. "Wow, the next day was I sorry I did that," laughed Thill.

Some of *Ward's* crewmen did not have to worry about what to do on liberty. They were married and their liberty time was spent with their families, which were living in Honolulu. Dave Morgan, WT1c, was one of these. His wife and son Jim moved to Honolulu in June 1941 and took up residence in a navy housing unit only a mile and a quarter from Pearl Harbor.

When Dave Morgan, already a 14-year navy veteran, had a liberty, he met the family and took them on a picnic or to one of the island's beaches. He was planning a week-long visit with them on Maui at Christmas, but the Japanese changed those plans. The navy shipped the dependents back to the States in February 1942, ending Morgan's family liberties. Jim Morgan returned to Honolulu several times after the war and in 1988 searched for the house he and his mother had occupied in 1941. It was still there.[10]

After the conversion of *Ward* to an APD in 1943, it passed through Pearl Harbor on its way to the war zone in the South Pacific. However, *Ward* never again returned to Hawaii and the sites of so many memorable liberties. *Ward's* next two years would be spent in combat areas and, with the exception of two trips, to Sydney, Australia, and several to Noumea, New Caledonia. In stark contrast to Pearl Harbor, *Ward's* crew would be taking most of their subsequent liberties in the South Pacific. These would be on hot, humid, and dank military bases on some of the world's least hospitable islands.

The only attraction at many of these locations was the two cans of warm beer that each sailor on liberty was entitled to on a shore liberty. These were usually drunk while sitting on the hot sand under a blazing sun or a driving rain. Females were non-existent. The contrast between these liberties and the fun-filled days of 1941 on Oahu could not have been greater.

During 1943 and 1944, men of *Ward* could only reminisce about their liberties in 1941. They had then been stationed in the perfect location at the perfect time. Sixty years later they would still smile when describing their liberties in Hawaii in 1941.

CHAPTER 9

First Year at War

When the first light of day arrived on January 1, it found *Ward* patrolling off Diamond Head with the same deadly determination of the past several weeks. Her crew hoped that morning would bring the beginning of a more promising year than the one they had just left. Although they recognized the seriousness of the war situation, the war had seemed somewhat remote since that first terrible day three weeks earlier. Young Ensign Frank Andrews welcomed the New Year officially by noting its arrival in the ship's Deck Log for January 1, 1942. He began his entry for the day with the following:[1]

> Ring out the Old, ring in the New,
> We're steaming on boilers one and two.
> Fifteen knots is standard speed,
> But seven knots is all we need.
> With one eighty seven revs per minute,
> Pearl Harbor's Restricted Area, we are in it.
> Patrolling the half that is to eastward,
> With the USS *Zane* in the one to the westward.
> Two things we wanted and didn't get this watch,
> Were a Japanese sub and a bottle of scotch.

Not to be outdone, Signalman 1c Jack Twitty made the next entry in the Deck Log with his version of poetry:[2]

> Upon the beginning of this solemn New Year's Day,
> Be it resolved that we doubly repay
> These outlandish attacks by the Japs
> And set this war right back in their laps.
> Though in doing this it may take long,
> But "Right is Might" and the Japs are wrong.

Although unofficial entries in the ship's Deck Log were prohibited, both Andrews and Twitty knew in advance that the captain allowed this traditional practice for the first log of the year. He had only been in command since December 5, but he already had a reputation as a CO who understood his men. Captain Outerbridge chuckled as he signed the log for January 1. The crew could use some levity after a stressful month of December.

January 1 was uneventful, possibly a sign that *Ward* would have a quiet year. Those notions were quickly dashed on the following day. Outerbridge began the day with four successive drills in the early morning. At 0930 *Ward* was in action in one of the more mysterious incidents of the year, one still not fully understood to this day.

Ward was proceeding westerly from her patrol area to investigate an oil patch on the water reported by a patrolling aircraft. Bingo! At 1015, as *Ward* arrived at the location of the oil, it picked up a solid sonar contact and went to General Quarters again. Eight minutes later she dropped a pattern of nine depth charges on the contact from her stern racks and Y gun. The charges brought up no evidence of a sub.

Ward's patrol partner, the *Allen*, was 2000 yards west of *Ward* observing the action. She had clearly seen *Ward's* signal flag indicating that she was making an attack, so the *Allen's* bridge personnel were all closely watching the incident through binoculars. Shortly after the depth charges exploded, *Allen's* commanding officer, Lt. D. B. Miller saw about 40 feet of a submarine's hull break the surface behind *Ward* and rise out of the water about eight feet. All of *Allen's* bridge crew witnessed the same sight. The sub then slipped beneath the surface and was not seen again.

Allen continued toward the spot where the submarine had disappeared to investigate. As it passed the location of the depth charging, her officers observed two rows of bubbles rising to the surface. *Allen* dropped two depth charges into the patch of bubbles, one set at 100 feet and one at 150 feet. Neither *Ward's* nor *Allen's* depth charges brought up any debris.

Allen's official Action Report to Headquarters following the incident clearly documents the momentary surfacing of the submarine following *Ward's* attack.[3] The report indicates that not only did *Ward* actually attack a submarine but that it may have sunk it as well. Defying explanation is the fact that although a number of men on the *Allen* observed the sub awash after *Ward's* attack, *no one on Ward saw it even though it was no more than 100 yards away.*

Ward's own Log includes no reference to a sighting but *Allen's* report does. Yet, how could *Ward's* crew miss seeing, at 100 yards, what *Allen's* crew saw at 1500 yards? Years after the war, Outerbridge was at a loss to explain what had occurred. He joked with his former crewmen that *Ward* may have sunk her second submarine that day. Japanese records indicate that none of their submarines were lost on January 2, 1942.[4] Was it a submarine? If so, whose? If it was a submarine belonging to another nation, that country surely would not have revealed it. This mystery will undoubtedly never be solved.

Ward now fell into a routine that left very little leisure time. The ship went to General Quarters for an hour at 0530 every morning as a precaution. Outerbridge conducted a series of drills every morning during this hour of GQ. The still vivid scenes of burned bodies and ships on December 7 brought a sense of urgency to the crew as they exercised their drills. But for a change in fortune, one of those burned ships could have been the *Ward* and those mangled bodies could have been theirs.

Ward was spending less time in the harbor now, sometimes only a few days and often just long enough to refuel. The destroyers doubled up on Inner Harbor Patrol with two ships in the Restricted Area at all times. *Ward's* crew was treated to the imposing sight of one of the large aircraft carriers passing through their patrol area with greater frequency now. *Lexington* and *Enterprise* were avoiding the harbor and patrolling the areas around the Hawaiian Islands.

January 8 was uneventful in the harbor but it had an unannounced visitor. In the very early hours of the morning, a float plane from the large Japanese submarine *I-19* criss-crossed the harbor photographing the various anchorages.[5] The Japanese were attempting to monitor the repair of ships damaged in the December 7 raid. They also wanted to determine the location of major ships of the Pacific Fleet, especially the aircraft carriers. The plane completed its flight undetected and returned to the *I-19*.

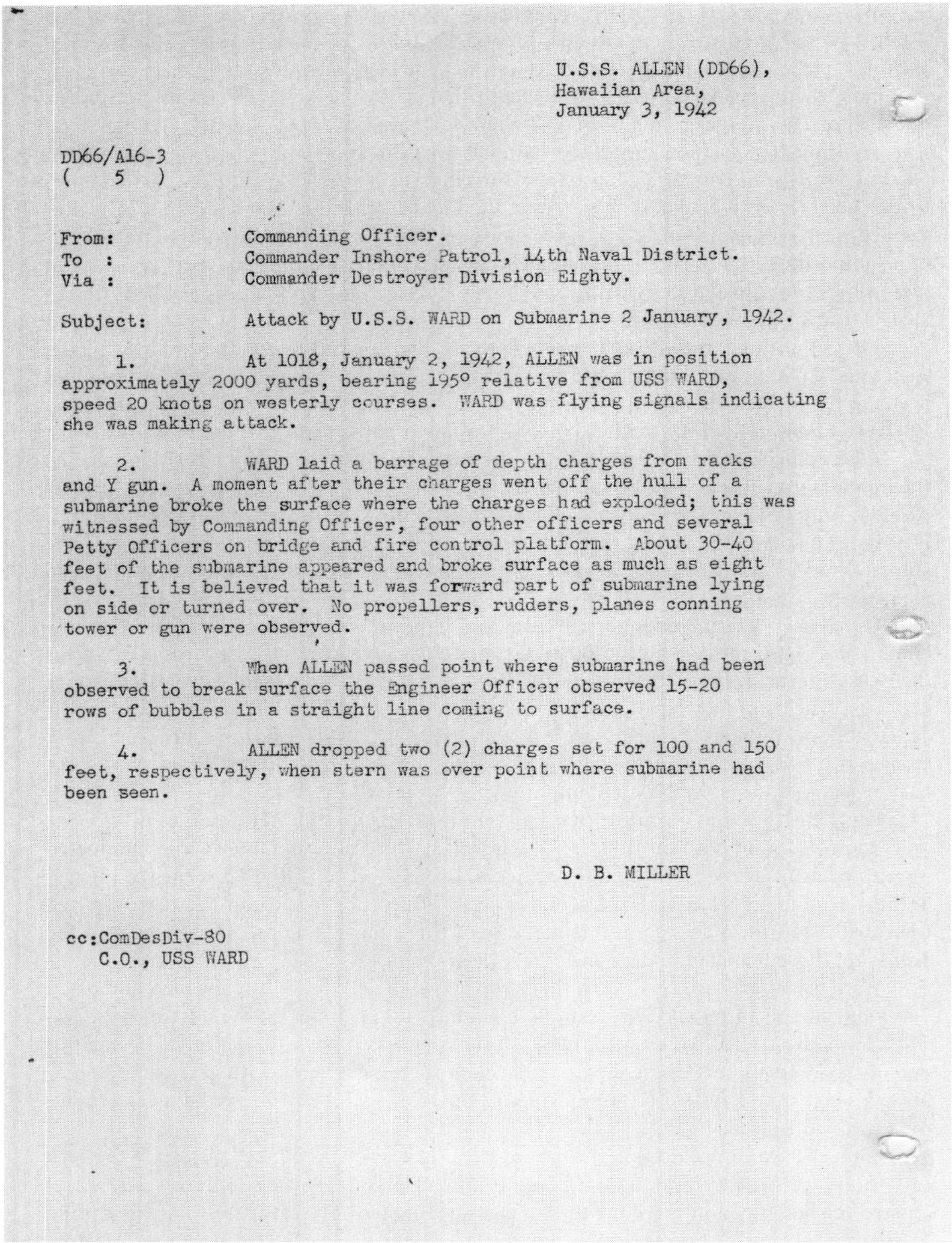

                                    U.S.S. ALLEN (DD66),
                                    Hawaiian Area,
                                    January 3, 1942

DD66/A16-3
(5   )

From: Commanding Officer.
To :   Commander Inshore Patrol, 14th Naval District.
Via :   Commander Destroyer Division Eighty.

Subject: Attack by U.S.S. WARD on Submarine 2 January, 1942.

     1.   At 1018, January 2, 1942, ALLEN was in position
approximately 2000 yards, bearing 195° relative from USS WARD,
speed 20 knots on westerly courses. WARD was flying signals indicating
she was making attack.

     2.   WARD laid a barrage of depth charges from racks
and Y gun. A moment after their charges went off the hull of a
submarine broke the surface where the charges had exploded; this was
witnessed by Commanding Officer, four other officers and several
Petty Officers on bridge and fire control platform. About 30-40
feet of the submarine appeared and broke surface as much as eight
feet. It is believed that it was forward part of submarine lying
on side or turned over. No propellers, rudders, planes conning
tower or gun were observed.

     3.   When ALLEN passed point where submarine had been
observed to break surface the Engineer Officer observed 15-20
rows of bubbles in a straight line coming to surface.

     4.   ALLEN dropped two (2) charges set for 100 and 150
feet, respectively, when stern was over point where submarine had
been seen.

                                    D. B. MILLER

cc:ComDesDiv-80
    C.O., USS WARD

Official report from USS *Allen* indicating that it believed *Ward* sank a sub on January 2, 1942.
(National Archives)

On January 20, a patrol plane spotted a submerged object two miles from *Ward* and marked its location with a smoke bomb. *Ward* raced to the spot and dropped 12 depth charges with no noticeable results. Activity was now picking up in the harbor approach. *Ward* was frequently acting as a target vessel for her division mate who would make simulated torpedo runs at her. When not patrolling or exercising with other fleet ships, *Ward* was now noting the almost daily arrival of merchant ships to Honolulu or Pearl Harbor as supplies began to pour into Oahu. Four transports carrying military personnel stood into Pearl Harbor on January 17.

Ward continued to exercise with Pearl-based submarines and, on January 21, it commenced two days of various drills with the sub *Triton* in the Lanai area 100 miles east of Oahu. On the 27th, *Ward* had a solid contact in the Restricted Area and dropped two depth charges. Maintaining contact, *Ward* made three more attacks, dropping 10 more depth charges with no visible signs of a sub. Outerbridge reluctantly concluded that the object may have been a whale. Only the most experienced sonar operators could distinguish between a submarine and a whale. In 1942, with sonar being relatively new, there were few experienced sonar operators with the Pacific Fleet.

Ward made another attack on January 29. As a convoy of merchant ships approached Honolulu Harbor, a patrol plane sighted an object underwater and dropped a smoke bomb. A patrolling PT Boat raced to the spot and dropped two depth charges. The destroyer/minelayer *Montgomery* followed with several more. *Ward* joined in with a full pattern of 10. As usual, the results were inconclusive. The harbor entrance area, with merchant ships bunched up and moving slowly without zig-zagging, was a submariner's paradise, so it was guarded tightly.

On February 6, *Ward* had another treat when fleet aircraft carrier USS *Yorktown* passed through her patrol area with a large escort and entered the harbor. *Ward* had not seen it before. It was originally assigned to the Pacific Fleet but then transferred to the Atlantic Fleet when the German navy began to exert itself. After the attack on Pearl Harbor, *Yorktown*, along with the carrier *Hornet,* was reassigned back to the Pacific Fleet to counter the large Japanese carrier fleet. Within months both would be involved in major actions that would have a huge impact on the war, but neither would survive the year.

Ward was in action again on February 14. After getting a solid sonar contact, it dropped nine depth charges. Shortly after the water disturbance subsided it regained the contact and dropped 10 more. No results were observed.

At 1113 on February 14, *Ward* witnessed the departure of a legendary ship and an old friend. The old cruiser, USS *Baltimore,* was towed out of Pearl Harbor on its way to Honolulu Harbor where it would be sold for scrap.

Built in 1888, *Baltimore* was the oldest ship in Pearl Harbor at the time of the attack. The cruiser participated in many notable events in both the Atlantic and the Pacific including the destruction of the Spanish fleet in Manila Bay in 1898. She was converted to a minelayer in 1914 and served in that capacity through World War I and up to September 1922, when it was decommissioned at Pearl Harbor. It had sat there ever since.[6]

The ship was of imposing size — 375 feet long with 4413-ton displacement. At Manila Bay it was Admiral Dewey's second largest ship, exceeded in size only by his flagship *Olympia.* At that battle she carried four eight-inch and six six-inch guns plus a variety of smaller weapons and five torpedo tubes. Her speed of 21.5 knots was impressive. The eight *Baltimore* crewmen wounded in the skirmish were Dewey's only casualties of the battle.[7]

After its decommissioning, the navy decided to anchor it in the open water of Aiea

Bay north of Ford Island. Here *Baltimore* would function as a fixed concrete mooring quay with up to five ships tied up to her. She was designated as berth X-5. For *Ward* and her sister ships of Destroyer Division 80, this was their assigned mooring site.

Baltimore usually had at least one of the division destroyers tied up alongside. On December 7, *Ward* was on harbor patrol and *Schley* at a navy yard dock. But *Allen* and *Chew* were moored to the *Baltimore.*

Orv Ethier remembers the *Baltimore* well even though it was just an abandoned hulk with no crew. "From time to time we'd climb up on her deck and wander around. It was quite an interesting ship to explore," recalled Ethier. "We weren't supposed to go up there but we did. It was fun inspecting her engine room, crew quarters, bridge, and other parts of the ship."

The 53-year-old cruiser had been a fixture at Pearl Harbor for 20 years. Now it had been sold and was leaving the harbor for its final time. The men of the destroyer were sorry to see the gallant ship leave.

Ward's heavy use of depth charges required her to replenish her supply on February 17 at the West Loch ammunition depot. With her patrol area being the most vulnerable spot around the harbor, *Ward* continued to use up depth charges. She took on 20 of the 300-pound charges as well as 51 boxes of 0.50 caliber ammunition and cases of 0.30 and 0.45 caliber small arms ammunition.

On February 24 neither *Ward* nor any other ship in the harbor detected any visiting aircraft, but it was there. A float plane released by Japanese submarine I-9 left the sub after dark out of sight of Oahu and flew directly to Pearl Harbor. It made several passes attempting to assess the status of repairs to the battleships damaged on December 7. It did not carry bombs, only cameras. If the U.S. had any radar operating in the harbor area, it was either not functioning that night or it could not differentiate between friendly and enemy aircraft.[8]

On March 3, *Ward's* crew began the huge task of unloading the ship's ammunition and commissary stores to railroad box cars on the dock siding. The ordnance was to be taken to the Lualualei Naval Ammunition Depot for storage while *Ward* was to be in dry- dock for overhaul.

That night the Japanese carried out the "second bombing of Pearl Harbor," although it went largely unnoticed.[9] In retaliation for U.S. carrier raids on their bases in the Marshall Islands in early February, the Japanese planned to bomb ships under repair in early March.

On the evening of the 3rd, they flew two of their largest aircraft, Kawanishi H8K flying boats, from Wotje in the Marshalls to French Frigate Shoals, a collection of 13 uninhabited rocky islands 500 miles northwest of Oahu. There they met two large Japanese I class submarines, I-15 and I-19, which refueled them, allowing them to reach Oahu and return to Wotje. The subs crews also armed each plane with four 550-pound bombs.

The aircraft, nick-named "Emily" by the Allies, flew together to Oahu. Crossing the northwest tip of the island they encountered clouds and rain, became separated, and proceeded to the harbor independently. One dropped its bombs through the rain at 0210, hitting only a grove of trees six miles east of the harbor. The second dropped its bombs at 0230, all four landing off shore.[10]

The aircraft were detected by radar this time, at 0055 while approaching the island. Four P-40 fighters took off from Wheeler Field and headed northwest into the rain to intercept them. Two PBY Catalinas were dispatched from Ford Island to seek out the aircraft carrier that was the assumed origin of the Japanese aircraft. The clouds that hid the harbor from the Japanese also hid the bombers from the P-40s and the Emilys made good their escape.

Reacting to the air raid sirens when the Emilys were first detected on radar, the *Ward* went to General Quarters for several hours. The Japanese plan worked. Had they used more bombers and had decent weather, they could have inflicted significant damage in this second bombing.

On March 3, *Ward's* crew disembarked from the ship and moved to a naval housing unit in Honolulu. They would be berthed there for approximately five weeks while their ship was in the repair yard. On the following day, while *Ward* was still unloading ammunition, Seaman 1c Gordon Hultman of St. Paul was severely injured while unloading depth charges. He was taken to the Pearl Harbor naval hospital with possible broken bones and internal injuries. He later recovered and returned to the ship.

By March 11, *Ward* had discharged most of her fuel oil to a yard oiler, YO-21, and major work lasting a month began on her engines. On April 11, tugs moved the ship into Dry-Dock No. 1, the largest of the yard's dry-docks, for two days' work on her hull.

During her month in the repair yard, *Ward* received an important addition to her armament, six single-barrel 20 mm anti-aircraft guns, which she test-fired on April 18.[11] Now, for the first time, she had a legitimate defense against aircraft. Had these been on her deck on December 7, she would have had a chance to shoot down the two aircraft that bombed her.

On April 16, the big carrier *Lexington* left the harbor with a destroyer and cruiser escort. It would be the last time that *Ward* or any other ship in the harbor would see the gallant "Lady Lex." She was on her way to meet the carrier *Yorktown* after which the two would steam to the Coral Sea north of Australia. Allied code breakers discovered that a Japanese invasion fleet was at sea intending to capture the strategic base at Port Moresby in New Guinea. If that occurred, Australia would be effectively cut off from reinforcement and would, itself, undoubtedly soon be invaded.

The two U.S. carriers met the three-carrier Japanese task force on May 7 and, in the first all-aircraft naval battle in history, the Japanese carrier *Shoho* was sunk and the invasion fleet turned back. *Lexington* was also sunk but New Guinea and Australia were saved. *Yorktown* was damaged and would return to Pearl Harbor three weeks later for emergency repair in one of the war's miracles.

Ward returned to patrol duty on April 16 after an absence of six weeks. She dropped two depth charges on another sonar contact on April 19 with no results. The following day *Ward* was ordered to one of the stations on the outer harbor line, the first time she patrolled the outer ring. She would alternate between inner and outer harbor patrol for the remainder of the year.

April 24 found *Ward* on inner harbor patrol again when a level of excitement rippled through the ship as it did on December 7.[12] The sonar operator picked up heavy screw noises at 2350 and reported it to the Officer of the Deck. Captain Outerbridge was immediately called to the bridge, slowed the ship to 10 knots and began echo ranging. The sound man soon reported in, "Submerged object ahead, bearing 080 degrees, range 3100 yards."

Ward continued tracking the object to within 500 yards when, as usual, the echo disappeared. Outerbridge ordered speed increased to 20 knots and a turn to port to lead the target, which was on a course of 260 degrees. "Drop depth charges," he shouted when he felt that *Ward* was directly in the sub's projected path.

At 0012 eight depth charges rolled off the stern followed by a smoke bomb to mark the location as *Ward* passed ahead of the sub. The Y gun projectors added to the attack with three pairs of depth charges to increase the coverage of the pattern. All charges were set to explode at 100-, 150-, or 200-foot depths. The sea erupted 14 times on both sides of the ship in a deafening barrage. It seemed incredible that a submarine caught in such a maelstrom could survive. In the dark it was impossible to see if the explosions brought up any debris.

When the disturbance subsided the sonar operator attempted to regain contact. The object was hovering near the edge of a submerged reef, making it difficult for the sound man to pick it up. Within a few minutes he was able to pinpoint it again and reported, "The object is now on course 180 degrees, range 700 yards, Sir." Apparently the sub was monitoring *Ward's* movements and trying to elude her by changing her own course and speed. The submarine was moving adjacent to the reef in relatively shallow water, not a good place to hide from an aggressive destroyer captain with a full complement of depth charges on board.

The sub was almost directly under the smoke float dropped with the first attack. Outerbridge decided to attack again and closed on it at a slower speed to better pinpoint the sub. "Eight knots," he ordered. The sonar operator could again hear screw noises. "I think she's deeper, captain," he shouted. With the sub located again, Outerbridge ordered, "Speed 15 knots. Commence attack."

Ward crossed the sub's path for a second time and dropped a pattern of 13 depth charges from the racks and Y guns. Because of the sonar man's suggestion, Outerbridge had the depths set for 200, 250, and 300 feet. Once more, the sea burst all around the sub's suspected position. Again, when the turbulence subsided, they could see no evidence of the sub or debris.

The officers on the *Ward's* bridge were stunned. It was unbelievable to think that a sub could have survived 27 depth charges, all dropped directly on her position. But it must have done just that. *Ward* continued to criss-cross the area but when daylight arrived, it revealed nothing. The sea seemed to have swallowed up the submarine. At 1922 the following evening, *Ward* picked up another possible contact and dropped six more depth charges without success.

Ward's most intensive attack ended inconclusively. A postwar review of Japanese records indicates that no Japanese submarines were lost on that day in Hawaiian waters. Yet, *Ward's* crew did not imagine the screw noises and sonar echoes. The ship was involved in a number of unexplained occurrences during her three years of combat in World War II. This latest had everyone on the ship baffled.

The first four months of 1942 proved to be relatively calm for *Ward*. She made many sonar contacts and dropped scores of depth charges, all without positive results to show for the efforts. It was impossible to know how many of the contacts were actual submarines and how many were other submerged objects. It was also not possible to determine how many submarines were deterred from their mission of attacking U.S. ships because of *Ward's* actions. Whether submarines were there or not, the patrols had been stressful because the threat of submarines was constant. When *Ward* returned to harbor, the crew was ready for a more relaxing time.

That feeling was not universal on *Ward*. There were some men whose work did not vary appreciably regardless of whether the ship was on patrol or moored in the harbor. The ship's complement was 135 but cooking and meal preparation was accomplished by a small group of ship's cooks, mess cooks, and mess attendants who had to provide meals no matter where the ship was.

Like so many other functions on *Ward,* meal preparation and service followed tradition. Officers ate in the wardroom and had their own cooks and mess attendants. Petty Officers ate in their own compartments while enlisted men ate in the crew compartments fore and aft, which also served as their mess hall.[13]

Enlisted men's meals were prepared by a Ship's Cook 1c and several cooks of lower rating. They were assisted by mess cooks who retrieved the food from storage, peeled potatoes, set up the tables, carried prepared food from the galley to the crew compartments, cleaned the tables and compartments, and washed the dishes.

Storing food was a major chore for mess cooks. Food arrived at the ship by whaleboat if the *Ward* was anchored in the harbor or on harbor patrol, or by delivery truck if *Ward* was moored at a dock. Mess cooks brought it on deck and stowed it below in the commissary hold. Whether it was 60-pound sacks of flour, 100-pound sacks of sugar, crates of canned vegetables, or frozen sides of beef, it all had to be stored.

Being a mess cook had its responsibilities but it also had rewards. Will Lehner held a fireman's rating but worked as a mess cook for six months before being given a Ship's Cook rating.[14] He enjoyed preparing food and, as a mess cook, he was relieved of his boiler room responsibilities.

Will had 17 men at the table he served. In addition to setting up the table and bringing the food down from the galley, he served as the table's waiter, bringing the men whatever they needed. If asked, he would run to the storeroom for a jar of pickles or a bottle of Worcestershire Sauce.

Mess cooks received an extra five dollars pay per month, but there were even more rewards. "If you took care of your table well," said Lehner, the mess captain, who sat at the table, put a dollar in a bowl and passed it around the table every payday. "He'd watch to see that everyone else put a dollar in as well. That was another $17 I made every payday and I could always use the extra money."

The cook prepared the meals on his duty days and assisted the other cook on his off-duty days. The duty cook usually prepared the evening meal, and breakfast and lunch on the following day. Then the other cook assumed the role of duty cook for the next 24 hours.

A Ship's Cook's day began about 0530 if he was the duty cook, and he immediately began preparing breakfast. As soon as breakfast was prepared he started on lunch. On some days, he worked on breakfast and lunch simultaneously. After lunch was completed, he started preparations for supper so the alternate duty cook could take over. He worked steady from 0530 to about 1900 and was ready for his bunk a few hours later.

Meal preparation on a Wickes-class destroyer like *Ward* was a major challenge due to the layout of the ship. Meals were prepared and cooked in a small galley in the galley deck house on the main or weather deck between the Number Two and Three stacks. It was then carried down to the crew compartments in stainless steel tureens. Up to five tureens were used and carried down to the crew in a wooden rack.

Enlisted men did not have a mess hall on a Wickes-class ship. Instead, permanent tables bolted to the deck in the crew compartment served as mess tables at mealtime. The lower bunks were raised and the crew's footlockers became the seats. When a meal was over, the table was cleaned off and became available for card playing or other activities. The footlockers were moved back and the room became a sleeping compartment and socializing center again.

Seating at the enlisted men's table was by rank. Lower ratings sat at one end while first- and second-class ratings sat at the other end.[15] Food was served family style from the tureens and started at the first-class end of the table. There were no exceptions to the seating arrangement.

The galley was unbelievably small for the size of crew it had to serve. It had an oil-fired range at one end with the width of the galley being not much greater than the width of the range. It also contained several steam kettles, a sink, a work table, flour, sugar, coffee bins, and a coffee maker.[16]

There were usually only two men working in the galley at a time, the Ship's Cook and the Officer's Cook. Dick Thill, one of the Ship's Cooks, recalled a third individual who worked in the galley at times. "We also had little Manuel Penetrante," quipped Thill. "He was a Filipino cook, one of the officer's cooks, and very small. He didn't take up much room in the galley."[17]

The perishables were kept in a big refrigerator on the weather deck, port side of the galley. There was no freezer on the ship. A butcher's table was bolted to the weather deck in the open near the galley. Meat came to the ship in quarters and had to be cut up on the table into chops or other usable smaller cuts. Pork loins were cut up into chops, roasts, and hams there on the deck. Chickens came frozen and de-feathered with the head and feet on and the insides still in. While in port, milk, meat, ice cream and other perishables were delivered each day. At sea, canned and dry foods were used.

The cooks usually worked from previously prepared menus which had been designed around the ship's food allowance of 54 cents per man per day. The menus were prepared on a weekly basis and repeated week after week depending on the availability of food items. Sailors could tell the day of the week by simply looking at the food on their plate. Most men agreed that, although the meals were not fancy and steak was not a common item, they were acceptable. Complaints were rare. An actual menu for a week in March 1941 is shown on the following page.

Breakfasts included such items as oatmeal, pancakes, eggs, and occasionally sausage or bacon. A Wednesday breakfast was usually beans, cornbread, figs, and tons of coffee. Lunches usually consisted of soup, sandwiches, luncheon meat, and fruit.

If the ship was in port or on harbor patrol, fresh fruit, including apples, oranges, bananas, and pineapples was always available from vendors. At sea, after the fresh fruit was used up, cooks relied on canned peaches or pears.

Suppers included some meat item such as roast beef, ham, chicken, or pork; potatoes, and canned vegetables. Other evening meals included chili, spaghetti with meat sauce, or the much discussed chipped beef on toast. Jello was a frequent dessert. Sunday nights were usually light meals and often included cold cuts, beans, and fruit.

The officers had their own menu but occasionally the officers and enlisted men shared a meat dish. Often when cooking pork chops, cooks for both officers and men would fix them all together. Mess attendants then served the groups separately.

At sea, fresh foods were eaten first, leaving canned or preserved foods for last. In 1941 and 1942, the longest voyage *Ward* made, other than the initial trip to Hawaii, was to other islands in the Hawaiian group. Fresh food lasted the duration of most of these cruises. Because of the humid climate, some items such as bread would show signs of mold before the cruise ended. Even mold on bread was not enough to start men grumbling, however.

Several of the 47th Division became cooks on *Ward*. Dick Thill held a Seaman 2c rating at the time *Ward* left for Hawaii in March 1941. Hearing that the ship was looking for

S. and A. Form No. 833
Revised Sept. 1930

BILL OF FARE FOR THE GENERAL MESS

U.S.S. WARD (139)

Week beginning .... March 31, ... 19 41

	BREAKFAST	DINNER	SUPPER
MONDAY	FRIED BACON SUNNY SIDE EGGS CREAMED POTATOES ORANGES BREAD, BUTTER, COFFEE.	TOMATO SOUP, ROAST PORK LOIN APPLESAUCE LYONNAISE POTATOES, GREEN PEAS BREAD, BUTTER, LEMONADE.	STEAMED FRANKFURTERS, HOMEMADE MUSTARD BOILED SAUERKRAUT FRIED POTATOES PLAIN CAKE BREAD, BUTTER, COFFEE.
TUESDAY	PORK SAUSAGE HOT CAKES TINNED HOT SIRUP FRESH GRAPEFRUIT BREAD BUTTER, COFFEE.	BEEF STEAK MASHED POTATOES BROWN GRAVY BOILED LIMA BEANS TINNED PINEAPPLE BREAD, BUTTER, LEMONADE.	MEAT LOAF BROWN GRAVY STEWED CORN CHOCOLATE PUDDING BREAD, JAM, COFFEE.
WEDNESDAY	BAKED PORK AND BEANS HOT CORNBREAD TINNED PRUNES BREAD, BUTTER, COFFEE	RICE TOMATOE SOUP ROAST VEAL MASHED POTATOES BROWN PAN GRAVY TINNED ASPARAGUS BREAD, BUTTER, LEMONADE.	BEEF CURRY AND RICE STEAMED. GOLD BAKED BEANS SLICED CHEESE PINEAPPLE CUSTARD BREAD, BUTTER, COFFEE.
THURSDAY	FRIED LUNCHEON MEAT FRIED POTATOES KETM ROLLED WHEAT CEREAL FRESH APPIES BREAD, BUTTER, COFFEE	POT ROAST OF BEEF BAKED POTATOES BROWN GRAVY STING BEANS TAPIOCA PUDDING BREAD, BUTTER, LEMONADE.	BAKED VIENNA SAUSAGE MASHED POTATOES TOMATO SAUCE BOILED KIDNEY BEANS BREAD, JAM, COFFEE.
FRIDAY	FRIED MEAT HASH TOMATO CATSUP SOFT BOILED EGGS TINNED FIGS BREAD, BUTTER, COFFEE	OYSTER STEW COLD TINNED SALMON MASHED POTATOES TOMATO GRAVY GREEN PEAS BREAD, BUTTER, LEMONADE	PORK CHOPS APPLESAUCE FRIED POTATOES STRING BEANS CORNSTARCH PUDDING BREAD, BUTTER, COFFEE.
SATURDAY	BAKED PORK AND BEANS TOMATO CATSUP HOT CORNBREAD TINNED APRICOTS BREAD, BUTTER, COFFEE	BEEF BROTH BOILED BEEF BOILED SPINACH BAKED POTATOES (JACKET) BROWN GRAVY BREAD, BUTTER, LEMONADE.	BROWN BEEF STEW COLD BAKED BEANS RICE PUDDING BREAD, BUTTER, COCOA.
SUNDAY	SCRAMBLED EGGS CREAMED POTATOES FRESH APPLES BREAD BUTTER, COFFEE	RICE TOMATO SOUP ROAST TURKEY SAGE DRESSING BOILED SWEET POTATOES GIBLET GRAVY ICE CREAM BREAD, BUTTER, LEMONADE.	COLD SLICED LUNCHEON MEAT POTATO SALAD SLICED CHEESE ORANGES BREAD, BUTTER, COFFEE.

Total estimated cost $422.92   Total estimated rations 805   Estimated ration cost per day $.5253

APPROVED: Respectfully submitted,

HUNTER WOOD, Jr.,   H. T. DOUGHTY,

Lieutenant Commander, ..., U.S.N.,   Lieutenant, ..., USN.
Commanding   Commissary Officer.

Ward's menu for the week of March 31, 1941. Note the cost per man per day of 53 cents for this menu. The maximum allowable cost was 54 cents. The sailors ate well this week. (Dick Thill) someone to train to be a cook, he volunteered. As a trainee he actually held the title of "Jack of the Dust," which was basically a commissary storeroom keeper. By November 1941, Thill, only 18 years old, was promoted to Ship's Cook 3c and began working in the galley.[18]

William Duval, Ship's Cook 1c and a regular navy man, was the chief cook and ruled the galley. Thill became a Cook 2c in 1942 and a Cook 1c in 1943. He served on the *Ward* until May 1944, when he was reassigned. He served in various locations including on the new cruiser *Savanah* when the war ended.[19]

Will Lehner became a mess cook in 1941 and a Ship's Cook in 1942. He reached the rank of Ship's Cook 1c in 1944. The chief cook missed *Ward's* departure from Hollandia in November 1944 and Lehner became chief of the galley until the ship was sunk. He continued as a cook in civilian life after discharge from the navy.[20]

As summer of 1942 approached, *Ward's* duties changed. Drills didn't change, however, and on May 3, the crew outdid themselves during a fire drill by playing a stream of water on a simulated fire only 65 seconds after the Fire Drill call was sounded.[21] *Ward,* however, was now spending much more of her time escorting convoys and less of her time searching for submarines.

Convoys of from two to 25 merchant ships from the mainland arrived in Hawaii with increasing regularity. They usually had their own destroyer escort and *Ward* provided additional escort in their passage through the harbor area when they were most vulnerable to submarine attack. A convoy of 24 merchant ships entered Pearl and Honolulu harbors on May 4 bringing more war materials to the island for future operations.

Passenger liners from the mainland, considered to be fast enough to out-run submarines, often traveled alone. A destroyer from Pearl Harbor would meet them approximately 100 miles out and escort them into the harbor. *Ward* drew this mission frequently.

Ward also served as escort to passenger liners and freighters plying the routes between Honolulu and other islands of the Hawaiian Island group. She would often escort them to Maui, Hawaii, Kauai, or Molokai, wait several hours while the ships unloaded, and escort them back to Honolulu.

In May, *Ward* began a new type of escort mission. When units of the U.S. Pacific Fleet entered or departed Pearl Harbor, they were at their maximum vulnerability because of their slow speed and inability to zig-zag in the confined area of the harbor approach. Lurking enemy submarines, using their sound detection equipment to pinpoint the location of the larger ships, could fire torpedoes with some degree of accuracy without actually seeing the ships. The navy devised a scheme to defeat this tactic.

As warships emerged from or approached the harbor, a line of destroyers would position themselves on either side of the ships and steam back and forth along the flanks of the formation. This would create another and louder sound for submarines to detect and thus mask the actual screw sounds of the warships. A submarine's sound detection equipment would be unable to pinpoint specific ships in the formation other than the destroyers creating the sound screen. Since a submarine lying in wait outside Pearl Harbor was unlikely to reveal its presence to torpedo a mere destroyer, this tactic was successful in protecting larger ships. *Ward* would participate in sound screens frequently during 1942.

The destroyers of Division 80 continued to hone their skills even though opportunities for actual combat diminished as the year wore on. On May 10 and May 15, all four ships conducted joint maneuvers culminated by the live firing of all 16 four-inch guns of the formation. All 3"/23 anti-aircraft guns fired star shells as well.[22]

On May 27 *Ward* was part of the sound screen for ships returning from the battle of

Coral Sea. These included one of the major combatants, the carrier *Yorktown*. The carrier had been hit hard by Japanese dive bombers and was limping into Pearl. Her arrival sparked one of the unsung miracles of World War II, one that played a critical role in reversing the direction of the Pacific war.

U.S. code breakers discovered that the Japanese planned to invade and occupy the outpost island of Midway in the Hawaiian chain during the first week of June. If successful, the Japanese would be in a position to threaten Hawaii itself. The Japanese force was known to include four aircraft carriers while, without *Yorktown*, the U.S. could muster only two.

Yorktown was desperately needed to improve the odds but the initial estimate of the time required to repair *Yorktown's* damage was three months. Admiral Chester Nimitz, Commander in Chief of the Pacific Fleet, gave the Pearl Harbor navy yard officials just three days to repair the carrier because it was going to leave the harbor for an important mission then, whether or not it was totally repaired.

As soon as the carrier was in dry-dock, 1400 repair men swarmed over her, cutting, welding, riveting, and repairing all her damaged areas. They worked through the nights and, unbelievably, on May 30 *Yorktown*, fully repaired and provisioned, left the harbor. [23]

Five days later the *Yorktown* played a decisive role in turning back the Japanese force at Midway and sinking four aircraft carriers in the process. Unfortunately, during the violent combat *Yorktown*, herself, was sunk. Without the miracle of the Pearl Harbor shipyard, the outcome of the battle of Midway may have been reversed.

Between patrol and escort duties, *Ward* was now spending very little time in the harbor. She needed to refuel at least once a week, even on patrol, but her stay in port was often only long enough to fill her fuel bunkers. Other times it was extended to take on supplies, but the men stayed on the ship and liberties would have to wait for another time.

On June 11, Ambrose Domagall, a member of *Ward's* Number 3 gun crew on December 7, and Robert Ball left *Ward* for transfer to the mainland, where they would be reassigned to another ship. The departure of the two crewmen was, in itself, usually not a noteworthy event, but signaled the inevitable dispersion of the 47th Division. Others would soon follow. Each loss by the tightly knit group was felt by the others.

Ward witnessed the triumphant return of the fleet units on June 13 from their decisive victory at Midway. She participated in the creation of a sound screen as the units began their entry into the harbor.

June 16 saw several promotions within the ship's officer ranks. Lt. Hartwell Doughty, Executive Officer, was promoted to Lt. Commander; Lt.(jg) Oscar Goepner, Gunnery Officer, was promoted to Lieutenant; and Ensign Louis Platt was promoted to Lieutenant (jg).[24]

Ward had now settled into the routine of patrolling and escorting. Although both missions were vital to the defense of the islands and the Pacific Fleet, as well as to the quality of life on Oahu, neither created the sense of excitement that impending combat would.

By mid-1942, with the defeat of the Japanese fleet at Midway, Japanese offensive initiatives including submarine forays into Hawaiian waters had diminished considerably. American intelligence and scouting capabilities, including improved radar, would prevent a repeat of the surprise attack of December 7.

The submarine menace still existed near Hawaii, but Japanese thrusts into the South Pacific were now the top priority for their submarine forces. The routine of anti-submarine patrols by the *Ward* had to be continued, but actual submarine contacts around Hawaii were infrequent after June 1942.

Ward's routine had significantly changed in the past six months. Patrols were constant, escort duty occurred almost daily, and stays in port were usually too short for any liberty. Even trips to the other islands were different. Previously *Ward* had laid over for at least one night to allow the crew liberty on an island. On escort trips after December 7, the ship often did not even enter the harbor after safely delivering a ship to her destination. She immediately turned about and returned to Pearl. If the *Ward* did dock, it allowed the crew only a very brief liberty ashore. Patrol and escort duty had become inherently tedious during the last half of 1942.

Although the opportunities for action were few during 1942, the officers kept the crew busy with drills and other duties. Engine room and fire room personnel were busy regardless of whether the ship was under way or not. There the 24 hours of each day were covered by three separate crews on a four-on, eight-off basis. Even on the off hours, black gang personnel had responsibilities. Fire room crewmen frequently spent their off hours scraping and wire brushing boilers that were not lit off.

Because opportunities for shore leave were less frequent in 1942 the *Ward's* own little store, or "gedunk" as the crew called it, became more important. Located adjacent to the galley in the galley deck house, it provided opportunities for the crew to purchase some basic necessities. Operated by Chief Commissary Steward Henry Minter in the tiny caged office, he dispensed cigarettes at five cents a pack, candy bars, and various toilet articles.[25]

Legitimate leisure time was infrequent on *Ward,* so finding activities to fill it up was not difficult. Card and dice games, usually poker and craps, could be found at any time of the day. Although gambling for money was prohibited on the ship, money found its way into almost all games. John Merthan was not a card player but used cards to profit anyway. A torpedo man buddy of his loved to gamble and hired Merthan to stand his watch on the depth charge rack so he could get into a poker or craps game. He gave John two dollars for the four-hour watch.[26]

On a cruise to Hilo, Hawaii, Merthan was on duty as a mess cook when the master of arms in the after crew compartment decided that it was time that John learned how to shoot craps. Predictably, an officer discovered them, reprimanded them and had Merthan's liberty card pulled when the ship reached Hilo. He restored the card for the last night in port so Merthan could spend some time ashore.[27]

Will Lehner was also caught by an officer shooting craps. "He could have put us on report but he didn't," recalled Lehner. "He just told us to knock it off and then went about his business."

All crewmen did their personal laundry during off-duty time. With the ship at war status, even laundry was done differently. Prior to December 7, crewmen were permitted to tie their clothes in a bundle, secure them with a line, and toss them over the side. The ship dragging them through the salt water cleansed them to the satisfaction of the men. Now they had to do laundry in buckets on the ship.[28]

War status also required the crew to dye their hats blue under the theory that a white hat could be seen by enemy pilots. They were permitted to wear white hats when off the ship, however.

Some men would lie on deck soaking up the sun or writing letters home. Cooks kept a bench on the weather deck just outside the galley. "We used to sit there and watch the flying fish. That would just fascinate me," quipped Dick Thill. Some men simply used the time to catch up on their sleep.

Before December 7, 1941, *Ward* crewmen had much more liberty time and more leisure time on the ship. Officers were more lenient towards the crew in their attempts to entertain themselves. Some men discovered a way to sneak beer on board in port which took some creativity. The MPs at the main gate would pat everyone down with a billy club before they entered the yard to prevent sailors from bringing in contraband such as beer. The men still smuggled beer on board. Once on the ship, the beer could not be stashed in the refrigerator to cool so the men improvised. They put the bottles in a sack at the end of a rope which they hung out of a porthole.[29] After December 7, the opportunities for this type of activity decreased dramatically.

On July 21, *Ward* was in action again. While on inner harbor patrol, she received a report from the gunboat *Almandite,* which claimed a possible sound contact at 1615 and dropped several depth charges. *Ward* immediately went to flank speed to close on the gunboat to assist. At 1637, *Ward* had a sonar contact itself and went to General Quarters. At 1715, with the contact now solid at a point 12 miles from the harbor mouth, *Ward* unleashed a 14 charge pattern. It was her first offensive action in three months but again, no evidence of an actual submarine was found.

She had another sonar contact on August 9, while escorting the submarine *Halibut* to Pearl Harbor. At 1302 she dropped a pattern of 15 depth charges and followed by another pattern of 14 a half hour later. When the sea stopped boiling, the results were the same as usual, no visible evidence.

Two days later, a major change occurred in the top staff of *Ward* when Lt. Oscar Goepner relieved Lt. Commander Doughty as the Executive Officer, or second in command of the ship. Doughty had been the Executive officer since the ship's commissioning in January 1941. He was now promoted to the post of Operations Officer for Destroyer Division 80.[30] He had been a strict disciplinarian on *Ward* but the men also considered him to be fair.

Three more of the original gang of St. Paul reservists left the ship on August 19, when F2c John Merthan, RM3c Judson Trimmer, and Sea1c Robert Stein all left for new assignments. Merthan finally got his wish to serve in the hospital corps with an assignment to the pharmacist's mate school in San Diego. He thought he would return to the *Ward* but was, instead, eventually sent to the 4th Marine Division. He saw the rest of the war from foxholes on various Pacific Islands.

On August 11, Ken Swedberg was taken to a Mobile Hospital 2, a Quonset hut in the hills above Pearl Harbor, with an appendicitis attack. He was still recuperating from his operation several weeks later when four wounded marines were brought in to his ward. They had just participated in a commando type raid on the Japanese-held island of Makin and were in need of medical attention.

Shortly, a silver-haired officer came to the ward and talked to each Marine about the raid to learn what they had seen and done. After thanking them for an excellent job on Makin, he turned to leave. As he did so, he smiled and waved to Swedberg and the other patients. His hair and appearance left no doubt as to his identity. He was none other than Admiral Chester Nimitz, Commander in Chief of the United States Pacific Fleet.[31] Nimitz enjoyed associating with enlisted men and later in the war, when he had established his headquarters on Guam, he often pitched horseshoes with them.

Ward had another sonar contact on September 24, after being alerted to the possible presence of a submarine by a patrol plane. She dropped 10 depth charges on the contact but again found no evidence of a sub even though she searched the area for two more hours with destroyers *Litchfield* and *Schley.* It would be *Ward's* last depth-charge attack as a destroyer.

On September 30, *Ward* lost one of its stalwarts and the crew lost its leader, mentor and friend when Lt. Commander Outerbridge was formally relieved as the commanding officer. His successor, Lt. Commander Robert Wilkinson, who had come on board four days earlier to orient himself, inspected the crew at quarters and then the entire ship with Outerbridge. At 1100 he read his orders to the assembled officers and formally assumed command.[32]

To a man, the crew was saddened by the departure of Outerbridge. To many he was the fatherly figure they expected from a commanding officer although he was only 36 years old himself. He was an old-school navy man but with a reputation of a captain with a heart.

Years later at ship reunions, which he often attended, he always spoke with the men on a first-name basis. Sixty years later, former crewmen consistently talked of him in glowing terms. Will Lehner, in recalling him, spoke reverently of Outerbridge. "He was only about five feet eight inches tall," said Lehner, "but he was a big man. I respected that man deeply."

After leaving *Ward,* Outerbridge was given command of a new 2200-ton destroyer, *O'Brien.* Outerbridge led the ship at the D-Day landings at Normandy in June 1944 where *O'Brien* provided close-in support. On June 25, while dueling with German shore batteries, *O'Brien* was hit just aft of the bridge by a shell that killed 13 of the crew and wounded 19 others. The ship continued on station until the mission was completed.

O'Brien was hit by a kamikaze off Okinawa on January 5, 1945 and again on March 26. The latter hit caused a huge explosion that killed 52 crewmen and wounded scores of others, including Outerbridge himself.[33] The crew saved the ship and took it back to Mare Island for extensive repairs.

Outerbridge continued in the navy, later commanding Destroyer Division 42 and the heavy cruiser *Los Angeles.* He retired as a rear admiral in 1957. By that time he had earned the Navy Cross, three Silver Stars, the Legion of Merit, Purple Heart, and Navy Unit commendation. Fate would bring Outerbridge and *Ward* together again in 1944 under bizarre circumstances he would rather have avoided.[34]

For *Ward,* the war that came so abruptly and violently at Pearl Harbor on December 7 continued to be largely invisible as 1942 wore on. Ships left the harbor for the war zone in the South Pacific at a remote place with the unseemly name of Guadalcanal. Some returned later with battle damage and holes to fill in their roster. Some ships did not return at all. A friend John Merthan had come to know well was stationed on the cruiser *Astoria.* It went down off Guadalcanal in a confusing night engagement with hundreds of lives lost.

For *Ward,* the war was a long way off. Except for the many sonar contacts she had picked up, she did not see the enemy again after that Sunday in December of 1941. For those in her crew who craved more excitement, 1942 was a difficult time. On some ships the absence of combat for such a prolonged time produced discontent among the crew, eventually leading to significant disciplinary problems.

This did not occur on *Ward* for several reasons. The leadership provided by Captain Outerbridge and his officers provided that delicate mix of firmness, fairness, and consistency that kept the crew relatively satisfied. In addition, the crew contained a nucleus of men from the nation's Upper Midwest reared in an environment of hard work and respect for authority. If there had been any troublemakers in the 47th Division, they would have been weeded out before they ever saw *Ward.*

Nevertheless, any group of 130 men confined on a small ship, called to muster for drills at any time of the day within sight of an island paradise just out of reach, can be expected to be less than totally happy. *Ward's* crew worked hard at keeping their ship in fighting condition 24 hours a day in a non-war zone, but they were men as well as sailors. On occasion they stepped over the line.

Many infractions were considered too minor for any official action to be taken. Thus, a mess cook caught playing cards during duty hours was simply told to break it up. Repeat behavior would have brought a sterner warning or an official reprimand for the offending sailor's file. Most *Ward* crewmen, given a break, were not likely to tempt fate again any time soon.

In 1941, *Ward* did have 18 incidents requiring formal discipline for more serious offenses. These did get into the individual's file and the ship's Deck Log. Half of these involved incidents on shore during a liberty including overstaying a liberty, disorderly conduct, and drunkenness. These were serious enough to warrant a Court Martial proceeding to determine guilt or innocence.

Specific sentences for guilt depended upon the nature, severity, and frequency of the offense. A typical sentence for these offenses ranged from a fine ($5 to $10 a month) to loss of liberty privileges, reduction in rank, and confinement on bread and water. Disrespect to a petty officer could earn a sailor confinement on bread and water in the Marine brig ashore, with up to 30 days for a repeat offender. This sentence allowed for full rations every third day of confinement.

On-ship conduct bringing disciplinary action usually involved disrespect, insolence, refusal to obey an order, or insubordination toward an officer. Typical sentences would range from being placed on report, fines, extra duty hours, or several days of confinement.

In 1942 the number of disciplinary actions decreased to 12. With an actual enemy to focus on and the possibility of combat on any given day, the men's attitudes changed. Because opportunities for shore leave after December 7 decreased, most infractions occurred on the ship. As before, these usually involved disrespect, insubordination, or failure to obey an order, with fines or extra duty hours the usual sentence. A fine of $10 per month for three months for failure to obey an order was a significant punishment to a sailor making only $40 a month.

The last three months of 1942 were devoted to more escort duty, exercises with U.S. submarines, and fleet exercises. These included escorting battleships during live firing of their 14-inch main batteries and five-inch anti-aircraft guns. *Ward's* crew always enjoyed the spectacle of the sounds and huge smoke clouds emitted by battleship salvos.

Ward also spent several days exercising with the submarine *Nautilus,* each using the other as the target. *Nautilus* made radar-directed attacks on *Ward* while *Ward* followed with a sonar-directed attack on the sub. The *Ward* was picking on a big one when it tangled with *Nautilus.* The sub was the biggest in the U.S. submarine fleet. It was considerably longer than *Ward* and, at over 2700 tons, was almost three times heavier. Its two six-inch guns gave it more firepower than that of the *Ward* and most other destroyers.

On November 24, *Ward* again lost one of its fixtures. Lt. Oscar Goepner, her Executive Officer who had been with the ship since January 1941, received a reassignment to the Submarine Chaser Training Center in Miami. Lt. Lloyd Benson assumed Goepner's duties.

On December 5, *Ward* received startling news from the headquarters of Destroyer Division 80. It spread like wildfire through the ship and the entire crew knew almost as soon as the officers did. The ship was ordered to proceed with *Schley* to Bremerton Naval Yard in Washington. There both ships would be converted to Auxiliary Personnel Destroyers, or APDs.

The ships would leave Pearl Harbor on December 13. After almost two years, the crew would have their first leave. It was a leave that would allow the men to return home for the first time since that bitter cold night of January 21, 1941.

Men were ecstatic as they prepared to return to the mainland. Those who had clothes in lockers at the YMCA were allowed to return there to retrieve them. Others made last-minute shopping trips to purchase gifts and souvenirs of the islands for family and friends. Everyone checked out their best dress uniform for the return home.

Ward refueled and provisioned on December 12 for the eight-day voyage. The ship and crew were ready to leave. At 0703 on the 13th, *Schley* left her berth alongside *Ward* in the navy yard and *Ward* pulled away from the dock four minutes later. Forty minutes later the ships passed the Pearl Harbor entrance buoy and began their journey home. As a destroyer it would be *Ward's* last look at the place that she had come to know well in the 20 months she had protected the harbor entrance. She would see it again later, but as an APD.

The two destroyers proceeded at a leisurely 12½ knots as they steamed eastward. There was a little bounce to the crew's step now as they carried out their duties and anticipated their upcoming leave.

Ward test-fired all of her four-inch and 20-millimeter guns in case she would encounter trouble on the way. The journey was without incident, however, and considerably different from the ship's westward passage. At 1135 on December 20, lookouts sighted land, and at 1310 *Ward* passed the entrance buoy to San Francisco harbor. At 1417 *Ward* anchored at Treasure Island Naval Base in San Francisco Harbor. Here TM2c Dan Lombardi left the ship to begin his 15-day leave. Others stayed on board.

An hour and a half later *Ward* and *Schley* weighed anchor and proceeded into San Pablo Bay to Mare Island Naval Yard. The *Ward* was back on the mainland but not yet ready to let her crew go.

The initial plans were for conversion of *Ward* to an APD to occur at Mare Island. After one stack was removed, the plans were changed. The stack was reinstalled so *Ward* could proceed to Bremerton, Washington, where the conversion would be made.[35]

The destroyers left Mare Island on December 22, stopped to refuel at Treasure Island and left San Francisco in their wake at 2122. Their final destination was Puget Sound Naval Yard at Bremerton, Washington.

With the crew so close to home, the ships sped along at 22 knots. At 1448 on December 24, the destroyers entered Seattle Harbor, where *Ward* moored at Pier 40 at 1522. It was Christmas Eve and the crewmen were not home yet, but they soon would be.

Ward's first tour of duty was over almost 22 months after it had begun. For both ship and crew there was still a war to be fought and they would be back in it shortly. Although *Ward* had already gained fame, her destiny still lay ahead. For now, it was time for visiting family and friends. The war could wait a little while longer.

CHAPTER 10

Ward Becomes an APD

Even as *Ward* settled in at Bremerton on December 24, workmen were poised to begin work transforming her to a different kind of ship. Time had finally caught up with the 24-year old four-stacker. Newer and more heavily armed destroyers were being added to the fleet by the dozens. These had up to six dual-purpose five-inch guns, 20- and 40-mm anti-aircraft guns, and the latest in radar and sonar equipment. They carried torpedo tubes and depth charges as did *Ward* but also carried a deadly new anti-submarine weapon, the "hedgehog" projectile, which did not explode unless it hit an underwater object.

The newer destroyers were much faster than the four-stackers and had a range that would allow them to travel with the fleet. Their versatility enabled them to perform any mission required of destroyers. In 1943 most four-stackers were to be phased out as destroyers and given different roles for the remainder of the war.

The old destroyers did have the speed and armament to perform other useful fleet functions, for which the navy did not have an excess of ships. Experimental conversions had proven that the four-stackers were very capable of serving in many other auxiliary roles critical to a modern navy.

Conversion of an old destroyer to another type of vessel would add a useful ship to the fleet at less cost and in less time than building a new one. The navy had decided in 1940 to add to their auxiliary fleet by converting four-stackers and, by 1945, had transfigured 129 of the old destroyers. This produced an additional 22 minelayers, 14 seaplane tenders, 18 minesweepers, 32 fast transports, 41 miscellaneous auxiliary craft, and 2 water barges. Thus, the useful life of these four-stackers was extended for several more years.

One of the greatest needs in the Pacific war in 1942 was for transport of men and supplies to the countless islands that littered the road to Tokyo. To reach Japan required an island-hopping campaign extending across the Pacific from its starting point in the Solomon Islands.

Experience in the Guadalcanal campaign of late 1942 revealed that the traditional navy concept of using large transports, each capable of carrying several thousand troops to a beachhead, had serious drawbacks. They were extremely vulnerable to enemy aircraft and submarine attacks during transit and while unloading. They were slow and could not defend themselves. They took days to unload, and the troops and vital supplies were at risk during this period when they sat off the beach.

Smaller, but faster transports, with anti-aircraft and anti-submarine weapons and capable of negotiating shallow waters to unload quickly, would be critically needed. In many upcoming landings, forces measured only in the hundreds of troops would be sufficient and did not justify the use of a large transport.

The concept of using destroyer-sized transports in combat had already been tested. At

Guadalcanal, the Japanese used destroyers to bring in supplies and fresh troops during the entire six-month campaign. In February 1943 they evacuated their entire remaining force of 11,000 men at night using destroyers, without the knowledge of nearby U.S. troops.

The U.S. Navy also toyed with the idea of developing a destroyer-transport. During the mid-1930s, the Marine Corps was seeking ships that could transport and land troops quickly, and notified the navy of this need. As an experiment the navy converted the old four-stack destroyer *Manley* (DD-74) to a destroyer-transport in 1938 to test the concept. It became (APD-1) and showed enough promise that the navy converted five more four-stackers in 1940.[1]

Four of the six conversions were used in the Guadalcanal campaign and, like the Japanese destroyers, proved the worth of small, fast destroyers in island warfare. The U.S. Navy had not yet mastered the art of night combat or the use of torpedo attacks at the time of Guadalcanal and experienced heavy ship losses in the first four months of the campaign. Included in the losses were three of the initial destroyer-transports, *Colhoun* (APD-2), *Gregory* (APD-3), and *Little* (APD-4).[2]

The navy had seen enough, however, and authorized the conversion of another 26 four-stackers to fast transports. The new designs were given the designation of Auxiliary Personnel Destroyers, or APDs. The name was later changed to Armed Personnel Destroyers although their crews often referred to them as "all-purpose destroyers." The ships to be converted were selected on the basis of their overall condition and a schedule developed for conversion at various U.S. shipyards. Ultimately the concept proved so successful that the navy converted 95 new destroyer-escorts, of which they had an excess, into Armed Personnel Destroyers late in the war.

Ward was not yet ready to let her men go when it reached Bremerton. On December 26 an ammunition barge came alongside and the crew turned to emptying the ammunition lockers. Before the day was over they transferred six torpedoes, 68 depth charges, 521 rounds of four-inch shells, 50 boxes of 20-mm ammunition, and 11,000 rounds of small arms ammunition onto the barge.

The following day the crew pumped all remaining fuel to a yard oiler. Now that the ship was ready for the conversion work to begin in earnest, the officers granted half the crew its first leave in two years, commencing at 1345 on December 28.[3]

Because the work would disrupt the crew compartments, *Ward's* crew was forced to temporarily shift their berth to the battleship *California,* which was in the yard on a re-modernization during *Ward's* entire stay.

The crew would spend the day on *Ward* standing their watch and cleaning up the ship from the previous day's work. At 1600 they left the ship. Some returned to the *California* for the evening meal. That half of the crew that had liberty caught a ferry across Puget Sound to Seattle. The ferries ran every hour on the hour. The liberty party had to be back on the dock by midnight to catch the last liberty boat back to the *California.*

This procedure continued until February 1943, when the conversion work was completed and *Ward* could again accommodate her crew. The crew shifted their berth to their own ship to get reacquainted with it.

The men had seen *California* before. The battleship was sunk at its mooring at Pearl Harbor, raised, and repaired sufficiently at Pearl to make her seaworthy enough for a voyage to the mainland. She sailed on her own power to Puget Sound in October 1942. She then underwent a year-long reconstruction of her damage as well as a complete re-modernization. This would bring her close to the standards for present-day battleships.

Because she did not berth her own crew during the reconstruction, her cavernous crew spaces were vacant. The only drawback to living on the *California* during this period was that the ship was not heated. The *Ward's* men spent a cold six weeks below decks on the battleship.

While the first contingent of men was preparing to begin their leave, workmen swarmed over the ship. They had just more than a month to transform *Ward* and *Schley* from conventional destroyers to APDs. Both ships would be converted simultaneously.

Ward's Number One and Number Two main battery guns were removed on December 30, with the Number Three and Four guns on the following day. The 12 torpedo launchers were next and the decks of the two ships became beehives of activity. Number One stack was taken down on January 1 and Boiler Number One lifted out of the hull. Number Two Boiler and stack were removed on January 2. Number Three and Four stacks were shortened to improve visibility and an iron ballast installed in the bilges to improve stability.[4]

Both destroyers were moved into Dry-Dock Number 5 on January 3, and the work continued with the destroyers now on blocks. The forward fire room was now cleared of all equipment and work began on erecting two levels of individual bunks. In only two weeks the ship's appearance had already changed.

In the midst of this work, *Ward's* captain, Lt. Commander Robert H. Wilkinson, was relieved as commanding officer by Lt.(jg) Lloyd G. Benson, temporarily. On January 15, Lt. Frederick W. Lemly assumed command as the next skipper of *Ward.* He would lead the ship into the South Pacific.[5]

The temperature in Bremerton was unusually cold for a winter in Washington as *Ward* settled in at her berth. The northern states were in the grip of a bitter cold spell as the ship's crew attempted to adjust to living in this climate. Russ Reetz knew that it would be cold while still on the voyage from San Francisco to Bremerton. "I was standing watch in the fireroom much of the time and even with the boilers fired up, I had to keep my pea coat on," laughed Reetz. "That had never happened before."

The temperature shock was the reverse of what the St. Paul men experienced when they left frigid Minnesota for sunny California in January 1941. Now, after two years of above-80-degree temperatures, they were suddenly cast into a below-freezing and bone-chilling climate.

The crew spent Christmas Eve and Christmas Day on board *Ward,* cold and tired, but happy to be only a train-ride from home. Thirty days had been allotted for crew leave. Half the crew, the port watch, would be given 15 days' leave beginning on December 28. The starboard watch would commence their leave after the first contingent returned. Thus, half of the crew would remain on board the entire time to maintain the fire and other critical watches even though *Ward* was docked.

With sea bags packed, including souvenirs and Christmas gifts, the port watch boarded trains to all parts of the country, including Minnesota. The group traveling on the Great Northern to St. Paul was considerably smaller than the group of 82 men who had left St. Paul 23 months earlier. Not only did half the crew remain on the ship, but a number of the original crew had previously been transferred off the ship and reassigned to other ships or stations.

Nevertheless, 29 crewmen climbed aboard the train anticipating a joyous reunion with family and friends. Included in this group were Ed Bukrey, Scotty Fenton, Ray Nolde, and John Peick of the crew of Gun Number 3 which had sunk the midget sub.

The men would not have as much time at home as they had anticipated. Their 15-day leave included travel time, and they had to travel halfway across the country twice. They would actually have just more than a week at home.

As the train chugged across the northern tier of states, the temperature continued to fall. The men wrapped their woolen pea coats even tighter around their bodies, if that was possible. The atmosphere on this train was totally different from that on their trip to San Diego. Card games were hard to find now and conversation was minimal. Men curled up in their coats and, despite the cold, tried to sleep.

Their sleep was interrupted frequently as the train stopped at almost every depot between Bremerton and St. Paul. The view through the ice-covered windows was bleak and unchanging, a snow-covered landscape that concealed any signs of life. The routine of sleep and muted conversation was broken only by trips to the dining car at mealtime.

In groups the men ate, the principal topic of conversation focusing on how each would unwind at home. Some of the sailors were disappointed at mealtime. On the *Ward* it was normal to have coffee available in unlimited quantity 24 hours a day. In the dining car they were limited to a single cup. After eating they retired to their seats, again to look forward to their next meal.

With the many stops, progress was painstakingly slow. Finally at 10:30 pm on December 30, the Great Northern Empire Builder pulled into Union Depot in St. Paul. To the surprise of the 29 men, a large crowd was waiting patiently in the cold, now well below zero. The trip from Bremerton had taken so long that reporters on the train had time to phone in their stories to the St. Paul newspaper for publication before the train arrived.[6]

As soon as the men began disembarking, the Great Northern Railway Drum and Bugle Corps, assembled for the occasion, broke out in stirring martial music. Men were mobbed as they stepped off the train. Soon the depot was a bedlam as friends and family attempted to reach their loved ones.[7]

St. Paul Mayor McDonough tried to shake the hand of every returning sailor he could find. He had difficulty reaching them all as the crowd of more than 2000 surrounded anyone wearing a blue uniform. The sea of humanity was a mob scene of hugging and kissing as mothers and fathers finally found their sons and cried unashamedly.

Harold Harris, one of the few married men returning, had last seen his two-and-a-half year-old daughter Gloria when she was seven months old. Now he was trying to make up for the lost time in one night. Friends of Gordon Hultman boisterously carried him around the depot on their shoulders, proclaiming him a hero.

The celebration was the biggest and loudest seen at the depot since the return of the Minnesota soldiers following the Armistice ending World War I. The frenzy continued for more than 20 minutes before it began to subside so that normal conversation could be heard. The men were stunned that 29 of them could have caused this massive uproar.[8]

The men began seven days of reunions and dinners with family, relatives and friends. Many found time to visit their former co-workers at the companies they had left in January 1941. Several of Orv Ethier's friends who had worked with him at Superior Packing left the company to join the army. They happened to be home on leave themselves when they learned that Orv was coming home. He took one night away from the family to join his friends in a big celebration at a fine St. Paul night club.

Some single men, such as Don Pepin and Ed Bukery, had left girlfriends behind when they went to Hawaii and now tried to find time for them between family visits. Bukrey was an avid cribbage player and recalled that "my dad and I played a lot of cribbage while I was home and he won every game."

All 29 men enjoyed at least two common activities—eating mom's cooking and sleeping in a real bed. The navy mattresses were only two inches thick and not easy to get accustomed to. The sailors had almost forgotten how restful a real bed could be until they were reunited with their own.

Russ Reetz did not waste any time when he finally got to his home at 2:30 in the morning. He immediately began confirming arrangements for his wedding. Two days later, tired and still short of sleep, he got married. Only then did Russ and his new bride begin the round of visits to his relatives just like all other returning crewmen.

Reetz had originally intended to get married in December 1941 in Honolulu. His fiancée had her airline ticket and was planning to fly to Hawaii in mid-December. A married shipmate lived in a two-bedroom house in Honolulu and was willing to share it with Reetz. The Japanese attack changed all of that when the navy prohibited wives from joining their husbands in Hawaii.

As it was, Reetz's wife returned to Bremerton with him a week after the wedding. She worked in a hospital there until *Ward* left for the Pacific, which is when she returned to St. Paul.[9]

The crew's leave passed swiftly and on January 10, most of the men reluctantly boarded the Empire Builder for a return to Bremerton and the war. Several of the 29 had been reassigned prior to their leave and reported for duty elsewhere. It was a most rested and relaxed group of sailors that rode the train west on the 10th.

Upon arrival at Bremerton, the men joined other crewmen coming off leave from all parts of the country. They reported on board on January 12, about 30 minutes before their leave expired.

The scene of two weeks earlier was now repeated, as the leave of the starboard watch commenced at 0930 on January 13. On January 16, four of the *Ward's* officers also left on 15-day leave. Like the enlisted men, the officers took their leave in two groups.

The train ride of the 21 men in the second group was a repeat of that of the initial contingent. Eight of the men would continue beyond St. Paul to destinations further east. A 14th St. Paul sailor, James Spratt, arrived in St. Paul on an earlier train. It was now much colder than the first group had experienced, temperatures now more than 20 degrees below zero.

As the train passed through North Dakota, a St. Paul reporter again boarded and filed stories by phone on the eminent arrival of the second group. When the reporter asked the men what would be the first thing they would do at home, the response was almost unanimous, "Get a good night's sleep." It was rare that any sailor answered with, "Have a night on the town." Later one of the men told the reporter that "it was fine to fire the first shot of the war but the war is not over. We have to go back and make sure we fire the last shot." That attitude was representative of the entire crew.

Karl Lasch, a member of the crew of Number 3 gun, was not sure whether or not his wife would meet the train. She was in the Women's Auxiliary Army Corps (WAACS) stationed in New York and needed to get a leave to meet him. Ken Ekblad and Dave Morgan were confident that their wives would meet the train. They had not been that sure a year earlier. Their wives were in Honolulu during the Japanese attack and it was days before they learned that their wives were safe.

Although the second contingent of returning sailors was smaller than the first, the crowd at Union Depot may actually have been larger. The welcome at the first event was so well publicized that it helped to draw additional spectators at the second welcome.

As the Empire Builder rolled into Union Depot at 10:30 pm on Friday, January 15, the mob scene of December 30 was repeated with the same program. The mayor, Great Northern Band, family, friends, and spectators all played their same roles.[10]

Dave Morgan was a former sergeant on the St. Paul police force, the first from the force to enlist. He was met by six St. Paul policemen, including his former partner, Sergeant Dan Pottgeiser, who gave him a roaring welcome. Ken Ekblad was met by his family and wife of 18 months. She had traveled to Honolulu in the summer of 1941 so the two could get married. With the outbreak of war she had to return to St. Paul. Karl Lasch was overjoyed to spot his wife in the boisterous crowd. His leave would now be a happy one.[11]

Although everyone wanted to know how the war was progressing around Hawaii, the men were reluctant to talk about it. Instead, they wanted to talk about the Minnesota athletic teams and how they were doing. They had lost track of the University of Minnesota football team and the St. Paul Saints baseball team since they left Minnesota.

Dick Thill's family chose not to battle the exuberant crowds at the depot. After he got off the train, he walked eight blocks in the biting cold to catch a streetcar to his home on St. Paul's west side. His parents welcomed him there. Thill's father took him to greet the relatives in the family car, a 1928 Chevrolet.

This group's allotted time also passed too quickly, and on January 23 they said their farewells and climbed aboard the Empire Builder again. There was still a war to fight and *Ward* was waiting for them.

Work continued feverishly while the second group of sailors was on leave. A new officer, Lt. (jg) Irv Fowler reported for duty on January 19. On January 25, with clean bottoms, *Ward* and *Schley* left the dry-dock. All remaining work would be completed afloat.

The second contingent reported back aboard on January 28 with the exception of several men who were late. They would be disciplined later. Davits and launching rails for the ship's landing craft were installed, as well as the new 3"/50 dual-purpose guns. Work below deck was completed by February 7, allowing the *Ward's* crew to leave *California* and move back to its own ship.[12]

On one of the last liberty nights before the *Ward* was completed, Walt Campion decided to have one final drink before the ship left for the war zone. Finding a quiet bar in Seattle, he noticed a lonesome looking soldier staring forlornly into his empty glass. Campion bought him a drink to cheer him up and the soldier returned the favor when Walt went to the rest room for a few minutes. That's the last thing he remembered. When he woke up, his wallet was empty and he realized that he had been given a "Mickey Finn." He would remember that lesson well.[13]

In just six weeks, *Ward* and the *Schley* had become different ships. They now had only two stacks and one boiler room with two boilers. The vacant space was filled with four-tiered bunks capable of accommodating 150 men with their personal armaments and packs. A temporary operating room was also added in the lower level troop space. *Ward* was the only one of the 32 APDs to have this feature. With only a few exceptions, all portholes were removed and the turbines and reduction gears in the engine room were repaired. New diesel oil tanks were installed in the space below the troop compartment for *Ward's* new landing craft.[14]

On deck the transfiguration was even more dramatic. The 12 torpedo tubes amidships were removed and replaced with four sets of Wellin davits, two to a side, each holding a standard navy LCP(R) landing craft, usually referred to as Higgins Boats, after the builder of the craft. The davits carried the boats high over the deck and out of the way. They could be launched relatively quickly by sliding down steel rails to the water.[15]

These four boats allowed *Ward* to serve the purpose for which it had been converted. These craft were 36 feet, 8 inches long and 10 feet, 10 inches in beam. Fully loaded they displaced only 3 feet, 6 inches of water. They were powered by a variety of engines, the most common being a 225-horsepower Gray marine diesel engine. This pushed the boat at eight knots with a range of 130 miles.[16]

The LCP(R) was manned by a crew of four consisting of a coxswain, an engineer, and two gunners. The gunners, sitting in individual cockpits in the bow, each manned a single 0.30 caliber machine gun. The boat could accommodate 25 fully armed troops or four tons of cargo. The troops sat on low benches on either side and debarked over a narrow bow ramp.

Other deck changes increased *Ward's* fighting capabilities. The biggest alteration was the removal of her four 4"/50 caliber single-purpose main battery guns which could not be elevated to fire at aircraft. They were replaced with four 3"/50 caliber dual-purpose guns.

These operated like the four-inch guns with a pointer and trainer each manually controlling the vertical or horizontal movement of the weapon. Although the gun fired a smaller and lighter shell, it was extremely versatile. With a maximum depression of 13 degrees and a maximum elevation of 85 degrees, it could fire at surface targets at close range or at aircraft almost directly overhead. Its shells could reach altitudes of 21,000 feet.[17] *Ward* carried four types of three-inch inch ammunition: anti-aircraft, common, armor-piercing, and illuminating.

She still retained five of the 20-mm single-barrel, rapid-firing anti-aircraft cannon that were installed in the summer of 1942. These would be supplemented with several more later in the war to give her a total battery of seven. Each of these guns was manned by a crew of five men and fed by drums holding 60 rounds of ball, tracer, high explosive, or incendiary ammunition. Together, the three-inch and 20-mm guns gave the ship a formidable defense against aircraft at almost any altitude.

Ward also retained its stern depth charge racks but four depth charge projectors were added. The projectors would throw a 300-pound depth charge 50 to 120 yards to the side of the ship depending on the size of powder charge used. Together with the stern racks, the projectors would allow *Ward* to fire larger depth charge patterns than she was able to do at Pearl Harbor. Ironically, *Ward* now had more overall firepower as a transport than she had previously had as a destroyer.

Ward received other equipment which would make it possible to survive in a combat zone. New and more sensitive sonar gear was installed and she now sported two new radar antenna atop her mainmast. A "bedspring" antenna served her air-search radar while a "derby hat" antenna provided the surface search capability. She could now detect submarines more quickly and would not have to rely on lookouts to detect surface ships or aircraft. Finally, all excess paint was removed below and above the deck to reduce fire hazard.

Ward was a complete ship again. Her hull, boilers, and engines were still 25 years old but her communications, detection, and weapon systems were up to date. She would now be able to hold her own in a fight, especially with aircraft, which would be her greatest threat.

After dock trials *Ward* was finally under way again under her own power on February 9. She conducted various sea trials to test her propulsion and other systems and test-fire her guns. On the 10th, an ammunition barge came alongside at 0530. *Ward* became a fighting ship once more when it took on 1200 three-inch shells, 62 depth charges, thousands of rounds of 20-mm ammunition, and various ordnance accessories. She also took on another new officer, Ensign Clifford Schroeder, Jr.

On February 11, *Ward* topped off her fuel tanks and dropped off all remaining yard workmen. On February 11, *Ward* and *Schley* left Bremerton bound for San Francisco. *Ward* would never again see Bremerton. *Ward's* new piping system caused some confusion for the black gang and someone opened the wrong valve, flooding the crew compartment with fuel oil. Clean-up would take a long time.

It was a somewhat different crew that took *Ward* to California at 20 knots. Although there were still many of the original 47th Division Reservists aboard, there were many new faces also. The ship was still *Ward* but the hull number as well as the appearance was now changed. The number on her bow was no longer 139, it was 16; for *Ward* was now officially APD-16.

She had already been assigned to Transport Division 22 and would meet her division mates in the Pacific. The ship had many new features to challenge the crew. They had to be mastered before *Ward* reached the war zone; their education began on the voyage to San Francisco.

The two destroyers anchored in San Francisco Bay at 0835 on February 13 and loaded for the long trek to the Pacific. *Ward* took on fuel, 15 new crewmen, four passengers, and 1000 bags of mail. At 2300 they were under way again at 15 knots on a bearing of 248 degrees. Two thousand miles dead ahead on that bearing lay Pearl Harbor.[18]

This visit to Oahu would be different from Ward's last trip. She would not linger there for almost two years this time but would continue on into the South Pacific. *Ward* was ready to fight again and was headed into harm's way.

CHAPTER 11

In the South Pacific at Last

It was a grim and subdued crew that took *Ward* out of San Francisco Harbor on February 13, 1943. Their confidence and composure was markedly different from that of the ship's first voyage to Pearl Harbor two years earlier. In 1941, with the world at peace, many saw the cruise to Hawaii as an extension of their reserve training and almost a paid vacation. For ten months it was. Then, two hours in December changed all of that.

The crew on February 13 was two years older now and had seen ships destroyed and men die. They had witnessed the enemy attempting to destroy *Ward* and had lost friends on other ships, some burned beyond recognition. However, with the exception of the one terrible morning, they had spent their time on an obsolete destroyer far from the exploding bombs, screaming shells, destruction, and death.

In 1941 they were young innocent sailors, looking for adventure where they could find it. Now, as the ship's twin screws put their homes and family 16 more miles behind them every 60 minutes, they had only to glance around them to see that this tour of duty would be different. They were no longer boys, but seasoned men ready to face a new and different war.

Not only was the crew different, the ship was as well. It now bristled with weapons. It carried radar antennas on its mast and new sonar gear. The most striking feature, however, was the four landing craft suspended above the deck amidships. Those landing craft would be *Ward's* greatest weapons in the new type of war she would fight. They would carry men or supplies and equipment to anywhere they were needed. It would be the movement of troops, supplies, and equipment to strategic locations in the chain of islands across the Pacific that would win the war. The APDs did not carry landing craft to hunt for submarines.

As the men tried to anticipate what lay ahead, they all recognized one reality. *Ward* would not be patrolling outside a harbor for months at a time again nor escorting ships between islands far from the sounds of battle. The landing craft she carried meant she would carry troops to landing beaches, some of which would be hostile. Hostile shores usually produced enemy responses to the landing and *Ward* could see violence as a steady diet in her new role.

The crew found one consolation in their new ship. They would not be sitting ducks as they were at Pearl Harbor. They were now about to carry the fight to the enemy on his own grounds. The United States Navy was going to do some of the bombing, strafing, and shooting, and *Ward* would be a part of it.

Somber thoughts also entered their minds. They felt reasonably secure on duty in Hawaii in 1942. Now, however, they realized that there was a chance that they may not return from this tour of duty. In 1942, the U.S. Navy sent four of the first six APDs in its

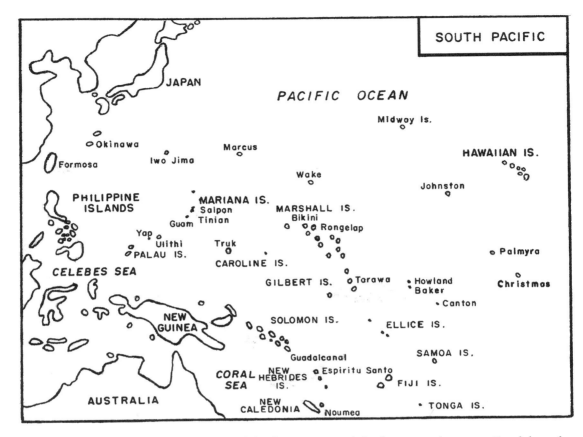

fleet to the South Pacific. Three of the four were sunk in fierce combat near Guadalcanal in the Solomon Islands.[1] Thirty-three men were killed on the three ships. Purvis Bay across the Sound from Guadalcanal would be *Ward's* new home within a matter of months.

The voyage to Pearl Harbor emphasized the seriousness of the war situation as *Ward* cruised silently at 15 knots. At night the ship was darkened as it steamed in a zigzag pattern. Her air and surface radar searched 360 degrees around the ship while her new sonar searched the depths from beam to beam.

Although *Ward* still resembled the destroyer DD-139, the many changes made in Bremerton required even the older hands to reacquaint themselves with their "new" ship. As *Ward* steamed toward Pearl Harbor, crewmen continued to familiarize themselves with the changes.

The crew's living quarters changed little. The Captain, Exec, and Engineering officers still had individual staterooms forward with the junior officers assigned two to a stateroom. Chief Petty Officers still had a group stateroom forward of the wardroom and enlisted men continued to have their crew quarters fore and aft.

Although the 20-mm guns were not new to the men, the three-inch dual-purpose guns were. Gun crews would soon be drilling daily on them against simulated aerial or surface targets. Before long the training would involve actual live targets. Crewmen would also be drilling with the new depth-charge projectors to become familiar with their operation and the various powder charges they used. The new air and search radar and sonar equipment was manned with newly trained crewmen who were already knowledgeable in their operation.

The cruise to Pearl Harbor was without incident this time but not without problems. Rough seas swept over the bow causing flooding in the officer's wardroom. It was discovered that the bolt holes from the old four-inch gun mounts had not been covered. The officers solved the problem temporarily by jamming pencils into the holes.[2]

Lookouts sighted Oahu at 0600 on February 20 and by 0850 *Ward* was moored at berth X-4 in Pearl Harbor. The ship had returned to a familiar haunt after a leave of three months. It was no longer the same ship, however, and some eyebrows were raised at the strange appearance of a familiar ship. *Ward* was still an old ship but looked different to all who knew her. She was about to change even more.

At 1400 a yard tug towed *Ward* to berth B-12 in the navy yard. While docked, yard workers swarmed over her, giving her a new appearance. Her standard blue-gray color was covered with a camouflage pattern designated as MS31L, meaning Dark Pattern System, Landing Craft. It consisted of a mottled pattern of light green, dark green, and brown on all horizontal surfaces, and haze green, navy green, and brown on all vertical surfaces.[3] She would now blend in with the surroundings on the jungle islands she would be visiting.

After taking on fuel and ammunition on February 22, *Ward* left the harbor with the four-stacker minesweeper *Robin* for two days of firing exercises off Oahu. She fired every gun she had, using various types of ammunition in her ammo locker, including star shells, in both day and night conditions. She returned to port at 1530 on February 23, ready for an assignment.

She had no sooner docked when a flurry of activity began. In the next 40 minutes, 38 men, including 8 coxswains, reported for duty. Shortly, 14 current crewmen left the ship for new assignments.[4] These included ten men of the original 47th Division reservists from St. Paul. The St. Paul contingent left on the *Ward* was gradually being whittled down. Most of the ten, like Ken Swedberg who transferred to the heavy cruiser *Salt Lake City,* went to other ships.

The personnel changes were due largely to *Ward's* transformation from destroyer to APD. With the reduction in boiler rooms from four to two, *Ward* needed fewer firemen and other boiler room crewmen. The new landing craft required new crewmen to operate and maintain them, ratings *Ward* did not previously have.

Ward left the harbor on the 24th for more gunnery exercises against surface and aerial targets. In this she was joined by the new escort carrier *Long Island*. The 11,300-ton *Long Island* was built by converting the hull of the freighter *Mormacmail* and adding a flight deck. She was the first of 86 escort carriers that the navy would build to supplement the large fleet carriers.[5]

Ward's anti-aircraft exercises were not entirely successful. When the three-inch batteries almost shot down the aircraft towing the target sleeve, Captain Lemly replaced the gunnery officer. Engineering Officer Farwell took over that responsibility even though he was not rated for a deck position. He would have to "grow into it."

Following the exercise, *Ward* and *Long Island* did not return to port but continued southwesterly at 15 knots. *Ward* led the carrier by 2000 yards to sweep for submarines on the journey. Their course of 190 degrees would take them to a South Pacific base in the war zone. *Ward* was rejoining the war.

The trip was uneventful until 0427 on February 26, when *Ward* sighted three unidentified ships at five-and-a-half miles. The ship went to General Quarters and took a protective position on *Long Island,* ready to fight if necessary. Tension gripped the *Ward* until the ships were identified as friendly.

At 1243 on the same day, *Ward's* sonar gear picked up an object dead ahead at only 650 yards. *Ward* suggested that the carrier change course while it investigated the contact independently. It could not regain contact but dropped a single depth charge at 1250 to keep any submarine down while the two ships left the area at 15 knots.

Ward sighted the U.S. outpost island of Palmyra at 0655 on February 27 and was safely moored in its harbor at 0825. After refueling *Ward* got under way again at 1040 and caught up with *Long Island,* which left the harbor first. With *Ward* leading once more, the ships continued driving for the South Pacific on course, 213 degrees at 15 knots.

An event of major significance occurred at 1539 on February 28 when *Ward* passed from north to south latitude as it crossed the equator. All maritime nations celebrate this event by requiring all polliwogs, those who have never crossed the equator before, to pay homage to King Neptune.

The required method of paying homage was determined by the shellbacks on the ship, those who had crossed the equator before. It usually involved some form of humiliation of the polliwogs, limited only by the creativity of the shellbacks. Since none of the St. Paul reservists had crossed the equator before, *Ward* had a large contingent of polliwogs. Many of them spent hours dressed in winter gear crawling through garbage or looking for icebergs using two empty beer bottles for binoculars. Even in wartime, most captains allowed these festivities to continue as long as they did not impair the ship's fighting alertness or capabilities. At the end of the day, *Ward* was free of polliwogs.[6]

With the entire crew now shellbacks, Ward and *Long Island* continued toward their destination at a steady 15 knots. At 1645 on March 3, *Ward* crossed the International Date Line and picked up a full day. This event, unlike the equator crossing, was not recognized by any formal celebration.

At 0725 on March 6, land was sighted 40 miles distant. These were the Fiji Islands, another island outpost that *Ward's* crew had never visited. The ship had finally arrived in the South Pacific. As was the custom with carriers approaching a base, *Long Island* launched her aircraft to fly to the island. *Ward* now took station aft of the carrier to protect her stern as she entered port.

The carrier anchored at Tomba Ko Nandi at 1222, *Ward* anchoring 23 minutes later in berth 47. The starboard watch of the *Ward* was given liberty immediately to inspect this strange new port. The port watch would have their liberty the following morning. *Ward* refueled from the *Long Island* the next morning, and at 1421 the two ships left Fiji on the final leg of their long journey. Again, *Ward* took station 2000 yards ahead of the carrier as the two ships steamed almost due west, zigzagging at 15 knots.

Dick Thill almost remained on the island when *Ward* pulled out. He had liberty in the morning and picked up a ride into town with an army truck. Returning to the ship several hours later, he missed the truck and started walking for the dock. Suddenly a rainstorm drenched the island forcing him to seek shelter in an unlit warehouse. A group of natives also hiding in the shed from the storm kept repeating "Ooola" to Thill. Not knowing what it meant and fearing for his safety, he could only stand there smiling but very apprehensive. He learned later that "Ooola" meant hello in the native tongue.

When the rain stopped, Thill resumed walking to the dock, at a brisker pace now. Fortunately another army truck came along and took him to the dock. The last liberty boat was ready to leave for the *Ward* and Thill came within minutes of being AWOL and stuck in Fiji.[7]

At 0607 on March 9, *Ward,* sighting land almost dead ahead at 20, miles, positioned herself astern of *Long Island* to protect the carrier on her entry into the harbor. *Long Island* anchored at 1440, *Ward* seven minutes later. They had reached Pallikulo Bay, Espiritu Santo in the New Hebrides Islands.

The New Hebrides were a group of islands 80 miles south of the newly secured island of Guadalcanal, where a six-month campaign finally wrested the strategic island from the Japanese. The island of Espiritu Santo was the most important of the Hebrides Islands because of its excellent harbor and airfield. In July 1942, it became the principal Allied base to support landings in Guadalcanal the following month. Buildup of supplies at Espiritu Santo began immediately and would be transported to the Solomon Islands and other forward bases for the next 18 months.

The following morning the *Ward* moved the short distance to Segond Bay, where the harbor was full of shipping. The crew recognized many ships they had seen before, such as the seaplane tender *Curtiss* that had been in Pearl Harbor on December 7, 1941.

Ward was put to work immediately, patrolling the northern approach to Espiritu Santo while at the same time acclimating her crew to the duties of an APD. *Ward* was now reunited with *Chew* and *Schley,* her sister ships from Pearl Harbor patrol days. She was already assigned to Transport Division 22, a group of APDs that would commence supply operations to the Solomon Islands shortly.[8]

Left behind as *Ward* began patrols was Seaman 2c Willie Woodward, who broke a leg while training to operate one of the landing craft hoists. He was transferred to the *Long Island,* which had the latest in medical facilities.

By March 16, *Ward's* crew began to wonder if anything had really changed besides the appearance of their ship. For a week since they arrived at Espiritu Santo they had been on harbor patrol similar to that which they performed at Pearl Harbor for most of 1941 and 1942. With frustration increasing, *Ward* was finally relieved on patrol by minelayer *Gamble,* another converted four-stacker, at 1225 on the 16th.

One welcome change did occur, however. *Ward's* crew was now able to have fresh bread, cakes, and other bakery items daily. Crewman Raymond Ballard received a Baker's rating and put it to use immediately in the galley house ovens. There were precious few reminders of home on a ship in the steamy South Pacific, and fresh bread would be one of the most cherished memories.

While refueling back in port, *Ward* received orders to escort a small convoy to Guadalcanal. At last she would enter the famed combat zone that her crew had been hearing about from crews of other ships. This is what they had trained for since they joined the reserves. *Ward* left the harbor at 1440 on March 18 to await her convoy, still in port. She would not only act as escort but as a transport as well. Her troop space was filled with men and her deck was piled with ammunition and supplies.

Thirty-seven minutes later, the freighter *Day Star* emerged from the harbor, followed by cargo ship *Adhara;* freighters *Lyman Beecher, Jig Turner;* and destroyers *Aaron Ward, Fletcher,* and minelayer *Gamble.* The convoy formed up and proceeded northwest on a course of 316 degrees at 11 knots. The war zone lay dead ahead, and that was *Ward's* destination.

A leak in a high pressure oil line forced *Ward* to drop out of the convoy at 2010 on March 19 to replace a blown gasket. Crewmen completed repairs in 15 minutes allowing *Ward* to steam at 25 knots to catch the convoy. At 2059 she was back in her assigned convoy station.

The Japanese discovered the convoy the following day when the *Fletcher* picked up a bogie on radar. She was ordered out to investigate it at 1036 and eight minutes later reported the intruder to be a two-engine bomber snooping on the convoy. At 1055 *Fletcher* fired a five-inch shell at the aircraft to pinpoint its location to the rest of the convoy. The bomber followed the convoy for another 20 minutes and all ships prepared for the inevitable raid which was sure to follow.

Suddenly, the aircraft dove at the convoy, dropping two bombs which near-missed the *Adhara*. Lemly ordered *Ward* to increase speed to 20 knots and to open fire on the bomber. All four three-inch guns cut loose and within a minute she added 23 rounds to the barrage put up by the escorts. Although angry black bursts of exploding shells surrounded the bomber, no hits were observed and the aircraft escaped to the north.

Sixteen minutes later, a PBY from Tulagi made an appearance over the convoy and stayed with it for some time. It would have been of little help if other Japanese planes appeared but it gave the convoy more eyes to locate additional trouble. The convoy reformed placing the four merchant ships in a single column with escorts ahead, astern, and on either flank. Convoy speed was maintained at 11½ knots with all lookouts scanning the sky for another attack. None materialized.

During the voyage, Lt. (jg) Richard Farwell, acting as Officer of the Deck during a mid-watch, received a lookout's report of a torpedo bearing 60 degrees relative. Seeing the phosphorescence from its wake, Farwell ordered "full right rudder" to comb the wake. Within minutes Captain Lemly was on the bridge and ordered full left rudder as the torpedo had now "changed course." The torpedo turned out to be a porpoise enjoying itself at the expense of *Ward's* crew.[9]

Early on March 21, the convoy sighted dark shapes in the dim light both to starboard and port. The shape to starboard was the Florida Island group; the mass to port became Guadalcanal, the jungle covered island which was the center of a ferocious six-month campaign of attrition of men, aircraft, and ships. In some of the most difficult fighting in history, United States forces finally wrested control from the Japanese over this inhospitable, hot, humid, and malaria-ridden piece of real estate.

The Japanese referred to Guadalcanal as "starvation island" and "the island of death" and it was exactly that. They lost more than 20,000 of the 32,000 men they committed to the ground combat with approximately half becoming the victims of disease and starvation. The Japanese evacuated 11,000 men by destroyers in a brilliant night operation barely a month before *Ward's* convoy appeared with additional men and supplies.

As dawn broke on the 21st, the convoy passed through Lengo Channel adjacent to the Guadalcanal shore. *Ward* escorted the *Jig Turner* to an anchorage along the shore for unloading. At long last *Ward's* crew gazed upon the island that had already become legendary in the South Pacific as the place where the Japanese advance had been stopped for the first time in the war. Veterans of that brutal campaign referred to it simply as "the canal."

Free of the *Jig Turner, Ward* steamed across the 20-mile-wide body of water between Guadalcanal and the Florida Islands now referred to as "iron bottom sound" or simply "the Sound." It was given that name in recognition of the many Japanese and American ships sunk in this area in the series of vicious and confusing night naval battles during the first four months of the campaign.

Guadalcanal did not have a natural harbor but there were several excellent anchorages across the Sound, including Purvis Bay, which became the home port of the U.S. Fleet in the lower Solomons. Various military installations, such as supply depots, hospitals, and administrative buildings had been constructed on nearby Tulagi Island. By 1012, *Ward* had

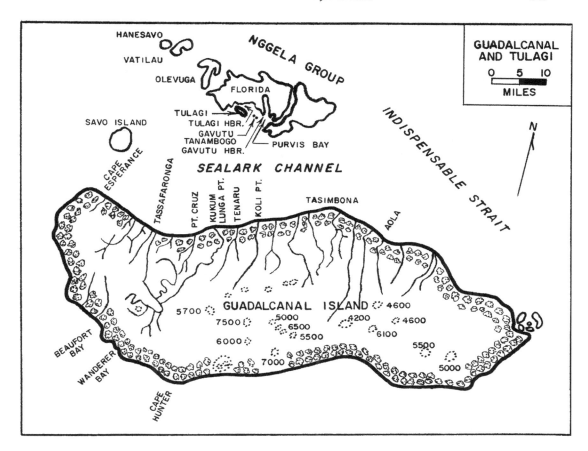

traversed the hallowed waters and safely anchored in Tulagi Harbor for replenishing. After refueling from yard oiler, YO-167, *Ward* moved the short distance to Purvis Bay to anchor for the night, her first in the war zone.

The following morning, *Ward* returned to the Guadalcanal shore to drop off supplies at Togoma Point and Lunga Bay. She was back at anchor in Purvis bay at 1532 of the 22nd.

On March 23, *Ward* returned to Togoma Point to pick up men and stores for the first of many supply runs out of Guadalcanal. With the big island now secure, the Allies poured troop, supplies, and equipment into it, creating a huge forward base. It would eventually replace Espiritu Santo as the advance base supplying the push through the Solomons. *Ward's* initial run would be to the newly occupied Russell Island group, 20 miles northwest of Guadalcanal.

The Japanese had used the Russells as a staging base for barge traffic to reinforce their garrison on Guadalcanal during the long campaign. When they evacuated Guadalcanal, they also left the Russell Islands. United States Army and Marine forces quickly followed the Japanese exit from the Russells by occupying it without resistance on February 21. From that day on, the Russells were provisioned by small landing craft escorted by APDs.[10]

Ward rendezvoused with LCT-159 at 1610 on the 23rd and escorted the landing craft toward the Russell Islands for 90 minutes. Then, APD *Sands* relieved her while *Ward* diverted to meet *Hopkins,* another converted four-stacker, now a minesweeper. *Hopkins* transferred to *Ward* sacks of mail destined for the Russells. With the mail stowed, *Ward* caught up with LCT-159 to resume escort duty.

At 2100 *Ward* observed anti-aircraft fire 15 miles away, signaling the presence of Japanese aircraft in the vicinity. She closed on LCT-159 to give her anti-aircraft protection and proceeded warily. She had not been attacked from the air since the Pearl Harbor raid but members of her crew who had been on board at the time remembered it well.

Anti-aircraft fire continued for several hours but always at a comfortable distance. *Ward's* gunners were tense as they watched explosions light up the sky to the north. At 2243, radar detected a plane approaching from starboard and all guns tracked on that bearing. Tensions increased as the aircraft continued toward the ship but relaxed when it was announced that the plane was a PBY on night patrol.

Ward and her small convoy continued on their way with all guns manned aware that they were vulnerable to attack by aircraft or submarine at any moment. The crew discovered that there was little time to relax in a war zone. This running of the gauntlet occurred often since supply runs consisting of several loaded landing craft escorted by an APD were made nightly.

This was *Ward's* initial run and she would make many more. The island-hopping campaign across the Pacific was just beginning and the Russell Islands was the first hop north from Guadalcanal. Construction of an airfield and buildup of the island as a supply depot had already begun. *Ward's* convoy reached the Russells without further incident and anchored in Renard Sound at 0050 on March 24.

LCT-159 was legendary in the South Pacific.[11] Commanded by Ensign John McNeill, the 114-foot landing craft with an 11-man crew had been a guinea pig in the scheme to transport LCTs across the Pacific by towing them behind freighters. The plan worked well until a severe storm parted the tow line. The crew was just barely rescued by a boat from the freighter as the landing craft disappeared in the driving wind and rain.

LCT-159 was not lost, however, and was found drifting near the Mexican coast. It was towed back to California and loaded on a liberty ship in sections for transport to New Caledonia, its original destination. McNeill, taken to Noumea after his rescue, spotted it arriving there and was reunited with it after both had almost perished in the storm. It was taken to Guadalcanal, where it became a workhorse for the navy.

The 159 made about 25 trips to the Russell Islands, carrying 150 tons of cargo on each trip. The routine was the same on every voyage. It loaded with men or supplies at Guadalcanal during the day and left for the Russells at dark with several other LCTs escorted by an APD. It arrived there early the following morning, unloaded, and returned to Tulagi the following evening. After one night's rest, the cycle would be repeated. Later, LCT-159 began making similar runs to New Georgia, where the shooting war was still being fought. Supply runs were always made after dark to avoid Japanese aircraft that prowled the area.

By 0731 on the March 24, LCT-159 was unloaded and left for Tulagi accompanied by *Ward*, destroyer *Sterrett*, and APD *Sands*. *Ward's* first mission was completed with only the distant anti-aircraft fire to keep it from being a "milk run." Before entering Purvis Bay, *Ward* took on provisions from transport *George Clymer* and refueled from transport *Fuller*.

Ward was on the move again on March 26, crossing the Sound to anchor off Togoma Point, Guadalcanal. She embarked Company K of the 169th Infantry Regiment and departed at 1919 with *Sands*, also loaded with troops of the 169th. With destroyers *Fletcher* and *Sterrett* escorting, the convoy made a cautious run to the Russells, anchoring in Polly Bay just after midnight. All four ships left Polly Bay as soon as the troops were unloaded.

The return trip was livened by anti-aircraft fire to starboard at 0319. The formation altered course and increased speed to 25 knots. At 0419 *Fletcher* cut loose with several five-inch salvos at an aircraft that *Ward* had not located. The aircraft flew off and silence returned once more. *Ward* anchored at 0635 on the 27th. With her second mission completed, she was filled with tension. The war had not yet come to the *Ward*, but it was getting closer.

On March 28, *Ward* again steamed across the Sound to Togoma Point, this time to pick up LCT-63 and LCT-323, which were still loading. The formation was under way at 1605 on the day's run to the Russell Islands. *Ward* led the LCTs and patrolled both flanks at 10 knots, searching with both sonar and radar. This voyage was totally uneventful and *Ward* led her convoy safely into Renard Sound at 0140 on the 29th. Seven hours later the landing craft were empty and *Ward* led them back to Purvis Bay, where they anchored at 1515.

Ward escorted LCTs 63, 159, and 323 to the Russells on March 30, once more on another quiet trip. Destroyer *Sterrett* provided additional escort on the return to Purvis Bay.

Another of the original 47th Division crew members left the ship on March 31. Anthony Ort, who was Gun Captain on Number One gun that fired the first shot of the war on December 7, 1941, was reassigned with orders to report to San Francisco.

Ward made the trip to the Russells again on April 1, on what was now becoming a routine. She was escorting LCT-159 but herself carried four officers and 75 men of the 103rd Provisional Anti-aircraft Battery. The troops were to staff and man several batteries of three-inch guns just set up on the islands.

Ward dropped off the men at Wernham Bay and led LCT-159 back four hours later. After dropping off two passengers at Lunga Point, Guadalcanal, *Ward* returned to Tulagi, where she refueled from oiler *Kanawha*. This would be the last time *Ward* would refuel from the oiler. In a week the *Kanawha* would be lying in deep water offshore Tulagi, the victim of Japanese bombers.

Ward picked up 63 navy personnel at Koli Point, Guadalcanal, on April 3, transporting them to Tulagi. On the 4th, *Ward* and *Sands* picked up officers and men of the 169th Infantry Regiment at Togoma Point for another run to the Russells, dropping them off at Pepesala Bay just after midnight.

On April 5th, *Ward* returned to Togoma Bay to pick up LCTs 60 and 62, which she took to Renard Bay in the Russells. On the return trip on the 6th, lookouts spotted a floating buoy. Captain Lemly used the opportunity to give his 20-mm gun crews some target practice. Guns One, Two, and Four fired 60 rounds apiece. In less than 24 hours, this practice would come in extremely handy.

Ward refueled from the *Erskine Phelps* as soon as she returned to Tulagi on the 6th and crossed the Sound immediately to rendezvous with LCTs 58, 182, and 369 off Lunga Point. At 1715 the convoy weighed anchor for another supply run. On the passage to the Russells, *Ward* observed anti-aircraft fire over Tulagi but reached Wernham Cove in the early morning of April 7 without further incident.

Lookouts were nervous, as it was apparent that Japanese aircraft were close by. While *Ward* was waiting for the LCTs to finish unloading, two Japanese bombers suddenly dove out of the darkness, dropping bombs on a ship only a mile away. While no damage was done, this attack was a harbinger of things to come. The day would get wild before it ended and men would die on both sides.

Destroyer *Aaron Ward* joined the convoy for the return to Tulagi and then left the formation for Lunga Point. It was the last time that *Ward* would see her namesake. *Ward* anchored at Tulagi at 1348 but her peace would be short-lived. She was about to become involved in a major Japanese air offensive, "Operation I."

Operation I was the last Japanese offensive in the Southern Solomons and planned by Admiral Yamamoto as a face-saving gesture for losing Guadalcanal. His goal was to destroy the newly won Allied bases in the Solomon Islands as a means of disrupting Allied plans for further moves up the Solomon chain.[12]

Yamamoto was able to marshal a sizeable aerial force for the offensive, consisting of 166 carrier planes plus 200 land-based naval aircraft. Under cover of Japanese fighters, Japanese troop reinforcements were landed on Kolombangara Island in the central Solomons on April 4 and 5.

Japanese submarines were involved as well but on April 5, submarine *RO-34* was discovered and sunk by destroyer *O'Bannon* in a surface battle. At noon on April 7, U.S. cruisers *Honolulu, St. Louis,* and *Helena* left Tulagi with six destroyers, with the intention of surprising some of the Japanese naval units reinforcing Kolombangara. Before the cruisers got very far from Tulagi, they received word that a huge force of Japanese aircraft were on the way to the Guadalcanal area. They were immediately ordered to head southwest out of the area at full speed.

There were more than 30 other Allied ships in Iron Bottom Sound, however, and they could not all flee. Many were in the process of unloading supplies. These would still make a lucrative target for the first large raid of Operation I.

At 1226 on April 7, Allied coast watchers on Bougainville observed large numbers of Japanese aircraft taking off from their airfields at Kahili, Buka, and Ballale on the southern tip of the island. They reported this to Guadalcanal immediately and Allied shipping was about to feel the fury of Operation I. The Japanese air armada included 67 dive bombers, several torpedo planes, and 110 escorting Zero fighters, a force larger than any they had assembled since the Pearl Harbor raid.[13]

With the advance warning provided by the coast watchers, 76 army and marine fighters were scrambled from the several airfields on Guadalcanal. They climbed immediately and orbited at various altitudes over the Sound awaiting the Japanese force some distance out. All the ingredients for a gigantic air battle were now in place. At 1400, the Russell Island radar station detected the bogies while they were still 75 miles from Guadalcanal. A tremendous battle was about to erupt and *Ward* would be in the middle of it.

All ships in the Sound were alerted to the incoming raid but no aircraft could be seen anywhere. *Ward* left Tulagi a half-hour earlier on her way to Guadalcanal and had been following the radio reports of the impending raid intently. When the reports placed the Japanese in the vicinity of Guadalcanal, Captain Lemly called the ship to General Quarters. *Ward's* radar operator, Joseph Strapp, first picked up the aircraft at 72,000 yards (41 miles) and notified the captain. Lemly realized that the attackers would be overhead in less than 15 minutes and ordered, "Speed 20 knots! Commence zigzag pattern!"

Minutes later it happened! The biggest air battle of the Solomons broke out over Iron Bottom Sound and sheer madness erupted.

Japanese dive bombers dove out of the cloud cover over Savo Island, and Yamamoto's wish for a major air battle was about to become reality. At 1512 *Ward's* lookouts spotted many fighters and bombers overhead. Lemly did not hesitate. "All guns fire independently! Commence firing!"[14] *Ward's* first fight for survival had begun.

Ward immediately opened up with all four three-inch guns. Three minutes later the range shortened and the 20-mm mounts commenced firing as well. The noise of all guns firing simultaneously shattered the quiet of the afternoon. This was a rare occurrence on the ship.

Will Lehner was a loader on the Number Four three-inch gun on the after deck house.

"The sky was black with planes," recalled Lehner. "We had no trouble finding a target and our gun was firing as fast as we could ram shells into it. It was pointing almost vertically. The planes did not bomb or strafe us but came over at a high altitude. They were dive bombing other ships all around us, however."

A Marine fighter chased a Japanese plane right past *Ward*. All guns that would bear fired at it and somehow missed both aircraft. The sky was now becoming a madhouse with several hundred aircraft zooming in all directions. Dogfights broke out everywhere and the intensity of the aerial combat was apparent even to those at sea level. The chatter of machine guns and 20-mm cannons was constant and provided an appropriate background for the angry bark of *Ward's* three-inch battery. Iron Bottom Sound was quickly transformed into a wild, noisy scene with hundreds of guns on the ships adding to the chaos.

Orv Ethier was a loader on a 20-mm mount and noticed a group of torpedo planes coming toward them. "I thought to myself, this is it, we've had it," he mused. "But they left us alone and flew right past us. They were after bigger ships than ours." *Ward's* gunners shot the tail off one of them and it crashed close astern. The others swerved right around the *Ward,* some flying past the bow, others past the stern, to attack other ships.

The presence of so many Allied ships in the Sound saved the *Ward* from serious damage or even sinking. There were simply too many larger targets between Guadalcanal and Tulagi for aircraft to pay much attention to an 1100-ton APD.

The pandemonium in the air now reached down to the water level as ships began darting in all directions to escape the madness in the sky. Aircraft streaming black smoke and flames were falling all around *Ward*. In many cases it was not even possible to know whether they were friendly or enemy, only that another pilot had been killed or seriously wounded. Two of them were Japanese bombers that *Ward* splashed herself with, direct hits from her three-inch guns.

Incredibly, with dozens of anchored or slow moving ships at their mercy, the Japanese armada scored relatively few hits. The 18-month old destroyer *Aaron Ward,* which had moved closer to LST-449 to give her some anti-aircraft protection was struck by several bombs. She was hit hard and immobilized while rescue boats surrounded her to fight fires and take off the crew. She would later sink while under tow.[15]

LST-449 was on a supply run from Espiritu Santo, bringing in a variety of equipment and stores for the buildup on Guadalcanal. It was also transporting a number of army troops and navy personnel. One of these was a young junior grade naval lieutenant who was assigned to a motor torpedo squadron based at Tulagi. He was eagerly looking forward to seeing combat action, but didn't expect it to occur while he was a passenger on the LST. He would soon experience combat at a much closer range than he wanted and would hold high public office later in life. His name was Lt.(jg) John F. Kennedy.[16]

The 14,500-ton oiler *Kanawha* also took two bomb hits that started huge fires. She had to be abandoned when it was apparent that she was in danger of sinking. Later she was towed to Tulagi and beached to keep her from sinking. The efforts to save her were suddenly halted when she slipped off the sand into deep water and was gone forever.

The New Zealand corvette *Moa* was fueling from the oiler *Erskine Phelps* and did not receive word of the impending raid. Bombers were attracted to the two ships lying side by side and quickly targeted them. Two bombs aimed at the oiler missed but hit the *Moa,* sinking her within minutes. Several other ships in the Sound were damaged by near-misses, including LST-449, and several by "friendly fire." Only the *Aaron Ward, Kanawha,* and *Moa* were actually sunk.[17]

Six 550-pound bombs landed within 75 feet of LST-449, one only ten feet off its bow. They lifted the ship and sprayed water and shrapnel over its deck. Fortunately no bomb hit the craft for among its deck cargo, in addition to Lt (jg) Kennedy, was a load of bombs. The ship took on water but damage was repaired within days. It left the Sound expecting further raids, and it was not until April 12 that it returned to unload cargo and passengers.

While maneuvering after the raid, LST-449 cruised by the wreckage of a Japanese bomber with its pilot in the water. With rescue on his mind the LST's skipper slowed to pick him up. When the pilot pulled out his pistol and fired several shots at the ship, soldiers at the rail riddled him with gunfire.

Although the attack appeared to those on *Ward* to last for hours, the sky was soon clear of Japanese aircraft. Several dozen smoke columns around the Sound marked the burial site of a bomber and pilot or one of the several Allied fighters downed in the fierce combat.

Ward emerged from the attack unscathed, the biggest scare caused by a stick of six bombs that exploded close astern in her wake. During the seven minutes of the most furious action, her gunners had fired 153 rounds of three-inch shells and hundreds of rounds of 20-mm ammunition. Among the 12 dive bombers shot down during the raid were three felled by *Ward*.[18] Twenty-seven Zeros were also knocked down by Allied fighters or anti-aircraft fire. Allied air losses were seven fighters but only one pilot.[19]

The Japanese conducted three more raids as part of Operation I, all in New Guinea. These accomplished very little and resulted in the loss of 21 more Japanese aircraft. Exaggerated claims by returning Japanese pilots led Admiral Yamamoto to conclude that the raids had achieved great success. On April 16 he called off the operation and recalled the aircraft to Truk. Two days later Yamamoto was dead.[20]

Calm returned to the scene by 1600, and by 1730 *Ward* took her station as escort to a convoy of five empty cargo ships. Three other destroyers, *Sterrett*, *Farenholt* and *Taylor* also joined the screen. Their destination was Espiritu Santo. The voyage was without incident except for a possible submarine which was investigated by *Sterrett*. It proved negative and the convoy moored in Segond Bay, Espiritu Santo at 0808 on April 10.

Ward took on fuel and ammunition and then tied up next to the destroyer tender *Dixie* for a week to receive a tender overhaul. Short of receiving a repair yard overhaul, a tender overhaul was the next best thing. Fully-equipped repair yards were rare in the South Pacific. Heavy maintenance and some overhaul could be provided by tenders designed for that purpose. *Dixie*, a 9450-ton tender, was a floating machine shop and equipped and staffed to repair, overhaul, and supply destroyers of all types. As part of the overhaul, *Ward* received another 20-mm gun on her forecastle.[21]

Orders for a new assignment came through on April 18 and *Ward* embarked three officers and 153 men of B Company, 4th Battalion, of the 1st Marine Raider Regiment for amphibious training. *Ward* took the men to Powell Point in the New Hebrides the following morning where they disembarked. The boats returned with the men, were hoisted aboard, and after cruising for several hours, the operation repeated. The landing was made for the third time after dark.

An event of enormous significance occurred in the Solomons on April 18 while *Ward* was conducting practice landings. Using intercepted Japanese messages Allied code breakers were able to discover that the Admiral of the Japanese Combined Fleet, Isoruku Yamamoto, would be making a trip to bases on the southern tip of Bougainville on the 18th. In one of the most daring and well planned aerial operations of the war, a flight of

P-38s, flying from Guadalcanal, intercepted Yamamoto's aircraft as it was preparing to land on Bougainville. They shot down the Betty bomber killing the mastermind of the Pearl Harbor attack and Commander in Chief of the Japanese Navy and another carrying a number of his staff.[22]

On April 20, the marines were landed once more, this time on Malekula Island, where they conducted combat exercises including a night maneuver. *Ward* finally returned the tired marines to Segond Bay on April 21. Even then, the marines were not done, and *Ward* dropped them off on Malekula Island again on April 22 and picked them up on the 23rd.

Ward took a break from landing exercises and joined *Schley* and *Crosby* in live firing exercises on April 26. Using their three-inch guns on a target towed by tender *Dixie*, the APDs made three runs in daylight and a fourth after dark using searchlight illumination. They followed with two more runs using star shells for illumination.

Drills continued on the 27th as the APDs again honed their combat skills. After conducting joint anti-submarine maneuvers they resumed anti-aircraft drills, firing on a sleeve target towed by a PBY. *Ward* used all four of her three-inch and all seven of her 20-mm guns. The APDs returned to Segond Bay for refueling following the exercise. It was obvious from the emphasis on anti-aircraft drills that *Ward* would be returning to the combat zone soon.

That came on April 29, when the three APDs joined by destroyer *Gwin* left Espiritu Santo and formed up as escort to a convoy of six merchantmen. The convoy proceeded at 9 knots on course 335 degrees, which would take it to Guadalcanal. Destroyer *Farenholt* joined the escort on May 1.

The convoy reached Iron Bottom Sound safely on May 2. *Ward*, *Schley*, and *Gwin* followed *Patapsco*, *Algorab* and *Weltevreden* which split off from the convoy to anchor off Tenaru Point, Guadalcanal. After providing a submarine screen while the ships unloaded, *Ward* steamed to Tulagi for refueling from *Eskine Phelps*. *Ward* returned to Guadalcanal to screen unloading operations until May 9.

Erskine Phelps, an oil-stained former four-masted schooner, was stationed at Tulagi as an immobile yard oiler. With only ten-foot stubs of her masts still showing, she was indeed a strange sight in the harbor. Her crews had endured many air raids and claimed four aircraft with their 20-mm guns.

After a quiet week, *Ward escorted* merchant ship *Vitus Bering* south out of Japanese aircraft range and rendezvoused with cargo ship *Libra* on its way to Guadalcanal from Espiritu Santo. *Ward* reversed course and escorted *Libra* northward.

At midday on May 13, *Ward* picked up a bogie on radar and tracked it as it approached. The aircraft remained out of sight until 1205 when it suddenly dropped out of the clouds and made a high speed pass at *Libra*. It was a two-engine bomber that dropped three bombs and climbed back into the clouds. The bombs landed 500 yards off the starboard bow of the merchant ship which managed to get off three rounds of anti-aircraft fire. Neither the bomber nor the *Libra* was damaged in the encounter.

Ward closed up tighter on *Libra* for the remainder of the voyage and both ships reached Guadalcanal safely on the following day. On May 15, after *Libra* had unloaded and *Ward* had refueled, *Ward* led *Libra* out of the Sound on the return trip to Noumea, New Caledonia.

Guadalcanal had hardly dropped out of sight astern when lookouts sighted a bogie approaching. *Ward* went to General Quarters and increased speed to 20 knots, anticipating an attack. At 1252 a Betty bomber dropped down from the clouds and dropped a single bomb that exploded 300 yards off *Ward's* starboard beam.[23] The bomber climbed back into the clouds and continued to track the ships for two hours before flying away. The ships arrived safely in Noumea on May 18 and *Ward* remained there for 22 days, her longest stay in any port during the entire war.

New Caledonia, a Free-French colony during World War II, was the principal of several islands administered from Noumea, its capital. Its inhabitants included both Europeans and Pacific natives. Noumea's harbor, Great Road, was an excellent anchorage and the island quickly became a main Allied staging base for the first two years of the war.

Noumea soon became known as the "Pearl Harbor of the South Pacific," with several bars, cafes, and parks.[24] The sleepy town of several thousand French colonial inhabitants and dusty tree-lined streets became an attraction for crews of every ship visiting the island. The streets soon filled with sailors, all looking for excitement and finding little. Government-licensed brothels, however, could be found by those seeking those services.

A USO and officers' clubs sprang up to serve the thousands of servicemen on the streets on a typical day. For officers, most visited the former Hotel du Pacifique. The picturesque hotel had been converted into an officer's club and became the social center for officers. The two-story building, with a walled compound and tree-filled courtyard, was jammed with men seeking cold drinks, something rare in the South Pacific. At 15 cents for a can of beer and 25 cents for a mixed drink, this was the ideal place for officers to make up for the lack of liquor aboard ship.[34]

Except for Pearl Harbor and Sydney, Noumea would be the most exciting liberty port that *Ward's* crew would visit in the Pacific. The crew used the time to explore the island and find entertainment and excitement where they could.

Ward was back in the war on June 9. She embarked 50 officers and men of the 97th Field Artillery Battalion and weighed anchor at 0725 on June 10. As it left the harbor all seven of her 20-mm guns conducted a live firing drill on a target sleeve towed by a PBY. Outside the harbor, *Ward* joined a convoy designated as TU (Task Unit) 32.7.2 consisting of LSTs 340, 341, 343, 395, 396, and 398 bound for Guadalcanal at nine knots. *Ward* and *Trever,* a four-stacker converted to a mine sweeper, provided the escort.

Anticipating Japanese air attacks when the convoy reached Guadalcanal, friendly aircraft conducted mock dive bombing attacks on the 11th. It was followed by live firing by all available anti-aircraft guns on sleeve targets. All of *Ward's* guns joined the action. The seas on the 12th were choppy, causing the LSTs to roll badly. Army personnel lined the rails to empty their stomachs in their first experience on an LST in rolling seas.

On June 13, LST-398 sighted an unidentified white object overhead. Although *Trever's* radar screen was clear, the LST's CO gave the LST permission to fire. After three rounds of three-inch fire, the Task Unit commander on LST-340 sent a terse message to LST-398, "Cease firing, you are shooting at the planet Venus." The incident provided some levity for the entire convoy and the story made the rounds of the entire South Pacific. Needless to say, LST-398 did not hit its target.[25]

On June 14, LST-397 and minesweeper *Hopkins,* which had diverted earlier to Espiritu Santo, were sighted and joined the convoy. Two friendly aircraft joined the escort for the remainder of the cruise. As darkness approached, the Task Unit commander issued orders prohibiting the ships from firing at aircraft in case of a night attack. Total concealment was a better defense than anti-aircraft fire.

At midnight the dark land mass sighted at 15 miles proved to be Guadalcanal. As dawn approached, nerves tightened. It was reassuring to see daylight, but it also increased the chance of an attack. None came and the convoy anchored off Lunga Point in a pouring rain on the afternoon of June 15.

After screening the LSTs for several hours, *Ward* started across the Sound to anchor at Purvis Bay for the night. Her radar suddenly picked up bogies in the vicinity and anti-aircraft fire erupted over Tulagi. For a half-hour the sky was lit up by streams of fire from ships and shore. Then the raid ended as quickly as it started, and *Ward* finally anchored for the night.

Japanese aircraft were over Guadalcanal or Tulagi almost every night, attempting to disrupt the buildup of supplies for additional landings further up the chain of islands. On some nights a single-engine aircraft would cruise over the island, keeping everyone on the ground awake. On other nights, a bomber, with its twin engines deliberately out of synchronization, would make pass after pass over the island dropping bombs on some passes. Eventually the Allies developed night fighters to deal with "Wash Machine Charlie" and "Louie the Louse" as the troops named them.[26]

On June 5, while *Ward* was in Noumea, 81 Zeros attacked the shipping and were met by 110 Allied fighters. Thirty-four Zeros did not return to their base that night. They sent another large force down the "Slot" on June 12 with similar results. On the morning of the 16th *Ward's* crew expected more trouble soon. It came later that very day.

The morning was unusually hot with few scattered clouds. After refueling from oiler *Monongahela, Ward* left for Guadalcanal for further orders. The day that had started out peaceful was about to turn ugly. At 1345 *Ward's* radar screen became active and showed blips to the north. The Captain called the ship to General Quarters immediately. Within minutes lookouts spotted dive bombers heading for the LSTs beached on Koli Point for unloading. "All guns, independent fire. Commence firing!" was the order from the bridge.

The aircraft took out their fury on *Ward* immediately. Three Val dive bombers came directly at the ship at 500- to 1000-foot altitudes.[27] The first plane straddled the ship's stern, throwing up three geysers no more than 50 yards away as all guns that could bear fired at it. The second plane approached even lower and again straddled the ship, this time near the bridge. Two bombs exploded to port, one to starboard. The explosions only 20 to 50 yards away showered the ship with shrapnel and spray. The third bomber dropped a single missile that barely missed the twisting ship to port.

Each plane also strafed *Ward* in its approach. Remarkably, neither the strafing nor the bombing caused a single casualty. *Ward's* luck continued to hold. The ship was fighting back hard with everything that would fire, creating a din that was continuous. She began extracting a heavy toll on her attackers.

Her Number Four 20-mm gun hit a Val in the engine cowling and cockpit area with about twenty rounds as it passed right over the ship. The plane rose to about 600 feet, shuddered, and then plunged straight down, splashing 800 yards off the starboard bow. It appeared that one of the shells had killed the pilot.

Number Seven 20-mm fired at a Val at about a 700-feet altitude with an accurate burst that chopped off its tail. It spiraled to the water tail-less about 1000 yards away.

Number One three-inch gun on the forecastle scored a direct hit on another Val's engine at a distance of 500 yards. The bomber disappeared in a spectacular explosion scattering debris over a wide area. The crew of Number Three three-inch gun spotted three bombers about 1300 yards away and closing. They hit one of them blowing its right wing off. It spiraled slowly into the sea a mile from *Ward*.

Other bombers also came close enough to *Ward* to feel her wrath. Her gunners hit three more but not hard enough to bring them down. All managed to flee but some may not have made it back to their base.

Every ship in the Sound was firing with all guns and filling the air with angry, black and deadly bursts. Destroyer *O'Bannon*, with her five five-inch guns and all anti-aircraft batteries blazing, looked like she was on fire.

Ward maneuvered close to the cargo ship *Celeno* to give her some anti-aircraft protection. Within minutes the *Celeno* took two bomb hits starting a huge fire that eventually destroyed most of her cargo. Will Lehner, on *Ward's* Number Four three-inch gun, saw the bomb explosions. "One bomb hit a pile of lumber on her deck," he recalled. "Wood splinters flew in all directions and sprayed *Ward's* deck."

Another bomb penetrated the deck and exploded in one of *Celeno's* holds. All of her holds contained bombs with the exception of one that contained medical supplies. That's where the bomb exploded. *Ward* was lucky again. *Celeno's* crew was able to beach the ship and, although badly burned, it was later salvaged.[28]

Two minutes after the *Celeno* was hit, LST-340, which the *Ward* had shepherded up from New Caledonia, was attacked by three bombers from a group of nine. It was crammed full of vehicles and troops. Three bombs hit among her deck cargo of jeeps, trucks, and gasoline, killing a number of men and starting a massive fire that threatened to destroy the ship. With power lost and the flames spreading, the troops abandoned the ship and swam toward nearby boats launched by a Seabee battalion. The LST had just enough forward motion to nudge its nose onto the sand of the Guadalcanal shore. LSTs 353 and 398 came alongside to help fight the fires and brought them under control four hours later.

At 1430, *Ward* ceased firing. In an 18-minute bedlam, the ship had fired 155 rounds of three-inch shells and more than 500 rounds of 20-mm ammunition. The Japanese had sent over 120 aircraft, their third largest raid of the war. Anti-aircraft fire and Allied fighters were credited with downing 107 of them in an air battle that lasted two hours.[29] Four of them belonged to *Ward*.[30]

Tensions were still high as *Ward, Schley, Dent,* and *Crosby* patrolled off Guadalcanal for the next four days. Japanese aircraft were spotted every day but only a handful at a time. *Ward* sent four rounds of three-inch shells at them on June 18 to keep them at a distance.

Ward now got a needed respite from the daily tension when she was assigned to TU 32.4.4 with *O'Bannon* and minesweeper *Skylark* to escort a convoy of freighters to Espiritu Santo. At 0955 on June 22, the escorts led *Aludra, Deimos,* and *Nathaniel Currier* out of Lengo Channel at 10 knots.

Trouble soon found *Ward* again. She was echo-ranging continuously and had both air and surface radars searching 360 degrees around the ship as the convoy plodded through the daylight and evening hours. Suddenly at 0445 of the 23rd, the silence was broken by two explosions ahead of *Ward*. From the bridge *Ward's* officers could see a steady white light on deck of the *Aludra* and black smoke pouring from the *Deimos*. There were no enemy ships or aircraft in sight to account for the explosions, however.

A hurried exchange of signals cleared up the mystery shortly. Both ships had taken a torpedo in the port side and were sinking.[31] Another torpedo fired at *Nathaniel Currier* just missed the ship's bow.

The convoy was thrown into even more confusion when a bogie aircraft was detected on radar. It ducked in and out of the clouds but did not attack. At 0500 two ships were picked up on radar as well, as that patch of ocean was becoming crowded. These were later identified as the Patrol Craft *YP-514* and *YP-518*.

The convoy commander ordered the *Ward* to escort *Nathaniel Currier* out of the area immediately and the two ships moved out at 12.6 knots, the freighter's best speed. The *Skylark* and other escorts remained to pick up the crew of *Aludra* and the *Deimos* from their boats and the water while *O'Bannon* searched for the sub. *Aludra* sank at 0733 and *Deimos* at 1233, both from gunfire from *O'Bannon*.

Twenty-five of the thirty-five army troops sleeping on deck of *Aludra* when torpedoed were killed along with three of her crew. A number of crewmen on *Deimos* were lost also. The sinkings were the work of Lt. Rickinosuke Ichimura in submarine *RO-103*.[32] He had penetrated Iron Bottom Sound and lay in wait for lucrative targets. The two ships were his only successes of the war. *RO-103,* itself, was sunk on July 28.

After picking up survivors *O'Bannon* sped off after the remnants of her convoy and rejoined *Ward* and *Nathaniel Currier* at 0737 on the June 24. The ships were safely moored in Segond Bay, Espiritu Santo at 0843 on the 25th. After refueling *Ward* left immediately for Noumea, New Caledonia, reaching the island base at 1117 on June 27. After refueling *Ward* nested alongside tender *Whitney* for overhaul and replenishment of supplies. She also filled her ammunition bunker taking on 350 rounds of three-inch shells and 4000 rounds of 20mm shells from ammunition ship *Lassen*.

On July 4 *Ward* moved into floating dry-dock ARD-2 in Noumea Harbor for cleaning and overhaul of her underwater surfaces. Her crew had the pleasure of celebrating a very hot Independence Day by scraping and steel brushing her bottom plates. When a crewman punched a hole through a plate, an inspector threatened to have the ship sent stateside as un-seaworthy. The captain, in rather strong language, rejected the suggestion and told him that they would repair the hole themselves.[33]

On July 6, *Ward* took on torpedoes, depth charges, 1000 rounds of five-inch ammunition, and other ordnance items all destined for Tulagi. She also embarked 150 troops for Guadalcanal. By July 9, a convoy was assembled and *Ward* joined destroyers *Gridley* and *Stringham* as escorts. Their charges were oiler *Cache* (AO-67) and cargo ships *Kenmore* and *SS Kotaagoeng*.

The formation, designated CTU 32.4.6, steamed north at 12.3 knots. A day out of Guadalcanal, destroyer *Ellet* joined the escort and the convoy anchored at Lunga Point without incident on July 13. After disembarking her troops, *Ward* took a screening position while the cargo ships unloaded.

Ward's baptism of fire was now over. She had transported hundreds of troops, countless tons of supplies, and escorted dozens of ships in and out of the combat zone in the past four months. In the process she had been strafed and bombed and had witnessed ships sunk and men killed around her. She had taken a toll of the enemy herself by shooting down at least seven aircraft.

Her crew, now battle-tested in the ways of the South Pacific, were bona fide combat veterans. One item was still absent from her combat record as an APD. She had net yet landed troops on a hostile shore. That was about to change.

CHAPTER 12

Amphibious Operations Begin

Although the crew of *Ward* did not know it, the ship had just ended one phase of her career and was about to begin another. For the past four months *Ward* had been carrying troops and cargo and escorting other cargo-carrying ships to Guadalcanal and the Russell Islands to build a huge supply depot there. The plan was to make Guadalcanal a staging base for future operations further up the Solomon's chain. While Guadalcanal was the first step on the road to Tokyo, additional steps were about to be taken.

Japanese aircraft and submarines still threatened shipping in the Guadalcanal and Tulagi area, as the gigantic raid of June 16 proved. That day, however, was the zenith of Japanese air attacks in the Solomons; these raids would diminish in frequency and intensity as the summer wore on.

Some of the Japanese airfields on southern Bougainville that were used to attack Guadalcanal were methodically being destroyed in preparation for amphibious landings on that island later in the year. Huge Japanese aircraft losses over Guadalcanal from April to June reached a level that Japanese air fleets could no longer sustain. They were losing the aerial battle of attrition at Guadalcanal just as they had lost the naval and ground battles of attrition there earlier.

Guadalcanal was about to become a backwater in the Pacific war as the Allies looked north. *Ward's* future missions would take her to new hotspots in the Solomon Islands and to New Guinea, where ground combat was still being waged fiercely.

During the past several months, it became apparent that *Ward* had fallen heir to some of the most skillful small-boat handlers in the entire navy. In February *Ward* picked up a contingent of coxswains in her brief stop at Pearl Harbor. These men would operate *Ward's* four landing craft. They had all either been skippers or first mates on shrimp boats in Florida before joining the service.[1] All were dedicated, fearless and extraordinary boat handlers. Four of them — Robert Ballantine, Louis Bennet, Arlo Beazley, and James Snead — would still be handling *Ward's* boats 22 months later on *Ward's* final day.

At 0849 on July 17, *Ward* anchored off Tetere, Guadcanal, where she took on 40 tons of field rations and personal gear followed by 154 officers and men of Company N of the 4th Marine Raider Battalion.[2] *Ward*, along with *Kilty, Waters,* and *McKean,* also loaded with troops, left Guadalcanal later in the day escorted by destroyers *Taylor, Ellet, Maury,* and *Gridley.* The APDs, designated as TransDiv22, were on their way to Enogai inlet on New Georgia Island in the Central Solomons.

This strategic island, only 90 miles northwest of Guadalcanal, was invaded by U.S. troops in June. Combat in the dense rain forest terrain of New Georgia was extremely difficult, with movement through the jungle almost impossible.

Earlier, a landing of 2600 men, under Colonel Harry Liversedge at Rice Anchorage on

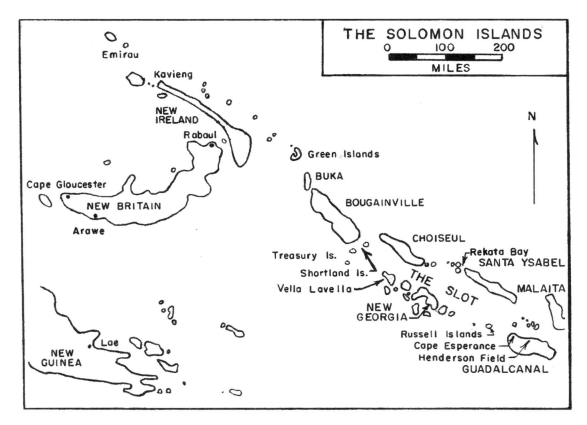

the island's northwest shore, was intended to stop the flow of Japanese reinforcements from nearby Kolombangara Island. Japanese troops and supplies were being barged across Kula Gulf nightly. Liversedge found conditions of supply so terrible that his men were reduced to eating captured Japanese rice. A supply run on July 11 helped, but his men were out of food and supplies soon again. The jungle quickly wore down the men and he needed reinforcements badly.

TransDiv22 was well aware that the Japanese also used naval units in Kula Gulf to bring in reinforcements to New Georgia. The Gulf had been the scene of two fierce night battles within the past 12 days resulting in the loss of cruiser *Helena* and destroyer *Gwin*. Several other U.S. ships were badly mauled. The Japanese also lost heavily.

The APDs hugged the coast of the jungle island and safely reached Enogai in total darkness at 0050 on July 18. They disembarked 700 marines in two hours and silently crept out of the Gulf at 0310. These reinforcements allowed Colonel Liversedge to maintain a critical blocking force for several additional days and turn the tide of the land battle. Trans-Div22 was back in Purvis Bay at 1434 on the 18th, ready for the next mission.

It came two days later. At Togoma Point *Ward* loaded supplies and 103 officers and men of an anti-tank company, 39 men of a service company of the 161st Infantry Regiment, and 24 men of Company A of the 25th Medical Battalion.[3] By 1745 *Ward* was under way with *Kilty, McKean, Waters, Stringham*, and *Crosby* of TransDiv22 escorted by destroyers *Stack* and *Lang*.

Proceeding cautiously but still making 18 knots, the ships cruised in two columns with 850 yards between the columns and 400-yard separation between ships. The convoy eased into Onaiavisi channel of the south shore of New Georgia and disembarked the troops at 0505 on July 21. The troops would reinforce ground units attacking the Japanese strongpoint at Munda, units that had been decimated by combat and jungle ailments.

Unloading was completed at 0625 and the convoy departed Onaiavisi to return to Tulagi. Seventeen minutes later *Ward* spotted unidentified aircraft and cut loose with 14 rounds from her three-inch guns to discourage them from coming closer. The APDs were safely at anchor at Tulagi at 1540.

Among the Allied craft based at Tulagi were several squadrons of PT boats. These small but speedy craft were assigned a variety of missions, including interdicting Japanese night supply missions. Because their own designated supply chain was not well defined, creative PT skippers borrowed supplies where ever they could, including APDs. *Ward* was often the object of their requests.

On a hot, windy day a young PT skipper approached *Ward* to borrow a bilge pump. Rough water had stove in a plywood patch on his squadron commander's PT boat causing it to take in water. The skipper, seeing an APD in the distance, was sure it would have a pump and lost no time in reaching it. Captain Lemly complied with the request and ordered a bilge pump brought on deck and transferred to the PT boat. With the pump on board, the PT boat raced back to its companion boat to save it from sinking. Transfer of the pump did not go smoothly and in the operation one of the PT boat crewmen suffered a broken kneecap and nose.[4]

The boat borrowing the pump from *Ward* would soon be sunk by a Japanese destroyer. It was PT-109; its young skipper who survived the incident was John F. Kennedy. In later years *Ward* crewmen remembered well the PT's youthful looking commanding officer. They had seen him several times but at that time he was just another PT sailor whose name they did not know.[5]

On July 24, *Ward's* number was called again and she steamed across the Sound to pick up LST-353 loaded with supplies and troops. This time they were bound for the newly occupied island of Rendova, across Blanche Channel from New Georgia. The two ships left Lunga Roads at 1437 with *Ward* making less than 12 knots to stay with the LST. The uneventful trip was highlighted only by the discovery of seven ships traveling a parallel course in the darkness. They turned out to be U.S. destroyers. *Ward* dropped off the LST and sped back to Purvis Bay alone.

At night, an APD carrying troops in enemy waters had no friends. All aircraft, ships, and submarines were assumed to be the enemy. On one of *Ward's* nighttime forays into the New Georgia area, she was attempting to clear the vicinity at her best speed when a deep booming voice was heard on the TBS radio. "TERRIERS, THIS IS BULLDOG, I HAVE TWO SKUNKS ON A BEARING OF...." The voice was immediately recognized as that of Arleigh Burke, legendary skipper of Destroyer Squadron 23, more commonly referred to as "31 knot Burke."

After several viscous night battles in the Solomons, Burke now was inclined to shoot first and ask questions later when picking up radar contacts in unfriendly waters. Apparently *Ward's* IFF identification system was not operating and her officers suspected that they were the "skunks" in Burke's message. They realized that the next message from Burke would be in the form of shells and torpedoes. They wasted no time in identifying themselves to him.[6]

TransDiv 22 was on the move on July 31, when all six APDs (*Ward, Kilty, Talbot, McKean, Stringham & Waters*) were ordered to Kukum beach to embark the 27th Regimental

A lookout on *Ward* keeps an eye out for enemy aircraft, submarines, or ships during one of her many supply missions in the South Pacific. Note the 20mm gun barrel above his head. (National Archives)

Combat Team of the 25th Infantry Division.[7] With destroyers *Maury, Gridley, Craven,* and *Dunlap* as escorts, the convoy left Kukum at 1741 heading up the Slot at 18 knots. It reached its destination, Oniaivisi on New Georgia, without incident at 0511 on August 1 and unloaded its troops. Anti-aircraft fire in the area indicated that they were not alone. They returned safely to Purvis Bay by 1755.

The following day the troops received word that a Tulagi-based PT boat failed to return from a night mission off Kolambangara attempting to stop Japanese reinforcements from reaching New Georgia. The boat, cut in half by the Japanese destroyer *Amagiri,* was PT-109 from the bilge pump incident. Its brash commanding officer, who would later be rescued and eventually returned to the U.S., would go on to become its 35th president.

Ward returned to Kukum beach on August 6 to pick up 128 officers and men of the 35th Regimental Combat Team for intensive landing practice. It put the troops through six landings at Kukum during the next three days before returning to Purvis Bay.

Ward and sub chaser *SC-733* revisited Rendova again on August 9, escorting LSTs 339 and 353 packed with reinforcements. The two escorts conducted anti-submarine patrols around Rendova for 10 hours the following morning, waiting for the LSTs to be unloaded. They guided the LSTs back to Purvis Bay on August 11.

Ward conducted more practice landings on the 13th with 214 men of Company F, 2nd Battalion of the 35th RCT. At dusk, Japanese torpedo bombers appeared to confirm that Guadalcanal was still a combat area. They had flown low over the water all the way from Buin on Bougainville to escape radar detection. The aircraft first dropped flares to silhouette any ships in the Sound and then made torpedo runs.

Three aircraft attacked the 9400-ton transport *John Penn,* one dropping its torpedo at close range. Immediately after releasing it, the plane was shot down, crashing into *John Penn* in a fiery explosion. Almost simultaneously, the torpedo slammed into the transport's side. The double hits took a heavy toll on the ship, killing 98 men and wounding 64 more before it went down.[8] Ultimately quiet returned to the Sound but *Ward,* with Company F still on board, spent another uneasy night.

Company F conducted a final landing practice on the morning of August 14 before *Ward* weighed anchor. At 1558 *Ward,* carrying Company F, joined APDs *Kilty, Dent, Talbot, Waters, McKean,* and *Stringham* of TransDiv12 and 22 in heading up the Slot at 18 knots.[9] They were accompanied by a heavy escort of *Nicholas, Corry, Pringle, Taylor, O'Bannon* and *Chevalier.* The convoy was destined to assault a new Japanese-held island.

With New Georgia practically secured, the next apparent step up the Solomons chain was the large island of Kolombangara directly across Kula Gulf from New Georgia. With an operating airfield at Vila, the island was considered by the Japanese to be the next Allied target. They had been moving in troops from Rabaul by destroyer to reinforce their garrison and now had a formidable force on the island to oppose any landing.

In the first test of the new Allied concept of leapfrogging in the Pacific, Admiral Nimitz decided to bypass Kolombangara and occupy the next island northerly, Vella Lavella. The Japanese troops on Kolombangara would thus serve no purpose and wither on the vine. For this operation, the Third Amphibious Force of APDs (TU 31.5.1), LCIs (TU 31.5.2) and LSTs (TU 31.5.3) was assembled at Guadalcanal.

Vella Lavella, a rugged jungle-covered island held no Japanese garrison and had no natural harbor. Nimitz, however, wanted a fighter base closer to Bougainville, the next major objective in the Solomons. Until now, the Japanese, with major bases on Bougainville to the north and Kolombangara to the south, had never considered it necessary to occupy Vella Lavella. Except for 2000 native islanders, the only inhabitants on Vella Lavella were survivors of downed aircraft and sunken ships of both sides.

Admiral Halsey's planners provided for a first-wave lightning strike on Vella Lavella by the 35th RCT carried by the seven APDs. The second and third waves would consist of 12 LCIs and three LSTs, respectively. Because of their slower speed, the LSTs left Guadalcanal ten hours before the APDs. All three waves were scheduled to land their troops on the designated beach at Barakoma, a shallow bay on the island's southeastern tip.

The APDs eased into Barakoma Bay at dawn on August 15 and encountered no opposition. A scouting party, carried to Barakoma by four PT boats four nights earlier, discovered that the only Japanese on the island were ship survivors of several naval battles in early August. With radar and sonar operators nervously watching for signs of the enemy, all APDs lowered their boats at 0622. Lookouts soon spotted a single Japanese aircraft, which did not attack but obviously radioed the news of the landing back to its base. An air attack could be expected later in the day.

It came at 0758, when the LCIs of the second wave had just nosed onto the beach. Six

Val dive bombers escorted by 48 fighters arrived on the scene to disrupt the operation. Allied fighters covering the landing were ready for them, and individual dogfights soon broke out right over the beachhead. The dive bombers circled to the east and dove at the destroyers out of the sun.

Three bombers missed *Corry* but sprayed her with water and shrapnel. Other bombers attacked the *Philip* and LST-395, barely missing both. Marine Corsairs from Guadalcanal downed three Vals and six Zeros within minutes, and army P-39s shot down several more. The remainder returned to Kahili airfield on Bougainville to report the results of their raid. None of the APDs were hit and left the beach area at 25 knots.

After the air attack the LSTs beached themselves and began unloading. The shallow lagoon made beaching difficult until bulldozers, the first vehicles unloaded, constructed earthen ramps for the wheeled vehicles.

All eyes were on the skies searching for the expected second Japanese raid, which was surely to come. It came in the afternoon in the form of 11 Vals and 48 Zeros. Seven of the Vals were quickly downed by the massed fire of ships' anti-aircraft guns and Allied covering fighters. This raid was followed by two raids later in the day, but when darkness closed over the beachhead not a single bomb had hit any U.S. ship. Incredibly, by day's end, the Japanese had thrown 140 fighters, 36 dive bombers, 23 medium bombers, and 20 seaplanes against the landing force without damaging a single ship.[10] The raids did cause some damage on the beach, killing 12 soldiers and wounding 50 more.

The landing stunned Japanese leaders, who expected that the next landing would be on Kolombangara. They would have to attempt to withdraw their troops there at night if they were to save them. This would be difficult, but the Japanese were masters at this type of operation. To facilitate this evacuation, they landed 400 troops at Horaniu on the north coast of Vella Lavella on August 18, to set up a barge staging base. They quickly brought in hundreds more from Bougainville, but by early October Vella Lavella was completely overrun by the Allies. The planned evacuation of Kolambangara was never accomplished, and the Japanese garrison troops were still there at war's end.

While Vella Lavella was captured without major Allied losses, there were still losses on land, in the air, and at sea. LST-396 exploded and sank on August 18 on a supply run to Vella Lavella. *Ward's* luck continued to hold as it came through the operation untouched.

Ward and *Waters* were busy again on August 19, each picking up 75 men of Carrier Aircraft Service Unit 14 at Kukumbona, Guadalcanal.[11] There they also rendezvoused with LCIs 23, 63, 64, 66, and 335 to escort them to Rendova. Arriving safely at 0601 on the 20th, the APDs screened the landing beach while the LCIs unloaded. The entire convoy was back in Purvis Bay on the 21st.

After almost continuous action since its arrival in the South Pacific in March, *Ward* now spent 10 days at anchor in Purvis Bay awaiting the next mission. Although the rest was welcomed, Purvis Bay was not the ideal place to be without activity for any length of time. Facilities were primitive and recreational opportunities almost non-existent.

Construction units did, however, build officer's and enlisted men's "clubs" on Tulagi to provide a site for the men to congregate on the island. But at Purvis Bay facilities were much cruder. There, on authorized liberties, crewmen could get two cans of warm beer provided by the ship at the enlisted men's shelter, located on what the sailors called "Whisky Point." Enlisted men referred to the place as the "Little Grass Shack."[12] Boredom was the real enemy at Tulagi and Purvis Bay.

The crew was happy to finally receive orders to pick up LSTs 397 and 488 off Kukum on August 31. With sub chaser *SC-761* as a second escort, the convoy left for Rendova at 1202 at 9.5 knots. *Ward* tested all three-inch and 20-mm guns on the way as her gunners had not fired them in many days. *Ward* dropped off her brood safely at 0631 on September 1, and all four ships were back at Guadalcanal the following day.

Ward's number was called again on September 9 for another escort assignment to Rendova. With minesweeper *Southard,* another converted four-stacker as escort, the two led LST-448 and 472, and LCIs 22, 63, 64, 68, and 69 to the forward base. This trip was also uneventful, with all safely back on September 11.

Ward's next assignment was another reinforcement convoy but this was a large one. She would join Task Group 31.6 consisting of LSTs 167, 448, 449, 472, 485, and LCIs 327, 328, 330, 331, 332, and 333. LST-485 was also towing an LCM. The convoy would have an unusually heavy escort of six destroyers—*Fahrenholt, Lardner, Lansdowne, Jenkins, Radford, and Woodworth,* and six APDs—*Ward, Crosby, Dent, Kilty, Talbot,* and *Waters.* The APDs would also carry troops and supplies. The convoy's destination was Vella Lavella, where the buildup of a forward base was in full swing. *Ward's* cargo on the trip was men of the 37th New Zealand Army Battalion.

The convoy loaded at Guadalcanal on September 16 and set sail at 0400 on the 17th. *Ward* again gave her gunners practice on the way. At 0700 on the 18th, the formation was off the beach at Maravari, Vella Lavella, three miles north of the original landings on September 15. All ships were unloaded by 1345 and the convoy departed for Guadalcanal without incident.

Ward was part of a return engagement by Task Group 31.6 to Vella Lavella a week later, this time with some opposition. On this trip TG 31.6 would consist of LSTs 167, 334, 448, 449, 472, 485, and APDs *Stringham, McKean, Talbot, Waters, Dent, Kilty, Ward,* and *Crosby.* Escorting would be destroyers *Selfridge, Ralph Talbot, Patterson, McCalla, Converse, Jenkins,* and *Radford.*

Ward embarked 146 officers and men of Company A of a Marine Transport Group Motor Division on September 23 at Guadalcanal and conducted a practice landing later that day. The convoy weighed anchor at 0400 the following morning and was lying off Juno River, Vella Lavella at dawn on September 25. *Ward, Kilty* and *Crosby* landed their troops by 0702 and patrolled the landing area while other APDs unloaded. By 0932 the APDs were under way for the return trip.

An hour after *Ward* left the beachhead, two groups of unidentified aircraft were detected by radar approaching the beach. At 1100 a flight of three Japanese bombers came in from the north, straddling LST-167. Nine minutes later four more flew over at 5000 feet. The LST was damaged severely by near misses that killed nine men, wounded others, and started a large fire. It was later towed back to Guadalcanal, stripped of useable parts, and left there to serve as an ammunition barge. *Ward* again escaped a combat incident without damage.

Ward remained at Purvis Bay until September 30, when it would tempt fate again. Task Group 31.6 was called on to make yet another reinforcement run to Vella Lavella. LSTs 334, 448, 449, 460, 485, and 488—accompanied by APDs *Stringhan, McKean, Talbot, Kilty, Crosby,* and *Ward*— would carry troops and supplies to the island. The escort would be heavy with destroyers—*Foote, Radford, McCalla, Patterson, Ralph Talbot, Converse,* and *Jenkins.*

Ward embarked 17 tons of supplies and 155 officers and men of Company G, 2nd Battalion of the 1st Marine Parachute Regiment at Tassafaronga, Guadalcanal at 0706 and formed up with the other APDs.[13] By noon the entire Task Group was assembled and proceeding at the best speed of the LSTs to Juno River. The convoy was off Baker Beach by 0600 the following morning and disembarked their cargo without incident. With empty troop compartments the APDs departed for Purvis Bay.

Again, *Ward* just missed a Japanese air raid when Val dive bombers appeared at 0930 and immediately dove out of the sun at the beached LSTs. LST-334 was hit by one bomb that penetrated her deck and exploded in the cargo hold, causing casualties and considerable damage.

LST-448 was hit by three bombs in quick succession, which caused secondary explosions and started a huge fire. The ship was abandoned when fire could not be brought under control. The ship suffered 17 killed and 14 wounded from her crew with additional casualties among the troops who were on board to unload cargo. The fire burned itself out and the ship was taken under tow by minesweeper *Bobolink.* En route to Purvis Bay on October 5, LST-448 settled and sank. LST-334 was able to make its way to Espiritu Santo for major repair.[14] *Ward's* luck was still holding.

In recognition of the possibility of having to tow an APD out of a combat zone, *Ward* and *Crosby* conducted drills on October 4 by alternately towing each other. On October 6 *Ward* was preparing for still another trip to Vella Lavella, loading 178 officers and men of the H&S Company of the 1st Marine Parachute Regiment at Tassafaronga.[15]

Forming two columns with APDs *Stringham, Crosby, McKean,* and *Waters,* the convoy departed Guadalcanal at 1040 and headed up the Slot. Destroyers *Taylor, La Vallette,* and *Ralph Talbot* provided the screen. At 1453 the formation rendezvoused with a slow convoy of LSTs 390, 446, 449, and 460 with an escort of destroyers *Nicholas, Fletcher,* and *Saufley.* At 1547 *Ward* stopped to retrieve the pack of one of its passengers who had inadvertently dropped it over the side. This was a sure sign that the submarine menace was considered negligible.

At 0545 on October 7, however, *Crosby* reported a sound contact and was ordered to investigate it with *Saufley. Crosby* dropped one depth charge and returned to its station. Nevertheless, the convoy commander ordered a change in course around the area. The convoy safely reached its destination, Uzamba Beach, Vella Lavella, at 0548 on October 8. After unloading, the APDs left the beached LSTs and returned to Purvis Bay at 23 knots.

Ward had another ten-day period of rest awaiting her next assignment. The captain took advantage of this to repair a faulty gyro compass and test it. Her only other mission during the rest was to rendezvous with the submarine *Guardfish* during the night of October 18. With all of the Allied anti-submarine measures in effect, the submarine could not have reached Purvis Bay safely alone, especially at night. *Ward* finally located *Guardfish* at 0400 in the dark and escorted her to Tulagi in the morning.

Guardfish was at Tulagi to play an important role in the next major Allied operation scheduled to begin in two weeks. She was to pick up two parties of Australian coast watchers and take them to Japanese-held Bougainville with radios. There, behind enemy lines, they would report on Japanese ship and aircraft movements in advance of Allied landings on the island. The coast watchers, Captain Eric Robinson and Sub-Lieutenant J. Keenan, who had both lived under the very noses of the Japanese on Bougainville for 15 months, were evacuated in July by submarine but asked to return.[16]

Ward received her next assignment on October 20, escorting a small convoy to New Georgia. With *Ward* leading and sub chaser *SC-760* patrolling 1500 yards astern, they guided LST-460 and LCIs 63 and 64 safely to the Munda area by the following morning. In late afternoon of the 21st, *Ward* rendezvoused with an LCT and took off 130 officers and men of the 27th Regiment of the 25th Infantry Division. She also picked up her convoy, LST-460 at Munda and the two LCIs at Rendova, now unloaded. All ships were back at Guadalcanal on the 22nd. *Ward* disembarked her passengers at Kukum for a period of R & R.

The Allies were about to make their next big move to secure the Solomons and further isolate the huge Japanese base at Rabaul on New Britain. With its excellent harbor and five airfields, Rabaul was the staging base for all Japanese air, ground, and naval forces in the Solomon's area. With that base neutralized, Japanese positions in the Solomons would wither and die without support and Japan's major units would be forced to retreat hundreds of miles.

Neutralization of Rabaul required the Allied possession of airfields within easy fighter range of the base. Fighter escorted raids could then systematically destroy Japanese aircraft and make Rabaul's Simpson harbor untenable for shipping. Airfields on Bougainville would be less than 200 miles from Rabaul and would serve this purpose. Bougainville thus became the next and climactic battle in the Solomon's campaign.

Allied planners scheduled the major landings on Bougainville for November 1 but two smaller landings would take place first. The Treasury Islands, two small outcrops 30 miles south of Bougainville, would be assaulted on October 27 to secure them as an advance base for small craft and PT boats. The following day minor Allied units would invade the large island of Choiseul southeast of Bougainville. This was to be strictly a feint to deceive the Japanese into believing that Choiseul, not Bougainville, was to be the major landing. The Choiseul assault troops were to be withdrawn after a few days.

The landing in the Treasury Islands was assigned to the 3700 men of the New Zealand 8th Brigade Group transported by a unit that included *Ward*. *Ward* would also be involved in the Choiseul raid.

On October 26 the APDs began the move. *Stringham, Waters, Talbot,* and *Dent* of TransDiv 12, with *Kilty, Crosby, McKean,* and *Ward* of TransDiv22, crossed the Sound to Kukum where they picked up troops and supplies. *Ward's* passengers were 198 officers and men of Company A of the 36th Battalion of the New Zealand Army with nine tons of supplies.[17]

All ships were loaded and under way in two four-ship columns at 20 knots at 1202. Their destination was the islands of Mono and Stirling in the Treasuries. Although the troops were veterans of combat in North Africa, Greece, and Crete, this would be New Zealand's first amphibious operation since Gallipoli in 1914. Their destroyer screen was *Eaton, Pringle,* and *Philip.*

All was quiet until nightfall. The night was unusually black with Japanese snooper aircraft searching the Slot. Despite the flares they dropped periodically, they did not spot the convoy. By morning the sky was heavily overcast, rain was falling and the day gloomy. It did hide the convoy, however.

The APDs reached the Treasuries safely and seven of them lay to 1300 yards off Stirling Island at 0540 preparing to disembark troops. Three minutes later the destroyers commenced a 38-minute bombardment of the landing beaches on both sides of the Blanch Channel, which separated the two islands.

In addition to the destroyer gunfire support, this operation saw the first use of LCI gunboats. LCIs 22 and 23 were equipped with two additional 20-mm, three 40-mm, and five 0.50 caliber guns and lay to off the beaches. They poured fire into any area that resembled a possible Japanese position.

At 0552 *Ward* disembarked 160 of her troops in the rain, using all four boats, and headed for the beach in the first wave. The bombardment stopped at 0621 with *Ward's* boats hitting the shore five minutes later. All eight machine guns of *Ward's* boats raked the jungle landing area with 0.30 caliber fire as they approached. In spite of the withering volley, return fire from shore hit a New Zealand officer in the boat carrying *Ward* Boat Officer Farwell. "I was standing next to him when he was hit," said Farwell. "His men carried him ashore to tend to him."[18] Allied fighter cover of 32 aircraft, which arrived at 0600, patrolled the sky over the island searching for targets.

Other landing craft came under fire from machine guns and mortars as they approached Mono Island. One boat was hit heavily, wounding 13 New Zealanders, but all boats continued on to the beach with their human cargo.

As LST-399 beached itself on Mono Island, it took several mortar rounds on its deck. When its ramps were lowered to discharge troops, the first three men down the ramp were killed by machine gun fire from a pillbox only 25 yards away. Further movement down the ramp stopped immediately. A New Zealand soldier, noticing a bulldozer in the hold of the LST, quickly climbed aboard. Raising the blade to deflect enemy fire, he drove it onto the beach and directly at the pillbox. Maneuvering around to its blind side, he lowered the blade and buried the pillbox.[19]

Ward's boats returned to the ship at 0658 and disembarked the remaining 40 men and all of the supplies. This was not without incident, however. The landing craft containing Lt. Farwell stopped after traveling only 500 yards. A bullet had pierced a fresh water heat exchanger and the boat had to be towed back to *Ward* by another of *Ward's* boats.[20]

By this time many of the Japanese guns were silenced and the second wave met little opposition. By 0757 the APDs had landed 1600 men, 150 tons of supplies, and had been hoisted aboard their ships.

On their return to the ship, *Ward's* boats carried a number of wounded men who needed immediate attention. *Ward's* medical officer was Lt. Commander Charles Cooper, who had previously been a surgeon at San Francisco General Hospital. He treated them all in *Ward's* small operating room and transferred them to a hospital upon returning to Purvis Bay.

The landings were a surprise to the Japanese and thus they had no naval units in the area to contest the operation. Their first reaction was to send a flight of Zeros down at mid-morning to harass the landing force. They were met by the fighters covering the landing causing a series of dogfights to break out over the islands. No damage was done on the ground by this raid.

A flight of 25 Japanese dive bombers from Rabaul arrived over the beachhead at 1530, again precipitating an air battle over the islands. Unloading operations were suspended for an hour as ground personnel sought cover. The bombers missed the transports but put two bombs into destroyer *Corry* killing eight crewmen and flooding her engine room. She had to be towed back to Tulagi but was saved.

Japanese artillery finally opened up and caused some difficulties on the beach. It hit LST-399 once more as well as a stockpile of ammunition on shore, resulting in a huge explosion.

The eighth APD, *McKean,* landed her troops on the opposite side of Mono Island where a high mountain peak provided an ideal site for a radar installation. The Japanese made their last stand on Mono in this area on November 2, and the Treasuries were secured after only two days. Additional troops were landed on November 6, and a PT base was quickly established. An airfield would follow shortly.

Ward was not done for the day. As soon as her boats were back on board, she formed up with *Kilty, Crosby,* and *McKean* to steam to Juno River on Vella Lavella on their next mission of the day. Destroyer Conway provided the escort. The remaining four APDs, TransDiv 12, would return to Guadalcanal. The APDs also exchanged landing craft with TransDiv 22 keeping the undamaged ones.

At 1832 on Juno Beach, boats from shore were already loaded and brought out to *Ward,* 180 men of Company B, 2nd Battalion of the 1st Marine Parachute Regiment plus 25 tons of supplies.[21] The other APDs embarked 545 more troops of the same Battalion and eight LCIs loaded additional marines, all bound for Choiseul. The four APDs were about to accomplish a feat that no other transports had done in World War II to date. They were to participate in landings on two islands 100 miles apart on the same day.

Occupation of Choiseul was not in the Allied plans. Because it was the next island up the chain from Vella Lavella, the Japanese expected some move toward this island. Admiral Halsey intended to strengthen this expectation with an invasion of light forces made to look like a major force.

The Choiseul formation in column astern, led by *Conway,* departed as soon as they were loaded but stayed close to the Vella Lavella shore until dark to avoid revealing their course to snooping Japanese aircraft. Then it headed at 15 knots into the dark, moonless night on a course headed directly for Vozo Village on Choiseul's northwest coast. Although the sea was calm, the convoy passed in and out of rain squalls most of the way.

Their presence was discovered at 2309 when a Japanese float plane spotted their fluorescent wakes and dropped two bombs, which exploded near one of the APDs but did no damage. On *Ward,* crewmen observed the explosions 1000 yards off their starboard quarter and waited nervously for more. None came.

The formation reached their destination and lay off shore of Vozo just before midnight. One of *Ward's* boats, under the command of Lt. Farwell, containing 21 face-blackened marines and a native guide, "Lt. Pete," was the designated reconnaissance boat.[22] It left the ship at 2352 and approached the shore by itself in total blackness. The boat engineer muffled the engine sound by running the exhausts underwater.

Marines and boat crew held their collective breaths, expecting a volley of machine gun fire to erupt from shore at any moment. Japanese campfires a short distance inland were clearly visible from the boat. With his knowledge of the area the guide was able to locate the exact landing site. The boat was quietly eased up to the beach and the ramp lowered. To the relief of everyone on board, the Japanese had no patrols around.

With the marines on shore, the boat crew slowly eased the boat off the beach. Using a hooded red light, Farwell signaled the waiting APDs to send their boats in. At 0019 the remaining 15 LCPRs silently made for the light. By 0220 the entire raiding force and supplies were ashore without incident.

An Australian coast watcher, C.W. Setan, was waiting on shore with 80 natives to carry supplies. A float plane spotted the ships as they were unloading and dropped a bomb, which near-missed *Conway.* It caused no damage but raised tensions further on all ships. Knowing that they could expect Japanese bombers at daylight, the APDs left the beachhead as soon as their boats were back on board. They headed for Purvis Bay at 23 knots and reached there safely at 1452. Choiseul held several thousand Japanese troops, who were soon made aware of the marines' presence. The marines moved along the coast destroying barges, warehouses, supplies and installations and creating the desired effect of a much larger force. Japanese troops moved into the area and firefights broke out in several places. By November

3 the marines had worn out their welcome and a withdrawal was in order. LCIs moved in that night and took off the troops at 0150. Of these marines, there were 9 killed, 2 missing, 14 wounded, and 1 captured, but they killed 143 Japanese troops.[23]

On November 1 the campaign to recapture Bougainville, the last Japanese held island in the Solomons, began in earnest. The U.S. 3rd Marine Division stormed ashore at Cape Torokina on the west shore of the 30 by a 120-mile, jungle-covered island. By afternoon 14,000 marines were ashore and had established a defensive perimeter. They were there to stay.

The Japanese reacted quickly by sending a task force of cruisers and destroyers to attack the transports lying offshore at the landing area. In a fierce gun battle designated the "Battle of Empress Augusta Bay," the following day the task force was turned back, having lost a cruiser and a destroyer.

The beachhead now had to be supplied and reinforced. This first reinforcement mission would be carried out by Task Group 31.6 consisting of five APDs of TransDiv 12 (*Stringham, McKean, Dent, Waters, Talbot*), three APDs of TransDiv22 (*Crosby, Kilty, Ward*), eight LSTs of TU31.6.1 (70, 207, 339, 341, 353, 354, 395, 488), and escorting destroyers *Eaton, Philip, Renshaw, Saufley, Sigourney,* and *Waller*. [24]

All APDs loaded troops and supplies at Tetere Beach, Guadalcanal, on November 4. *Ward's* share was 25 tons of supplies and 198 officers and men of the 19th and 21st Marine Regiments and 75th Seabee Battalion.[25] After a practice disembarking, the APDs were under way at 1722 in two columns. At 0618 on the following morning, they rendezvoused with the LSTs and their escort making the resultant convoy an impressive sight.

The formation reached Bougainville at 0600 on November 6, and unloading began immediately. In order to accelerate unloading, for the first time the LSTs contained loaded trucks and trailers. At the beach the trucks drove off the landing craft, pulling loaded trailers to storage areas. Even with this new technique, the LSTs were not completely empty until 0300 the following morning. They backed off the beach, joined the waiting APDs and escorts and lumbered back to Guadalcanal. The convoy brought 3500 troops and 5000 tons of supplies to the beachhead.

The mission was uneventful, except for what could have been a disastrous collision on the way to Bougainville. LST-488 missed a signal when the convoy made a 90-degree turn in the dark. Luckily, a sharp-eyed Boatswains Mate saw a dark shape ahead and alerted the captain who ordered, "Full speed astern!" Otherwise LST-488, loaded with gasoline, explosives, and troops, would have collided at full speed with another LST carrying the same cargo.[26]

Ward remained at Purvis Bay only long enough to refuel and, on the morning of November 8, was off Kukumbona, Guadalcanal, embarking troops and supplies for another run to Bougainville. It picked up 147 officers and men of the 2nd Battalion, 21st Marines and the 75th Seabee Battalion, plus 25 tons of supplies.[27] After the usual practice landing, *Ward* and the other APDs of TransDiv12 and 22 were under way at 1742 on November 9. At 0629 on November 10 they joined a convoy of LSTs 334, 390, 397, 398, 446, 449, 472 and 477, with the same six escorts as the previous convoy. The combined force was designated Task Group 31.7 and carried 3600 additional troops and 6000 tons of supplies to the beachhead.

Although Japanese aircraft were over the Slot every night, this convoy reached Bougainville at 0641 on the 11th without incident. The ships were all safely at anchor at Guadalcanal on November 13. By November 14 the Allied beachhead now held 34,000 troops. The reinforcement operations were running smoothly, but that was about to change.

TransDiv12 and 22 were called on again on November 15 to join the next major convoy to Bougainville as part of Task Group 37.6. Their passengers on this run would be men of Company I, 3rd Battalion of the 21st Marine Regiment.

The eight APDs departed Tetere beach, Guadalcanal, at 1744 on the 15th in the usual two columns, 500 yards apart. TransDiv 12 was in the starboard column, TransDiv22 in the port column, with 1000-yard separation between ships of a column. They steamed through the darkness at 19 knots searching for the formation of eight LSTs that had left Guadalcanal earlier because of their slower speed.

At 0448 on the 16th they finally sighted the LSTs (70, 207, 339, 341, 353, 354, 395, and 488) plodding along at nine knots. Their escort was the same destroyer squadron of six ships that had guided the previous supply convoys. The ocean-going tug *Pawnee* (ATF-74) joined up soon after. The Task Group continued up the Slot unmolested the rest of the day and into the night.

Tensions rose with the loss of daylight as the skies were clear. Japanese aircraft could be expected over the Slot every night that weather permitted, and the weather on the 16th was good. Bombers could be expected to fly over the beachhead dropping flares and bombs to harass men on ship and shore. Gun crews slept very little once the formation left Guadalcanal. The threat from possible submarines added to the tension.

Japanese headquarters at Rabaul already knew of the presence of TG37.6 from their spotter planes, which located it during the afternoon. Their first response was to dispatch a group of nine dive bombers and five torpedo bombers timed to attack the task force when it was off the Bougainville beach.

The LSTs occupied the center of the convoy with APDs stationed around the LSTs as an inner screen. The destroyers formed the outer screen. The formation approached to within 20 miles of the beachhead at 0300 on November 17, when radar screens began picking up blips to the north. Because of the darkness, the aircraft were unable to coordinate their bombing runs and were forced to attack individually throughout the night.

Gunners all around the screen held their fire in accordance with standing orders not to fire at night and give away their position. For almost 50 minutes a cat and mouse game was played off Bougainville with aircraft searching for targets and trying to entice the ships to fire. At 0348 the game ended abruptly.

A low-flying Betty bomber spotted a wake and turned into the convoy, veering first at *Talbot* and then at *McKean*. *McKean* turned hard to port to present a smaller target and opened up with a 20-mm gun. That immediately pinpointed the ship's position. Gene LaMere, one of *McKeans* electricians manning a searchlight on the mainmast, saw the aircraft approach.

"It was dark," he recalled, "but I had a good view from the mast. I saw the aircraft drop its torpedo and could see the torpedo wake head for the aft section of the ship starboard. When the torpedo hit, it knocked the searchlight right off the mast and stunned me."

The torpedo hit *McKean* at 0350 and exploded in the after magazine and depth charge storage. That ruptured the diesel fuel tanks, throwing burning oil all over the ship. All crewmen stationed aft were killed instantly. The only exceptions were three sailors who were blown off the ship.

The 20-mm gun continued to fire at the bomber as it passed over the ship and scored damaging hits, possibly killing the pilot. It crashed not far from the *McKean* just after the torpedo hit. *McKean's* captain, Lt. Commander Ralph Ramey, ordered "Abandon ship," and then made a quick inspection to see that no one alive was still on the ship. Then he went over the side at 0412.

The water was alive with the 153-man crew and 185 Marine passengers who survived the explosion. *Ward* was not far from *McKean* when it went down but could not stop to help the men in the water. All APDs were ordered to continue on to the beach. The 1400 Marine passengers in their collective troop compartments were too valuable to risk to further attacks by aircraft still circling the convoy.

Able-bodied men in the water pulled burned and wounded crewmen and troops onto life rafts and other floating debris to await rescue. Some men who left the ship too soon actually burned to death in the flaming oil covering the water. Destroyers *Sigourney* and *Waller* along with *Talbot* were ordered to pick up survivors. The rescue proceeded smoothly despite additional attacks by the aircraft on a sea now illuminated by *McKean's* fires.

McKean sank stern first at 0418 with two of her depth charges exploding as she settled. It was an ironic tribute to a gallant ship that had made many such missions in the war.

McKean's loss was costly. Sixty-four of her crew were killed, along with 52 Marine passengers. Many more were injured or burned. Five of the attacking aircraft were downed before they were driven off at dawn by U.S. fighters.[28]

Ward had been called to General Quarters as soon as *McKean* was hit. Her crew watched the action around them intently. Her gunners peered into the darkness but did not fire. As they watched McKean burn, many thought to themselves, "That could have been us."

Several bombs exploded 1500 yards off *Ward's* port quarter and at 0442 a shell ricocheted only 50 yards off the port bow. Once more Lady Luck looked down upon *Ward*.

After the attacks, *Ward* continued on to the beachhead and began disembarking her first troops at 0557. A bomb suddenly exploded off her port quarter at 0657 causing some anxious moments. Six minutes later *Ward* disembarked her second wave. *Ward's* medical officer went ashore with this wave to help with wounded on shore. He was later recalled when *Ward* was ready to depart.

At 0755 Japanese dive bombers were spotted over the ship. *Ward's* 20-mm guns opened up along with those of every other ship close by. Within minutes a bomber spiraled down, trailing black smoke, crashing 2500 yards off *Ward's* port beam. Attacks continued sporadically throughout the day as the APDs cruised off shore waiting for the LSTs to unload. At 1808 the LSTs backed off the beach and the convoy reformed for the return trip to Guadalcanal. Only the *McKean* was missing. During the return, *Ward's* engineers discovered burned bearings and notified the captain. The ship lay dead in the water for several hours while repairs were made.

Upon approaching Guadalcanal, *Ward* peeled off from the convoy and diverted to the Russell Islands to make permanent repair to her bearings. By 0825 on November 19 *Ward* was at anchor in Sunlight Channel in the Russells after a harrowing mission. It was a saddened crew that could finally relax. They had lost friends on *McKean*.

While at anchor, workers also relocated two of *Ward's* 20-mm mounts for better fields of fire. The crew was given eight days to rest while the work was done on her engines. They discovered that the Russell Islands were not much different from their usual home at Purvis Bay. Sipping the customary warm beer was the only form of recreation available here as well.

At 1107 on November 28 *Ward* was finally on the move but not back to Purvis Bay, as the crew had anticipated. The ship was headed south at 16 knots to Noumea, New Caledonia, away from the Solomons and combat zone. *Ward* reached Noumea at 0830 on November 30 after an uneventful voyage. Two more of the original 47th Division crew, Ed Zechmann and Maurice Hurley, left the ship here for reassignment.

While moored at Noumea, *Ward's* crew received astounding news that swept through the ship like wildfire. *Ward* was ordered to Sydney, Australia, for ten days. Sydney was known as a fantastic liberty port. *Ward's* crew would have an opportunity to confirm that shortly.

Ward weighed anchor at 1004 on December 1 to put Noumea behind it. On the way out of the harbor, it suddenly encountered minesweeper *YMS-119* cutting across its bow. *Ward* had to quickly reverse its engines to avoid a collision and mess up its liberty cruise. That done, it could now point its bow toward Sydney and make 22 knots to an anticipated ten days of fun.

Ward's engines were still creating problems and, on the following morning, they lost fuel oil suction three times. Each time the ship had to stop for temporary repairs. At 1200 on December 3, land was sighted and at 1400 *Ward* entered Jackson Harbor, Sydney. A pilot came aboard at 1417 to guide the ship to an anchorage. At 1532 *Ward* was moored next to heavy cruiser *Tulsa* in Wooloomooloo Bay.[29] A five day liberty would begin the following morning for half the crew.

Orv Ethier recalled the entry into Sydney Harbor. "The harbor is one of the most beautiful places we could imagine. It looked like two mountains with an opening between them protected by big breakwaters. Its narrow opening was not visible until a ship approached the breakwaters. Once past them, the huge magnificent harbor opened up like in a picture book. We tied up at a place called 'Man 'o War Steppes' near a big outdoor amphitheater. Across a little bay from us was Hyde Park, a beautiful park with crowds of people walking around. We could step off the ship and walk a short distance to the park, go through it, and pick up a trolley to downtown Sydney. This was a far cry from the jungles we had been staring at for eight months."

What amazed Don Pepin the most was the big double-decker buses and subways in Sydney. "There weren't many American cities with subways in 1943," recalled Pepin. "I never realized how modern a city Sydney was. It also had a lot of big dance halls and we got to see some big name bands while we were there."

Dick Thill was impressed with Sydney's beauty, great food, and friendly people. He was further impressed with a monument that the city had built near the harbor to honor the U.S. Navy. "It was in appreciation for stopping the Japanese in the Battle of the Coral Sea in May of 1942. This probably saved Australia from being invaded."

Ethier had to serve on Shore Patrol for a 24-hour period during *Ward's* stay. He did not enjoy this duty, as he encountered his own crew mates boisterous and drunk and had to deal with them. Shore Patrol was conducted by groups of four men carrying night sticks. It consisted of a U.S. soldier, sailor, and Marine, and an Australian policemen. One of the U.S. men would be an officer following the Patrol in a jeep and empowered to arrest U.S. servicemen if necessary. Because most U.S. servicemen on liberty carried considerable cash, they were told not to walk alone, to prevent assaults.

Ward's crew had not seen bright lights or women since February. With the influx of U.S. servicemen on leave, there were not enough women to go around. Taverns were plentiful, however. There were relatively few Australian men around since most were in the service fighting in North Africa, New Guinea, or other places.

This caused the inevitable friction between local men and U.S. servicemen. Will Lehner recalls a donnybrook between the two groups in a tavern one night. Several men were tossed through the tavern's front window before the evening ended.

Lehner and Dick Thill both met women they continued to see throughout the liberty. They would meet for coffee in a restaurant and bring their own liquor to spike it. Lehner became close to the woman he met and continued to correspond with her after *Ward* had left Sydney. He visited her family on *Ward's* next visit to Sydney six months later. Their friendship continues to this day.[30]

Liberty for all crewmen ended at 2400 on December 12, with a number of men straggling in after midnight. At 0806 on December 13, *Ward* fully fueled and provisioned, got under way with a refreshed crew. Her sister APDs, *Stringham* and *Dent,* which also had coincident ten-day leaves, accompanied her. The three proceeded north at 19 knots but not back to Purvis Bay. They were bound for a new theater, the Southwest Pacific, where combat had been going on for a year and a half.

Their destination was the huge jungle island of New Guinea. The strategic island, second in size in the world only to Greenland, was the location of a dirty and fierce ground campaign to wrest control from the Japanese. The fighting was similar to that of Guadalcanal, where disease and the climate caused as many casualties as the Japanese. Combat was generally confined to a narrow fringe of jungle along the coast. Because the dense, impenetrable interior would simply not allow movement of troops, General MacArthur was attempting to force his way up the island's eastern coast line.

On December 14 Captain Lemly held mast and handed out discipline for the 20 men who reported late to the ship in returning from liberty. Most were less than an hour late, some only a few minutes, but they all received extra duty hours. Several of those with more serious violations received a reduction in rank. After an uneventful voyage, the APDs reached Milne Bay at the extreme southeastern tip of New Guinea on December 17 where they anchored at 1419. Lemly immediately reported to the Commander of Task Force 76 for orders and *Ward* was given a new assignment.

Ward left Milne Bay on December 19 and steamed up the coast to Cape Sudest near Buna, where it anchored at 1810. Here it was reunited with her sister APDs from the Solomon's campaign. That had not changed.

Ward's role had not changed either. On the 20th, *Ward* embarked 142 men of Company I and L of the 3rd Battalion, 7th Marine Regiment, and promptly conducted a practice landing. *Ward* repeated this on December 22 with 151 men of the same units on a remote beach with *Stringham, Kilty, Crosby,* and *Dent* also taking part. All were back at Cape Sudest in late afternoon.

Ward's crew knew from the landing drills that another amphibious operation was soon expected but they had no idea where. Because their passengers were marines, they knew that this would not be a reinforcement but a landing on a hostile shore, and that they would be in the first wave.

December 24 did not resemble any other Christmas the crew had experienced before. At 1440 *Ward* embarked 143 men of I and M Companies of the 3rd Battalion, 7th Marine regiment.[31] The ship remained at anchor through the night with 300 men packed on it. The heat was intense and sleep came hard to crew and passengers. The following day would be Christmas and everyone's thoughts were of Sydney, home, family, and Christmases past. But tomorrow they would take the fight to the enemy once more.

Men of *Ward* also thought about how lucky they had been so far. In the past eight months *Ward* had been hit by bomb fragments and machine gun bullets but nothing bigger. All bombs and torpedoes had missed, although ships near them had been struck by both and sunk. Friends of theirs had been killed. They wondered to themselves, "How long can this continue? Would Lady Luck finally look the other way? Would tomorrow bring death and destruction to *Ward?*"

It was an uneasy sleep for men of *Ward* on Christmas Eve.

New Britain and New Guinea

Dawn was just breaking as *Ward* weighed anchor off Cape Sudest on a hot and humid Christmas morning in 1943. The anchorage was full of ships all now stirring as they maneuvered to find their stations in a cruising formation. *Ward* was one of nine APDs designated as Task Unit 76.1.2 (TU 76.1.2) that formed two columns. *Stringham Kilty,* and *Crosby* joined *Ward* as TransDiv22 in the starboard column. *Brooks, Gilmer, Humphreys, Sands,* and *Noa*) comprised TransDiv12 in the port column.[1]

These ships would constitute the first wave of the invasion force scheduled to land on a hostile shore in 24 hours. Behind them were ten LCIs and four LSTs that made up the second wave. Additional LSTs at Cape Sudest would follow later in the day. In all, seven waves of various types of landing craft would hit the beach within a 24-hour period. Their destination was Cape Gloucester on the northwestern tip of New Britain. At 0648 the Task Unit was in motion.

Early in the war President Roosevelt and the U.S. Joint Chiefs of Staff had decided to follow two general paths across the Pacific, both ending in Japan. One would island-hop across the central Pacific, beginning at Guadalcanal in the Solomon Islands. This campaign would be led by U.S. Admiral Chester Nimitz, Commander of Allied forces in the South Pacific.

The second route would run northwesterly along the eastern shore of the huge island of New Guinea and jump across to the Philippine Islands. This campaign would be directed by U.S. Army General Douglas MacArthur, Supreme Commander of Allied forces in the Southwest Pacific.

Until early December 1943, *Ward* was assigned to Admiral Halsey's Third Fleet under Admiral Nimitz. When she returned from Sydney, Australia, on December 17, she was reassigned to the Seventh Fleet Amphibious Force, General MacArthur's naval force. She would remain in that assignment for the remainder of her life.

Although army Generals usually do not have naval forces under their command, as Commander of the Southwest Pacific Theater, MacArthur needed the capability to transport troops and supplies over water and bombard enemy positions. For most of 1943 he scoured the Pacific searching for ships that were not already committed to other operations. By mid-December he had amassed an impressive fleet. It included four cruisers, 22 destroyers, nine APDs, 23 LSTs, 19 LCIs, 12 LCTs, and 14 LCMs. MacArthur's Navy, as it was called, had grown.[2]

New Guinea was one of the least hospitable places in the world. Its terrain was largely mountainous and covered by a dense rain forest. Its hot and humid climate and ferocious natives made it an area to avoid. Yet, the Japanese, recognizing the island's strategic location, established bases along its entire eastern shore to control the island and the surrounding sea lanes.

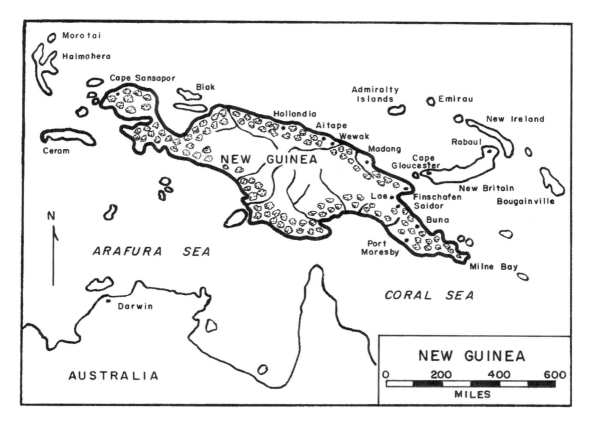

Because of New Guinea's difficult terrain, ground transportation along its 1500-mile long coast line was impossible. Roads did not exist nor could any be constructed. Any advance up the coast would, of necessity, have to be by water, by leapfrogging troops from harbor to harbor.

This concept could work but only if the Japanese airfields on the western end of New Britain island were neutralized. All allied shipping along New Guinea's coast had to pass through the 50-mile wide strait separating New Guinea and New Britain. MacArthur decided to eliminate this threat by invading Arawe on the south coast of New Britain on December 15 and Cape Gloucester on the northern coast on December 26.

Operational planners did not respect the calendar when scheduling amphibious operations. Critical factors, such as weather forecasts, tides, ship and troop availability, and intelligence information determined landing dates. Holidays had little role in planning.

Holiday season on not, Cape Gloucester would be assaulted on the day after Christmas. Will Lehner on the *Ward* wondered about the timing. "Geez," he asked, "do we really have to make a landing at Christmas?"

New Britain, like New Guinea, was a mountainous jungle island with no roads. Although the big Japanese base at Rabaul at the eastern end of New Britain had 90,000 troops, it was not a threat to an invasion force at Cape Gloucester. Reinforcement from Rabaul 280 miles away from Cape Gloucester was possible only by sea or air. With Allied control of the air, those options were no longer feasible. The 7500 Japanese troops on the western end of New Britain were on their own.

Christmas morning was hot and humid with rain clouds ahead of the formation as the APDs steamed almost due north at 12 knots, aiming for Vitiaz Strait. A Japanese coast watcher on New Guinea and a Japanese reconnaissance plane spotted the convoy. However, because Japanese planners at Rabaul assumed that it was headed for New Britain's south coast to reinforce the Allied troops that had landed there ten days earlier, they did not become alarmed.

The convoy passed through the strait and, at midnight, changed course to the east to follow New Britain's north coast. At 0530, when it was off the designated beach, the morning silence was shattered when cruisers and destroyers commenced a heavy bombardment of the airfields five miles from the beach to prevent its use during the landings. *Ward* disembarked her troops into her four boats while she lay 9000 yards off the beach. As soon as the boats were in the water, other cruisers and destroyers, assigned to provide gunfire support, opened up on the beach.

The landing saw the inaugural use of a new weapon when LCIs fitted out as rocket-firing platforms unleashed a heavy five-minute bombardment of the beach with hundreds of projectiles. At 0705 a flight of B-24 heavy bombers passed over the landing area, covering it with a dense pattern of 500-pound bombs. Nineteen minutes later B-25 bombers came in just over the tree line, bombing and strafing the beach.

The boats of TransDiv 12 reached shore on the narrow strip of sand designated as Yellow Beach 1 just after 0800, landing 720 men of the 3rd Battalion of the 21st Marine Regiment.[3] The remaining five APDs landed the 1st Battalion simultaneously on nearby Yellow Beach 2 to the east. The tremendous shore bombardment had cleared the beachhead of whatever Japanese troops were there, ensuring that the landing would be unopposed. By the time *Ward's* boats were back on board at 0845, the troops she landed were already making their way westward through the jungle toward the airfields.

By day's end 13,000 Allied troops were ashore on Cape Gloucester and more were to come. Confident that a Japanese response was soon to follow, the APDs left the beachhead at 22 knots at 0945.

The first Japanese reaction was in the form of 50 fighters and bombers at 1430. They attacked three destroyers maneuvering eight miles off the beach. Several bombs crashed into destroyer *Brownson* near her stack, killing 108 of her crew and damaging her mortally. She could not be saved and sank a half hour later.[4]

Destroyer *Shaw,* which rose out of the ashes at Pearl Harbor and had to be completely rebuilt to fight again, was near-missed by three bombs that killed 4, wounded 31, and caused flooding below deck. The destroyer *Mugford* was also near-missed, and endured casualties.

Ward's luck held again. In an operation where ships were sunk and men killed, she came through untouched, and was back at anchor off Buna, New Guinea, at 2259. Disembarking there was Patrick Robinson, a war correspondent for the International News Service, who had gone along to Cape Gloucester for the ride.

By the 27th, *Ward* was ready to return to Cape Gloucester, having embarked 200 men of Company B, 1st Battalion, of the 5th Marine regiment.[5] At 1427 *Stringham, Ward, Kilty* and *Crosby* (comprising Task Group 76.1.2), along with *Brooks, Gilmer, Sands, Humphreys,* and *Noa* (forming Task Group 76.1.1) were traveling at 15 knots for a return to Cape Gloucester. Destroyers *Hutchins* and *Lamson* provided the escort. Although there were numerous reports of enemy aircraft in the vicinity, the task force was not molested on the voyage.

The APDs were off the beach at 0600 on December 29 and their boats were away at

0655. While the APDs left the transport area to await the return of their boats, army B-25s pounded the airfield and other targets. *Ward's* boats were hoisted aboard by 0815 and TG 76.1.2 left the beachhead to return to Buna. *Ward's* role in the Cape Gloucester operation was over. *Noa* remained at the beach for several hours to embark Marine casualties and rejoined the task force later.

The ground fighting at Cape Gloucester was some of the most difficult of the war to date. While opposition was only moderate, the jungle terrain became a nightmare for the troops because of almost continuous rains following the landings. Clothing rotted within a matter of days and vehicles became bogged down in mud that defied travel. By January 16, 1944, the area was secured and Cape Gloucester became another backwater area. General MacArthur, however, was now free to begin his push up the New Guinea coast.

It began on December 31, when the nine APDs were ordered out at 0456 and cruised down the coast to Goodenough Island to pick up the 126th Regimental Combat Team of the 32nd Infantry Division.[6] The APDs would take them to Saidor, where the Japanese held an airfield near the mouth of Vitiaz Strait. The airfield, in Allied hands, would prevent Japanese use of the strait and any interference with upcoming landings.

At 1627 the APDs embarked the troops for a practice landing with *Ward*, taking 126 men of Company I. She also took on Robert Eunson, a war correspondent for the Associated Press. At 0601 on January 1 the APDs were under way at 20 knots in a double column, followed by two LSTs and a group of LCIs. Destroyers *Beale, Mahan, Flusser, Reid, Lamson, Drayton, Hutchins,* and *Smith* accompanied the task force to provide escort and fire support.

At 0615 on January 2, after a 175-mile voyage, the formation, off Saui Point, prepared to land their troops. Bad weather prevented the planned air cover from putting in an appearance and pre-landing support rested with the destroyers. At 0645 all eight destroyers opened up on the beach area and pounded it for 32 minutes. At 0656 the APD's boats were in the water and headed for the beach, even as the bombardment continued. When the destroyers lifted their fire, the landing craft themselves raked the beach with withering machine gun fire.

By now the beach was covered by a heavy pall of smoke and dust, making observation from the ships impossible. By 0749 the boats were back at the APDs and a force of 2400 troops was on the shore pushing toward their objectives. A flight of army B-24s now joined the battle, making a pass over the Saidor airfield to bomb targets there.

By the time Japanese bombers from Wewak, New Guinea, arrived over the beachhead at 1600, all the ships had already departed. The bombers accomplished nothing except to crater the beach area. *Ward* was back at anchor at Buna at 2133. Again, she returned her crew from a landing without injury. By January 3, Saidor airfield and the surrounding area were in Allied hands and Vitiaz Strait was secure.

On January 5 APDs *Stringham, Ward, Kilty, Crosby,* and *Noa* departed for the long trek to Espiritu Santo, stopping off at Milne bay for refueling. They anchored in Segond Channel, Espiritu Santo, on January 9 for 11 days of cleaning and restoring the ship to fighting condition after a month of amphibious operations. The crew was finally able to take a shore leave without the usual jungle backdrop.

Ward and *Kilty* returned to the war on January 20, escorting merchant ships *SS William Howell* and *SS James Baker Francis* to Guadalcanal. Returning to Espiritu Santo on January 26 with destroyer-escort *Harmon, Ward* remained there only long enough to refuel and headed back to Guadalcanal the same day, this time escorting oiler *Kankakee* (AO-39). This voyage was also without incident, the only excitement coming in the form of live target practice for the three-inch and 20-mm guns at an aircraft-towed sleeve. On the 28th, *Ward* nested next to destroyer tender *Whitney* in Purvis Bay, where she received routine servicing and repair along with 1500 gallons of fresh water.

On January 31, Lt. Richard Farrell moved up in rank on the ship with an appointment to Executive Officer. He relieved Lt. Lloyd Benson, who was appointed to be the new commanding officer on the *Crosby*. Benson was a graduate of the U.S. Naval Academy and Farwell was grateful to him for teaching him celestial navigation in only a week's time.[7]

Ward was called on again, on February 2, to escort merchant ship *SS Santa Cruz* and seaplane tender *Chandeleur* to Munda. Minesweeper *Zeal* came along as a second escort. *Ward* escorted *Chandeleur* back to Purvis Bay on February 10 without incident.

After a week of inactivity, *Ward* received orders to participate in another amphibious operation. The Allies were ready to move further up the Solomons chain. On February 13, *Ward* picked up 15 Marine Corps officers and other men at Guadalcanal and sailed to Vella Lavella with APDs *Kilty*, *Crosby*, and *Dickerson* of TransDiv 22 in one column and APDs *Stringhan*, *Talbot*, *Waters*, and *Noa* of TransDiv 12 in a parallel column.

There, at Juno River on February 14, *Ward* embarked 105 men of B Company of the 35th New Zealand Battalion, 74 men of the 30th New Zealand Battalion, and 47 men of various New Zealand and U.S. Marine units. Her troop spaces were packed tight. Ninety minutes later the troops disembarked in a practice landing near Juno River. Taking the troops aboard again, the APDs left Vella Lavella at 1253 for the Green Islands.[8]

The Green Islands were a small group of coral outcroppings north of Bougainville and only 115 miles from Rabaul. Besides Rabaul, several other Japanese airbases were within range of the Green Islands. An Allied airfield on the Green Islands would be a major step in isolating Rabaul, and Admiral Halsey decided in early January to occupy them.

A reconnaissance on the evening of January 30 revealed that Nissan Island, the largest of the Greens, had excellent beaches and was suitable for an airfield. It also discovered that the islands were lightly fortified. Because the islands were the home of 1200 friendly natives, it was decided to omit the usual pre-landing bombardment.[9]

Destroyers *Fullam*, *Guest*, *Bennett*, *Halford*, and *Hudson* led the APDs up the Slot at 20 knots. They were followed by 12 LCIs, seven LSTs, and four LCTs with additional troops and supplies. Off Bougainville they rendezvoused with more landing craft that loaded at the Treasury Islands. A formidable force was on its way.

Japanese aircraft were detected around the convoy during the night, making nerves taut. Although no landing craft were damaged, the Japanese singled out the cruiser *St. Louis* for attention. She was hit by one bomb and near-missed by three others, killing 23 sailors and wounding 28 more.

The APDs were off Nissan Island in the morning, disembarking their troops at 0632. Their boats were forced to pass single file through a narrow passage between reefs surrounding the Nissan Island lagoon. This was the only route to the landing beach and Japanese fortification of this passage could have caused heavy casualties among the landing force. Luckily the passage was not fortified and opposition on Nissan was light.

Ward's lookouts spotted six aircraft attacking the LCIs and LSTs ten miles away at 0640. They came in without fighter escort, however, and were immediately intercepted by Marine fighters from Bougainville. The marines quickly downed two; heavy anti-aircraft fire drove off the others.

At 0715, *Ward's* boats returned and immediately disembarked a second wave destined for a different beach. At 0820, the boats were back again and hoisted aboard. The APDs lined up and, at 20 knots, left for the Russell Islands for reinforcements. As soon as the APDs pulled out, the LCIs and LSTs beached themselves on Nissan to unload. By nightfall, 5800 New Zealand troops were ashore and these landing craft were on their way back to Purvis Bay. The 102 Japanese troops on Nissan were quickly overcome and within two days a PT-boat base was operating on the island.

Since most of Nissan's coconut groves and gardens would be displaced by the new airfield, the U.S. military decided to relocate the natives. The navy transported 1147 natives by LST to Guadalcanal for temporary living there in what the natives considered "a fantastic experience." They would reside there until the Allies no longer needed the airfield.[10]

At 1802 on February 18, *Ward* left for Nissan with 203 men of the navy's 33rd Construction Battalion on board.[11] APD *Dickinson* also picked up Seabees and left with *Ward*. Just after midnight, APDs *Stringham, Waters,* and *Talbot* rendezvoused with *Ward* and *Dickinson* and formed two columns with destroyers *Anthony, Braine, Terry, Wadsworth,* and *Halford.* Twelve LSTs and two LCIs also joined the formation now designated as Task Group 31.5.1.

At 2025, while steaming at 18 knots, *Ward* collided with an unknown submerged object that shook the ship. Will Lehner, below deck aft at the time felt it. "I heard a loud 'kaboom' and thought we had been torpedoed," recalled Lehner. "The ship began vibrating badly and you could actually hear every rotation of the screws." The collision smashed the *Ward's* sonar dome and damaged both screws. Although vibration was extreme, *Ward* was able to continue at 17 knots and remain in formation.[12]

The APDs were off Nissan at 0600 on the 20th and disembarked their troops at Red Beach 45 minutes later. At 0659 a U.S. fighter plane covering the landing dove into the sea near the ships. One of the escorting destroyers raced to the spot and rescued a shaken pilot.

By 1600 all APDs and landing craft had unloaded troops and supplies and were heading for the return to Purvis Bay escorted by destroyers *Renshaw, Bennett, Guest, Fullam, Hudson* and tug *Menominee.* All craft were safely in port the following day.

In Purvis Bay *Ward's* hull was inspected by a variety of repair personnel. The results were not good. Her sonar head and badly bent port propeller could not be repaired. Both needed replacement. This work required a dry-dock and when news of this spread through the ship, *Ward's* crew envisioned a cruise to Pearl Harbor, Sydney, or some other excellent liberty port with a dry-dock. They were all disappointed to learn that *Ward* had, instead, been ordered to Espiritu Santo, which had the closest dry-dock available.[13] It was not an exciting liberty port but it would provide a change of scenery.

Before leaving for Espiritu Santo on February 28, the port screw was locked and *Ward* would proceed on one engine. *Ward* picked up 30 navy and Marine passengers bound for Noumea, New Caledonia, on leave or reassignment. She made a short detour there before heading to Espiritu Santo. She arrived at Noumea on the 28th and disembarked her passengers. *Ward* lost another of the 47th Division Reservists here as Herbert Raubig left the ship for reassignment to Gunner's Mate school in San Diego.

Ward proceeded to Espiritu Santo at 14 knots, vibrating all the way. At 0904 her own landing craft pushed her into floating dry-dock ARD-5 and assisted in mooring her. Repair yard workmen swarmed over her before the dry-dock was pumped dry. Unwanted excitement broke out ten minutes later when a repair worker's welding torch started a fire in the lower sonar room. A fire and rescue party from the destroyer tender *Dixie* was immediately summoned. Their quick response several minutes later had the fire extinguished shortly and limited damage to the loss of some confidential charts and maps.

As soon as the dock was pumped dry, *Ward's* crew went over the side to scrape the hull while yard workers began replacing the sonar head and port screw. A new screw and sonar head had been flown in from the mainland and were waiting on the dock. All damage was repaired by March 4 and *Ward's* boats and several yard tugs nudged her out of the dry-dock. *Ward* nested alongside the *Dixie* for further overhaul work.

On March 14 *Ward* was fully repaired, overhauled and ready for the war again. She weighed anchor at 1652 and headed for Guadalcanal. Nine war correspondents were riding along as passengers. Back in her old home at Purvis Bay on the 16th to await a new assignment, she got one almost immediately. She would participate in another amphibious campaign, this one relatively close to Rabaul.

Original Allied plans provided for occupying Kavieng on the northern tip of New Ireland by April 1, 1944. This would have been a major operation requiring the marshalling of considerable resources. In line with its strategy of bypassing major Japanese strongholds to save time and reduce casualties, the U.S. Joint Chiefs of Staff cancelled the operation. Planners instead substituted Emirau Island for Kavieng. Emirau, 80 miles northwest of Kavieng, would give the Allies an airfield close to Rabaul without having a major fight for it.[14]

The Japanese, in occupying other nearby strongholds, had disregarded Emirau and had no troops there. They would soon pay for that mistake. *Ward's* role in the Emirau operation would be to transport units of the 4th Marine Regiment now resting in Guadalcanal.

Ward and her eight sister APDs were under way from Tassafaronga, Guadalcanal, with the 4th Marine Regiment at 1656 on March 17. *Ward's* passengers were 208 men of Company B of the 1st Battalion and a *Life Magazine* war correspondent.[15] *Ward* was joined by *Kilty, Crosby, Dickinson,* and *Noa* in the port column with *Dent, Talbot, Waters,* and *Stringham* making up the starboard column. Destroyers *Terry, Woodworth, Anthony,* and *Braine* escorted the formation. Two days later they rendezvoused with Task Group 31.12.1 composed of LSDs and an APA attack transport.

The voyage was completed without incident and the force disembarked the troops at Emirau on March 19. No pre-landing bombardment was needed and the operation went

Boats carrying the 4th Marine Regiment on their way to the landing beach at Emirau on March 20, 1944. The *Ward* is in the foreground. (Naval Historical Center.)

down without any hitches. *Ward's* boats made one run with troops and a second with supplies. When her boats were hoisted aboard she patrolled offshore until 2000, awaiting the unloading of other landing craft. After an at-sea fueling by all APDs from oiler *Chikaskia*, the task group made their way back to Guadalcanal without incident.

Although landings may have occurred without opposition, they were not always without excitement. Friendly fire was the cause of casualties at more than one beachhead. On occasion, friendly fire would occur before the troops even left the ship. Dick Thill recalled when a soldier was displaying his BAR to others in *Ward's* troop compartment. He accidentally fired several rounds, which went through the deck above them nicking several men. The ship's doctor treated them for minor gunshot wounds but the BAR man received several lectures, both official and unofficial.[16]

At anchor at Purvis Bay, *Ward* was inactive for 12 days, waiting for the next operation. Days were long as the officers searched for activities to keep the crew busy. One of the biggest events on board was a fire in an officer's stateroom on March 27. He had inadvertently dropped hot cigarette ashes in the waste basket igniting some scrap paper. A fire party was called and quickly extinguished the fire but, the officer was the butt of jokes among the crew for days.

Another of the original 47th Division Reservists, GM2c William Scholtes, left the ship on the 27th for reassignment to the Advanced Gunner's Mate School in Washington, D.C.

Orders finally came down from Third Fleet Headquarters on April 2. *Ward, Dent, Talbot,* and *Crosby* were needed for upcoming operations in New Guinea and sailed for Milne Bay on April 4. *Noa* and *Kilty* joined them the following day. At 2204 that night a U.S. freighter, traveling alone, blundered into the path of the convoy, requiring all APDs to make an emergency turn to starboard to avoid a disaster.

Lt. Lloyd Benson, left, and Lt. Com. Fredrick Lemly, commanding officer, review *Ward's* battle flag following the Emirau landing. The flag was hung from the bridge wing when entering a port. (Naval Historical Center.)

USS *Dent* (APD-9), a sister ship of *Ward,* is under way after conversion to an APD. Although few full-length photos of *Ward* were taken as an APD, she resembled *Dent* closely. (National Archives)

The convoy reached Milne Bay on April 6 without further incident but was immediately ordered to proceed to Cape Cretin up the New Guinea coast. They anchored in Dreger Harbor on April 8. The following morning *Ward* embarked 140 officers and men of the 163rd Regimental Combat Team of the 41st Infantry Division for amphibious training. *Ward* joined eight other APDs and several LSTs, all designated Task Group 76.6.1, and sailed for Lae, New Guinea. There on April 10 they conducted a practice landing for all troops.

During the exercise a U.S. patrol bomber dropped several depth charges on a suspected submarine only five miles away. *Kilty* and destroyer *Hopewell* left the beachhead to investigate but found nothing. All boats were back aboard the APDs by 1600 which then anchored for the night. They returned to Dreger Harbor the following morning.

On April 18 the next operation up the coast of New Guinea was beginning. *Ward* again boarded the 163rd Regimental Combat Team and joined *Kilty, Schley, Dent, Talbot, Noa, Crosby, Kane,* and *Dickinson* along with Dock Landing Ship *Epping Forest* comprising Group G of Echelon R-1 of Task Group 77.3. Their destroyer screen consisted of *La Vallette, Stemble* and *Hopewell.* The task force was bound for Aitape, where they would take that area from the Japanese.

On the 19th *Ward* held abandon-ship drills for her passengers and test-fired her anti-aircraft guns as was the usual practice for all APDs on their way to an amphibious landing on a hostile shore. At noon, the formation grew larger when Group G rendezvoused with Group H. On the 20th TG 77.3 rendezvoused with TG 77.1 and 77.2, and for the first time Task Force 77 was assembled.

It was an imposing sight, one which awed even the *Ward* crewmen. Spread out all around them were eight large transports, 14 APDs, one LSD, one AK, 32 LCIs, and 21 LSTs carrying two full infantry divisions of about 35,000 troops. Their screen consisted of 18 destroyers. Nearby but detached was a covering force of eight escort carriers screened by 17 more destroyers. The triple-pronged attack involved 215 ships of all types and was the largest force MacArthur had assembled to date.[17]

Unbelievably, the Japanese did not discover the armada as it continued toward the New Guinea coast. At 1800 on the 21st, Task Group 77.3 split off from the main convoy and proceeded to Aitape. On *Ward,* crewmen wondered where the remainder of the convoy was headed. What they did not know was that Task Groups 77.1 and 77.2 were bound for Hollandia, 125 miles further up the coast.

As part of the overall Allied strategy to occupy all Japanese strong points on the New Guinea coast by the end of 1944, MacArthur had decided on an aggressive next step. He would bypass the major Japanese base at Wewak and attack three strongholds simultaneously.

Aitape, with its nearby airfield, would be assaulted by TG 77.3 while Humboldt and Tananmerah Bays, two fortified areas with several excellent airfields halfway between them at Hollandia, would be invaded by TG 77.1 and TG 77.2, respectively. Capture of these airfields would ensure that the Allies maintained air control over most of New Guinea. All Japanese forces on most of the island would be in jeopardy. D-Day for all three areas was set for dawn on April 22.

Tananmerah Bay was assigned to the 24th Infantry Division while the 41st Infantry Division, minus its 163rd Regimental Combat Team, would take Humboldt Bay. The 163rd would be storming the beach at Aitape.

Minesweepers *Perry* and *Hamilton* cautiously moved into the approaches to Aitape to clear any mines from the transport area. The APDs followed and were lying off the beach at 0527. *Ward's* boats were on the way 27 minutes later.

Since Allied intelligence was not able to determine Japanese troop strength at Aitape, the entire 1200-yard-wide beach and four offshore islands had to be neutralized prior to landing. All ships, including the APDs, were utilized in the shore bombardment and given a specific target area. *Ward's* assigned area was the small island of Tumleo, a mile and a half off the beach.[18]

Ward's three-inch guns were not designed for shore bombardment but her gun crews were eager to put her guns to use. At 0601 her Number One, Number Three, and Number Four guns opened up on Tumleo at a range of 2600 yards while *Ward* lay motionless and broadside to the target. Her shells threw up geysers of dirt and debris all over Tumleo as the guns searched for installations and troops. While a three-inch shell would not damage a ship to any extent, it could still kill men, damage equipment, and rearrange the landscape.

At 0630 naval gunfire ceased and aircraft from the escort carriers took over bombing and strafing the beach for ten minutes. When *Ward* lifted her fire on the island she noticed what looked like a small landing barge southeast of the island. Her gunners pummeled that for five minutes before it became apparent that the landing barge was, in fact, a coral reef.

Ward's boats hit the beach in the first wave at 0645. Two minutes later she resumed her fire on Tumleo and ceased fire for good after eight minutes of shooting. She expended 324 rounds of three-inch ammunition on the island and kept any Japanese there from interfering with the main landings.

Leaving the beach area, *Ward* conducted anti-submarine patrol around the LSTs for several hours. At 0927 *Ward's* boats were hoisted aboard, with *Noa*, *Schley*, and *Kane* headed back to sea to rendezvous with the First Reinforcement Group consisting of a transport, six LSTs and various other ships all carrying the 127th Regimental Team. At 1800 the four APDs met the Group and took them slowly back to the beachhead.

At 0557 on the 23rd, the ships were off the beachhead ready to unload their troops. *Ward* dispatched all four of her boats to the attack transport *Ormsby* to take off her troops for a landing on Tumleo. As the boats left the Ormsby, *Ward* opened up again on the island, this time using Number One, Number Two, and Number Four guns. She ceased fire as the boats neared shore, confident that her 311 rounds of three-inch fire left no Japanese alive on the beach.

Army troops occupying the island later confirmed that the *Ward's* bombardment had caused damage in the landing area, but the only fatality they could find was a solitary cow. *Ward* left Aitape later in the day, escorting TG 77.4.3 back to Cape Sudest.[19]

The beaches at Aitape were quickly secured at a cost of two killed and 13 wounded. Most of the 1000 Japanese troops retreated into the jungle when the bombardment began. Tadji Airfield was put into operation as a fighter base two days later. Japanese response to the landing was a single raid by three aircraft on the night of April 27 that scored a torpedo hit on the freighter *Etamin* but did not sink her.

Ward replenished her three-inch ammunition from the ammunition ship *Pyro* and refueled from the Australian tanker *Robert F. Hand* on April 27. Then it left on an escort run. Joining *Kane* and *Noa* and destroyers *John Rogers*, *Reid*, and *Kalk*, the group met Transport Task Unit 76.12.8 at sea on the 28th. The Unit, comprising transports *Harry Lee*, *Virgo*, *Windsor*, *Zeilen*, *Centaurus*, and *Ormsby*, was carrying needed reinforcements to Cape Saidor and Aitape.

TTU 76.12.8 disembarked a portion of the troops at Saidor on the 29th and sailed immediately for Aitape. With the escorts forming a protective screen 14,000 yards off the beach, the transports unloaded the remaining troops and cargo at Aitape on May 3. The convoy left later on the 3rd for a return to Cape Sudest after an incident-free voyage.

On the return, *Ward* received orders to proceed alone to Dreger Harbor at Cape Cretin. Nearing the harbor, *Ward* received an SOS call from a disabled small boat outside the harbor. Spotting the craft, the Captain ordered *Ward's* Number Two boat into the water to tow the craft into the harbor. It was just another of the odd jobs that APDs were called on to do.

Ward had no sooner refueled when it was ordered out on another escort mission. Acting as a destroyer she joined a five-ship screen to take TU 76.2.85 to Humboldt Bay with troops and supplies. She rendezvoused with U.S. transport *Henry T. Allen* and Australian transports HMAS *Minoora*, HMAS *Kinimbla*, and HMAS *Westralia* for what would be a routine cruise. The convoy was back at Cape Cretin at 1115 on May 9. An hour later *Ward*, along with destroyer *Swanson* and APDs *Herbert*, and *Dickerson*, continued on to Cape Sudest with three of the transports.

After five days of inactivity at Cape Sudest, *Ward* headed down the coast to Port Harvey, where she anchored two hours later. She was in need of routine overhaul work and the destroyer tender USS *Dobbin* was anchored there. Port Harvey was not a good liberty stop but at least the crew was able to feel solid ground under their feet again. S1c Charles Benge discovered that sometimes the toughest part of a liberty was the boat ride. Jumping into the Higgins boat for the return trip to the *Ward*, he fractured his leg. Her overhaul completed, *Ward* returned to Cape Sudest.

On the move again on May 21 *Ward,* in company with *Herbert,* cruised up the coast to Humboldt Bay with orders to pick up the Panamanian tanker *SS Alcibiades.* The tanker was not at its designated position, and the APDs were forced to search four hours before they located it. Continuing along the coast, the APDs encountered a steady stream of ship traffic, making it apparent that the Hollandia landings had now created one of the world's major coastal shipping lanes. The tanker was safely anchored in Humboldt Bay on May 24.

At Humboldt Bay, Captain Lemly learned that *Ward* would participate in still another major amphibious operation. The Allied march up the New Guinea coast was almost complete, with only a few Japanese strongholds remaining at the western end of the big island. When these were captured MacArthur would be able to leapfrog to the Philippines, his major goal.

One of the strongholds was the 45-mile-long island of Biak, lying 60 miles off the New Guinea coast. Biak's three airfields controlled the air over the gigantic Vogelkop peninsula at the west end of New Guinea and had to be taken. The 10,000 Japanese troops on Biak could make its capture difficult. MacArthur planned to land at Bosnik on Biak's southern shore on May 27. The landing would be carried out by units of the 41st Infantry Division carried by LSTs, a variety of smaller landing craft, and five APDs.

Bosnik was selected because of its proximity to the airfields, the relatively flat land behind the beaches, and its long stone jetties that could accommodate shipping. As the administrative center of the former Dutch colony on New Guinea, Bosnik was also now the headquarters of the Japanese occupation army.[20]

On the morning of May 25, *Ward* embarked 129 men of various units of Company K of the 186th Regiment of the 41st Infantry Division.[21] At 1630 she was travelling with *Kilty, Schley, Crosby,* and *Herbert,* comprising Task Unit 77.4.3. Outside the harbor they rendezvoused with TU 77.4.2, consisting of a group of LSTs. Soon, TU 77.4.4, with a formation of LCIs and escorts, joined the convoy making an impressive array of ships moving up the New Guinea coast. Japanese snooper aircraft spotted the convoy but no attacks resulted, suggesting that either the Japanese were short of aircraft or they were conserving them for a later attack.

On May 26, as Task Force 77 prodded along toward Biak, a U.S. Navy photographer, travelling on *Ward* as a passenger to photograph the invasion, talked to several crewmen. He was intrigued to learn that there were still 18 men on board who had been on the ship on December 7 at Pearl Harbor. He asked that the 18 men congregate on deck for a photo.

Even more startling was the fact that 15 of the men were members of the original 47th Division reserves, which took over the ship in February 1941 after its recommissioning. The remainder of the original crewmen who had left the ship did so because, having gained valuable experience on *Ward,* they were reassigned to newer or bigger ships.

Task Force 77 was off the shore of Biak at 0629 on May 27 and a minute later proceeded to commence a 45-minute bombardment. Cruisers *Boise, Phoenix,* and *Nashville* unleashed more than 1000 six-inch shells, which pulverized the terrain for a 15-mile length of coastline. Destroyers pounded the actual landing beaches with five-inch shells to destroy anything close to the water's edge. At 0725 a formation of 25 B-24 bombers joined in, raking the beaches with anti-personnel bombs.

The effect was awesome. It appeared that no one could live through the devastating barrage. In the dead calm of the morning a heavy smoke cloud from the naval and aerial bombardment hung low over the island obscuring the view of the shore from the ships.

On the *Ward,* troops were ready. The ship's cooks fed them at 0400, before the ship's

Photo taken on *Ward* en route to the Biak landing in May 1944. These 18 men were the only crewmen who had served on the ship since its commissioning in January 1941 and had been on the ship on December 7 at Pearl Harbor. Fifteen were members of the 47th Division Reserve unit from St. Paul. Bottom row, from left: James Spratt, Alfred Fink, Orville Ethier, Clarence Fenton, Donald Pepin, Giles LeClair, Frederick Hughes. Top row: Ray Nolde, William Griep, Howard Gearing, Harold Harris, Howard Paynter, James Lovsted, William Duval, Irvin Holley, William Lehner, EdWard Bukrey, Frank Fratto. (Naval Historical Center)

crew was fed. At 0541 crews manned the boats as *Ward* moved to the debarkation area. She lowered her boats at 0629 and loaded the men. The boats were away at 0728 with boats from all APDs making up the fifth wave. They disappeared into the smoke and hit the beach at 0735.

Although *Ward's* boats received no fire from shore, other ship's boats did. Japanese machine-gun fire hit several boats, and shore batteries scored hits on a number of transports. The smoke and dust from the bombardment became so thick that coxswains were having difficulty finding their designated beach. Some APD's boats landed considerably west of their beach and caused much confusion until the error was discovered. Ground units, once on shore, were forced to move through other units to continue toward their designated targets.

Eventually all enemy beach opposition was silenced and landings continued without return fire. *Ward's* boats were back from the beach at 0818 but were immediately sent to the LSTs to assist in taking supplies from the huge landing craft to the beach. By 0954 her boats were back on board and the five APDs left the area to return to Hollandia. By 1715, 12,000 troops had been put ashore along with tanks, artillery, and 2400 tons of supplies.

By the end of the day the beachhead was secure and troops were advancing on the airfields. Although fighting was fierce, Japanese strongholds were captured one by one. The airfields were taken in early June and quickly made operational. Once again *Ward* came through a major contested landing without damage or casualties.

On the return trip *Crosby* lost fuel suction and lay dead in the water while the engine room gang made repairs. *Ward* stood by her on anti-submarine watch until *Crosby* was able to move again. Both ships were back in Humboldt Bay on May 28.

On June 1, while on anti-submarine patrol outside Humboldt Bay, S1c Rudolph Thurmond fell overboard while loosening a turnbuckle on a lifeline. Number Two boat was immediately lowered and Thurmond was back on board shortly. A similar misfortune would occur months later with much different results.[22]

With all of the activity at Biak and other locations along the New Guinea coast, Humboldt Bay had quickly become a major Allied anchorage. British, Dutch, Australian, New Zealand, and U.S. ships ranging in size from heavy cruisers to landing craft dotted the seascape, a lucrative target for submarines. Ship arrivals and departures were continuous. *Ward* and other APDs spent three weeks patrolling for submarines outside the harbor.

On June 21 *Ward* was ordered to a base the crew had not yet seen, Seeadler Harbor on Manus Island in the Admiralty Islands. The Admiralties, lying northwest of Rabaul, were occupied by MacArthur's forces on February 29. This gave the Allies the major base they would have had if they had taken Rabaul itself. Capturing Rabaul from the 90,000 Japanese who held it was an opportunity the Allies decided to pass up.

The Admiralties, with only 2000 troops on it, was a preferable substitute. It had all the attractive features of Rabaul, including airfields and a magnificent harbor. Seeadler Harbor was 15 miles long and four miles wide, much larger than Pearl Harbor, and one of the finest anchorages in the entire Pacific. Its capture completely sealed off Rabaul from the outside.

Ward arrived at Seeadler Harbor on June 22; two days later she nested alongside her old friend, destroyer tender *Dobbin*. Here she received the benefits of another tender overhaul.

Fresh from her overhaul she took on 705 rounds of three-inch shells and fuel from tanker *Leopard*. She was ready for the war again on July 4 and left for New Guinea on the following day. She was safely back in Dreger Harbor, Cape Cretin, on July 6 but stayed only long enough to exchange boats with *Schley*. *Ward* left immediately for Milne Bay, at the very southeast tip of New Guinea, where she arrived on July 7.

Here *Ward* turned in Schley's battered boats to the Amphibious Training Command and received four reconditioned boats in exchange. She also took on 184 naval officers and men for transportation to Cape Cretin, where she dropped them off on July 10. She rendezvoused with *Schley* to again exchange boats with her, thus providing her sister ship with newly conditioned landing craft.

Ward was moving again on the afternoon of the 10th, this time to Alexishafen, New Guinea, for three days of various systems maintenance. She returned to Cape Cretin on the 17th, just in time for a vicious wind and rain storm. The Australian transport *HMAS Kinimbla* dragged her anchor in the howling gale and was soon aground. Captain Lemly feared that *Ward* would suffer the same fate and took the ship out of the harbor, where she could face the wind bow on. Seven hours later, when the storm subsided, *Ward* returned to the harbor.

On July 19 *Ward* left Cape Cretin independently for simulated battle exercises at sea. She fired all of her three-inch and 20-mm guns and dropped depth charges. Her depth charges were old and deteriorating and would have had to be disposed of in any case had they not been used now.

The crew was treated to a rare occurrence at 1733 on July 20 when they observed a full

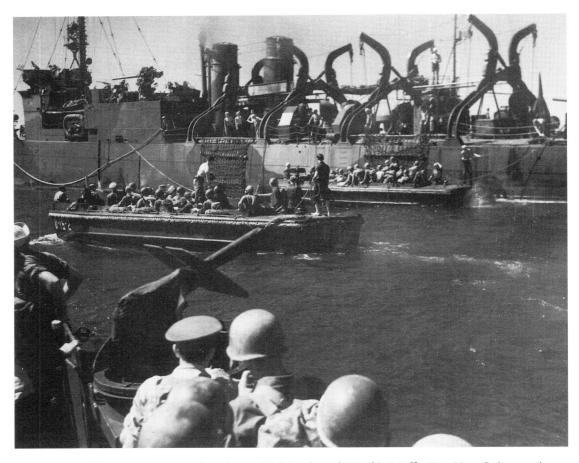

Troops of the 1st Regiment, 6th Infantry Division board *Ward* in Maffin Bay, New Guinea, using *Ward's* boats before the Allied landing at Cape Sansapor, July 30 . 1944. (National Archives)

solar eclipse.[23] The deck was full of crewmen curious to witness something they had never seen before.

Ward entered Humboldt Bay on July 21 for a few days of quiet. On July 22 Captain Lemly was appointed temporary commander of Transportation Division 22 but would still retain command of *Ward*. Later in the day, with *Ward* leading and acting as navigator, the ship joined *Kilty, Crosby, Schley,* and *Herbert,* minesweeper *Vireo* and four other minesweepers in escorting 20 LCIs to Maffin Bay. The convoy reached the destination safely on the 22nd.

At Maffin Bay, *Ward* began preparations for her next amphibious landing. On the 23rd she embarked 94 men of Companies E and F of the 1st Regiment of the 6th Infantry Division for practice landings. The APDs took the troops to a beach near Toem, New Guinea, for landing drills and returned on the 24th.

With practice over, on the 27th, *Ward* embarked the same men, along with three Australian war correspondents, for the real thing. The five APDs joined 19 LCIs and eight LSTs in a convoy escorted by 11 destroyers and four sub chasers. Each of the LSTs in turn towed an LCM. The convoy was carrying the entire 1st Regiment.[24]

The force was part of "Operation Globetrotter," which was assembled to seize an important airfield site at Cape Sansapor near the extreme westerly tip of New Guinea. Cape Sansapor was selected because of its fine beaches and excellent airfield locations. With an airfield here, New Guinea would essentially be entirely under Allied air control.

Scouting parties had already discovered an absence of Japanese troops in the area so resistance, if any, was expected to be light. No pre-landing bombardment was planned. Despite this, *Ward* test-fired all anti-aircraft guns and conducted drills en route to the landing. Enemy aircraft were reported in the vicinity of the convoy but none closed in on the convoy.

At 0626 on July 30 the Task Group was off the beach at Cape Sansapor. *Ward's* actions in the landing were a model of perfection. After feeding the troops first and then the ship's crew, the boat crews were at their stations at 0600. The troops were on deck ready to load at 0615, the boats in the water at 0628 and the troops loaded by 0630. All boats were in position at the line of departure at 0650 and the first wave commenced their run for the beach at 0655. The boats were on the beach at precisely their designated time of 0700 and backed off empty at 0702. All four boats were hoisted on board at 0720 and *Ward* was under way at 0725 for the return to Hollandia.

Making this achievement more remarkable was the need to tow one of *Ward's* boats back to the ship. It had bent its rudder in landing but crews on the ship repaired it within an hour.

The entire landing of six waves was carried out in an hour without any opposition. All landing craft were unloaded by late afternoon and on their way back for reinforcements. Passing Biak Island on the return trip, the APDs noticed anti-aircraft fire over the island for an hour. No aircraft bothered the convoy as it continued, now in darkness.

The Cape Sansapor operation was concluded within a month with a total of no more than 43 men killed and 85 wounded. This was the final landing in New Guinea; General MacArthur's next move on the way back to the Philippines would be the Island of Morotai in the Dutch East Indies. The allied movement, in which *Ward* had an active role, had now progressed almost 1000 miles up the rugged New Guinea coast in only four months.

After seven months of continuous action up and down the coast of New Guinea, without a leave or meaningful liberty, *Ward's* crew received exciting news on August 3. The commander of the Seventh Amphibious Force ordered the ship to Sydney for an overhaul and ten-day liberty. On August 4, *Ward* took on six naval officers and 20 enlisted men also bound for Sydney as passengers. *Kilty* and *Crosby* received identical orders and would travel with her.

At 2008 the three APDs were heading for the land down under, with brief stops at Finschafen and Milne Bay. *Ward* led the way at 19 knots. *Ward* dropped off one passenger at Finschafen, picked up fuel and 34 more naval officers at Milne Bay, and later transferred some of them to the *Kilty* and *Crosby* to better distribute the load.

The APDs were finally on their way on August 8 and had now picked up *Schley* and *Herbert* as well. Captain Lemly acted as commander of the Division for the cruise. The group encountered rough weather immediately, and rough seas on the 9th tore the ready locker for Number One gun loose from the deck. It ripped a hole in the weather deck that took in water. *Ward* slowed to 10 knots while a crew made repairs.

The officer in charge of the naval passengers told the *Ward's* officers to treat his men as if they were troops on a mission and assign them menial duties on the ship. One navy lieutenant objected to officers having to work and refused to do any at all. Upon hearing this, the passenger's commander ordered the officer not to leave *Ward* when it reached Sydney.

Instead, he would be put on the first available plane back to New Guinea. Other passengers quickly got the message.

The inviting sight of beautiful Sydney welcomed the crew at 1030 on August 12 as sailors lined the deck for a glimpse of the harbor. *Ward* disembarked all of her passengers with the exception of the disgruntled officer.

For *Ward's* crew it was a repeat of the earlier trip to Sydney. Men who had not seen a western city, neon lights, restaurants, tavern, or women for eight months now had time to catch up. Before leaving the ship they were strongly reminded that they were representatives of the navy and the United States and must conduct themselves in a manner reflecting well on both. Most men did that. Several, however, returned to the ship with an assortment of injuries, obviously acquired from fighting.

Some used the liberty to renew friendships made on the first trip to Sydney. Will Lehner spent much of the time visiting his friend Valerie and her family. The liberty passed too quickly and the crew was saddened to see it end.

Ward was overhauled and made ready for another series of landings. It was a refreshed crew that mustered on the ship on August 22 for the return to New Guinea. A number of men who reported to the ship late from liberty would have to explain their actions at a Captain's Mast. Their sentence, in most cases, would be extra duty hours.

Ward left the serenity and beauty of Sydney behind at 1406 on the 22nd and, with her four sister ships, pointed her bow north for the war zone. Although they did not know it, the coming months would be the most dangerous of the war for U.S. naval vessels. They would face a new weapon, used by the Japanese in desperation, for the first time. *Ward* would soon see that weapon, for which there were few defenses. The Japanese called it "divine wind." United States sailors called it "kamikaze."

CHAPTER 14

Leyte

Crewmen were still reminiscing about the liberty as the five APDs steamed north from Sydney at 19 knots. It was 1944, and the *Ward* was carrying 90 naval passengers back to their posts in New Guinea to resume the war. On August 26 she received a message for *Schley* to reduce speed to five knots. A sailor on the *Schley* was diagnosed with appendicitis and needed an immediate operation. A Pharmacist's Mate would perform the operation but needed a steady operating table. All five ships immediately slowed to five knots. Two hours later, Schley notified all ships that the operation was successful and all resumed normal speed.

The convoy arrived in Milne Bay on the 27th without further incident. *Ward* dropped off 21 passengers, picked up 214 more bound for bases further up the coast, and resumed her voyage. She dropped off 74 men at Finschafen on the 28th and continued to Humboldt Bay, Hollandia, arriving at 0600 on August 30. After discharging her remaining passengers she was ready to get back into the war.

Ward's stay at Hollandia did not last long. On September 1 she was ordered to join *Kilty* in escorting LSTs 181, 459, 467, and 472 down the coast to Aitape. On September 3 *Ward* embarked 135 men of Company A of the 124th Regiment of the 31st Infantry Division for landing exercises. The following day, in company with *Kilty, Crosby, Schley,* and *Herbert* she rendezvoused with TU 77.3.1 for what turned out to be a successful drill on a secluded beach near Aitape.

These preparations were for the next operation, which would take the Allies beyond New Guinea. After clawing their way up the big island's coast in some of the worst terrain in the world, the Allies were ready to leap to a stepping stone halfway to the Philippines. Their destination was Morotai, a 25-mile by 44-mile-island in the Dutch East Indies. It would be a staging base for the planned invasion of Mindanao, which was to be the first Philippine Island to be recaptured.

Halmahera Island was the first choice for the staging base until it was discovered that it contained excellent natural defense lines, with 25,000 Japanese troops defending its nine airfields. By contrast, intelligence had learned that only 500 troops defended Morotai. Its single airfield was only partially constructed but it could be completed quickly. [1]

A force of 28,000 Allied troops, with the 31st Infantry Division as its nucleus, would assault Morotai. Troops and the mountain of supplies needed to sustain the force would be carried in a gigantic convoy, including two Australian attack transports, five APDs, 45 LSTs, 24 LCIs, 20 LCTs, and one LSD. [2]

The force would be assembled at both Hollandia and Biak and be screened by 24 destroyers, four frigates, and assorted other ships. Distant cover and support would be provided by a naval force that included several escort carriers. TransDiv22 would furnish the five APDs.

Ward was under way at 0710 on September 10, as part of TU 77.3.1, with 157 men of Company A of the 124th Regiment on board.[3] The force rendezvoused with TU 77.3.2 on the following day, creating an imposing sight. One of *Kilty's* crewmen apparently was so impressed with the view that he fell overboard. LCI-578, following *Kilty* picked him up. On September 13, TU 77.3.3 and a cruiser bombardment squadron both joined the formation, making the invasion force whole for the first time.

On the afternoon of the 13th, several troops on LCI-225 needed medical attention. *Ward* was ordered to pick them up and transfer them to the command ship *Wasatch*. She lowered Number One boat and made the transfer. Several hours later Number One boat was sent to LCI-970 for the same purpose. At 1652 *Ward's* medical officer made a third trip, this time to look at several men on LCI-25. He treated them on the LCI without need to transfer them.

The armada reached the coast of Morotai at 0630 on September 15 and prepared to land. The cruiser force had already shelled suspected enemy positions on neighboring islands for an hour without receiving return fire. Australian ships commenced bombarding the landing beaches, stopping just before the landing craft hit the shore.

The 20 boats of the APDs landed their troops as scheduled at exactly 0830 as part of the first wave. As expected, the landing was unopposed. The APDs retracted their boats and reformed outside the transport to provide anti-submarine screening while the LCIs unloaded. At 1430 the APDs shepherded the LCIs into a convoy for the return to Cape Sansapor.

Although the landing was free of opposition, it was not without problems. Because of the gradual slope of the beach, the APD's boats grounded 80 yards off shore. Men stepped off the boats into armpit-deep water and waded ashore in a thick gumbo mud. Many vehicles had to be pushed ashore by bulldozers brought in by the LSTs.

The beachhead was totally secured by noon and sporadic combat occurred for the next 30 days. Army fighters were operating from the Morotai airfield by October 4, and it quickly became the principal base for raids on Leyte Island.

On September 19 *Ward*, *Kilty* and *Schley* escorted 23 LCIs down the coast to Humboldt Bay, where they would be loaded with reinforcements for Morotai. On the afternoon of the 19th, an army P-38 fighter crashed 1500 yards off *Ward's* starboard quarter although no enemy aircraft were in the vicinity. The plane sank immediately but the pilot escaped and was seen shortly floating in a life jacket.

Ward headed for the scene at full speed and lowered Number One boat as soon as she approached the pilot. At 1447 the boat picked up 1st Lt. Edgar Scott of the 18th Fighter Group and returned him to the *Ward* uninjured.[4] With Scott and Number One boat safely aboard, *Ward* resumed her position in the convoy screen.

Scott, from Corvallis, Montana, was one of the tough-luck pilots of the war. On this day he was hit by anti-aircraft fire over Halmahera Island while on a strafing mission. He managed to nurse his aircraft out to sea where he could ditch near a friendly ship. This was the fourth time he had been shot down.

He would be downed one more time on January 31, 1945, while on a mission over Formosa. Again the anti-aircraft fire knocked out one of his plane's two engines. His remaining engine carried him 90 miles out to sea before it quit running. He bailed out safely and rescue planes were on the scene shortly. The rough seas, however, prevented them from picking him up and he was never seen again.[5]

In the early hours of September 21 the convoy experienced some scary moments. *Ward's* radar picked up two unidentified ships approaching the convoy in the darkness from dead ahead. Twenty-seven minutes later, as the first ship passed close by the convoy on the starboard side, *Schley* directed the ship to veer to port to clear the LCIs. It did as directed but the second ship, seemingly confused, veered to port and then back to starboard directly into the path of the LCIs.

The ship, now identified as a U.S. Army tanker, passed only 700 yards to starboard of *Ward,* continuing to ignore *Ward's* directions. Although the LCIs now turned on their running lights at *Ward's* order, the tanker severed a tow line between LCIs 1014 and 1015 and crashed into LCI-578. By sheer luck, a major disaster was averted. The 5000-ton tanker could have easily demolished several of the 200-ton LCIs or the 1100-ton APDs. As it was, damage was confined to LCI-578 and it was able to continue on with the convoy. At 0558 all ships were back in Humboldt Bay, shaken but safe.[6]

After *Ward* had dropped off Lt. Scott and several wounded army troops, it made a test run outside the harbor to check out a suspected problem. The test confirmed that her reduction gears were misaligned and in need of emergency repair. Fortunately destroyer-tender *Dobbin* was stationed in the harbor and *Ward* anchored alongside. *Ward* remained nested to the tender for nine days while her repair workers took *Ward's* engines apart.

During *Ward's* stay in Hollandia, Ensign Guy Thompson, an officer newly assigned to the ship, was attempting to make connections with it. He waited in a Quonset hut for more than a week, checking daily with operations and intelligence officers to determine the location of *Ward.* It rained continuously the entire time. Having no success, he checked with the mail distribution center and learned that *Ward's* mail had been picked up every day. He waited at the mail center the next day and made connection with the men picking up the ship's mail. He finally arrived on board on September 28, soaked to the skin. *Ward's* officers, from Captain Lemly on down, welcomed Thompson and provided dry clothes. His first impression of the ship and officers was more than positive.[7]

On October 1 the overhaul was completed and *Ward* gave the engines a thorough test in open water. Results were satisfactory and *Ward* was again ready for war.

On October 5 she led TransDiv 22 (*Schley, Kilty, Crosby,* and *Herbert*) south to Finschafen to pick up troops. On the 6th *Ward* stopped to transfer her doctor to *Kilty* for an emergency operation. The formation reached Dreger Harbor on October 7 but high winds, rough seas and poor weather postponed the loading of ammunition and supplies until the 8th. On the 9th she embarked 148 officers and men of Companies E and F of the 6th Ranger Battalion.

The formation left for Humboldt Bay in the afternoon with *Ward* leading the column. On the morning of October 11 TransDiv 22 reached Humboldt Bay, where all APDs refueled from tanker *Villalobos.* The harbor was already full of ships of all types and more were arriving by the hour. On the 12th, U.S cruisers *Boise, Nashville, Phoenix,* and Australian cruisers *Shropshire* and *Australia* stood in for fuel.

At 1514 on October 12 Task Group 78.4, including the *Ward,* was on the move. The British minelayer-transport *HMS Ariadne* was functioning as fleet guide. This was, indeed, a momentous day. Although the Japanese did not know it yet, the liberation of the Philippines was now imminent. In keeping with her role of being first in major actions, *Ward* would again be first in this historic event. She and her sister APDs would take the initial step in the invasion of the Philippines. They would land troops three days before the main landings took place on Leyte Island.

The original Allied plans provided for invading the huge southern Philippine Island

of Mindanao on November 15. This would allow the establishment of air fields to support the invasion of Leyte in the central Philippines on December 20. Airfields on Leyte would, in turn, permit landings on the main island of Luzon scheduled for February 20, 1945.

Several unforeseen factors led General MacArthur to recommend a revised Philippine schedule to the Joint Chiefs of Staff in the fall of 1944. U.S. carrier raids in the Philippines in the summer of 1944 encountered unexpectedly weak opposition from Japanese aircraft indicating that Japanese land-based air power was no longer a major force in the islands.

In addition, large U.S. carrier forces in 1944 developed quite rapidly and their use in other amphibious operations was extremely successful. It became apparent to naval planners

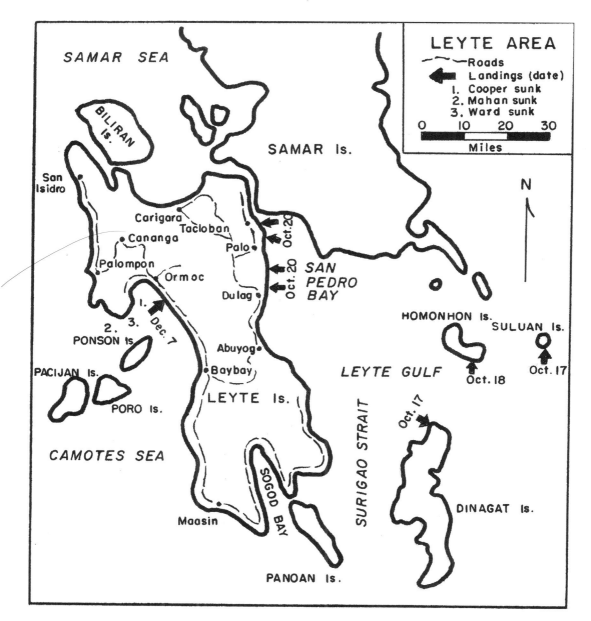

that the previously held concept of establishing land-based air power in order to ensure air control over the next amphibious landing operation was no longer valid. Navy airpower from aircraft carriers alone was now capable of establishing air control over any area.

The reliance on ground airfields had previously limited the length of leap frog amphibious operations to the range of ground-based aircraft, usually several hundred miles. Use of aircraft carriers for air power, however, allowed a leap frog of almost any distance. Invading Mindanao was no longer a prerequisite for a landing on Leyte, allowing the Allies to now assault Leyte as the first step in the Philippines. They would simply bring their floating airfields with them. The landing was scheduled for October 20, cutting two months off the original schedule.[8]

Accelerating the schedule for Leyte was a logistical nightmare but by early October, 738 ships were assembled at Hollandia and Seeadler Harbor in the Admiralty Islands. The size of the armada assembled was exceeded to date only by that used to assault the beaches at Normandy, France, in June 1944.[9]

The task force included 420 amphibious ships to land an initial force of 145,000 men and a follow-up of 55,000 additional troops. It would also bring the huge amounts of supplies and equipment needed to sustain this enormous army. Once loaded, the fleet had a 1250-mile journey from Hollandia and an 1800-mile trip from Seeadler Harbor. The nine-knot LSTs left Seeadler on October 10 in order to arrive off Leyte on October 20.

TransDiv 22 was carrying the 6th Ranger Battalion and Company B of the 21st Infantry Regiment but they would not be going to Leyte Island. Nor would they be waiting until October 20 to get into action. They had been given a special assignment and would be the first U.S. troops to land in the Philippines since the war began.

The entrance to Leyte Gulf, the site of the main landings, was divided by several islands containing Japanese radio and radar installations that guarded Leyte. Allied planners decided to destroy these important installations three days before the assault on Leyte itself. This task was entrusted to the 6th Ranger Battalion, carried to their destination by TransDiv 22.

Below deck of the APDs, the troops made preparations for combat as they bided their time. When the ships were converted to APDs, extra blowers were installed in the new troop compartments for added comfort. However, the air in the compartments still became oppressive. Packing 150 men into a compartment for days in a humid tropic environment quickly created a "lived in" odor that blowers simply could not dissipate. Shower facilities aboard ship were far from luxurious and restrictions on water use compounded the problem of keeping clean.

As junior officer of the watch, Ensign Thompson was required to make a ship's tour, including all berthing spaces, every hour between sunset and sunrise. Although the compartments were lighted at night by several red lights that created a very dim twilight, strolling through the compartment was not without risk. Until an officer learned where all the obstructions were, making the rounds for the first few times was guaranteed to produce a mass of shin bruises.

Of even greater concern to Thompson were the troops themselves, most of them battle-hardened veterans. As he put it, "It was nerve racking to walk through the troop compartment at night. The troops all slept in their skivvies with no sheet covering them. Most men had, as sleeping companions, one or two grenades, a jungle knife and maybe a sidearm. Considering that they were highly keyed up, when walking through the compartment one had to be damn careful not to jiggle a berth or arouse a nervous sleeper."[10]

As Task Group 78.4 proceeded towards Leyte, a rendezvous with tankers *Salamoni*, *Chepachet*, and *Winooski* was scheduled on October 15 to refuel the minesweepers, escorts, and APDs. The rendezvous was made but the weather turned sour and a driving rain with 30-knot winds raked the area. Hooking up to the tankers was extremely difficult and refueling took hours to complete. October was the stormy season in the Philippines, and the stormy spell the fleet encountered while refueling would remain through the landings.

The minesweepers (TG 77.5) and the APDs (TG 78.4) steamed together at 10 knots through the rough seas on October 16 with no indication that they had been spotted by Japanese search planes. Suddenly, at 0558 on the 17th, a flare popped above them silhouetting every ship in an eerie white glare. They could no longer count on the element of surprise and an attack could be expected at any time.

At 0635, as the force neared Dinagat Island, the minesweepers moved to the van of the formation and began sweeping a channel for the APDs. At 0838 destroyer *Lang* and frigate *Bisbee* opened fire on shore targets. The battle for the Philippines had begun.

The APDs followed the minesweepers in a column astern to a point 1000 yards off the Dinagat beach, designated as "Black Beach," where they anchored. Their luck held out and although they were in range of any shore guns, they received no fire. The weather was still terrible, howling winds causing the driving rain to blow horizontally, complicating the loading of boats. At 0900 *Ward's* boats were in motion with Company E, heading for the beach. The LCPRs had difficulty maneuvering in the seas that tossed water over their sides as the men huddled out of the wind. All boats managed to reach the shore without drawing enemy fire.

Ward's boats pulled away from the beach and returned to the British minelayer *Ariadne,* functioning as a transport. They took off the troops she was carrying since the *Ariadne* had no boats of her own. At 0924 *Schley's* boats came alongside *Ward* to take off remaining troops from Company F. *Ward's* passengers were now all disembarked.

The first opposition emerged in the form of several aircraft, but the massed anti-aircraft fire drove them off. At 1101 *Ward's* boats took ammunition and supplies to the beachhead. During the commotion of the landing, a fire broke out in *Ward's* forward crew compartment necessitating calling the ship to fire quarters. A fire crew extinguished it before it could do much damage.

The rough seas and tidal currents now made it difficult for the *Ward* to stay within the swept channel and were threatening to tear the anchor windlass from the ship. At 1143 she weighed anchor and moved out to open water. The gale-like winds sweeping directly into the beach and rising in intensity had now created havoc on shore.

The wind pushed *Ward's* Number One, Two, and Four boats onto the beach, stranding all three. Number Three boat, with full power straining the engine, was able to extract itself and backed off the beach. It also managed to tow Number One boat off the sand, but Number Two and Four boats were stuck fast. Number One boat made it back to the *Ward,* but Number Three boat could make it only as far as the *Schley,* which took it aboard. *Ward,* in turn, hoisted aboard one of *Schley's* boats that could not get back to her because of the rough seas.[11]

Ward now left the beach area and joined others in screening for another mine sweeping operation. The weather continued to deteriorate as winds howled and the seas rose. Skies darkened even though it was only mid-day. Ed Bukrey had the 1400 to 1600 wheel watch and saw drifting mines freed by the sweeping. "We tried to hit them with our 20s to detonate them but the ship was tossing so badly we couldn't hit anything. I thought we were going to flounder," recalled Bukrey. The weather remained bad at the beachhead for the remainder of the day and night.

The weather had made operations almost impossible for the LCPRs. By nightfall *Ward* still had her two boats high and dry on the beach. *Schley* had one boat beached and one sunk while *Kilty* had two beached and one sunk. *Crosby* lost all four of her boats.

When it became apparent that *Ward's* two boats could not return to the ship, Boat Officer, Ensign Guy Thompson, who had only joined the ship three weeks earlier, requested and received permission to dig in for the night on the beach. Thompson gathered together his two boat crews, plus the crew of *Schley's* boat, to dig a series of foxholes for the 19 men. Before darkness fell, an army officer warned the sailors to stay put, as his soldiers would shoot anything moving above ground during the night.

The boat crews spent a miserable night with the storm still howling above them. Two buckets, one for sanitary purposes and one filled with oil-soaked sand to brew coffee in the morning were the only amenities in the foxholes. The crews requisitioned the boat's emergency rations, which were the sole supply of food. A case of peaches discovered in one of the boats provided an unexpected treat.

The crew removed one of the boat's 0.30-caliber machine guns and tied it to a log for a mount. Thompson's side arm was the only other weapon; it gave the crewman standing watch a small measure of reassurance by holding on to it.[12]

By morning the weather had improved somewhat and the APDs returned to the beach to complete the unloading. *Ward* was a mess. The deck was littered with debris and every flag had been ripped from the masts. She then grounded temporarily on a reef but later floated off with the tide. She was still missing two boats.

At 0730 *Ward's* Number One boat left for the beach with supplies and *Schley's* Number One boat came alongside for a load of supplies also. At 0950 lookouts spotted two Val dive bombers coming in over the hills of Dinagat four miles away. *Ward* went to General Quarters immediately and opened up with all guns. One bomber made a strafing run at the ships but was driven off by heavy fire. The second, seeing this, did not attack at all.

Ward sent a salvage party ashore in the afternoon of the 18th to recover her boats and their crews. Number Four boat was badly damaged but refloated and towed back to the ship. With the help of a boat pulling from offshore, boat crews pushed Number Two boat off the beach and, although damaged, made it back under its own power. The boat crews were cold and hungry but otherwise made it through the harrowing experience with a few new stories to tell.

On the morning of October 19 *Ward* transferred her two remaining undamaged boats to the *Crosby* to pick up one company of Rangers off the beach at Suluan Island and take them to Dinagat. *Crosby* had no useable boats at all.

Suluan was actually the first of the Leyte Gulf islands to be assaulted when Company D of the 6th Rangers hit the beach at 0820 on the 17th. The troops soon disposed of the 32 Japanese on the small island and destroyed the lighthouse being used as an observation post. It was here that all four of *Crosby's* boats were rammed onto the beach by 50-knot winds.

The weather prevented the Rangers from landing on the third island, Homonhan, until noon on the 18th. They found the island unoccupied. Thus, by the afternoon of October 18, the entrance to Leyte Gulf was secured, compliments of the 6th Ranger Battalion and the APDs. The next two days would be spent sweeping Leyte Gulf itself of mines before the 145,000 troops poured in on the 20th.

On the evening of the 19th the APDs left the beach area to screen and patrol. On the following morning they were ordered to steam to newly acquired Babelthaup in the Palau Islands. A massive shore bombardment of Leyte's beaches had begun on the 19th and at 1000 on the 20th, the recapture of the Philippines began in earnest.

A tragedy struck *Ward* on October 20. While standing at their position under Number One boat davit during a collision drill, seven sailors not involved in the drill were holding on to a life line. Suddenly it gave way. Without warning two men were pitched into the sea.

Other crewmen immediately threw life jackets to them and the ship turned sharply to close on them. Sailors quickly lowered Number Four boat with Lt. Railsback in command to pick them up. APD *Herbert's* Number One boat, however, was the first to reach the men. When it was within 10 yards of them, one of the men in the water yelled that he was fine but that his crewmate was having difficulty. A sailor dove off the boat, grabbed the man in trouble, S2c William Behme, and pulled him to safety.[13]

The other sailor in the water, WT3c Paul (Eddie) Duchin from Chisholm, Minnesota, was an excellent swimmer and had won swimming contests in high school. He was seen sinking beneath the water before anyone could reach him. Crewmen from *Herbert's* boat indicated that Duchin did not appear to be injured. That boat returned Behme to *Ward,* where he was given artificial respiration and treated for shock and immersion. He soon recovered from the near drowning. The two LCPRs searched for Duchin for an hour in the area without any further sign of him.[14]

Ensign Thompson, the Boat Officer, was in one of the standby boats watching the incident. He observed a huge shark approaching Duchin and then dive under the water. Said Thompson, "I've seen a lot of sharks in my time at sea but this was the largest I ever saw."[15]

The Captain held an investigation into the accident and although there were some crewmen who unofficially felt that the two sailors had been sitting on the lifeline before it gave way, an action that was strictly prohibited, none testified to that effect during the proceedings. The Mast hearing concluded that a turnbuckle had loosened, causing the lifeline to give way.[16]

In three years of combat during which *Ward* had been bombed, strafed, and crashed by a kamikaze and sunk, the ship had not lost a man to hostile fire. Duchin was the only fatality and he was lost in an accident. The incident shook the crew but they still realized how lucky they had been throughout the war. They knew that crewmen's lives would eventually be lost if *Ward* continued in combat, but the loss of Duchin still hit the small crew hard.

Ward, Schley, and *Herbert* pulled into Kossol Roads in the Palau Islands on October 22. For the *Ward* it would be her only visit there. With the extra 147 passengers on the long cruise from Hollandia to Leyte and Palau, Ward had run out of food. The officers found a merchant ship in the harbor with a load of individual "C" rations still on board and arranged to requisition enough to get *Ward* back to Hollandia. *Ward's* cooks opened countless tins of the rations to make up a meal for the entire crew.[17]

On October 24 the three APDs were ordered to rendezvous with TG 76.6, consisting of attack transports *Crescent City Windsor, Hercules, Warren,* and destroyer *Howorth,* and take them to Humboldt Bay. The convoy was safely anchored at their destination on October 27.

Another changing of the guard on *Ward* took place at 1130 on October 28, when Lt. Richard Farwell, the ship's Executive Officer, relieved Lt. Commander Fredrick Lemly as commanding officer. Lemly was well liked and respected by the entire crew and, in the tradition of previous commanding officers of the ship, was a bold and decisive leader who did not shy away from combat or difficult decisions.

Will Lehner recalled the saying the *Ward's* crew affectionately applied to Lemly: "Lemly, Lemly, he's our man. He'll get us killed if anyone can." But Lemly, more than any other single individual, was responsible for instilling in the crew the discipline and sense of dedication that had taken the crew through some difficult times without losing a man in combat.

Years later, Guy Thompson paid further tribute to Lemly. "The absence of a death rate on *Ward* attests to the leadership of Lemly in training of the crew," said Thompson. Lt. Norman Stewart was appointed the new Executive Officer. Lemly left the ship in a formal ceremony on October 29 to take on a new assignment as the Executive Officer of the Naval Training Station in Miami. He retired years later as a Rear Admiral.

Farwell's first mission was to take *Ward* to Morotai along with *Kilty,* on October 30, to escort LSTs 660, 706, and 748. The convoy reached their destination safely on November 3. *Ward's* boats were busy all day on the 4th taking liberty and mail parties ashore and running various errands. Morotai was another typical, unattractive and uninviting South Pacific location for a liberty. Its only attribute was that it offered a change of scenery as the crew enjoyed their usual two cans of warm beer.

The routine of the stay at Morotai was interrupted at 0300 on November 5 with a message that enemy aircraft were expected shortly. *Ward* went to General Quarters immediately. Ten minutes later shore-based anti-aircraft batteries opened up. Within minutes, flares appeared over the airfield, followed by sticks of bombs.

At 0325 a searchlight caught a Japanese bomber in its beams attracting fire from ships all over the harbor. The sky was filled with anti-aircraft bursts, but unbelievably, the bomber managed to escape.

At 0545 *Ward and Kilty* led the three LSTs out of Morotai harbor to rendezvous with a convoy bound for the Leyte beachhead. Rendezvous was made at 1335 on the 6th with TG 76.4, a large convoy in seven columns. *Ward* joined as part of the screen. Convoy speed was limited to the nine knots of the LSTs.

No activity was encountered until 2055 on November 11, when anti-aircraft fire was spotted by a number of ships, including *Ward.* The convoy remained on alert the remainder of the night and entered Leyte Gulf on the 12th with no attacks materializing. It was *Ward's* first visit to the site of the huge assault on October 20.

At 0520 a group of LSTs left the convoy and proceeded to Dulag beach to unload. Minutes later, anti-aircraft fire broke out over the gulf and a Japanese aircraft spun out of the sky, leading a long trail of black smoke. It crashed in a spectacular explosion directly ahead of the LSTs. The aircraft must have been alone; no further attacks followed.

Later in the day *Ward* received reports of 50 to 60 Japanese aircraft approaching the beach. The aircraft apparently selected a different target and no attack occurred for the remainder of the day. *Ward* took advantage of the calm to refuel from tanker *Arethusa.*

Minutes after refueling, the alert sounded and *Ward* returned to General Quarters. This time it was real and Japanese bombers appeared over the Gulf heading for the transports. Every gun on ship and shore opened up in a tremendous barrage. Two bombers were hit immediately and fell onto the gulf, burning all the way down.

One bomber made a pass over the repair ship *Egeria* without attacking, turned around, flew at the ship again upside down. It deliberately crashed into its side in a huge explosion which produced a large fireball. Minutes later another bomber crashed into the repair ship *Achilles,* starting several fires.[18]

Ward remained at General Quarters almost continuously as bombers appeared singly or in groups throughout the day. At 1720 a bomber attacked a group of LCIs unloading on the beach. Eight minutes later *Ward* opened fire on a bomber directly above her. The aircraft suddenly dove into an LST near the beach.

At 1734 three bombers flew directly toward the *Ward* at 1500 feet altitude. *Ward* opened fire with all guns, concentrating the fire on the leading bomber. The plane began smoking heavily and losing altitude as it veered away from the ship. It did not get far, however, and crashed into the Gulf several miles away. The remaining two bombers flew low toward Dulag, where they both crashed into Liberty ships, setting them on fire.[19]

The Gulf became a huge, confused battlefield with aircraft now coming in from all points of the compass and the sky blackened with shell bursts. Columns of smoke arose from either downed aircraft or burning ships. Just when tired crewmen wondered if it would end soon, it increased in ferocity.

Additional aircraft appeared and anti-aircraft fire became even more intense. The battle was approaching sheer madness. Three more aircraft slashed into the Gulf, trailing fire as they crashed. Another attempted to crash into an LST but missed. Finally, at 1830 the air was clear of aircraft and crewmen slumped to the deck at their guns, totally exhausted. They looked at each other, too tired to speak, but their looks conveyed the same thoughts. They were glad to be alive at the end of a wild and vicious battle.

It had been an incredible afternoon. Three freighters, an LST, and a salvage vessel continued to burn and other ships were damaged. At least 12 aircraft had been destroyed. Thousands of rounds of ammunition were expended.

For the crew of *Ward,* the combat was different from any they had previously experienced. They had observed only one bomber actually dropping a bomb. All others attempted to crash into a ship with their bomb still attached. Deliberate suicide by a pilot was difficult for them to understand. Worse yet, it was a frightening weapon to fight. Shooting down an aircraft, diving directly at a ship at several hundred miles an hour, was practically impossible. If the Japanese continued to use this weapon, many more ships would be hit and countless lives lost.

As soon as the attack ended *Ward* formed up with TG 76.4, composed of LSTs and liberty ships bound for Hollandia. It was a miserable night with the crew dead tired and a driving rain that limited visibility to about 200 yards. Nerves were further strained when bogies lit up the radar screens. The aircraft followed the convoy for the next 36 hours, keeping to the fringes but occasionally making a feint toward the convoy. At times, lookouts observed heavy anti-aircraft fire at the stern of the convoy. Sleep was sporadic and men stayed at their guns, catching a few minutes of sleep when they could.

On November 15, just as aircraft contacts were tapering off, *Ward* picked up a submarine contact at 0939 and charged out to investigate it. She lost it a few minutes later but picked it up again at 1017 at a range of 3200 yards. Charging forward with a grim determination, she loosed nine depth charges set for various depths. The sea boiled and rose into the air in angry geysers of black and green water. When the turbulence subsided, the contact was gone and *Ward* returned to her station.

The convoy spent several days steaming through a series of rain squalls, followed by aircraft and surface contacts. It was with much relief that it sighted the friendly shore of Hollandia at noon on November 18.

It was a drained crew that manned the ship as the convoy slowly eased into the harbor and anchored. Men who, for weeks, had not slept more than several hours at a time looked forward to a sleep uninterrupted by an air raid, a submarine contact, or a General Quarters announcement.

Leyte Island was not yet secured but Allied troops held much of it, and it was only a matter of time before it would be fully occupied and become another backwater area. To a man, *Ward's* crew hoped that this would occur before they had to make another run into the area infested with kamikazes. They did not get their wish. They would be called upon to return to the island of kamikazes within several weeks. Their destination would be a place called Ormoc, and they would visit it on a December day already made infamous at another island several thousand miles away. *Ward* was there also.

CHAPTER 15

Destiny's Date Repeated

Hollandia, with its incessant rain, oppressively humid climate, and lack of amenities for sailors on liberty, still looked good to the crew of *Ward* after a solid month of combat. The ship had emerged from a stressful period in which the crew witnessed and participated in a form of battle that was not like anything they could have imagined or trained for. They were now fighting to stay alive while being attacked by men who wanted to die. They would soon return to that battlefield but could first unwind for a few days in Hollandia.

While *Ward* spent a number of days on resupplying and refueling, the crew took advantage of the limited recreational facilities that the base provided for relaxation. Warm beer, movies on ship, and looking up long-lost friends were the usual activities.

Ward, like most other ships, ran port and starboard liberties. The boat division had exhausted themselves making almost continuous mail, liberty, supply, personnel, and other official runs, in addition to their harrowing experience on Dinagat. As Boat Officer, Ensign Thompson wanted his men to have liberty together. He pulled some strings to make it happen and the entire boat division went ashore on their own boats, operated by the deck division. It was probably the only time in *Ward's* history that an entire division had liberty at the same time.[1]

Ashore the men had the usual liberty of two beers, three Cokes, and softball if they wanted it. Non-drinkers could trade their beers for Cokes. Sailors could relax for a few hours if it didn't rain. When asked how often it rained in Hollandia, Ensign Thompson replied, "The word 'often' doesn't do it justice. The rainfall occurrence was a lot closer to continuous than to often."

Some sailors made their own fun. Ship's cook Will Lehner learned that his cousin was a Chief on the amphibious command ship *Rocky Mount* and kept an eye out for it wherever *Ward* went. He finally caught up with it in Humboldt Bay at Hollandia and the two were able to share a few beers.

On November 19 another officer, Lt.(jg) Russell Baldwin, a medical officer, joined *Ward.* He replaced Lt. Charles Cooper who had been the ship's doctor since April 1943. Cooper, well respected by the crew, had several idiosyncrasies. He liked to make salads and went ashore to get the heart of palm from a palm tree whenever he could. This, however, did not do the tree any good. As a surgeon he felt that he was not getting enough surgery to stay in practice, so he always kept his eye open for opportunities for surgery in any form. Baldwin's tour of duty on *Ward* would be short but unforgettable.

Orders came through shortly and *Ward* was at sea on November 22 to escort another convoy to Leyte Gulf. She joined TG 76.4.2, consisting of three tankers and 14 merchant ships in five columns. The convoy screen consisted of *Ward, Kilty, Schley,* and destroyer-escorts *Newman* and *Eichenberger.* With a convoy speed of only 9.5 knots, the voyage took almost a week but it was free of aircraft or submarine contacts.

Destroyers *Fletcher, Howorth,* and *LaVallette* came out of Leyte Gulf on the 27th to reinforce the escort as it neared dangerous waters. On the 28th the convoy narrowed to two columns wide to enter the Gulf. Although no aircraft were spotted, there were alerts throughout the next eight days. *Ward* sat at anchor until December 6, while planning continued for the final operation needed to secure Leyte.

In the six weeks since the main landings at Leyte Gulf, Allied forces had captured the southern and eastern sectors of Leyte Island. The Japanese, however, had decided to fight the decisive battle of the Philippines at Leyte and continued to move in reinforcements. They brought in troops to the ports of Ormoc or Carigara on the northwestern end of the island and marched them across the island to combat.

As long as the Japanese held these two ports, they could continue to wage a war of attrition on Leyte. Allied efforts to stop the flow of troops were limited to air attacks. The narrow waterways prevented the use of larger ships from operating on the west approaches to Leyte and PT boats were not capable of stopping Japanese convoys.

Lt. jg Russell Baldwin, medical officer, joined *Ward* six weeks before it was sunk. (Byron Baldwin)

General MacArthur's next major operation was to be the invasion of Mindoro Island, 250 miles northwest of Leyte on December 5. That date would have to be pushed back because of the strong Japanese opposition on Leyte. He would have to secure Leyte quickly or the Mindoro and subsequent landings would be delayed even further.

The Japanese already had 70,000 troops on Leyte with more arriving weekly through Ormoc and Carigara. Incessant rains and mud had slowed the Allied advance on Leyte to a crawl and prevented the newly captured Leyte airfields from being used for direct ground support missions. MacArthur's solution was to land almost a full division of troops at Ormoc, cut the island in half, and sever the flow of reinforcements for good. Then Japanese troops already on the island could be dealt with.

Planning for this operation was hastily completed and the date of December 7 for D-Day was selected only a week earlier. The army division to be used, the 77th Infantry Division, was already on its way to garrison the now backwater island of Guadalcanal when it was stopped in transit, turned around, and returned to Leyte Gulf. Their R and R duty would have to wait.

The Ormoc operation would be similar to those *Ward* had participated in throughout the South Pacific. Troops would be carried by some type of landing craft rather than large transports. Eight APDs would be used and supplemented by 27 LCIs, 12 LSMs, and four LSTs. Larger transports were not available on such short notice. This force would be designated as TG 78.3, the Ormoc Attack Group. Twelve destroyers would serve as the escorts and fire support units. Opposition, if any, from Japanese naval units was expected to be light. The principal threat would be from kamikaze attack.

While at Dulag, *Ward* was ordered to remove her coding machine and all secret material from the ship and transfer it to command ship *Mt. McKinley* for storage. The only exception was the Operations Order, which was kept in a weighted sack on the bridge. This concerned Captain Farwell. "I wondered just how hazardous this operation was expected to be," he explained.[2]

At 1000 on December 6, *Ward* embarked 108 officers and men of the 77th Infantry Division off the beach at Dulag in Leyte Gulf.[3] At 1320 TG 78.3 was on its way to Ormoc under Rear Admiral Struble for what would be an eventful trip for the *Ward*. As the crow flies, Ormoc was only 25 miles from Dulag across Leyte Island. The convoy, however, had to cruise south for 80 miles along the eastern shore of Leyte, and then crawl its way 80 miles north again along the west shore.

It was a voyage filled with apprehension as Japanese aircraft tracked it the entire way, relaying its position back to their airfields. All crewmen knew that the landing would not be a surprise.

Sunset on December 6 was an extraordinary sight but common to the Pacific. The sky, in a series of successive events, changed in color from pale blue to burnt orange and red, to shades of violet and deep purple as dusk settled around the convoy. The serenity of the phenomenon belied the violence and death that the following day would bring.

The convoy proceeded through the night at nine knots with sleep elusive to most crewmen and passengers on *Ward*. Although the formation was not attacked, Japanese snoopers made their presence known, dropping flares periodically. Anti-aircraft fire was observed just ahead of *Ward*, stretching nerves even further. Men tried to sleep at their gun positions and if sleep came, it was only for a few minutes, interrupted by the raucous "bong-bong-bong" of the General Quarters alarm.

At 0440 an unidentified aircraft passed down the starboard side of the column without attacking, obviously attempting to draw fire. Ahead of the formation, minesweepers had completed clearing a lane to the beachhead. They found it to be free of mines.

Aircraft were now being reported all around the convoy. At 0500 the destroyer *Smith* reported a near miss from a bomb. A flare suddenly illuminated destroyer *Hughes*, Admiral Struble's flagship. Struble had earlier advised the convoy that they could expect heavy Allied air cover during the landing. Just as dawn was breaking, he alerted the ships that heavy rains had made Leyte's airstrips inoperable and air cover would be light at best.

Dawn broke on December 7 as one of the few decent days in weeks. It blossomed forth with clear skies, calm seas, and a gentle breeze. It would have been a topic of conversation anywhere but Ormoc Bay. As the destroyers moved into their bombardment positions, several were straddled by extremely accurate fire of a three-inch shore battery. Gunfire would shortly knock it out.

At 0626 *Ward* lowered her boats to the "high rail" position. Eleven minutes later she lowered them to the water. The troops filled them quickly and were away for the line of departure at 0642. The boats were ordered to the beach at 0653 and the 16 boats of the APDs, making up the first wave, headed shoreward to White Beaches One and Two. The Ormoc landing was on the move. The remaining 16 APD boats followed as the second wave. The LCIs and LSMs comprised the third, fourth, and fifth waves.

Destroyers began pounding the beaches with five-inch shells at 0640. At 0702 four LCIs, designated as LSMRs, equipped as rocket launching platforms, unleashed an incredible barrage saturating the beach with explosions. Through binoculars men on the bridge could see Japanese defenders scampering for high ground beyond the beach as rockets pulverized the beach area, Destroyers ceased their fire at 0710 and the rocket barrage terminated two minutes later.

In one of *Ward's* boats, commanded by Ensign Thompson, the troops kept watching the beach as the boat neared the shore. Thompson told the sergeant in charge of the troops to order the men to lower their heads. To make his point clearer, Thompson told the sergeant, "I'll shoot anyone who sticks his head above the gunwale!" To reinforce his statement, Thompson pulled out his 0.45 pistol. Years later Thompson explained, "I didn't want the Japs to see us coming in with a boatload of men. There was a feeling that they did not shoot at boats that were carrying supplies or equipment. But my main reason for that outburst was to allow the coxswain to have a good view of the sea behind the boat."[4]

A flight of P-40s flew low over the LCPRs as they neared the beach. Several LCPR bow gunners, thinking the aircraft were enemy, cut loose with their machine guns. When P-38s flew over a few minutes later, gunners recognized their distinctive shape as friendly aircraft. The P-40s continued to receive fire with one barely able to return to its field because of heavy damage.[5]

With a pall of black smoke and dust rising over the beach, Ormoc Bay suddenly became strangely silent. Within minutes, the first-wave boats hit the shore and troops scampered inland without return fire.

By 0751 all of *Ward's* boats were hoisted aboard and she moved out from the beachhead to assume an anti-submarine station between Leyte and Ponson Island at the head of Ormoc Bay. Destroyer *Mahan* and minesweepers *Saunter* and *Scout* joined *Ward* in screening the five-mile stretch of water.

After *Ward's* boats were back on board, Boat Officer Thompson went to the radar shack just off the bridge. The shack served as the ship's Combat Information Center (CIC) and contained two radar men, a sonar man, and Thompson, along with two radar screens, a fathometer, and a sonar stack. All of this was housed in, as Thompson described, a room the size of a hall closet.[6]

Thompson's stool in the CIC was a tool box and, for a desk, he balanced a piece of plywood on his knees. This held his maneuvering board on which he plotted the action occurring around the ship. His tools were rudimentary as well. Designers of *Ward* had not envisioned the need to track the action of surface ships, submarines, aircraft, and shore operations occurring simultaneously in the vicinity of a ship.

Ashore, the troops of the 77th Division advanced against no opposition to secure the beachhead and block the important road leading south from Ormoc. Offshore, conditions were markedly different.

Ward had been on anti-submarine patrol for more than an hour without incident when at 0940 her lookouts spotted nine twin-engine bombers coming in from the northwest at a 4000-foot altitude. Captain Farwell immediately called for 20 knots and began evasive maneuvers. All four ships opened fire as the aircraft passed overhead without dropping any bombs. The bombers were quickly attacked by a group of army P-40s and P-38s, which had been covering the beachhead area.

Ward's No. 2 boat hooking up to the falls to be hoisted aboard after the Ormoc landing on December 7,1944. Conversing are Boat Officer, Ensign Guy Thompson (wearing helmet) and SM3c Jesse Trotter. (Bernhardt Jungkind)

The bombers circled to the south, where they were temporarily out of sight. Minutes later the bombers, now joined by four Zero fighters, returned and dove at the *Mahan*, maneuvering at high speed five miles southwest of the *Ward*. P-38s followed them down in their dives, firing all the way. Three fighters fell immediately and two bombers began trailing smoke.

All nine bombers continued toward the *Mahan* attacking one at a time. *Mahan* fought back hard, her 20-mm guns knocked the first one down in flames only 50 yards from the ship and hit two others, which crashed before they got close. She splashed a fourth making a strafing run. Then, her luck ran out.

In quick succession, she was crashed by a kamikaze just aft of the bridge and two more in her side, one right at the waterline. The ship immediately burst into flames which spread so quickly that the magazines could not be flooded. With an explosion imminent, the *Mahan's* captain ordered the ship abandoned at 1001. It was later sunk by the destroyer *Walke*. *Mahan* suffered 10 dead and 32 wounded in the attack.[7]

At 0955 three twin-engine bombers broke away from a larger group at 3000 feet and sought out a ship. Below them was the *Ward* on a base course of 100 degrees, fishtailing at 20 knots to present a more elusive target. A signalman, who had been observing the

Captain Richard Farwell on the *Ward's* port bridge wing watches her boats being hoisted aboard following the Ormoc landing. The *Ward* had only hours left. (Bernhardt Jungkind)

approaching aircraft, now astern of the ship, through the ship's large telescope twice identified them as American planes. Suddenly he shouted, "Jap planes! Jap planes!"[28]

"Full left rudder," yelled Captain Farwell. As *Ward* began to swing to port the bombers dove at her in a line abreast formation with the center plane leading. A P-38 followed them closely, scoring hits on the leading bomber, and set it smoking.

"All guns commence firing!" was Farwell's next command. The bomber, still smoking heavily, leveled off, caught up with the *Ward* and, with a deafening roar it crashed into her port side just above the waterline. It entered the boiler room and troop space which, several hours earlier, had been filled with men preparing to land. The bomber's port engine, jarred loose by the impact, shot completely through the troop space and exited through the starboard side. Other parts of the aircraft shattered the compartment but remained in the ship.[8]

Port side of *Ward* shortly after being struck by a kamikaze. Note the gaping hole near the waterline just below the column of smoke where the plane entered the ship. (Bernhardt Jungkind)

A second bomber came in right over the ship's bow seconds later and crashed into the sea 200 yards off the starboard bow. The third aircraft splashed 600 yards astern of the *Ward*. The pilots of both of the planes must have been killed or severely wounded by *Ward's* anti-aircraft barrage.[9]

Will Lehner was on the Number Four three-inch gun on the after deck-house and could clearly see the first bomber coming in. He could also see that *Ward's* guns were hitting it hard. "I thought that it would crash into the deck and skid along it, killing everyone there including me. That's what happened to others off Leyte," he recalled. "But this one was trying to sink us instead, so it hit us right at the water line where it could have the best chance of doing that."

Don Pepin was in communications in the aft steering station near Lehner when the bomber hit and exploded. "Pepin didn't waste any time," laughed Lehner. "When the flames poured out of the boiler room, he jumped over the side, earphones and all." A boat later picked up Pepin and others who had jumped into the water. Lehner went below deck to help fight fires until someone told him to get out.

Orv Ethier was on the throttle in the engine room when the kamikaze hit. The jar was so great that it knocked him on his rear end. In discovering later on where the bomber had hit the *Ward*, Ethier philosophized, "If we had to take a hit, we could not have picked out a better spot. If it had hit six feet higher it would have wiped out a lot of gun crews and everyone on the bridge. If it had hit further back, it would have hit the engine room and killed the entire black gang, including me. On the other hand, the troop compartment was empty. Of course, if it had hit us there three hours earlier it would have killed the 108 troops waiting to land. We surely were awful lucky."[10]

FM2c Peter Bevelaqua was at his battle station with the forward damage control party when the bomber hit. The explosion threw him into a bulkhead causing injuries to his hands, arms, and face. Coxswain Arnold Wendt was a trainer on a 20-mm mount on the galley deckhouse. He could see the tracers going into the bomber as it approached. Moments later the bomber crashed into the ship right below Wendt's 20-mm mount. Wendt claimed that he saw a body fly right over the ship at impact. None of the gun crew was injured in the crash or explosion.

Lt.(jg) Russell Baldwin, the ship's new medical officer, would normally have been at his battle station in the small operating room off the troop compartment. Since there were no patients there, he was on the bridge observing the events unfolding in Ormoc Bay. As the bomber approached the *Ward,* Baldwin ducked behind the wheelhouse. Seconds later the aircraft struck amidships and exploded. He suddenly realized that had he been in the operating room, he would have been killed instantly. From that day on he felt that he had been reborn and celebrated an additional birthday on December 7 of every year.[11]

Ensign Thompson was also on the bridge when the bombers approached and was certain that the first bomber would crash into the bridge. The sharp maneuvering threw it off enough and it hit 20 feet aft and 30 feet below the bridge. The explosion knocked him into a bulwark but he still saw the following two bombers smash into the water.

Thompson immediately ran aft to lower some boats and was probably the last man to do that. Within seconds of the explosion the flames amidships prevented any further movement between the fore and aft sections.

The bomber's fuel tanks exploded on impact, sending sheets of flame through the troop compartment. The aircraft carried no bombs, having dropped them earlier. This saved *Ward* from an even greater disaster and loss of many lives. *Ward's* uncanny luck was still holding despite the hit she had taken.

The initial explosion started immediate fires in both the boiler room and troop compartment which were then fueled by the Ward's own ruptured tanks. Boiler fires flared back as the fire room lost pressure and the forced draft blower was knocked from its mounting, falling into the fire room. Within minutes the ship lost all communications systems and power.[12]

Steam pressure dropped to less than 100 pounds and the ship now lost all headway. With the loss in power, most fire and bilge pumps and other fire-fighting equipment became inoperative. Some of the fire-fighting equipment was stored in the galley deck house, which was soon surrounded by flames making it impossible for crews to reach it.

At 1005 Farwell ordered Number One and Two boats into the water to assist in fire-fighting through the holes in the side made by the bomber. Boat Officer Thompson lowered two boats but two others were jammed in their davits. Without power, the boats could not be raised enough to pull the stops. All the coxswains had battle stations forward and could not get to the boats, so Thompson manned the two boats with the first boatswain's mates he could find. However, the boats' gasoline-powered billy pumps quickly became clogged and were of little use. Farwell also ordered the ship's life rafts into the water in case the ship had to be abandoned.[13]

Gasoline and diesel storage tanks beneath the troop compartment which had ruptured from the aircraft's impact now added their fuel to the raging fire. Lack of water pressure not only made fire-fighting extremely difficult but made questionable whether the ship's magazines could be flooded. This doubt would soon influence decisions regarding the fight to save the ship. Crewman Albert Fink went below to open the magazine flooding valves but he could not confirm that the magazines were really flooded.[14]

Within minutes, the *Crosby, O'Brien, Saunter,* and *Scout* were on their way to help *Ward. Crosby* and *Scout* lowered boats to pick up men in the water. At 1018, *O'Brien* tucked its bow in close to *Ward* and began fire-fighting operations.

Ward burning as seen from the destroyer *O'Brien* on left. *O'Brien* put her bow against the *Ward* to fight fires and later take men off. She then was ordered to sink *Ward* by gunfire. (National Archives)

USS *Ward* burns furiously after being struck by a kamikaze on December 7, 1944, following successful landings in Ormoc Bay, Leyte. Incredibly, not a crewman was lost in this incident. (National Archives)

Black smoke poured out of the burning troop space and boiler room engulfing much of the ship. Topside, flames were moving forward past the galley house and threatening the bridge. BM1c Clarence Fenton cut away an awning over the well deck to dissipate the smoke and, although it helped, flames kept inching forward.

Further complicating the fire-fighting were the 1000 rounds of ready ammunition for the 20-mm guns stored under the galley deck house. Intense heat made it impossible to jettison the ammunition, and rounds were now being set off. Soon, the heat set off a belt of Very signal gun ammunition stored in the wheelhouse, starting a fire there.[15]

The explosions and fire and smoke amidships had created two islands of men, one forward of the fire, one aft. There was no communication between the two groups and movement between them was impossible.

Farwell was now concerned that the exploding ammunition and possibility of a magazine explosion posed a greater danger to the crew than the fires. At 1024 he gave his last command, "Prepare to abandon ship!" Hearing that order the crew proceeded orderly to the rail to climb down into *Ward's* own boats and rafts or boats from the *Crosby* and *Scout*. Others simply dove off the ship.[16]

Some men had duties to complete before they could leave the ship. Gunners' Mates had to check the depth charges to confirm that they were on "safe" and would not explode when the ship sank. Others threw ready ammunition in their guns overboard. Officers gathered confidential papers from the bridge and radio shack, shoved them into a weighted sack and gave them to the Communications Officer for safe keeping. Other papers locked in the wardroom safe would go down with the ship. When the officers determined that the men were all off, they followed them into the boats.

SoMM3c Fred Hughes, on radar watch on the bridge, found himself with only the captain and the helmsman. Everyone else had gone. Because he had never attended a navy boot camp, he never learned to swim. He was not about to jump overboard and decided to stay. Climbing down to the well deck, he spotted two mess attendants and decided to stick with

them. One said, "Let's jump on the count of three." At the count of one, both jumped, leaving Hughes alone again. Since flames prevented him from going aft, he went forward to the anchor chain to wait. He knew a boat would probably come by to pick up the captain and he'd wait for that. Luckily, for him, one came along.[17]

While waiting for the crew to leave the ship, Captain Farwell decided to fight back. He grabbed a 20mm gun and fired at a Japanese plane in the vicinity. He then removed his gun belt, helmet, and binoculars in case he had to jump overboard. Shortly, a boat came alongside and he slid down a mooring line to safety. During the initial attack, he had been nicked in the hand from shrapnel from strafing by the aircraft that crashed into the ship.[18]

The crew was not all off the ship, however. On the stern, a group of ten men were still busily engaged in fighting the flames. With all communications out and separated from the forward section by the

S2c Frederick Hughes. (Dorothy Hughes)

fire, they were not aware of the "abandon ship" order. The only officer with them was the Assistant Engineering Officer, John Carney, who was below deck looking for a hose. The group included Orv Ethier, Will Lehner, Jake Lundstead, Howie Payner, Frank Fratto, Todd Hayes, and several others. Ethier explained later, "No one ordered us to keep fighting the fire. That was our job and we were going to keep doing it until someone ordered us to stop."[19]

They were still at it when a boat containing Captain Farwell and other officers maneuvered around the stern on its way to the *O'Brien*. Farwell was surprised to see that men were still on *Ward* fighting fires. He was certain that he had been the last man off the ship, as tradition dictates.

In the boat with the officers was Ray Nolde of Number Three gun fame, Gene Heiberger, and Fred Hughes. They were the last enlisted men left on the forward part of the ship when the officers left. Farwell yelled to them, "This is the last boat, sailors. You better jump in now."

Seeing the men on the stern, Farwell told them in forceful terms to abandon ship now. Since his own boat was full, he directed one of *Ward's* boats to pick up the men. Ethier did not mind being ordered off the ship. "We weren't making much headway against the flames anyway," he said.

The *O'Brien* was now only about 60 feet away and her crew had lowered cargo nets over the side. They yelled to the *Ward* men to jump in and swim to the nets. No one did. There was now burning oil on the water all around the ship and the men did not relish the thought of getting wet or burned. Will Lehner had another reason for not swimming to the *O'Brien*. "I kept thinking about Eddie Duchin, who fell overboard several weeks earlier," said Lehner. "A shark got him. I was sure that if I jumped in a shark would take a bite out of me so I stayed put."

The men instead waited on the fantail for the ship's boat to come alongside. "Getting off the ship was actually pretty easy," recalled Orv Ethier. "We just climbed down to the screw guard and stepped right into the Higgins boat. We didn't even get our feet wet."

Ethier still laughs about leaving *Ward*. "The captain is supposed to be the last man off the ship but I was the last one off. I also took over as engineer of the boat when I got in because the coxswain who had been alone in the boat had difficulty running the engine and the boat by himself. That was one of my jobs anyhow."

The men in the water waited for one of the boats to pick them up. As they treaded water they watched an aerial battle between P-38s and Zeros right above them. Bullets splattered the water around them but nobody was hit.

Ed Bukrey was one of the men in the water. He had been at his station on the galley deck and watched the first bomber dive directly at the ship. He, too, saw the 20-mm hits all around its cockpit and was sure that the pilot was dead. "I was convinced that the plane would hit the galley deck and started backing off," he recalled. "Instead, it hit right below me and the next thing I know is that I'm in the water."

Don Pepin did not swim well but had a life preserver on. Bukrey noticed another sailor who could not swim, struggling without a life preserver. Bukrey, who was a good swimmer, took his own life preserver off in the water and managed to slip it on the sailor. Soon a small boat picked them up and took them to one of the minesweepers. When the minesweeper's captain noticed Bukrey without a preserver on, he walked over to him immediately. "He started to chew me out until one of his own men explained why I had no preserver on," Bukrey said.[20]

Lehner still was not sure he was safe even after the boat took his group off *Ward*. Soon after leaving the ship a Japanese plane, a victim of the air battle raging above Ormoc Bay, crashed into the water near *Scout.* He wondered to himself, "Geez, are we going to be hit again?" However, none of the rescue boats were damaged and eventually the surviving Japanese aircraft left.

Some of the rescue boats took the *Ward* survivors to the *O'Brien.* Bevelaqua was in this group and received medical attention for his injuries immediately. Lt.(jg) Baldwin treated several crewmen for burns before they were taken to the *O'Brien.* Sixty-six survivors were taken to the *Scout.* Others, including those on Ethier's boat, went to the *Crosby.* When all of the men in his boat were safely aboard the *Crosby,* Ethier pulled the floor plug to allow the Higgins boat to sink. With all four of her own boats on board, *Crosby* had no room for another boat. *Crosby* accelerated the sinking by firing 20-mm shells into the boat's bottom.

Ensign Thompson was also taken to *Crosby.* Before he climbed out of the boat, he insisted on off-loading a spare set of boat screws. Boats carried two sets of differently pitched screws, one for use in port and a quieter set for use in landings. These screws were no longer in the supply chain and Thompson knew that *Crosby* could use them. Although *Crosby's* Executive Officer was yelling at him to get on board, Thompson made sure the screws made it to the Crosby as well.[21]

When Ethier climbed aboard *Crosby,* one of the first men he saw was Arnie Laettner, who, like Ethier, was from St. Paul. "I didn't know Laettner," said Ethier, "but I knew of him. "His family owned Laettner Fuel and Ice in St. Paul and the company is still in business today. Arnie gave me a shirt, toothbrush and stuff like that. We came to the *Crosby* with nothing but the shirts on our back and those were burned and torn. We needed some necessities until we could get back to Hollandia."[22]

Some of the *Crosby* crewmen asked Ethier why his group was still on *Ward* when everyone else had left. "Hell," said Ethier, "we were just trying to save the ship."

Incredibly, when a tally was taken of *Ward* survivors on the various rescue ships, it was discovered that not a single man was killed. Several crewmen were burned, one, coxswain James Snead, seriously, by the initial explosion following the aircraft's impact. Their injuries were not life-threatening and they were treated immediately by the medical personnel of the rescue ships and Ensign Baldwin of *Ward.*

The boat containing Captain Farwell and other officers took them to the *O'Brien.* As soon as he was on board, Farwell asked to be taken to the ship's captain. He urgently wanted to inform the captain that *Ward's* magazines may not have been flooded and that there was risk to the *O'Brien* and her crew by remaining close to *Ward.*

When Farwell reached *O'Brien's* bridge he was stunned upon meeting her captain. It was none other than William Outerbridge, *Ward's* commanding officer and Farwell's superior on December 7, 1941. As an ensign during Outerbridge's tenure on *Ward,* he respected Outerbridge as did everyone else on the ship.

Farwell immediately advised him about the uncertainty of *Ward's* magazines being flooded. Hearing that, Outerbridge immediately ordered *O'Brien* to back away from *Ward* while he requested instructions from Admiral Struble, the commander of TG 78.3. Struble already knew of Ward's plight, having earlier received a message from *Ward* over a battery-powered radio. Outerbridge wanted a chance to save *Ward* and relayed that request to Struble. It had been his first command and he had spent 10 months as well as the beginning of the war on the ship.

The short response soon came from the Admiral. They were words that both Farwell and Outerbridge dreaded to hear, "Sink by gunfire!"[23]

When Outerbridge heard the terrible order, he yelled to no one in particular, "No! No! I did not hear that! Our radio is out!" He waited, hoping to hear a different order from Struble. The same message came back loud and clear but he again hesitated. He had just been given the most heart-wrenching order a commanding officer could receive. He was being ordered to sink the first ship he had ever commanded. He thought it still could be saved and wanted desperately for an opportunity to do that. Finally, the message was repeated a third time and he realized that he had no choice.

After he collected himself, he ordered all other ships to leave *Ward* and directed the *O'Brien* to stand off 800 yards from the ship. Minutes later he ordered *O'Brien's* guns loaded and trained. As he peered across the water separating the two ships he hesitated once more as though he wanted to give *Ward* a few more moments to live. Then, with a firmness befitting his character and position, he gave the fateful order, "Fire!"

O'Brien's gunnery officer had previously served on a four-stacker and knew exactly where the aft magazine was. That was the aiming point. The first salvo from *O'Brien's* five-inch guns was a bulls eye and hit the magazine squarely. The ship exploded in a fiery display, throwing debris in all directions. When the smoke cleared, the entire aft section of the ship was gone. Only the bow was visible and it was pointing up, as if it was giving a final salute of good-bye to her crew.

As the ship slowly disappeared, Farwell and Outerbridge stood side by side on the bridge, misty-eyed, each alone with his thoughts. Not a word was said as they watched *Ward's* final moments together. Then it slipped beneath the waves at 1125 and was gone forever. Its resting place was 120 fathoms below the surface of Ormoc Bay at 10 degrees 50' 42" North latitude, 124 degrees 32' 30" East longitude.[24]

From the decks of the rescue ships, *Ward's* crewmen watched in silence as *Ward* slowly slipped beneath the waters of Ormoc Bay. They stood for a few moments alone in their thoughts, all feeling as if their hearts had suddenly been wrenched from their bodies. The *Ward* was not just a ship; it was men as well, a closely knit group of men. They were inseparable and a part of them had just disappeared. For some, like Will Lehner, Orv Ethier, Ed Bukrey, Don Pepin, and Clarence Fenton, it was the only home they had known for almost four years.

Men and officers alike stood

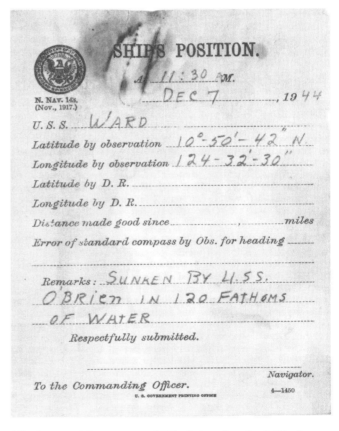

SHIP'S POSITION.

N. NAV. 143,
(Nov., 1917.)

At 11:30 a.m.

DEC 7 , 1944

U. S. S. WARD

Latitude by observation 10°-50'-42" N.

Longitude by observation 124-32'-30"

Latitude by D. R.

Longitude by D. R.

Distance made good since , miles

Error of standard compass by Obs. for heading

Remarks: SUNKEN BY U.S.S. O'BRIEN IN 120 FATHOMS OF WATER

Respectfully submitted.

Navigator.

To the Commanding Officer.

U. S. GOVERNMENT PRINTING OFFICE

4—1450

The last position report of *Ward* showing the latitude and longitude of her sinking in Ormoc Bay. (First Shot Naval Vets of St. Paul) watching *Ward's* final moments, gripped in anguish with tears streaming down their faces. As Ensign Thompson on the *Crosby* brushed the tears from his face a sailor, himself crying unashamedly, said to him, "Don't cry, Mr. Thompson, we'll make them pay for every rivet." [25]

A short time later Farwell recalled to Outerbridge two items that went down with *Ward* that would be missed. He had $150 stored in his safe and there were ninety cases of beer stored in the forward peak tank. These were to be doled out to the crew at beach parties. [26]

Minutes after *Ward* disappeared from view Outerbridge overheard his gun crew gloating over their great shot that blew up *Ward's* magazines on the first salvo. Walking over to them, still feeling the pain of the loss of his first ship, he said to them, "What do you guys want to do now, paint an American flag on your turret?" He wanted no crewmen of his bragging over the sinking of *Ward*.

Seven miles away, *Mahan* also sank. Sinking of *Ward* and *Mahan* so close together and within minutes of each other did not end the violence in Ormoc Bay on December 7. Another wave of Japanese aircraft swarmed in for an attack just as the Mahan went down. Four bombers singled out *Liddle,* another APD. She hit three, which exploded in the air, but the fourth crashed into her flying bridge at 1120, killing 37 men, including all 17 on the bridge. [27] She would live to fight again, however.

With additional Japanese reported on their way to join this assault, Admiral Struble ordered TG 78.3 to leave the area. It would leave behind two warriors. One of them, the *Ward,* finally had used up all of her luck. Even in death, however, her luck held for a last time. While other ships had lost up to hundreds of men in a kamikaze attack, she was probably the only ship lost to a kamikaze without losing a single man.

Built in record time in 1918 to fight submarines, she was too late for that war and too old for the following war. Nevertheless, resurrected in 1941, she fired the first shot of World War II; sank the first ship; made many amphibious landings, some under fire; was the target of strafing, bombs, and kamikazes; and did it all without losing any men in combat.

She went down three years to the day of her baptism of fire at Pearl Harbor with her flag flying high. She was a proud ship, manned by a fighting crew of proud men. The name and exploits of the USS *Ward* (DD-139/APD-16) will never be forgotten.

CHAPTER 16

Eilogue

Ward was gone and her crew scattered on the various rescue ships that assisted her during her final moments. For some of them, their home of almost four years was now 700 feet below the waters of Ormoc Bay. All realized that they had just come through a disaster with better results than they could have hoped for. While other destroyers had lost much of their crew to kamikaze hits, *Ward* did not lose a man and had only a few injured. The men were shaken but thankful for their good fortune.

However, for the first time in years their future was uncertain. They were still sailors, they were still in the Pacific, and the war was not over. What would become of them?

Some of the uncertainty was resolved quickly. All rescue ships were already on their way back to Tacloben on the original Leyte beachhead. There they would make arrangements for a return to Hollandia. The voyage to Tacloben was not without incident as Japanese aircraft savagely attacked the formation three times. On board *Scout*, Lehner nervously watched a Japanese plane hit the water near the minesweeper. None of the rescue ships were hit but escorts *Lamson* and *Liddle* nearby were crashed by kamikazes.

Liddle was hit in the flying bridge and suffered 58 casualties, including her captain. *Lamson's* toll was 21 dead and 50 injured two hours later when a plane crashed on her deck starting a huge fire and wiping out many of her deck crew.[1] Seeing this, *Ward's* survivors were even more convinced that Providence had been looking down upon them earlier in the day.

By dusk of the 7th the attacks were over and the formation rounded the southern tip of Leyte heading north into Leyte Gulf. The ferocity of the latest attacks was evidenced by the ammunition expenditure of the escorts. They collectively fired 4320 rounds of five-inch, 6809 rounds of 40-mm, and 6224 rounds of 20-mm against kamikazes *after* they left Ormoc Bay. The ships put into Tacloben the following morning.[2]

On December 8, *O'Brien* transferred the wounded to LST-464 which was serving as a temporary hospital ship. She sent the remaining six officers and 39 surviving men to *Crosby* which had more accommodations for them as an APD than did *O'Brien*. Before leaving for Hollandia the men were given dungarees and shirts to replace those they were still wearing from *Ward*. *Crosby* and several other rescue ships left for Hollandia with the survivors of *Ward* and *Mahan*. Captain Farwell, Ensign Thompson, and several others who were still making arrangements for the crew, missed *Crosby* but caught a plane later and reached Hollandia ahead of the crew.

Thompson arranged for berthing for the men and visited the base chaplain to discuss the crew's spiritual needs. He also wanted to obtain a supply of Rosaries and New Testaments. When the crew arrived several days later, Thompson canvassed them to see if they wanted either item. Almost the entire crew felt that they had a need to express thanks and accepted a Rosary or Bible. The men also received survivor clothes consisting of green dungarees, blankets, and personal items. They would be billeted in Quonset huts during their stay in Hollandia.[3]

One of the first persons that Ed Bukrey met after landing in Hollandia was Al Sundberg, his basketball coach at Johnson High School in St. Paul. Sundberg was with the Red Cross and passing out clothing, cigarettes, toilet articles, and other badly needed items. The two spent much of the following week together.[4]

While waiting for transportation back to the mainland, the crew helped to unload ships for two weeks. One of these was the former cruise ship *SS Monterey* now taken over as an army transport. When it was unloaded, it embarked several thousand men from all branches of service and army nurses who were being rotated home. These included survivors from sunken ships like *Ward* returning home for reassignment.

The *Monterey* made the 16-day trip to San Francisco unescorted, zigzagging much of the way. Don Pepin recalled the trip well. "The food was absolutely great with two full meals a day. There were so many people on board that we had to eat standing up. There were crap games all over the ship and I spent a lot time watching them," he laughed. The ship celebrated two Christmas days, one on either side of the International Date Line. They received only one Christmas dinner however.[5]

Ensign Thompson was assigned the responsibility of getting the men to the Receiving Station at Treasure Island, San Francisco. There the crew laid over for three weeks and were issued full uniforms. They were all given 30-day survivor's leave and dispersed to all parts of the country. Most of the original 47th Division men returned to St. Paul although several men, such as Dave Morgan, met their wives in San Francisco. Orv Ethier used his leave time to marry his sweetheart Patricia.

Following their leave, *Ward's* survivors returned to Treasure Island for reassignment. A few returned to sea. Lyle Perkins, a radio man joined *Crosby,* the ship that picked him up after *Ward* went down. Most were assigned to shore duty at one of the many naval bases in the United States. Will Lehner was sent immediately to the naval hospital in San Francisco with a severe case of battle fatigue. The many hours he had spent as cook or at battle stations caused him to sleep little over the past year and to lose 53 pounds. After almost five months in the hospital he was granted a medical discharge.[6]

Many of those who left *Ward* earlier served on other ships. Ken Swedberg saw combat in the Aleutians in which his ship, the heavy cruiser *Salt Lake City,* battled a superior Japanese force but survived. Ship's cook Dick Thill served on the light cruiser *Savannah* where he cooked for 1350 men and had cooks working for him although he was the youngest cook on the ship. During a tour, *Savannah* carried President Roosevelt to Malta in 1945 prior to the Yalta summit meeting with Stalin and Churchill.

Walter Campion served on the new destroyer escort *Osterhaus* and other ships. Maurice Hurley was assigned to the amphibious command ship *Mount McKinley.* Russ Reetz spent a year at a small boat base on Purata Island just offshore of Bougainville. John Gill and John Entemann, who were sent home from the *Ward* for being under age, later enlisted again as soon as they were old enough. Entemann became an Air Force pilot.

With the end of World War II, a number of *Ward* crewmen stayed in the service. These included Frank Hadju, Don Jones, Fred Phenning, and Dave Morgan of the 47th Division reservists. Morgan later reached the rank of Lt. Commander. Ensign Baldwin spent the remainder of the war on the ammunition ship *Mauna Loa.* Ensign Thompson went on to an excellent career including various sea and shore assignments, including commanding

Two of *Ward's* commanding officers with families in a lighter moment aboard a destroyer. Lt. Com. Richard Farwell, wife Mae and child, left, and Captain William Outerbridge with wife Grace. (First Shot Naval Vets of St. Paul)

officer of PCE-897.[7] Captain Farwell commanded several ships before his detachment from the navy in March 1947.

A number of the crew stayed in the naval reserve. Orv Ethier found his way back to a destroyer, *Chevalier,* during the Korean War. Ed Zechmann left the navy but joined the marines in 1946, serving in Korea and other places for 13 more years.

Most of the crew left service at war's end and made the transition to civilian life. Although individual careers ultimately scattered them across the country, many of the original reservists stayed in the Upper Midwest where they reside today.

The strong sense of unity, loyalty, patriotism, and pride that bonded *Ward's* crew did not diminish after VJ Day. Like so many other military units, the men of the original 47th Division did not want the memory of their ship lost in the backwash of the war. The movement to create a mechanism to keep the ship's memory alive began in St. Paul where a nucleus of the crew still resided.

On February 27, 1947, a group of 47th Division members met at the American Legion Hall in St. Paul with men of the 11th Battalion Headquarters to discuss forming an organization. Shortly after, an organization of former crewmen became official with duly elected officers. George DeRosia was selected to be the first president. The group's name was "First Shot Naval Vets."[8]

Because of logistics, the group's active membership consisted largely of 47th Division reservists. In this sense, the group differed from typical organizations of former ship's crewmen which encompassed all alumni who served on the ship. *Ward* was different in that 70% of her initial crew trained together and came to the ship as a group.

In the early years, meetings were held regularly with *Ward's* role in World War II being the predominant order of business. An annual reunion was the major activity of the year; invitations were sent to all 47th Division crewmen who could be located. It was held on December 7 to commemorate the major events in *Ward's* career.

As time passed, more of the original crewmen relocated out of Minnesota but a strong and active nucleus remained in Minnesota and adjoining states. The principal focus continued to be the sinking of the midget sub at Pearl Harbor. Soon, locating the Number Three gun that had sunk the sub emerged as a priority issue for the organization.

After agreeing that the appropriate location for the gun was St. Paul, the group approached the navy to determine its location and status. In 1951, the navy advised the organization that the gun was currently being stored in the Navy Yard in Washington, D.C. and was ultimately destined for the Smithsonian Institute.

This prompted an intensive effort by Minnesota's congressional delegation to allow the gun to be displayed in St. Paul, the home city of the gun crew and most of *Ward's* men in 1941. Here, it was argued, the gun could more appropriately be displayed as the symbol of what *Ward* achieved on December 7.

After rounds of discussion involving the navy, Smithsonian Institute, and Minnesota officials, the navy consented to transfer custody of the gun to the State of Minnesota, providing that the state arrange and pay for its move and accept responsibility for maintaining the gun in excellent condition.[9]

That accomplished, the First Shot Vets looked for assistance in moving the gun. They, themselves, had no planning or financial resources for an effort of that magnitude. Although they could not fund it entirely themselves, the St. Paul Veteran's of Foreign Wars agreed to take it on as a project.

The VFW Department Adjunant/Quartermaster, Lowell Eastlund, aware that the State of Minnesota would celebrate its Centennial in 1958 approached the Minnesota Centennial Planning Committee. He suggested that relocation and dedication of the gun be part of the Centennial activities. The committee agreed to provide financing and appointed Eastlund to chair a subcommittee to relocate the gun.

Transportation of the six-ton gun produced an exhibition of inter-service cooperation rarely seen in the post-war period. The navy prepared the gun for moving and delivered it to Andrews Air Force Base outside Washington, D.C. There, the Air Force loaded it into a C-119 Flying Boxcar aircraft and flew it to Wold-Chamberlain Field, now Minneapolis-St. Paul International Airport. Minnesota National Guard units picked it up there and trucked it to its display site on the State Capitol grounds in St. Paul, where it was placed on a prepared concrete base.[10]

The formal dedication ceremony on May 9, 1958, took almost as much planning. Admiral E. P. Forrestal, Commandant of the Ninth Naval District, addressed the crowd of almost 1000 onlookers. After outlining the history of the gun, he officially presented it to Minnesota Governor Orville Freeman, who accepted it on behalf of the State. A centerpiece of the ceremony was the introduction of the nine-man crew of the gun who then took the respective positions at the gun that they had occupied on December 7, 1941.

Although locating several who lived out of state had been challenging all nine men were present. It would be the last time the nine men would be together. The excellent Great Lakes Training Station band from Chicago was flown in to add further ceremony to the occasion. The gun was finally "home."[11]

Keeping a naval rifle with a 17-foot long barrel in a condition commensurate with its status as a cherished World War II Memorial is a continuing challenge. It must be painted periodically to prevent rust and corrosion and at intervals the multiple coats of paint must be removed for repainting; volunteers have usually stepped forward from the ranks of the area veteran's organizations. In 1967, a group of naval reservists, including Maurice Hurley, a 1941 *Ward* crewman, cleaned and repainted the gun.

The navy demands this attention since it still owns it. The president of the First Shot Naval Vets is required to submit an annual statement to the navy confirming that the gun is being properly maintained.[12]

In the mid–1970s the First Shot organization decided to obtain for public display a four-inch shell identical to that fired by Number Three gun. Since the navy no longer had four-inch guns in their arsenal, they did not stock four-inch ammunition. They did agree to lend the First Shot Vets an empty four-inch shell casing usually displayed at the U.S. Naval Academy Museum in Annapolis. They shipped it to St. Paul, where the organization arranged to have a facsimile made with an inert warhead.

Former Captain Outerbridge, wearing fur cap, visiting Number 3 gun on a 1974 trip to St. Paul, Minnesota. Ken Swedberg is directly behind Outerbridge, Will Lehner to the far left. (First Shot Naval Vets of St. Paul)

During the organization's reunion on December 7, 1974, Rear Admiral William Outerbridge (retired) presented the facsimile shell to the State of Minnesota on behalf of the First Shot Naval Vets. It was initially displayed at the Veteran's Service Building on the State Capitol grounds but later moved to the Minnesota Military Museum at Camp Ripley.[13]

In the 1970s the First Shot Naval Vets undertook another major project, one to make the story of *Ward's* achievements available to more people. After several years of research compiling photographs and information from archives, former crewmen and other sources, they published a booklet in 1981 entitled, "USS *Ward*—First Shot." The book encompassed *Ward's* career from its initial construction in 1918 to its sinking in 1944. Many writers contributed to it, including William Outerbridge, who wrote the Foreword.[14]

The book was sold wherever *Ward* members participated in events and was the organization's principal source of income. In 1981 the group published an expanded edition under the title, "USS *Ward* Fires First Shot—WORLD WAR II," with additional text and photographs. Until the book in hand was written, the First Shot book was the principle published source of information on *Ward*. It is still being sold today.

Many of the original 47th Division reservists in *Ward's* initial crew of 1941 attended the early reunions. William Outerbridge, living in Georgia after World War II, had an open

William Outerbridge, left, receives a plaque from the First Shot Naval Vets at a banquet in St. Paul on December 7, 1974. Emcee Bernard Kinderman, former *Ward* crewman, is at right. (First Shot Naval Vets of St. Paul)

invitation and attended a number of the events. He was usually a house guest of a *Ward* crewman during his stay in St. Paul.

On December 7, 1981, for the 40th anniversary of the Pearl Harbor attack, the First Shot Naval Vets invited both Admiral Outerbridge and Captain Richard Farwell and their wives to attend commemorative ceremonies in St. Paul. Both couples were house guests of Ken Swedberg during their visit. The festivities included a visit to the Minnesota State Capitol and an audience with Governor Albert Quie where all First Shot Vets signed a memory book. A gala dinner party concluded the momentous long weekend.[15]

The Swedberg's friendship with the two former *Ward* skippers continued to flourish and the couple was invited to visit the Outerbridges in Georgia and the Farwells in California. Ken recalls the enjoyment of sailing in Farwell's 39-foot sailboat. Both former captains insisted on being called by their first names, confirmation that on "happy" ships, time and age erase all rank.[16]

As the years progressed, the unpredictability of Minnesota winters created hardships for those attending reunions in early December. The organization moved the event to mid-September where it continues today.

With the passage of time the number of surviving crewmen has dwindled and reunions reflect this. The meetings continue to be held annually in St. Paul and media coverage ensures that the achievements of *Ward* and her crew will not be forgotten.

Former *Ward* crewmen in the office of Minnesota Governor Albert Quie in 1981. From left: Russell Reetz; Don Pepin; Richard Farwell, former commanding officer; unidentified governor's aide; Will Lehner; Quie; William Outerbridge, former commanding officer; Ken Swedberg; Joseph Dyrda; Bernard Kinderman; unidentified wearing cap; Orville Ethier. (First Shot Naval Vets of St. Paul)

Will Lehner, Ken Swedberg, the author, and Dick Thill in front of *Ward's* Number 3 gun at the 2004 reunion of the First Shot Naval Vets of St. Paul. (First Shot Naval Vets of St. Paul)

Reunion of First Shot Naval Vets in St. Paul, September 2000. From left: Robert Ball, Donald Jones, Donald Pepin, Robert Jones, Orville Ethier, Gordon Huefmeier, Ambrose Domogall, Edward Bukrey, Dick Thill, Ray Nolde, Will Lehner, Russell Reetz, and Ken Swedberg. (First Shot Naval Vets of St. Paul)

In 2003 the Minnesota State Senate passed a resolution honoring the actions of the ship and its crew on December 7, 1941. At the 2003 reunion the First Shot Naval Vets were presented with the "Citizens Patriot Award" by the United States Department of Defense for their exceptional service to the country as a citizen organization.

Former *Ward* crewmen are very active in military and related observances. They are sought out to participate in remembrance activities on Memorial Day, Veteran's Day, and Pearl Harbor Day. They are often speakers or panelists at seminars, workshops, or historical programs on World War II. Several, including Dick Thill, Will Lehner, Orv Ethier, and Ken Swedberg are frequently asked to speak to high school students.

"I enjoy speaking to them," said Lehner. "The kids are genuinely interested in hearing about Pearl Harbor because they don't get many opportunities to read about it. My message is usually the same. Freedom is not free. I remind the kids that for them to be able to sit in school and learn, someone has to sacrifice from time to time. Although our ship only lost one man in protecting their freedom, thousands of other men died for them."

Over the past 30 years, television networks and cable channels have produced many documentaries describing the attack on Pearl Harbor. Most include interviews with participants on both sides of the battle. Because of *Ward's* role in the attack, her crewmen are often interviewed in such programs.

In 1991, during the 50th anniversary commemorative program at Pearl Harbor, Orv Ethier was a panelist along with many noted Pearl Harbor participants from both sides. This publicity made *Ward* one of the most well-known destroyers of World Ward II.

Also in 1991, Ken Swedberg and Ed Bukrey attended a commemorative seminar at the Admiral Nimitz Museum (now the National Museum of the Pacific) in Fredricksberg, Texas. One of the speakers was Kazuo Sakamaki, captain of the midget submarine captured during the Pearl Harbor attack and now displayed at the museum. The two former *Ward* men met Sakamaki, who was quite friendly until they disclosed that they were on the *Ward* that fateful morning.

Swedberg was featured on a network program hosted by Oliver North in October, 2002, in which he described *Ward's* role in the sinking of the midget submarine. In August 2003, History Channel filmed a documentary on *Ward's* role during the attack and on the sinking of the sub. Swedberg accompanied the film crew to Hawaii and participated in the program's production. It aired on December 7, 2003.

Will Lehner and Russell Reetz were invited to accompany famed underwater explorer Robert Ballard in his effort in 2000 to locate the midget that *Ward* claimed to have sunk on December 7 and production of a TV documentary to corroborate the search. In 2003 Lehner was a participant in a documentary on the finding of the midget in 2002 and was able to visit the sub in one of the research vehicles of the Hawaii Undersea Research Lab that found the sub.

Despite the eyewitness accounts of *Ward's* attack on the midget sub by various crewmen through the years, much skepticism remained. No evidence of a sinking had been found and *Ward* would not have been the first destroyer to claim a sinking simply because a submarine disappeared. Although *Ward* was credited with a sinking, doubters questioned whether a 23-year-old destroyer could sink a modern submarine. The disbelievers included some of the navy's own officers.

Without corroborating evidence *Ward* crewmen could offer only their personal recollections to counter arguments that they did not sink the sub. The answer to the question lay 1200 feet below the surface, off Pearl Harbor's channel entrance, and was not easily accessible.

Serious efforts to search for the sub did not begin until the 1980s when deep sea research vehicles reached a sophisticated level of development. Elsewhere, the vehicles with their sensitive electronic equipment had scored some dramatic successes. In 1985 undersea explorer Robert Ballard found the famous liner *Titanic*, which sank in the Atlantic on her maiden voyage in 1912. In 1989 Ballard made another historic find when he located the legendary German battleship *Bismarck,* sunk in 1941 by British naval forces after a massive effort to hunt it down.

In the Pacific in 1980, the National Oceanic and Atmospheric Administration's (NOAA) National Undersea Research Program at the University of Hawaii now incorporated the newly established Hawaii Undersea Research Lab (HURL) as its operating arm. Their overall mission was science research and exploration. By 1985 HURL's need for a submersible with a deeper diving capability led it to a warehouse in Scotland, where 16 manned vehicles were sitting idle. Of these, Pisces V had the deepest capability and HURL acquired it in 1986. After some rebuilding, it was ready for diving in 1987.[17]

Prior to commencing its annual underwater scientific research program, HURL always conducted several days of test dives. These dives served to check out equipment, personnel, procedures, and support operations. The area they selected for the test dives was the "defensive sea area" at the mouth of the Pearl Harbor channel.

The defensive sea area was an ideal location for the test dives. It was close to HURL's home port of Snug Harbor on Sand Island, away from the heavily traveled sea lanes to Honolulu Harbor, and the sea bed was littered with debris of World War II vintage. After it became known to HURL that the midget sub allegedly sunk by Ward in 1941 in the defensive sea area had never been found, they used the annual test dives to search for it.

In 1992, HURL's Operations Director and Chief Pilot Terry Kerby, on a test dive, discovered a midget sub in the defensive sea area. His hopes that he may have located *Ward's* midget were quickly dashed. The sub was in several pieces, had been mechanically disconnected, and obviously could not have been the one *Ward* sank.[18]

National Geographic funded a search for the midget in 1991 on the fiftieth anniversary of the Pearl Harbor attack. Using an unmanned research vehicle, the search turned up nothing. National Geographic made another major effort to locate *Ward's* midget in 2000 using Ballard's underwater research team. After two weeks of searching in the defensive sea area, he was unsuccessful and called off the search. Russell Reetz and Will Lehner, *Ward* crewmen invited on the expedition, both suggested to Ballard that he was searching too far from shore. Their advice went unheeded and Ballard lost a great opportunity. Said Lehner, "How do you convince the man who found the *Titanic* and *Bismarck* that he is looking in the wrong place?"[19]

Terry Kerby, Operations Director and Chief Pilot for the Hawaii Undersea Research Laboratory who led the search for the midget sub. Kerby has been conducting deep-sea dives in Hawaiian waters since 1976. (Hawaii Undersea Research Laboratory)

Since Ballard's failures to find his prey were rare, his inability to find the missing sub served to fuel the skeptic's arguments. *Ward* crewmen continued to face occasional looks of disbelief when describing the sub's sinking.

HURL was having no success either. Although Kerby was convinced that the sub would be in the southeastern corner of the defensive sea area, he was not very optimistic about finding it. "With only three test dives a year, and with the seabed covered with debris and rocks, it would take years to look behind every rock," he explained. It would take some kind of break to locate the sub.[20]

HURL got that break in 2001 when it acquired a side scan sonar device for use in conducting sea bottom fish habitat surveys. The sonar gave operators an accurate estimate of the size and shape of underwater objects. Since the device had to be tested before it could be used in the research program, Kerby suggested to Dr. Christopher Kelley, HURL's chief biologist, that it be tested in the defensive sea area where it could assist in the search for the midget.[21]

Kelley agreed and in March 2002 the new sonar mapped the southeast corner of the area, including locations just outside the defensive sea area. The mapping identified 39 objects that had potential for being the midget sub. One of these looked especially promising, being cylindrical in shape and an estimated 80 feet long, the exact length of a midget sub. "Although 39 individual objects were identified for closer inspection, this cylinder immediately became our number one priority," said Kerby.

Because of budget limitations, HURL could not conduct any test dives until its diving season began in August. Even then, with the cost of deep sea dives at $18,000 a day, HURL could devote only three days to test dives before they had to start on their actual research program. If the sub was not found within those three days, their search would have to be shelved for another year.

"At HURL we were holding our collective breaths all summer hoping that no one else would stumble on to the object," said Kerby. "We kept its existence our own secret." They were aware that there were others in the world like Ballard who had the interest and means to dive for the sub if they learned of its location.

The secret was kept and HURL conducted its first day of test diving on August 24, 2002. This time they not only had their initial deep sea vehicle, Pisces V, but a second vehicle, Pisces IV as well. The two vehicles could each hold three people and had a depth capability of 6500 feet. The 1200-foot depth at the diving site would pose no problem.

Both vehicles searched for

One of HURL's two Pisces deep-sea research vehicles being put into the water by the control ship Ka'imikai-o-kanaloa. HURL used two of these vehicles with a diving depth capability of 6500 feet to locate the sub. (Hawaii Undersea Research Laboratory)

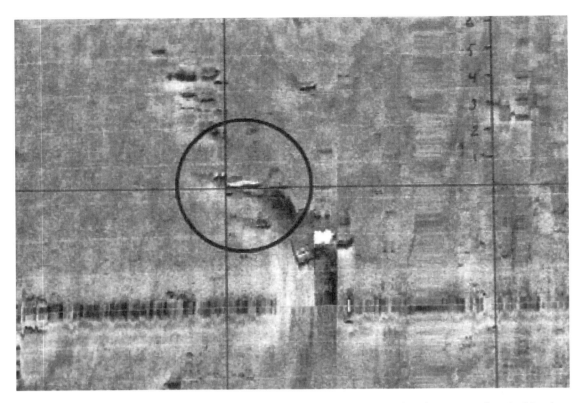

An image from the side-scan sonar of the Hawaii Undersea Research Laboratory taken in March 2002. The circled object is the midget submarine facing due east 1200 feet below the surface. Budget restraints prevented HURL from diving on the object to confirm its identity until August 2002 (Hawaii Undersea Research Laboratory)

eight hours on the 24th without success. The crews were confident, however, that they would be able to locate the cylindrical object on their final days of diving.[22]

The second dive was made on August 26 with the intent to inspect four promising objects located some distance apart. Pisces V encountered a battery problem as soon as it was on the sea bed and had to abort its dive. Pisces IV searched alone and located three of the objects, none of which was the midget. Only one test dive remained before the search would have to be abandoned for another year.[23]

On August 28 the two submersibles dove on their last test dive of the year. In Pisces IV was chief pilot Kerby, pilot-in-training Colin Wollerman, and Al Kalvaitis from the National Undersea Research Program Office. Manning Pisces V were pilot Chuck Holloway, Chris Kelley, and Rachel Shackelford, HURL's new Data Department Manager.[24]

After successfully conducting a tracking exercise on the bottom, they headed for the estimated location of the primary target object. On the way, Pisces IV became entangled in a large nest of coiled steel cable, a potential disaster in the making. Getting a deep sea vehicle stuck in debris is one of the greatest fears of divers. Kerby ordered Pisces V to back away, but to stand to render assistance if necessary. Seven minutes later Pisces IV was free.

An hour and a half later Kerby came upon a large rock which showed up clearly in the sonar mapping. Knowing that the target object should lie just to the southeast, Kerby suggested that Pisces V could move toward it while the crew of Pisces IV completed some

The first view of the midget submarine in 61 years as seen by the crew of the research vehicles of HURL on August 28, 2002. It was found on the last dive HURL made for the sub in 2002. (Hawaii Undersea Research Laboratory)

housekeeping chores. Shortly, Rachel Shackelford, monitoring the sonar screen, noticed a long, slender object. Pisces V moved toward it and within minutes the bow of a small submarine came into view.

"We got it! We got it!" yelled Rachel Shackelford in Pisces V joyfully. Others exclaimed, "Oh my gosh, look at that!" Chris Kelley also in Pisces V added, "Tell Terry that we've got a midget submarine here." Lab researchers in the control ship on the surface monitoring the conversations from below filled the room with cheers as they heard the astounding reports.

When Pisces IV arrived at the spot, both vehicles illuminated the object with their powerful lights. Details could now be clearly seen. Except for marine growth, the hull appeared to be in excellent condition. Sand-laden currents may have helped to keep the hull relatively clean. Its bow still contained two torpedoes and it listed slightly to starboard. A four-inch hole was clearly visible at the base of the conning tower on its starboard side and no damage from depth charges was apparent. There was no exit hole from the shell visible on the port side and by positioning the two submersibles on either side of the conning tower with the floodlights on, it was confirmed that the shell did not pass completely through the sub.

A closeup of the conning tower of the midget submarine discovered in August 2002 off Pearl Harbor. Note the shell hole made by *Ward's* Number 3 gun. This and the presence of torpedoes still on board identified this sub as the one *Ward* sank in 1941. (Hawaii Undersea Research Laboratory)

Since three of the original five midgets had previously been found, this was one of the two still missing. One of the two was the midget from I-16 that had radioed to Tokyo on the evening of December 7, 1941, that its attack was successful. This meant that it had fired it torpedoes. The midget that *Ward* had sunk was attacked before it could fire its torpedoes. "The fact that this sub still had its torpedoes and displayed a shell hole in the conning tower was unmistakable proof that this was *Ward's* midget," said Kerby. "After 61 years the men of the *Ward* are finally vindicated."

Its discovery several miles from where *Ward* hit it in 1941 can easily be explained. A submarine with only a four-inch hole letting in water, with stern diving planes in the up position, and with the rudder hard to starboard requires considerable time and travels some distance in descending 1200 feet.

Word of the discovery spread quickly around the world. The Hawaii Undersea Research Lab was deluged with requests for information and photographs as the significance of the finding became apparent. No one was more excited than *Ward's* former crewmen in St. Paul. The crew members were kept busy for days handling media calls from around the country.

On August 11, 2003, an independent television station engaged HURL to make another dive on the sub, this time carrying a former member of the *Ward's* crew. Will Lehner was selected to make the descent.

Some questioned whether Lehner, 84, should be making such a dive. He explained that the opportunity to see the sub once more would be one of the highlights of his life that he could not pass up. And it was. He explained further.

"As I peered out of the window of the research vehicle and saw the midget lying on the seabed, the hairs on the back of my neck stood straight up. I was living the entire experience again. I saw the sub 61 years ago on the surface and then saw it going down. Now I was seeing it again. It was a great thrill and I could not have passed up the opportunity to see it once more. People used to tell me that we just thought that we sank a sub but we really didn't because there was never any evidence. Now I can show them the photographs and tell them that this is the evidence and I saw it myself."

His voice now almost trembling, he continued. "You can't believe how relieved we are with the discovery of the sub. It brings a closure to something that was hanging over *Ward's* crew for our entire lives. We will never again be doubted when we describe what we did. Now the case is finally closed."[25]

The crew of the control ship Ka'imikai-o-kanaloa gave Lehner an impromptu salute as he climbed out of the research vehicle following its ascent to the surface. They gave him a standing ovation in recognition of his role in *Ward's* achievement of sinking the midget 61 years earlier.

Although some facets of the submarine episode were over, others were just beginning. Discovery of the submarine within the territorial limits of the United States, and sunk while attacking before war was even declared, raises some interesting legal questions. At

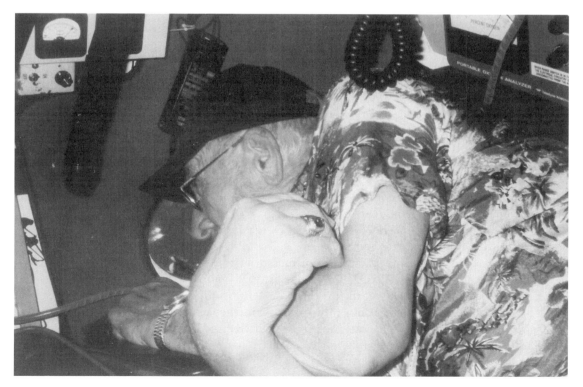

Former Ward crewman Will Lehner viewing the midget sub thru the porthole of the HURL research. Vehicle in 2003. The small confines of the vehicle require its crew to lie down while using the portholes. (Will Lehner)

Bow-on view of the Ward's midget sub on the seabed taken by former Ward crewman Will Lehner from a HURL research vehicle on his visit to the sub in 2003. Note torpedoes still inplace. (Will Lehner)

the top of the list are: What does the discovery prove? Who owns it? And what should be done with it?

Its finding confirms what did not need confirming. Japan's attack on Pearl Harbor was planned long in advance. It proved that the United States, not Japan, fired the first shot of the war and confirms that *Ward's* crew members were correct when they claimed that they sank a submarine.

The question of ownership seems to be resolved by long-standing precedent. It provides that sunken ships of war, including remains of crewmen, belong to the original owner even if found within the territorial limits of another belligerent. Thus, the midget remains the property of Japan and any action taken relative to its ultimate disposition needs the concurrence of the Japanese government.[26]

Some possible scenarios for the midget's future have already been identified. They include allowing the sub to remain where it is and designated a memorial, raising it for return to Japan and for display as a joint memorial at Pearl Harbor. There are undoubtedly others as well. If the sub is left on the seabed, ultimately it will deteriorate and disappear, leaving nothing.

Although technically feasible, raising the sub introduces a whole range of knotty problems. Its torpedoes and scuttling charge are still active and pose a threat to any operation. This is probably solvable as it was when another midget was discovered in 1960. If raised, the sub must quickly be immersed in a tank of fresh water at 10 degrees Centigrade and subjected to cathodic protection for a year to preserve it from corroding. This would involve considerable cost.[27]

Since the two-man crew is still on board, the sub is also a grave site and the Japanese have a strong cultural mandate for returning fallen servicemen to their homeland, especially when they are considered heroes. Steps would have to be taken to provide for this if the midget is brought to the surface.

Returning the remains may be the most compelling argument for raising the sub. Although it would surely be a meaningful memorial in either Japan or the United States, both countries already have one of the original five Pearl Harbor midgets on display. Japan displays hers at the Maritime Self-Defense Force Academy at Eta Jima. This is the midget discovered in Ke'ehi Lagoon outside Pearl Harbor in 78 feet of water in 1960. After its torpedoes were removed, it was raised and returned to Japan.

At the National Museum of the Pacific, formerly the Admiral Nimitz Museum, in Fredricksberg, Texas, the United States displays the midget carried by I-24. It grounded near Bellows Field and was captured on December 8, 1941. Whether either nation would find a second midget sub memorial necessary is arguable.

Also surely to be discussed at some future time will be the ultimate disposition of both the I-24 midget and *Ward's* Number Three gun. The gun, on display at the Minnesota State Capitol grounds in St. Paul since 1958, was brought to Minnesota when no one else really wanted to display it. Neither the Arizona Memorial nor the Arizona Visitor Center was constructed at Pearl Harbor yet and World Ward II memorials in any form were relatively few.

Today, however, memorials are an integral part of Pearl Harbor's landscape as well as other areas of Oahu. With a million and a half visitors annually to the Arizona Memorial, a meaningful artifact of the Pearl Harbor attack would be more accessible to the masses there than anywhere else. The current locations of the I-24 midget and the Number Three gun are appropriate for the near future. However, the question of where the gun and the sub should be permanently located to best honor the *Ward,* her crew, and all other participants of the Pearl Harbor attack should be addressed before long.

History will not allow the saga of *Ward* and the midget sub to rest. Even after 64 years the interest in the incident remains high and the quest for more information continues. A Japaneses television network produced a documentary on the five midget submarines and their crews in 2004. Their research included a visit to the *Ward* reunion in St. Paul and a trip to see the spot where *Ward* encountered and sank one of the midgets. Students at Hawaii Pacific University are making a similar documentary in 2005 and met with *Ward* crewmen in St. Paul in April 2005 to gather information. Several *Ward* crewmen will travel to Honolulu in December 2005 to accept a plaque honoring their achievement of December 7, 1941.

Discovery of *Ward's* midget sub in 2002 did not completely close the curtain on the midget sub episode of December 7, 1941. One midget, the one carried by the I-16, is still unaccounted for. If and when it is found, the remaining questions surrounding the use of these five subs may finally be answered. Whether or not that happens, *Ward's* role during the attack and her heroic achievements in World War II are now documented and a matter of record. The extraordinary career of the courageous ship with two faces and three lives spanning 26 years is no longer concealed by the archives or by 1200 feet of blue Pacific waters.

Appendices

USS Ward *Technical Data*

	DD-139	APD-16
DISPLACEMENT		
Standard (tons)	1060	1190
Full Load (tons)	1257	1600
DIMENSIONS		
Length (Overall)	314'- 4½"	314'- 4½"
Beam (w.l.)	30'-11½"	30'-11½"
Draft (f.l.)	9'- 8⅛"	11'- 4"
ARMOUR		
Belt	none	none
Deck	none	none
ARMAMENT		
Main Battery	4- 4"/50 cal	4- 3"/50 cal
Anti-aircraft	1- 3"/23 cal	5/9- 20-mm
Machine Guns	2- 0.50 cal	2- 0.30 cal
Torpedo Tubes	12- 21"	none
Depth charges	Stern racks + projectors	Stern racks + projectors
MACHINERY		
Boilers	4 Mormand 250 psi sat	2 Normand 250 psi sat
Engines	2 Parsons Geared turbines	no change
Shaft Horsepower	26,400	26,000
Screws	2–3 bladed	no change
Rudder	1 balanced	1 balanced
Fuel oil cap.	394.4 tons	440.3 tons
Diesel oil cap	none	9.0 tons
Generators	2–25kw West.	2–60kw Parsons
Max. Speed	34.2 K	28.7 K
NORMAL COMPLEMENT		
Officers	8	8
Enlisted men	125	140
TROOP CAPACITY	none	150/200

Evolution of Armament of USS Ward

	1918	12/41	7/42	12/42	3/43	1/44	4/44
MAIN BATTERY							
4"/50	4	4	4	4	0	0	0
3"/50	0	0	0	0	4	4	4
ANTI-AIRCRAFT							
3"/23	2	1	1	0	0	0	0
20-mm	0	0	6	6	5	9	7
0.50 cal.	2	2	0	0	0	0	0
0.30 cal.	0	0	0	0	0	2	2
TORPEDO TUBES							
21" Tubes	12	12	12	12	0	0	0
DEPTH CHARGES							
Stern Racks	2	2	2	2	2	2	2
Y gun	1	1	1	1	0	0	0
Projectors	0	0	4	4	6	6	6

Chronology of Major Events of USS Ward

March 4, 1917	Construction was authorized
May 15, 1918	Keel laid at Mare Island shipyard, Vallejo, California
June 1, 1918	Launched
July 18, 1918*	Commissioned, Commander Milton Davis commanding
December 2, 1918	Left Mare Island for sea duty
May 5–7, 1919	Participated in historic first cross-Atlantic flight by aircraft
September 13, 1919	Participated in Naval Review by President Wilson in Seattle
June 5, 1922*	Decommissioned at destroyer base, San Diego, California
January, 1941	Taken out of Reserve Fleet, began overhaul, San Diego
January 15, 1941	Recommissioned, Lt. Hunter Wood commanding
February 10, 1941	Made first sea trial, San Diego, California
February 28, 1941	Left Mare Island Navy Yard, California, for Pearl Harbor
March 9, 1841	Arrived Pearl; Harbor Naval Base, Hawaii
December 5, 1941	Lt. William Outerbridge became the commanding officer
December 7, 1941	Fired first shot of World War II. Hit and sank Japanese submarine outside Pearl Harbor before the air arrack
January 2, 1942	Attacked strong submarine contact outside the harbor
September 30, 1942	Lt. R.H.Wilkinson became the commanding officer
December 13, 1942	Left Pearl Harbor for U.S. mainland
December 24, 1942	Arrived Puget Sound Naval Yard for conversion to APD
January 8, 1943	Lt. (jg) L.S. Benson became the commanding officer
January 15, 1943	Lt. Fredrick Lemly became the commanding officer
February 11, 1943	Departed Puget Sound Naval Yard as APD-16
February 13, 1943	Departed San Francisco for Pearl Harbor loaded with mail
February 24, 1943	Arrived Pearl Harbor, given new camouflage paint scheme
February 28, 1943	Crossed the equator for the first time
March 3, 1943	Crossed the International Date Line
April 7, 1943	Heavy Japanese air attack on Guadalcanal and Tulagi. Ward shot down three enemy aircraft
June 16, 1943	Heavy Japanese air attack on Guadalcanal. Ward shot down four enemy aircraft

June, 1943	Lent a bilge pump to PT boat skipper Lt. John Kennedy
August 15, 1943	Participated in invasion of Vella LaVella
October 27, 1943	Participated in invasion of Treasury Islands
October 28, 1943	Participated in diversion landings on Choiseul Island
November 17, 1943	Participated in landings on Bougainville Island
December 3, 1943	Began 10-day liberty in Sydney, Australia
December 26, 1943	Participated in invasion of Cape Gloucester, New Britain
January 2, 1944	Participated in landings at Saidor, New Guinea
February 15, 1944	Participated in landings at Nissan in the Green Islands
March 20, 1944	Participated in the invasion of Emirau Island
April 22, 1944	Participated in invasion of Aitape, New Guinea
May 27, 1944	Participated in invasion of Biak in the Schouten Islands
July 30, 1944	Participated in landings at Cape Sanspor, New Guinea
August 13, 1944	Began a second 10-day liberty in Sydney, Australia
September 15, 1944	Participated in invasion of Mototai, Dutch East Indies
October 17, 1944	Participated in landings on Dinagat Island, Philippines
October 20, 1944	Suffered only fatality of entire war (accidental)
October 30, 1944	Lt. Richard E. Farwell became commanding officer
December 6, 1944	Loaded troops at Leyte Gulf
December 7, 1944	Participated in invasion of Ormoc, Leyte Island; hit by kamikaze aircraft in Ormoc Bay. Sunk by U.S. destroyer *O'Brien* (DD-724) at 1130
August 28, 2002	*Ward's* midget sub sinking confirmed with discovery of sub on sea bottom by Hawaii Undersea Research Lab

*Although many sources indicate that the initial commissioning date of *Ward* was July 24, 1918, and its decommissioning date was June 21, 1921, the official U.S. Navy Deck Logs for *Ward*, however, clearly show that *Ward* was commissioned on July 18, 1918, and decommissioned on June 5, 1922.

Amphibious Landings—USS Ward *(APD-16)*

Date	Location	Unit Carried	No. of Troops
July 18, '43	Enogai, New Georgia	4th Marine Raider Bat.	150
July 21, '43	Enogai, New Georgia	161 Inf. Reg.	166
August 15, '43	Vella Lavella	35th RCT- 25th Inf. Div.	214
October 27, '43	Treasury Islands	Co. A, 36th Bat., N.Z. Army	198
October 28, '43	Choiseul Island	Co. B, 2nd Parachute Bat.	180
November 17, '43	Bougainville Island	Co. I, 3rd Bat. 21st Marines	167
December 26, '43	Cape Gloucester, NB	Co. I/M, 3rd Bat., 21st Mar.	143
January 2, '44	Saidor, New Guinea	126 RCT, 32nd Inf. Div.	147
February 15, '44	Green Islands	30th & 35th New Zealand Bat.	212
March 20, '44	Emirau Island	Co. B, 1st Bat. 4th Marines	208
April 22, '44	Aitape, New Guinea	163 RCT, 41st Inf. Div.	137
May 27, '44	Biak Island, New G.	186th Inf. Reg.	129
July 30, '44	Cape Sansapor, N.G.	Co. E/F, 1st Reg. 6th Inf. Div.	99
September 15, '44	Morotai Island, N.E.I.	Co. A, 124th Reg. 31st Inf. Div.	124
October 17, '44	Dinagat Island, Leyte	Co. E, 6th Ranger Bat.	147
December 7, '44	Ormoc Bay Leyte	77th Inf. Div.	108

Note: In addition to the above landings, which were made on islands under Japanese control, *Ward* made scores of trips to various bases under Allied control. *Ward* carried equipment, supplies and personnel, often being attacked by Japanese aircraft en route.

USS Ward *Citations Earned in World War II*

Battle Star—For actions at Pearl Harbor — December 7, 1941

Battle Star—For operations in the Southern Solomons— April 7 to June 16, 1943

Battle Star—For occupation of Vella Lavella Island — August 15, 1943

Battle Star—For operations in the Northern Solomons (Treasury Is., Choiseul Is., Bougainville Is.)
    October 27 to November 17, 1943

Battle Star—For operations at Cape Gloucester, New Britain — December 26–29, 1943 and Green
    Islands— February 15–19, 1944

Battle Star—For occupation of Saidor, New Guinea — January 2, 1944

Battle Star—For operations at Hollandia, New Guinea — April 21 to May 29, 1944

Battle Star—For operations at Biak — May 27, 1944, and Cape Sanspor, New Guinea — July 30–31,
    1944, and landings at Morotai Island — November 5 to 18, 1944

Battle Star—For operations at Leyte — October 17, 1944 and Ormoc Bay — December 7, 1944

Navy Unit Commendation — For exceptionally meritorious service against enemy aircraft, shore
    batteries and submarines. Operating in contact with the enemy attack, the USS *Ward* per-
    formed her duties as a destroyer and high speed transport, constantly maintaining a superior
    degree of efficiency in the performance of her assigned tasks. From the time she fired the first
    shot of the war at Pearl Harbor until mortally wounded by a kamikaze attack in Ormoc Bay
    three years later, the USS *Ward* contributed materially to the success of the Pacific Campaign
    by the offensive action that resulted in the destruction of enemy submarines and several
    enemy planes. Her courageous determination and effort were in keeping with the highest tra-
    dition of the United States Naval Service.

Four-Stackers Converted to Aux. Pers. Destroyers (APD)—32

APD No.	Name	Former DD No.	Original Com. Date	Sunk or Decom.	Fate
1	Manley	74	10/15/17	11/19/45	Scrapped
2	Colhoun	85	06/13/18	08/30/42	Sunk by airc.
3	Gregory	82	06/01/18	09/05/42	Sunk by dest.
4	Little	79	04/06/18	09/05/42	Sunk by dest.
5	McKean	90	02/25/19	11/17/43	Sunk by airc.
6	Stringham	83	07/02/18	11/09/45	Scrapped
7	Talbot	114	07/20/18	10/09/45	Scrapped
8	Waters	115	08/06/18	10/12/45	Scrapped
9	Dent	116	09/09/18	12/04/45	Scrapped
10	Brooks	232	06/18/20	08/02/45	Scrapped
11	Gilmer	233	04/30/20	02/05/46	Scrapped
12	Humphreys	236	07/21/20	10/26/45	Scrapped
13	Sands	243	11/10/20	10/19/45	Scrapped
14	Schley	103	09/20/18	11/09/45	Scrapped
15	Kilty	137	12/17/18	11/02/45	Scrapped
16	Ward	139	07/18/18	12/07/44	Sunk by airc.
17	Crosby	164	01/24/19	09/28/45	Scrapped
18	Kane	235	06/11/20/	01/24/46	Scrapped
19	Tattnall	125	06/26/19	12/17/45	Scrapped
20	Roper	147	02/15/19	09/15/45	Scrapped
21	Dickerson	157	09/03/19	04/04/45	Scuttled
22	Herbert	160	11/21/19	09/25/45	Scrapped
23	Overton	239	06/30/20	07/28/45	Scrapped
24	Noa	343	02/15/21	09/12/44	Sunk-Collision
25	Rathburne	113	06/24/18	11/02/45	Scrapped
29	Barry	248	12/28/20	06/21/45	Sunk by airc.
31	Clemson	186	12/29/19	10/12/45	Scrapped

APD No.	Name	Former DD No.	Original Com. Date	Sunk or Decom.	Fate
32	Goldsborough	188	11/26/20	10/11/45	Scrapped
33	Geo. E. Badger	196	07/28/20	10/03/45	Scrapped
34	Belknap	251	04/28/19	08/04/45	Scrapped
35	Osmond Ingram	255	06/28/19	01/08/46	Scrapped
36	Greene	266	05/09/19	11/24/45	Sunk-typhoon

Four-Stackers Converted to Destroyer-Minelayers (DM)—22

DM No.	Name	DM No.	Name	DM No.	Name
1	Stribing	9	Ingraham	17	Montgomery
2	Murray	10	Ludlow	18	Breese
3	Israel	11	Burns	19	Tracy
4	Luce	12	Anthony	20	Preble
5	Maury	13	Sproston	21	Sicard
6	Lansdale	14	Rizal	22	Pruitt
7	Mahan	15	Gamble		
8	Hart	16	Ramsay		

Four-Stackers Converted to High Speed Minesweepers (DMS)—18

DMS No.	Name	DMS No.	Name	DMS No.	Name
1	Dorsey	7	Howardt	13	Hopkins
2	Lamberton	8	Stansbury	14	Zane
3	Boggs	9	Chandler	15	Wasmuth
4	Elliot	10	Southard	16	Trever
5	Palmer	11	Hovey	17	Perry
6	Hogan	12	Long	18	Hamilton

Four-Stackers Converted to Misc. Auxiliaries (AG)—42

AG No.	Name	AG No.	Name	AG No.	Name
18	Stoddert	87	MacLeish	107	Stansbury
19	Boggs	91	Dahlgren	108	Chandler
20	Kilty	95	Litchfield	109	Zane
21	Lamberton	96	Broome	110	Trever
22	Radford	97	Simpson	111	Hamilton
24	Semmes	98	Ramsay	112	Breckinridge
28	Manley	99	Prebble	113	Barney
80	Dupont	100	Sicard	114	Biddle
81	J. Fred Talbott	101	Pruitt	115	Ellis
82	Schenk'	102	Babbit	116	Cole
83	Kennison	103	Upshur	117	Whipple
84	Hatfield	104	Eliot	118	McCormick
85	fox	105	Hogan	119	John D. Ford
86	Buhmer	106	Howard	120	Paul Jones

Four-Stackers Converted to Seaplane Tenders (AVD)—14

AVD No.	Name	AVD No.	Name	AVD No.	Name
1	Childs	6	Hulbert	11	Thornton
2	Williamson	7	Wm. B. Preston	12	Gillis
3	George C. Badger	8	Belknap	13	Greene
4	Clemson	9	Osmond Ingram	14	McFarland
5	Goldsborough	10	Ballard		

Four-Stackers Converted to Water Barges (YW)—2

YW No.	Name	YW No.	Name
56	Turner	57	Walker

Four-Stackers Traded to Great Britain in September 1940—50

DD No.	Name	DD No.	Name	DD No.	Name
70	Conway	140	Claxton	195	Welborn C, Wood
72	Conner	143	Yarnell	197	Branch
73	Stockton	162	Thatcher	198	Herndon
75	Wickes	167	Cowell	252	McCook
76	Philip	168	Maddox	253	McCalla
78	Evans	169	Foote	254	Rodgers
81	Sigourney	170	Kalk	256	Bancroft
88	Robinson	175	MacKenzie	257	Welles
93	Fairfax	182	Thomas	293	Laub
89	Ringgold	181	Hopewell	258	Aulick
108	Williams	183	Haradan	264	MacLanahan
127	Twiggs	184	Abbot	265	Edwards
131	Buchanan	185	Doran	268	Shubrick
132	Aaron Ward	190	Satterlee	269	Bailey
133	Hale	191	Mason	273	Swasey
134	Crowninshield	193	Abel P. Upshur	274	Meade
135	Tillman	194	Hunt		

Commanding Officers of USS Ward (DD-139)

USS *Ward* was commissioned at Mare, Island, California, on July 18, 1918

Com. Milton S. Davis	July 18, 1918	to	December 21, 1919
Lt. John F. Bates	December 19, 1919	to	June 19, 1920
Lt. C.J. Reno	June 19, 1920	to	July, 1920
Lt. T.P. Kane	July, 1920	to	October, 1920
Lt. W.J. Lorenz	October, 1920	to	September 16, 1921
Lt. F.C. Denebrink	September 16, 1921	to	November 12, 1921
Lt. H.A. Harrison	November 12, 1921	to	November 21, 1921
Ens. C.J. Christopherson	November 21, 1921	to	January 23, 1922
Ens. Clyde A. Coggins	January 23, 1922	to	March 24, 1922
Lt.(jg) Marcus L. Kurtz	March 24, 1922	to	June 5, 1922

Ward was decommissioned on June 5, 1922, and remained in
the Reserve Fleet in San Diego until January, 1941.

Lt. Hunter Wood	February 13, 1941	to	December 5, 1941
Lt. William Outerbridge	December 5, 1941	to	September 30, 1942
Lt. Com. R.H. Wilkinson	September 30, 1942	to	January 8, 1943

Ward was converted to an auxiliary personnel destroyer (APD) in
Bremerton, Washington, in January 1943 and recommissioned on January 15, 1943.

Commanding Officers of USS Ward *(APD-16)*

Lt.(jg) Lloyd G. Benson	January 8, 1943	to	January 15, 1943
Lt. Fredrick W. Lemly	January 15, 1943	to	October 30, 1944
Lt. Richard E. Farwell	October 30, 1944	to	December 7, 1944

USS *Ward* was sunk on December 7, 1944

Roster of Personnel

Because of the interest in the Ward by former crewmen, relatives and friends of crewmen, as well as many others, a complete roster of all who served on the ship from its recommissioning on January 15, 1941, to its sinking on December 7, 1944, was deemed to be useful.

Although all Deck Log and Muster Roll reports for this period were reviewed thoroughly, the exact dates of arrival or detachment from the ship were not available for every crewman. Some men were simply not logged aboard or logged off. Others left the ship temporarily for hospitalization or schools and never returned, but were then not accounted for in the reports. For those men, only the month or year of detachment is listed. Other men came aboard temporarily for reassignment to another ship, transportation to some specified military base or another ship, or to participate in an exercise. Those men are not considered part of the *Ward's* crew and not included in the roster. The author regrets if any member of the crew was mistakenly omitted from the roster for that reason.

Because of the many inquires as to the makeup of the crew at various important milestones in the ship's career, the roster also indicates in the final column who was on the crew at these times. The following letter designations are used to indicate this:

I — Initial sailing on February 13, 1941, after recommissioning

P — Japanese Attack on Pearl Harbor on December 7, 1941

S — Sinking in Ormoc Bay, Leyte by kamikaze attack on December 7, 1944

F — Died while on board

* — Members of the 47th Reserve Division

The roster indicates that 50 officers and 454 enlisted men served on *Ward* during this period. The author welcomes additions, deletions, or corrections to the roster for use in any future revised edition.

Officers

Name	Date Arrived	Rating	Date Detached	Rating	Notes
Andrews, Frank Von D.	1/15/41	Ens.	9/30/42	Lt. jg	(I) (P)
Austin, Robert A.	12/1/43	Ens.	1/2/44	Ens.	
Baker, Bernard R.	5/17/42	Ens.	3/7/43	Lt. jg	
Baldwin, Russell E.	11/19/44	Lt jg (MC)	12/7/44	Lt. jg (MC)	(S)
Bell, Arthur S.	4/17/42	Ens.	8/6/42	Ens.	
Benson, Lloyd G.	6/18/42	Lt. jg	2/6/44	Lt.	(C)
Borland, William F.	6/18/42	Ens.	8/23/43	Ens.	
Brink, Bruce M.	9/17/44	Lt.	9/24/44	Lt.	
Carlin, James V.	11/2/42	Lt. jg	12/42	Lt. jg	

243

Name	Date Arrived	Rating	Date Detached	Rating	Notes
Carney, John B.	1/13/44	Ens.	12/7/44	Ens.	(S)
Condit, P. K.	11/14/42	Lt. (MC)	12/42	Lt. (MC)	
Cooke, S. C.	11/21/44	Ens.	12/7/44	Ens.	(S)
Cooper, Charles E.	4/27/43	Lt. (MC)	11/21/44	Lt. Com. (MC)	
Crummey, Ralph S.	11/10/42	Ens.	12/12/42	Ens.	
Doughty, Hartwell T.*	1/29/41	Lt.	8/11/42	Lt. Com.	(I) (P)
Edwards, Robert C.	10/9/43	Ens.	12/7/44	Ens.	(S)
Gale, Winsor C.	1/15/41	Lt.	2/1/41	Lt.	
Gay, James E.	3/30/44	Lt.	7/7/44	Lt.	
Green, James P.	3/27/44	Lt, jg	7/10/44	Lt. jg	
Grefe, Theodore F.	1/29/41	Ens.	12/4/41	Ens.	(I)
Farwell, Richard E.	10/29/41	Ens.	12/7/44	Lt.	(C) (P) (S)
Goepner, Oscar W.	1/31/41	Ens.	11/24/42	Lt.	(I) (P)
Gordon, Clarence E., Jr.	2/1/42	Lt.	2/19/42	Lt	
Hastings, James R.	8/23/43	Ens.	3/6/44	Ens.	
Haynie, Donald B.*	1/29/41	Ens.	2/26/42	Ens.	(I) (P)
Ierardi, William J.	10/28/43	Lt. jg	10/29/44	Lt. Jg	
Jungkind, Bernhardt F.	9/1/44	Ens.	12/7/44	Ens.	(S)
Larson, E. A.	11/21/44	Ens.	12/7/44	Ens.	(S)
Law, Louis E.	5/28/43	Ens.	11/29/44	Lt. jg	
LeGros, Emile E.	8/27/43	Ens.	12/7/44	Lt. jg	(S)
Lemly, Frederick W.	1/11/43	Lt.	10/28/44	Lt. Com.	(C)
May, Wayne	4/10/43	Ens.	6/21/44	Lt. jg	
McKinnell, J. F.	10/13/41	Ens.	Dec. 1942	Ens.	(P)
McManus, Edward J.	4/6/42	Ens.	5/18/42	Ens.	
Morford, Alan V.	10/3/44	Lt. jg	12/7/44	Lt. jg	(S)
Outerbridge, William W.	12/5/41	Lt.	9/30/42	Lt. Com.	(C) (P)
Peck, George S.	7/31/42	Ens.	3/28/44	Lt. jg	
Platt, Louis F.	7/8/41	Ens.	5/28/43	Lt.	
Railsback, Edward N.	12/24/43	Ens.	12/7/44	Lt. jg	(P)
Redmond, R. L.	10/12/43	Lt. jg	12/10/43	Lt. jg	
Rowe, Hilary C.	1/15/41	Lt. jg	6/23/41	Lt. jg	(I)
Schroeder, Freeman C.	2/10/43	Ens.	2/25/44	Ens.	
Scott, Alan R.	1/18/44	Ens.	3/6/44	Ens.	
Sieg, R. L. Jr.	2/17/42	Ens.	4/9/42	Ens.	
Stevenson, Robert G.	6/18/42	Ens.	11/4/42	Ens.	
Stewart, George B. III	3/10/41	Ens.	4/24/43	Ens.	
Stewart, Normon R	9/30/44	Lt.	12/7/44	Lt.	(I)
Thompson, Guy E.	9/28/44	Ens,	12/7/44	Ens.	(S)
Wilkinson, Robert H.	9/27/42	Lt. Com.	1/8/43	Lt. Com.	(C)
Wood, Hunter Jr.	1/15/41	Lt. Com.	12/5/41	Lt. Com.	(C) (I)

Note: (C) in last column denotes Commanding officer

Enlisted Men

Name	Date Arrived	Rating	Date Detached	Rating	Notes
Adams, Clemmie J.	2/13/43	S2c	12/7/44	S1c	(S)
Adams, Joseph T.	7/4/43	S1c	8/21/44	Cox	
Adams, Raymond M.	2/9/42	AS	12/7/44	GM2c	(S)
Adkins, Marvin G.	10/19/43	F3c	12/12/43	F3c	
Ainsworth, Thomas	2/23/43	MoMM2c	1/30/44	MoMM1c	
Alford, Marcus D.	2/13/43	S2c	12/7/44	S2c	(S)

Name	Date Arrived	Rating	Date Detached	Rating	Notes
Allen, George S.	9/20/42	AS	12/10/42	S2c	
Alvarado, Gilbert	9/20/42	AS	12/12/42	S2c	
Anderson, Albert C.	2/23/43	Cox	5/28/43	Cox	
Anderson, Clayton F.*	1/29/41	S2c	3/1/41	S2c	
Anderson, George	5/28/43	CBM	10/27/44	CBM	
Angle, Frank R.	10/28/44	S2c	12/7/44	S2c	(S)
Aquino, Rudolph G.	2/23/43	S2c	10/15/43	S1c	
Arndt, Walter H.	2/23/43	MoMM2c	5/28/43	MoMM2c	
Austin, Gilbert A.	9/20/42	AS	12/7/44	EM3c	(S)
Avera, I. C.	1/12/42	EM3c	12/10/42	EM2c	
Axel, Laverne M.	10/6/42	S2c	2/22/43	S2c	
Baca, Richard C.	2/13/43	S2c	12/7/44	S1c	(S)
Bachman, Robert L.	2/23/43	S2c	12/7/44	RdM2c	(S)
Badger, William D.	9/20/42	AS	12/12/42	S2c	
Baker, Kenneth D.	10/28/44	S2c	12/7/44	S2c	(S)
Ball, Robert L.*	1/29/41	S2c	6/12/42	S1c	(I) (P)
Ballantine, Robert D.	2/23/43	Cox	12/7/44	BM2c	(S)
Ballard, Raymond A.	1/12/42	S2c	12/7/44	Bkr2c	(S)
Barfuss, Carl; A. *	1/29/41	S2c	9/30/42	SF3c	(I) (P)
Baxter, George A.	1/15/41	CPhM	4/4/42	CPhM	(I) (P)
Beazley, Arlo O.	2/23/43	Cox	12/7/44	BM2c	(S)
Beedle, Clarence C.	10/6/42	S2c	12/12/42	S2c	
Behme, William H.	9/30/44	S2c	12/7/44	S2c	(S)
Bell, Francis G.	9/20/42	AS	11/19/44	EM2c	
Bellevance, Joseph A.	11/5/42	SM1c	12/12/42	CSM	
Belt, Edward C.	7/19/43	Cox	9/4/44	BM2c	
Benge, Charles M.	2/13/43	S2c	11/22/44	S1c	
Bennett, Louis C.	2/23/43	Cox	12/7/44	BM2c	(S)
Bensinger, Charles O.	1/15/41	S2c	6/18/42	SM3c	(I) (P)
Bently, Arthur G.	10/28/44	S1c	12/7/44	S1c	(S)
Berard, Henry E.	1/15/41	CGM	2/6/41	CGM	
Berlier, John C.	9/14/42	SM1c	12/12/42	SM1c	
Berryhill, Joseph N.	2/13/43	S2c	12/7/44	F1c	(S)
Betsch, William H.	9/20/42	AS	12/7/44	S1c	(S)
Bevelaqua, Peter J.	9/30/44	S2c	12/7/44	S2c	(S)
Bier, Burton A.	9/20/42	AS	12/7/44	S1c	(S)
Blakely, William A.	9/20/42	AS	12/12/42	S2c	
Blanchard, West C.	9/20/42	AS	1943	S2c	
Bloomer, Gale D.	12/11/41	F1c	11/29/44	CWT	
Blum, Arthur E.	9/20/42	AS	12/12/42	S2c	
Bone, Joseph J.	9/20/42	AS	12/7/44	WT2c	(S)
Border, Fred L.	1/15/41	WT1c	9/14/41	WT1c	(I)
Boudreaux, Wilmer J.	9/20/42	AS	7/14/44	WT3c	
Boughton, Walter J.	11/5/42	SK1c	12/12/42	CSK	
Boyd, Albert E.	11/5/42	SK3c	12/12/42	SK3c	
Boyett, James N.	2/22/44	S2c	12/7/44	S1c	(S)
Brannen, Harrold	1/15/41	S2c	2/6/41	S2c	
Brockelhurst, Ralph S.	2/6/41	MM1c	8/21/41	MM1c	(I)
Brown, Fredrick D.	4/22/43	SoM3c	12/13/43	SoM3c	
Brown, James D.	3/24/44	EM1c	12/7/44	EM1c	(S)
Brurud, Willard V.	10/28/44	S1c	12/7/44	S1c	(S)
Brunner, Charles J.	9/1/44	S2c	12/7/44	S2c	(S)
Buckener, Joseph J.	10/6/42	S2c	12/10/42	S2c	
Buckland, Joseph J.	9/1/44	S2c	12/7/44	S2c	(S)

Name	Date Arrived	Rating	Date Detached	Rating	Notes
Buckmaster, J. C. Jr.	1/6/42	S2c	2/17/42	S2c	
Buell, Oliver D.	1//9/43	PhM1c	8/17/43	PhM1c	
Bukrey, Edward J.*	1/29/41	S1c	12/7/44	GM1c	(I) (P) (S)
Burckhardt, Arthur L.	9/1/44	S2c	12/7/44	S2c	(S)
Burdett, G. W.	9/1/44	S2c	12/7/44	S2c	(S)
Burger, Howard J.	9/1/44	S2c	12/7/44	S2c	(S)
Burgess, Roy L.	9/1/44	S2c	12/7/44	S2c	(S)
Burnett, Harry	1/15/41	F1c	10/13/41	SF1c	(I)
Byers, Edwin	9/1/44	S2c	12/7/44	S2c	(S)
Byle, Harry G.	9/1/44	S2c	12/7/44	S2c	(S)
Cain, Francis O.	9/1/44	S2c	12/7/44	S2c	(S)
Callahan, Donald L.	2/6/41	F3c	10/8/42	F2c	(I) (P)
Camilleri, Francis	9/1/44	S2c	12/7/44	S2c	(S)
Campbell, Clyde W.	1/15/41	BM2c	2/27/41	BM2c	
Campion, Walter A. *	1/29/41	S2c	2/23/43	TM2c	(I) (P)
Cancienne, William J.	2/13/43	S2c	12/7/44	S1c	(S)
Caputo, Rocco C.	9/1/44	S2c	12/7/44	S2c	(S)
Carlilse, Roger W.	1/18/41	F3c	2/6/41	F3c	
Carota, Julius	9/1/44	S2c	12/7/44	S2c	(S)
Carter, Edward W.	9/1/44	S2c	12/7/44	S2c	(S)
Carter, Richard	9/1/44	S2c	12/7/44	S2c	(S)
Castillo, Joseph	2/13/43	S2c	12/7/44	Cox	(S)
Castle, Joseph P.	9/1/44	S2c	12/7/44	S2c	(S)
Casto, Francis P.	9/1/44	S2c	12/7/44	S2c	(S)
Cavanaugh, Gerald A.	9/1/44	S2c	12/7/44	S2c	(S)
Caves, Rhodell C.	6/13/41	MM1c	1941	MM1c	
Cederberg, Laurence D.	9/1/44	S2c	12/7/44	S2c	(S)
Chalk, George F.	9/1/44	S2c	12/7/44	S2c	(S)
Champion, Flay O.	9/1/44	S2c	12/7/44	S2c	(S)
Chapman, Edward L.	9/1/44	S2c	12/7/44	S2c	(S)
Chapman, Hubert D.	12/11/41	F2c	12/12/42	MM2c	
Chinn, Richard B.	7/17/42	ROM3c	8/30/42	ROM3c	
Christensen, Gunnar M.	9/1/44	S2c	12/7/44	S2c	(S)
Christensen, Robert L.	9/1/44	S2c	10/4/44	S2c	
Christopherson, George H. *	1/29/41	F1c	2/23/43	Bmkr2c	(I) (P)
Christy, Peter	9/1/44	S2c	12/7/44	S2c	(S)
Clark, Marvin R.	2/13/43	S2c	12/7/44	Cox	(S)
Clark, Robert L.	2/23/43	MoMM2c	12//7/44	MoMM1c	(S)
Cole, Lionel L.	2/23/43	Cox	5/28/43	Cox	
Colin, Alvin G.	2/23/43	SC3c	1943	SC3c	
Collins, Allen M.	2/22/44	MoMM3c	12/7/44	MoMM2c	(S)
Collyard, Henry V. *	1/29/41	S2c	2/23/43	TM1c	(I) (P)
Conklin, Kenneth R.	10/4/43	CMM	12/30/43	CMM	
Conley, Gene S.	1/18/41	S2c	2/6/41	S2c	
Conner, Harold E.	10/6/42	S2c	12/12/42	S2c	
Conover, Henry C.	2/23/43	Y2c	1943	PhM2c	
Conroy, William E. *	1/29/41	CQM	3/22/42	CQM	(I) (P)
Cowgill, Paul L.	1/15/41	CMM	1/6/42	CMM	(I) (P)
Curry, Chesley J.	2/23/43	Cox	5/28/43	Cox	
Cyrus, John H. *	1/29/41	Matt2c	1942	Matt1c	(I) (P)
Daniel, Ernest R.	4/28/41	CEM	10/20/41	CEM	
Daniels, Lloyd B.	2/12/44	S1c	12/7/44	RM3c	(S)
Day, Warren	1/15/41	MM1c	2/6/41	MM1c	
Delay, Archie J.	1/18/41	F3c	2/6/41	F3c	

Name	Date Arrived	Rating	Date Detached	Rating	Notes
Denonno, Joseph	11/16/42	AS	12/4/42	S2c	
DeRosia, George H. *	1/29/41	CWT	2/23/43	CWT	(I) (P)
Derouin, Clifford J.	11/16/42	AS	12/4/42	S2c	
DeSalvo, Joseph	11/16/42	AS	12/4/42	S2c	
DeSantell, Arthur L.	11/6/42	AS	12/4/42	S2c	
DeServe, Joseph	11/16/42	AS	12/4/42	S2c	
Dionisopoulos, Panogiotes A. *	1/29/41	S2c	10/15/43	QM2c	(I) (P)
Dismuke, Auldrag R.	10/19/43	F3c	12/7/44	F1c	(S)
Dolan, Owen C. *	1/29/41	S2c	9/23/42	Cox	(I) (P)
Domogall, Ambrose A. *	1/29/41	S2c	6/11/42	CMM	(I) (P)
Donnolly, Michael	10/6/42	S2c	12/10/42	S2c	
Dornheim, Walter H.	1/15/41	CMM	1942	CMM	(I) (P)
DuBose, Carroll L.	4/13/42	CPhM	12/12/42	CPhM	
Duchin, Paul E.	10/23/43	F3c	10/20/44	WT3c	(F)
Dumdie, Robert N.	8/22/43	PhM1c	12/7/44	PhM1c	(S)
Dunstan, Edward A.	2/23/43	Cox	5/28/43	Cox	
Duval, William H.	1/15/41	SC1c	11/22/44	CCS	(I) (P)
Dyrda, Joseph P. *	1/29/41	S1c	12/12/42	GM2c	(I) (P)
East, William H.	8/27/44	CM3c	12/7/44	CM2c	(S)
Echols, Harry I.	8/26/43	StM2c	12/7/44	StM1c	(S)
Efaw, Fred S.	10/20/41	CEM	3/12/44	CEM	(P)
Eichman, Reuban J.	12/11/41	WT2c	11/24/42	WT1c	
Ekblad, Kenneth W. *	1/29/41	MM1c	3/11/44	MM1c	(I) (P)
Ellsworth, Guy E.	9/1/44	S2c	10/4/44	S2c	
Elsa, James	2/6/41	F1c	7/17/41	F1c	(I)
Ely, Robert N.	2/23/43	S2c	10/15/43	S2c	
Entenmann, John R. *	1/29/41	F3c	6/8/41	F3c	(I)
Erickson, Edward F.	2/23/43	MoMM2c	5/23/43	MoMM2c	
Ethier, Orville S.*	1/29/41	F3c	12/7/44	MM1c	(I) (P) (S)
Falgout, Henry J.	10/6/42	S2c	12/7/44	S1c	(S)
Fenslage, John E.	10/28/44	MMS3c	12/7/44	MMS3c	(S)
Fenton, Clarence W. *	1/29/41	S2c	12/7/44	BM1c	(I) (P) (S)
Ferguson, Henry M.	1/18/41	S2c	2/6/41	S2c	
Ferrante, Rudolph M.	10/19/43	S2c	12/7/44	S1c	(S)
Fetty, Edwin M.	10/19/43	S2C	12/7/44	SF3c	(S)
Fickel, Paul E.	10/19/43	S2c	8/12/44	S1c	
Fink, Alfred J. *	1/29/41	S2c	12/7/44	GM2c	(I) (P) (S)
Fischer, George J.	5/28/43	QM1c	9/4/44	CQM	
Flanagan, Harold P. *	1/29/41	S12c	8/29/42	TM3c	(I) (P)
Fletcher, William	2/18/42	AS	12/7/44	S2c	(S)
Fluegel, Joseph V. *	1/29/41	S1c	5/28/43	GM1c	(I) (P)
Fong, Mon S.	6/3/43	QM3c	10/15/43	QM3c	
Forsythe, Carl E.	2/18/42	AS	6/18/42	S2c	
Foster, Napoleon	5/17/42	Matt3c	6/26/42	Matt3c	
Frantz, Albert	2/13/43	S2c	12/7/44	WT3c	(S)
Frasieur, Jack L.	2/6/41	F1c	10/22/41	F1C	(I)
Fratto, Frank L.*	1/29/41	F1c	12/7/44	MM1c	(I) (P) (S)
Frederickson, Kenneth	5/28/43	CBM	8/1/44	CBM	
Fritts, Harold N.	2/18/42	AS	12/7/44	RM2c	(S)
Fritz, Leo L.	1/12/42	S2c	4/23/42	F3c	
Fritz, Robert	2/18/42	AS	1942	F2c	
Fritzham, Peter B. *	1/29/41	SC3c	4/6/41	SC3c	(I)
Frizell, James W.	2/23/43	S2c	10/15/43	S1c	
Funk, Robert W.	2/18/42	AS	12/12/42	Cox	

Name	Date Arrived	Rating	Date Detached	Rating	Notes
Furmall, James	10/19/43	F2c	12/7/44	F1c	(S)
Gabaldon, Arthur P.	10/8/42	SoM3c	12/12/42	SoM3c	
Garner, Wade	4/23/42	S2c	10/16/43	RM2c	
Gatewood, Maurice E.	1/15/41	RM3c	9/30/42	RM1c	(I) (P)
Gearin, Howard F. *	1/29/41	S1c	12/7/44	SM1c	(I) (P) (S)
Gerner, Louis O. *	1/29/41	CM3c	9/30/42	CM2c	(I) (P)
Gibbons, Thomas R.	2/23/43	MoMM2c	8/21/44	MoMM1c	
Gibson, Elmer T. *	1/29/41	CY	9/7/42	CY	(I) (P)
Gilbreath, Cloves W.	10/6/42	S2c	12/10/42	S2c	
Gill, John K.*	1/29/41	S2c	1/6/42	S1c	(I) (P)
Gordon, Fred J.	2/23/43	S2c	12/7/44	WT3c	(S)
Gorman, Robert H. *	1/29/41	S2c	1943	SM2c	(I) (P)
Graff, Louis J.	1/15/41	WT1c	8/19/42	WT1c	(I) (P)
Grant, Albert D.	2/23/43	S2c	1943	S2c	
Gray, Harvey C.	10/19/42	S2c	12/7/44	FC3c	(S)
Grendsya, Leonard J.	10/19/42	S2c	12/7/44	GM2c	(S)
Griep, William G. *	1/29/41	S2c	12/7/44	BM2c	(I) (P) (S)
Griffen, Albert E.	2/23/43	Bm2c	1/17/44	BM1c	
Grindall, Basil J. *	1/29/41	S2c	1943	S1c	(I) (P)
Groxton, James A.	10/6/42	S2c	2/23/43	S2c	
Gruening, Donald W. *	1/29/41	S2c	5/28/43	RM1c	(I) (P)
Guin, Franklin	2/12/44	S1c	12/7/44	QM3c	(S)
Haes, Dean D. *	1/29/41	RM3c	5/28/43	RM1c	(I) (P)
Hajdu, Frank M. *	1/29/41	S2c	12/12/43	EM2c	(I) (P)
Halebrink, M. C.	1942	Matt2c	12/12/42	Matt2c	
Hall, Charles W.	11/19/44	F3c	12/7/44	F3c	(S)
Hamel, Alfred J.	11/3/42	F2c	12/7/44	Mm2c	(S)
Hanley, George T.	10/6/42	S2c	8/21/44	Cox	
Hanson, Carl P.	2/6/41	BM2c	5/28/43	CBM	(I) (P)
Hanson, R. L.	11/19/44	S1c	12/7/44	S1c	(S)
Harriman, James E.	2/24/43	S2c	12/7/44	RM3c	(S)
Harris, Buckner H.	1/15/41	CRM	3/24/41	CRM	(I)
Harris, Harrold J. *	1/29/41	F1c	12/7/44	MM1c	(I) (P) (S)
Haugner, William F.	11/3/42	F2c	12/7/44	RdM3c	(S)
Hayden, Laurence E.	11/3/42	F2c	12/7/44	MM2c	(S)
Hayes, Richard J.	2/9/42	AS	3/14/44	MM1c	
Hayes, William P.	2/23/43	S2c	9/7/43	S1c	
Hayward, James F.	11/3/42	F2c	12/7/44	WT2c	(S)
Head, David D.	2/9/42	AS	11/29/44	MM2c	
Heffner, George M.	1/8/42	MM1c	1942	MM1c	
Heiberger, Gene G. *	1/29/41	S2c	12/12/42	SK2c	(I) (P)
Heick, John G.	3/30/44	SK2c	4/17/44	SK2c	
Herbert, Eugene	2/14/41	EM1c	10/20/41	EM1c	(I)
Hicks, Edward C.	1/15/41	CY	2/6/41	CY	
Hill, John G.	1/15/41	MM1c	4/27/41	MM1c	(I)
Hodges, William W.	2/22/44	F2c	12/7/44	F1c	(S)
Hoegerl, Marcellus	10/6/42	S2c	12/7/44	S1c	(S)
Holder, Raymond L.	2/23/43	S2c	10/15/43	S1c	
Holley, Harrold E.	2/23/43	S2c	10/15/43	S2c	
Holley, Irvin E.	1/15/41	SK3c	12/7/44	CSK	(I) (P) (S)
Holst, Floyd N.	1/12/42	S2c	12/12/42	SM3c	
Horn, William J. Jr.	3/16/44	EM2c	8/21/44	EM2c	
Horstman, Arthur H.	5/28/43	BM1c	8/21/44	BM1c	
Horton, John R.	9/30/44	S2c	10/4/44	S2c	

Name	Date Arrived	Rating	Date Detached	Rating	Notes
Houk, Robert N.	9/14/42	F1c	12/12/42	F1c	
Houston, Grover J.	2/13/43	S2c	12/7/44	GM3c	(S)
Howat, Albert J. *	1/29/41	F1c	5/28/41	F1c	(I)
Hueffmeire, Gordon W. *	1/29/41	S2c	3/24/41	S2c	(I)
Hughes, Frederick V. *	1/29/41	S2c	12/7/44	SoM3c	(I) (P) (S)
Hughes, Invin	11/24/42	MM2c	2/23/43	MM2c	
Hultman, Gordon R. *	1/29/41	S2c	2/23/43	TM3c	(I) (P)
Humphries, John A.	2/9/42	AS	11/20/44	WT2c	
Hunt, Charles R.	10/6/42	S2c	12/7/44	SC2c	(S)
Hunt, Harvey E.	1/15/41	TM2c	2/1/42	SM3c	(I) (P)
Hurley, Maurice J. *	1/29/41	F3c	12/1/43	WT2c	(I) (P)
Hutchins, Major C.	12/10/42	Matt2c	12/12/42	Matt2c	
Hutton, Clyde	7/24/44	GM3c	12/7/44	STM2c	(S)
Hyde, Adriel	12/12/42	CPhM	12/31/42	CPhM	
Inman, John A. Jr.	2/23/43	S1c	5/20/44	S1c	
Ivosevich, Theodore Jr.	9/30/44	S2c	10/4/44	S2c	
Jacobs, Henry L.	5/28/43	MM2c	12/30/43	MM1c	
Jankowski, Leo F.	1/18/41	F3c	1943	CGM	(I) (P)
Johnson, William E.	1/18/41	F3c	2/6/41	F3C	
Jones, Donald B. *	1/29/41	S2c	1943	Cox'	(I) (P)
Jones, Harley W.	2/23/43	S2c	10.15.43	S1c	
Jones, Roberet E.	2/23/43	S2c	12/7/44	RdM3c	(S)
Kay, Fred D.	2/9/42	AS	6/18/42	S2c	
Kearns, Jack R.	1/15/41	Mamth1c	2/6/41	Mamth1c	
Keely, Thomas H.	1/15/41	GM2c	2/6/41	GM2c	
Kelley, Kermit E.	10/19/42	S2c	2/23/43	TM3c	
Kinderman, Bernard J. *	1/29/41	F1c	1943	E1c	(I) (P)
Kitchens, Jesse L.	8/29/42	QM2c	5/28/43	QM2c	
Knapp, Russell H. *	1/29/41	BM2c	8/27/42	BM1c	(I) (P)
Knott, Ray L. Jr.	10/27/44	SF3c	12/7/44	SF3c	(S)
Koenke, Albert	1/15/41	MM1c	1943	MM1c	(I) (P)
Krack, Ronald M.	5/28/43	GM2c	12/30/43	BM1c	
Kramolisch, Jerome W. *	1/29/41	F3c	5/13/41	F3c	(I)
Lance, Albert	7/23/44	CSM	9/23/44	CSM	
Larson, Lester L.	2/23/43	RM3c	12//7/44	RM2c	(S)
Lasch, Karl C. J. *	1/29/41	Cox	1943	BM1c	(I) (P)
Leber, William G.	12/22/41	F1c	12/27/42	MM2c	
LeClair, Giles J.*	1/29/41	S2c	12/7/44	SoM2c	(I) (P) (S)
Lee, Harold D.	10/6/42	S2c	12/7/44	S1c	(S)
Lehner, Willet S. *	1/29/41	F1c	12/7/44	SC1c	(I) (P) (S)
Lester, Claudius, O.	1/15/41	OC1c	4/20/41	OC1c	(I)
Lindsey, Paul J.	10/6/42	S2c	12/12/42	S2c	
Linn, Peter A. *	1/29/41	WT1c	4/7/42	WT1c	(I) (P)
Loos, Francis G.	1/15/41	Sc3c	2/6/41	FC3c	
Lombardi, Daniel J. *	1/29/41	S2c	2/23/43	TM2c	(I) (P)
Long, Leonard H.	7/20/41	MM1c	11/5/41	MM1c	
Lovsted, Kames K.	1/15/41	F1c	12/7/44	CMM	(I) (P) (S)
Lundquist, Donald D.	2/5/41	FC3c	5/23/41	FC3c	(I)
Lunn, Frank E.	3/24/44	F3c	12/7/44	F2c	(S)
Lunsford, Earl N.	10/6/42	S2c	12/12/42	S2c	
Lusson, Victor W.	1/15/41	CMM	11/22/42	CMM	(I) (P)
Mahan, Dennis	1/15/41	CEM	3/24/41	CEM	(I)
Mancini, Joseph	3/24/44	F3c	12/7/44	F1c	
Mansell, Frederick L.	9/30/44	S2c	10/4/44	S2c	

Name	Date Arrived	Rating	Date Detached	Rating	Notes
Marien, Alfred	2/6/41	MM2c	10/11/41	MM2c	
Marlar, Owens L.	10/6/42	S2c	12/10/42	S2c	
Marshall, Earl E.	1/15/41	MM3c	2/6/41	MM3c	
Martin, Harrold W.	1/5/42	AS	12/7/44	WT2c	(S)
Maskeawitcz, William C.	1/15/41	TM1c	12/12/42	CTM	(I) (P)
Mason, Albert L.	1/12/42	MM1c	12/12/42	CMM	
Mayer, Walter L. *	1/29/41	CGM	3/22/42	CGM	(I) (P)
McAdams, James C.	6/2/42	S2c	12/12/42	RM3c	
McCue, Maurice J.	1/15/41	MM1c	12/31/41	MM1c	(I) (P)
McGrath, John P.	1/22/41	CBM	8/14/41	CBM	(I)
McPhee, John D.	2/6/41	MM1c	12/12/42	MM2c	(I) (P)
McPheeters, Paul A.	11/3/42	S2c	2/1/43	S1c	
Mead, Richard G.	9/20/42	SoM3c	12/12/42	SoM3c	
Merthan, John R. *	1/29/41	F3c	8/19/42	F2c	(I) (P)
Miller, James D.	9/14/42	F1c	12/12/42	F1c	
Miller, Lacon E.	6/26/42	Matt2c	12/7/44	St3c	(S)
Minter, Henry A.	1/15/41	CCStd	1942	CCStd	(I) (P)
Mitchell, Paul	1/15/41	CWT	2/6/41	CWT	
Mollere, Louis P.	1/15/41	MM1c	9/7/42	MM1c	(I) (P)
Mondo, Gust J. *	1/29/41	GM3c	12/2/41	S1c	(I)
Monett, Arthur L.	2/22/43	S1c	12/7/44	SM2c	(S)
Moore, Billie	9/28/44	S1c	10/4/44	S1c	
Morgan, David J. *	1/29/41	WT1c	2/20/43	WT1c	(I) (P)
Mortenson, Leon R.	8/8/41	Msmth1c	1/6/42	Msmth1c	(P)
Moss, Barney	1/15/41	MM2c	10/10/43	CMM	(I) (P)
Mroszak, Edward A. *	1/29/41	S1c	2/23/43	TM2c	(I) (P)
Muehlmann, Frank C. Jr.	10/19/43	F3c	12/7/44	WT3c	(S)
Mundell, Eugene V.	1/15/41	F1c	4/1/42	F3c	(I) (P)
Murray, Woodrow S.	11/19/44	EM1c	12/7/44	EM1c	(S)
Myers, Burgess	2/23/43	S1c	11/20/44	CM2c	
Myers, Ellie B.	3/8/42	Matt3c	1/18/44	StM1c	
Nabors, Samuel M.	12/22/41	F2c	12/6/42	F1c	
Nadeau, Thomas C. *	1/29/41	F3c	2/23/43	WT2c	(I) (P)
Navarro, Jose	9/9/43	Ck2c	8/21/44	Ck2c	
Nelson, Howard H. *	1/29/41	WT2c	10/22/41	WT2c	(I)
Nicandro, Zosimo	2/23/43	S2c	12/7/44	St1c	(S)
Noble, Sidney E.	10/10/41	SF2c	10/19 42	SF2c	(P)
Nolde, Raymond B. *	1/29/41	S2c	12/7/44	SF2c	(I) (P) (S)
Noonan, John J.	10/19/43	S1c	12/7/44	S1c	(S)
Oliver, John W.	2/23/43	S2c	12/7/44	F1c	(S)
Olson, Olaf A.	12/11/41	F1c	1942	F1c	
Olson, Robert E.	2/23/43	S2c	12/7/44	QM2c	(S)
Ort, Anthony	2/6/41	Cox	3/31/43	CBM	(I) (P)
Palmer, Ben F.	2/23/42	QM1c	4/9/42	QM1c	
Park, Charles W.	2/23/43	S2c	10/15/43	S1c	
Parker, Joseph E.	10/6/42	S2c	12/10/42	S2c	
Paynter, Howard K. *	1/29/41	F1c	9/1/44	CMM	(I) (P)
Peacock, William C.	11/5/42	Y2c	12/12/42	Y2c	
Pearl, Gerald O.	1/15/41	Y3c	1/23/44	CY	(I) (P)
Peick, John A. *	1/29/41	SC1c	1/11/43	GM3c	(I) (P)
Penetrante, Manuel	10/6/41	OC1c	12/30/43	CCK	(P)
Pepin, Donald R. C. *	1/29/41	S2c	12/7/44	SM2c	(I) (P) (S)
Perkins, Lyle C.	10/19/43	S1c	10/8/44	RM3c	
Peterson, George A.	10/9/42	EM3c	11/3/43	EM2c	

Name	Date Arrived	Rating	Date Detached	Rating	Notes
Peterson, John E. *	1/29/41	S2c	12/12/42	BM2c	(I) (P)
Peterson, L. V.	11/19/44	S1c	12/7/44	S1c	(S)
Pfaff, Kenneth L. *	1/29/41	S2c	4/23/42	RM3c	(I) (P)
Pfeifer, Carroll	8/10/42	S1c	2/23/43	TM3c	
Phenning, Fred P. *	1/29/41	F3c	5/28/43	MM2c	(I) (P)
Pope, Marshall W.	12/11/41	F3c	6/28/43	MM2c	
Probst, Paul W. *	1/29/41	SC1c	5/23/41	SC1c	(I)
Pruitt, Raymond E.	1/18/41	Matt1c	3/12/42	Matt1c	(I) (P)
Przedwojewski, Benedict P.	9/30/44	S2c	10/4/44	S2c	
Race, George W.	12/22/41	F1c	12/12/42	MM2c	
Rader, Tony L.	12/11/41	F1c	5/28/43	MM2c	
Raeubig, Herbert E. *	1/29/41	S2c	2/28/44	GM3c	(I) (P)
Ramey, Martin M.	9/27/43	StM2c	12/7/44	StM2c	(S)
Rawdon, Ted	2/22/44	F2c	12/7/44	MoMM3c	(S)
Redd, Charles	1/15/41	Matt3c	1/6/42	Matt3c	(I) (P)
Reed, James M.	12/22/41	WT2c	1/23/44	CWT	
Reetz, Russell A.*	1/29/41	F3c	5/28/43	MM2c	(I) (P)
Reeves, McKinley K.	1/15/41	OS1c	2/23/43	OS1c	(I) (P)
Rice, John W.	2/23/43	F3c	12/7/44	MM3c	(S)
Richardson, Robert E. *	1/29/41	S2c	7/6/41	S2c	(I)
Ritenour, R. W.	10/3/44	F1c	12/7/44	F1c	(S)
Roberts, Donald E.	11/20/42	FC2c	5/28/43	FC2c	
Roberts, Roy J.	6/12/42	S2c	12/7/44	RM2c	(S)
Robertson, James M.	6/4/43	S2c	10/15/43	S1c	
Robinson, Melbourne A.	9/23/44	CCS	10/1/44	CCS	
Rodrigue, Davis A.	2/9/42	AS	5/10/44	S1c	
Rogers, Harrpld J.	1/15/41	GM2c	11/21/42	GM1c	(I) (P)
Rohan, James M. Jr.	1/15/41	EM2c	7/31/42	EM1c	(I) (P)
Romans, James P.	4/23/42	AS	12/7/44	WT1c	(S)
Rominger, R. V,	4/23/42	AS	12/7/44	RdM2c	(S)
Rothweiler. Roy E.	4/23/42	AS	12/7/44	BM2c	(S)
Ruigomez, Charistobel C.	4/23/42	AS	12/7/44	SK3c	(S)
Russell, Eugene G.	4/23/42	AS	6/13/44	SF3c	
Salas, Louis	4/23/42	AS	12/10/42	S2c	
Sanders, Carl R.	5/28/43	Y2c	10/27/44	Y1c	
Sanford, Alan C. *	1/29/41	S2c	8/27/42	RM3c	(I) (P)
Sanford, Harrold R.	4/23/42	AS	12/7/44	CM1c	(S)
Sargent, Kenneth M.	4/23/42	AS	11/29/44	CM2c	
Saunders, Orval P.	2/6/41	SM1c	4/14/42	SM1c	(I) (P)
Sayre, Charles A.	4/23/42	AS	5/20/44	S1c	
Schmitt, Carol E. *	1/29/41	S2c	11/13/42	Y2c	(I) (P)
Scholtes, William A. *	1/29/41	S2c	3/28/44	GM2c	(I) (P)
Schook, Robert N.	9/30/44	S2c	10/4/44	S2c	
Secor, David M.	4/23/42	F1c	12/7/44	GM2c	(S)
Seip, Keith L.	2/23/43	S2c	12/7/44	S1c	(S)
Sexton, Robert E.	6/27/41	SM3c	7/16/41	SM3c	
Seydel, Richard J. *	1/29/41	F3c	6/27/41	F3c	(I)
Shields, Martin L.	2/13/43	S2c	12/7/44	F1c	
Shutter, Thomas P.	3/30/44	SK2c	7/7/44	SK2c	
Siegel, Edward L.	11/5/42	EM3c	12/10/42	EM3c	
Simmering, Robert J.	8/10/42	TM3c	8/28/42	TM3c	
Skubitz, Nicholas	9/1/44	Y3c	12/7/44	Y3c	(S)
Sloan, Shannon B.	5/28/43	FC3c	12/7/44	FC3c	(S)
Smith, Sam B.	1/15/41	WT1c	7/31/42	WT1c	(I) (P)

Name	Date Arrived	Rating	Date Detached	Rating	Notes
Smorowski, Wilfred A.	1/15/41	F1c	1/15/43	WT1c	(I) (P)
Smuke, Edward A.	9/30/44	S2c	10/4/44	S2c	
Snead, James F.	2/23/43	Cox	12/7/44	BM2c	(S)
Southward, Harry *	1/29/41	S2c	12/12/42	SC2c	(I) (P)
Spratt, James L. *	1/29/41	S2c	11/29/44	MM2c	(I) (P)
Stan, George	10/19/43	S2c	12/7/44	S1c	(S)
Stanford, William O.	10/19//43	S2c	12/7/44	S1c	(S)
Stark, Alan J.	10/19/43	S2c	12/7/44	S1c	(S)
Stefanou, Robert A.	6/2/42	S2c	5/28/43	RM3c	
Stein, Robert E. *	1/29/41	S2c	8/19/42	S1c	(I) (P)
Stephens, William H.	10/19/43	S2c	12/7/44	S1c	(S)
Stephenson, Burkitt R.	10/19/43	S2c	12/7/44	Cox	(S)
Stephenson, Harrold O.	10/19/43	S2c	12/7/44	S1c	(S)
Steubing, John D.	10/19/43	S2c	12/7/44	S1c	(S)
Stivers, Wilfred P.	1/15/41	CQM	2/6/41	CQM	
Stocks, Gerald H.	10/19/43	S2c	12/7/44	F2c	(S)
Stokes, James E.	2/12/44	S1c	12/7/44	S1c	(S)
Stolen, Harrold M.	1/8/42	S2c	5/8/43	Cox	
Stout, Merrill O.	1/3/42	QM2c	2/25/42	QM2c	
Strapp, Joseph P.	2/13/43	RT2c	8/27/44	RT1c	
Streip, Fred W.	2/6/41	MM1c	7/8/41	MM1c	(I)
Swedberg, Kenneth C. E. *	1/29/41	F1c	2/23/43	WT2c	(I) (P)
Sweeny, Edward J.	5/28/43	PhM2c	12/7/44	PhM2c	(S)
Swisher, Morton D.	2/23/43	Cox	5/28/43	Cox	
Sylvester, Truman J.	1/12/42	QM1c	8/26/42	CQM	
Szakacs, John Jr.	9/30/44	S2c	10/4/44	S2c	
Tapp, Alongo	1/15/41	Matt3c	2/6/41	Matt3c	
Terkle, Milan V.	9/22/42	S2c	12/12/42	S2c	
Terpin, Troy T.	10/1/42	TM3c	2/23/43	TM3c	
Thibault, George E.	9/14/42	CMM	11/21/42	CMM	
Thill, Richard J. *	1/29/41	S2c	5/20/44	SC1c	(I) (P)
Thomas, William A. Jr.	10/12/44	Y2c	12/7/44	Y2c	(S)
Thompson, Samuel W.	7/19/43	F3c	12/7/44	MM3c	(S)
Thompson, William D.	2/28/44	EM3c	9/1/44	EM3c	
Thornton, Herbert C	2/23/43	S2c	10/15/43	S1c	
Thurmond, Rudolph	2/12/44	S1c	12/7/44	S1c	(S)
Tido, John Jr.	1/15/41	S1c	9/3/42	BM2c	(I) (P)
Todd, Harold S.	1/15/41	F3c	12/30/43	MM1c	(I) (P)
Tourell, Audrey C.	2/6/41	QM3c	8/19/42	QM2c	(I) (P)
Tredennick, Rolling N.	7/6/44	Y1c	11/21/44	Y1c	
Trimmer, Judson P. *	1/29/41	RM3c	8/19/42	RM3c	(I) (P)
Trotter, Jesse J.	2/22/43	S1c	12/7/44	SM3c	
Tucker, Julius R.	10/6/42	S2c	2/23/43	S2c	
Turk, Adelbert W.	8/18/41	CBM	3/20/42	CBM	(P)
Twitty, Jack O.	1/15/41	SM2c	9/30/42	CQM	(I) (P)
Ulmer, Fredrick J.	10/6/42	S2c	10/15/43	QM3c	
Urbanski, George D.	1/15/41	S2c	2/6/41	S2c	
Vaughn, Joseph A.	1/7/42	S2c	2/28/44	CM1c	
Warren, Lawrence E.	2/18/42	S2c	12/12/42	F2c	
Waugh, Charles E.	2/23/43	S2c	3/7/43	S2c	
Weathers, Raymond A.	10/6/42	S2c	12/10/42	S2c	
Weber, George E.	1/6/42	GM2c	9/23/42	GM2c	(I) (P)
Wells, Horace O. *	1/29/41	S2c	2/8/43	S1c	(I) (P)
Wendt, Arnold A.	2/13/43	S2c	12/7/44	S1c	(S)

Name	Date Arrived	Rating	Date Detached	Rating	Notes
Wenzel, Frank M.	2/22/44	S2c	12/7/44	S1c	(S)
Wheeler, George F.	10/1/42	CMM	2/23/43	CMM	
White, John E.	2/13/43	S2c	12/7/44	S1c	(S)
White, William R.	2/22/44	S2c	12/7/44	S2c	(S)
Wilbur, Mason	1/15/41	F2c	2/6/41	F2c	
Willis, James M.	2/23/43	Cox	5/28/43	Cox	
Wilson Ben	2/23/43	S2c	12/7/44	S1c	(S)
Wilson, Gordon L.	2/23/43	S2c	12/7/44	S1c	(S)
Winter, Lyle J.	1/15/41	TM3c	12/12/42	TM1c	(I) (P)
Wood, David F.	1/12/42	S2c	8/19/43	EM2c	
Wood, Russell W. *	1/29/41	S2c	6/15/42	S1c	(I) (P)
Woodward, Harrold H.	1/15/41	QM2c	7/6/41	QM2c	(I)
Woodward, Willie L.	2/23/43	S2c	3/11/43	S2c	
Wooldridge, General T.	8/13/43	MM2c	12/7/44	MM1c	(S)
Woolworth, Lloyd M.	10/6/42	S2c	4/2/44	S1c	
Zapata, Andrew J.	2/23/43	BM2c	12/30/43	BM1c	
Zayon, Sidney	1/17/44	BM1c	12/7/44	BM1c	(S)
Zechmann, Edward A. *	11/8/41	F3c	12/1/43	WT2c	(P)
Zechmann, Robert A. *	1/29/41	F3c	12/12/42	SK3c	(I) (P)
Zuniga, Rudolph F.	2/13/43	S2c	12/7/44	F1c	(S)
Zwizanski, Myron	2/23/43	MoMM2c	9/7/43	MoMM2c	

Chapter Notes

Chapter 1

1. Dickey, *A Family Saga,* p. A-2.
2. *Ibid.*
3. *Ibid.*
4. Preston, *Destroyers,* p. 9.
5. Friedman, *U.S. Destroyers, An Illustrated Design History,* p. 9.
6. Preston, *Destroyers,* p. 11.
7. *Ibid.*
8. Friedman, *U.S. Destroyers, An Illustrated Design History,* p. 14.
9. *Ibid.* p. 428.
10. *Ibid.* p. 16.
11. *Ibid.* p. 24–28.
12. *Ibid.* p. 28–37.
13. First depth charge installations were made in 1917 using stern slings. In 1918 stern depth charge tracks were first used.
14. Dickey, *A Family Saga,* p. A-10.
15. *Ibid.* A-16.
16. *Ibid.* A-17.
17. Friedman, *U.S. Destroyers, An Illustrated Design History,* p. 37.
18. *Ibid.* p. 39.
19. *Ibid.* p. 39–40.
20. Alden, *Flush Decks and Four Pipes,* p. 13.
21. FAS, *Military Analysis Network,* p. 1.
22. Kinderman, *USS Ward Fires First Shot WW II,* p. 3.
23. *Ibid.*
24. Bonner, *Final Voyages,* p. 21.
25. Kinderman, *USS Ward Fires First Shot WW II.* p. 3.
26. *Dictionary of American Naval Fighting Ships (DANFS),* Vol. VIII. p. 99–100.
27. Many sources, including DANFS, show the commissioning date of *Ward* to be July 24, 1918. The ship's Deck Logs clearly show that *Ward* was commissioned on July 18, 1918.
28. Deck Log USS *Ward,* July 18, 1918.
29. *Ibid.*
30. Bonner, *Final Voyages,* p. 21.

Chapter 2

1. Deck Log USS *Ward,* July 24, 1918
2. *Ibid.* July 25, 1918
3. *Ibid.* August 31, 1918
4. *Ibid.* July, 1918
5. *Ibid.*
6. Kinderman, *USS Ward Fires First Shot-WW II,* p. 20.
7. *Ibid.*
8. Deck Log USS *Ward,* September 2, 1918.

9. *Ibid.* December 8, 1918.
10. Bonner, *Final Voyages,* p. 22.
11. *Ibid.*
12. Deck Log USS *Ward,* December 17, 1918.
13. *Ibid.* December 26, 1918.
14. *Ibid.* January 3–4, 1919.
15. *Ibid.* January 12, 1919.
16. *Ibid.* May 4, 1919.
17. Alden, *Flush Decks and Four Pipes,* p. 11.
18. Caras, *Wings of Gold,* p. 64–69.
19. *Ibid.*
20. Deck Log USS *Ward,* May 16, 1919.
21. *Ibid.*
22. Alden, *Flush Decks and Four Pipes,* p.11.
23. *Dictionary of American Naval Fighting Ships,* Vol. VIII, p. 101.
24. Deck Log USS *Ward,* April 21, 1921.
25. Many sources, including the *Dictionary of American Naval Fighting Ships* show the decommissioning date of *Ward* to be June 21, 1921. Although *Ward* was in Reserve status at that time, the ship's Deck Logs clearly show that *Ward* was decommissioned on June 5, 1922.

Chapter 3

1. Morison, *Rising Sun in the Pacific,* Vol. III, p.16–18.
2. Wilmott, *Pearl Harbor,* p. 40–42.
3. Dickey, *A Family Saga,* p. 64.
4. First Shot Naval Vets of St. Paul, files.
5. Dick Thill, interview.
6. First Shot Naval Vets of St. Paul, files.
7. *Dictionary of American Naval Fighting Ships,* Vol. VIII
8. *Ibid.* Vol. V.
9. Ed Bukrey, interview.
10. Orville Ethier, interview.
11. Will Lehner, interview.
12. Deck Log USS *Ward,* January 15, 1941.
13. *Ibid.* January 29, 1941.
14. Clark, *The Famed Green Dragons,* p. 52.
15. Deck Log USS *Ward,* February 27, 1941.

Chapter 4

1. Deck Log USS *Ward,* February 28, 1941.
2. Kinderman, *USS Ward Fires First Shot WW II.*
3. Deck Log USS *Ward,* March 1, 1941.
4. Muster Roll USS *Ward,* March, 1941.
5. Deck Log USS *Ward,* March 3, 1941.
6. Cohen, *East Wind Rain,* p. 26.
7. *Ibid.* p. 2.

8. *Dictionary of American Naval Fighting Ships,* Vol. VIII.
9. Burlingame, *Advance Force Pearl Harbor,* p. 93.
10. *Ibid.* p. 101–102.
11. United States Coast Guard, Historian's Office.
12. Deck Log USS *Ward,* April 28, 1941.
13. Letter, Capt. Richard Farwell to LCDR Arnold Lott, April 12, 1976.
14. Wilmott, *Pearl Harbor,* p. 76–77.
15. Deck Log USS *Ward,* December 4, 1941.
16. Klobuchar, *Pearl Harbor:Awakening a Sleeping Giant,* p. 37.
17. *Dictionary of American Naval Fighting Ships,* Vol. VII, p. 35 & 189.

Chapter 5

1. Morison, *Rising Sun in the Pacific,* Vol. III, p. 19.
2. Wilmott, *Pearl Harbor,* p. 46.
3. *Ibid.* p. 45–47.
4. Burlingame, *Advance Force Pearl Harbor,* p. 155.
5. Wilmott, *Pearl Harbor,* p. 43.
6. *Ibid.* p. 72.
7. *Ibid.* p. 95.
8. Burlingame, *Advance Force Pearl Harbor,* p. 160.
9. *Ibid.* p. 161.
10. *Ibid.*
11. *Ibid.* p. 162.
12. Burlingame, *Advance Force Pearl Harbor,* p. 130. The Japanese used Tokyo time during the entire operation. Thus the attack occurred on the morning of December 8, Tokyo time.
13. *Ibid.* p. 72.
14. Prange, *December 7, 1941,* p. 69–72.
15. Burlingame, *Advance Force Pearl Harbor, p.* 60–70.
16. Wilmott, *Pearl Harbor,* p. 93.
17. Burlingame, *Advance Force Pearl Harbor,* p.168.
18. *Ibid.* p. 169.
19. Ken Hackler, historian.
20. Burlingame, *Advance Force Pearl Harbor,* p. 170.
21. Deck Log USS *Ward,* December 7, 1941.
22. Ken Swedberg, interview.

Chapter 6

1. U.S. Navy Bishop's Point Radio Log, December 7, 1941.
2. *Ibid.*
3. Burlingame, *Advance Force Pearl Harbor,* p. 172.
4. *Ibid.*
5. *Ibid.* p. 179.
6. *Ibid.* p. 182.
7. *Ibid.* p. 212–215.
8. *Ibid.* p. 186.
9. *Ibid.*
10. Kinderman, *USS Ward Fires First Shot WW II,* p. 30.
11. Ken Swedberg, interview.
12. Russell Reetz, interview.
13. Prange, *December 7, 1941,* p. 232.
14. Cohen, *East Wind Rain,* p. 110–112.
15. Ken Swedberg, interview.
16. Burlingame, *Advance force Pearl Harbor,* p. 220.
17. Robert Crerar, crewman of USS *Cummings.*
18. Cohen, *East Wind Rain,* p. 221–223.
19. Deck Log USS *Ward,* December 7, 1941.
20. *Ibid.*

21. Cohen, *East Wind Rain,* p. 46.
22. *Ibid.*

Chapter 7

1. Kinderman, *USS Ward Fires First Shot WW II,* p.20.
2. Burlingame, *Advance Force Pearl Harbor,* p. 256–257.
3. *Ibid.* p. 255–256.
4. *Ibid.* p. 258.
5. *Ibid.* p. 259–260.
6. Deck Log USS *Ward,* December 11, 1941.
7. Arroyo, *Pearl Harbor,* p. 120.
8. Burlingame, *Advance Force Pearl Harbor,* p. 220.
9. Ken Swedberg, interview.
10. Burlingame, *Advance Force Pearl Harbor.* P. 154.
11. *Ibid.* p. 425–426.
12. *Ibid.* p. 269–279.
13. Prange, *December 7, 1941,* p. 366.
14. Deck Log USS *Ward,* December 13, 1941.
15. *Ibid.* December 14, 1941.
16. Burlingame. *Advance Force Pearl Harbor,* p. 263.
17. John Merthan, interview.
18. Robert Ball, interview.

Chapter 8

1. Orville Ethier, interview.
2. Dick Thill, interview.
3. Will Lehner, interview.
4. Ken Pfaff, interview.
5. History Channel, *Hotel Street,* 2001.
6. Orville Ethier, interview.
7. Ken Swedberg, interview.
8. Robert Ball, interview.
9. Russell Reetz, interview.
10. James Morgan, interview.

Chapter 9

1. Deck Log USS *Ward,* January 1, 1942.
2. *Ibid.*
3. Report, Commanding Officer of USS *Allen* to Commanding Officer, Inshore Patrol, 14th Naval District, "Attack of USS *Ward* on Submarine," January 3, 1942.
4. Watts, *Japanese Warships of WW II,* p. 376–383.
5. Burlingame, *Advance Force Pearl Harbor,* p. 364.
6. *Dictionary of American Naval Fighting Ships,* Vol. 1.
7. Ibid.
8. Burlingame, *Advance Force Pearl Harbor,* p. 364.
9. *Ibid.* p. 364–365.
10. *Ibid.*
11. Deck Log USS *Ward,* April 18, 1942.
12. Report, Commanding Officer, USS *Ward* to Commander In Chief, U.S. Fleet, "Attack of Enemy Submarines," May 3, 1942.
13. Clark, *The Famed Green Dragons,* p. 52–53.
14. Will Lehner, interview.
15. *Ibid.*
16. Clark, *The Famed Green Dragons,* p. 53.
17. Dick Thill, interview.
18. *Ibid.*
19. *Ibid.*
20. Will Lehner, interview.
21. Deck Log USS *Ward,* May 3, 1942.

22. *Ibid.* May 27, 1942.
23. Morison, *Coral Sea, Midway, and Submarine Actions,* Vol. IV, p. 81.
24. Deck Log USS *Ward,* June 16, 1942.
25. Don Pepin, interview.
26. John Merthan, interview.
27. *Ibid.*
28. Will Lehner, interview.
29. John Merthan, interview.
30. Deck Log USS *Ward,* August 11, 1942.
31. Ken Swedberg, interview.
32. Deck Log USS *Ward,* September 30, 1942.
33. Tracy White, historian.
34. *Ibid.*
35. Letter, Capt. Richard Farwell to LCDR Arnold Lott, April 12, 1976.

Chapter 10

1. Alden, *Flush Decks and Four Pipes,* p. 45–47.
2. McGee, *The Amphibians Are Coming,* p. 42.
3. Deck Log USS *Ward,* December 28, 1942.
4. *Ibid.* January 1–2, 1943.
5. *Ibid.* January 15, 1943.
6. *St. Paul Dispatch,* December 31, 1942.
7. *Ibid.*
8. *Ibid.*
9. Russell Reetz, interview.
10. *St. Paul Dispatch,* January 16, 1943.
11. *Ibid.*
12. Deck Log USS *Ward,* February 7, 1943.
13. Walter Campion, interview.
14. Kinderman, USS *Ward Fires First Shot WW II,* p. 32.
15. *Ibid.*
16. Adcock, *WW II US Landing Craft,* p.7.
17. Dickey, *A Family Saga,* p. 20.
18. Bonner, *Final Voyages,* p. 23.

Chapter 11

1. The APDs sunk at Guadalcanal were *Colhoun* (APD-2), *Gregory* (APD-3), and.
Little (APD-4). Morison, *The Struggle for Guadalcanal,* Vol. V, p. 109–110, 117–120.
2. Letter. Capt. Richard Farwell to LCDR Arnold Lott, April 12, 1976.
3. Dickey, *A Family Saga,* p. 37.
4. Deck Log USS *Ward,* February 22–23, 1943.
5. Silverstone, *U.S. Warships of World Ward II.* P. 50–53.
6. Deck Log USS *Ward,* February 28, 1943.
7. Dick Thill, interview.
8. Other ships in Transport Division were *Schley* (APD-14), *Kilty* (APD-15), & *Crosby* (APD-17).
9. Letter, Capt. Richard Farwell to LCDR Arnold Lott, April 12, 1976.
10. Hoyt, *The Glory of the Solomons,* p. 39.
11. McGee, *The Amphibians Are Coming,* p. 87–92.
12. Hoyt, *The Glory of the Solomons,* p. 59.
13. *Ibid.*
14. Deck Log USS *Ward,* April 7, 1943.
15. McGee, *The Amphibians Are Coming,* p.137.
16. Donovan, *PT-109,* p. 17–21.
17. McGee, *The Amphibians Are Coming,* p. 137.
18. Action Report USS *Ward,* April 7, 1943.
19. McGee, *The Amphibians Are Coming,* p. 137.

20. Hoyt, *The Glory of the Solomons,* p. 64.
21. Deck Log USS *Ward,* April 17, 1943.
22. Hoyt, *The Glory of the Solomons,* p. 67–77.
23. Deck Log USS *Ward,* May 17, 1943.
24. McGee, *The Amphibians are Coming,* p. 161–162.
25. *Ibid.* p. 167.
26. Hoyt, *The Glory of the Solomons,* p. 152.
27. Action Report USS *Ward,* June 16, 1943.
28. McGee, *The Amphibians Are Coming,* p. 177.
29. *Ibid.*
30. Action Report USS *Ward,* June 16, 1943.
31. Deck Log USS *Ward,* June 23, 1943, and McGee, *The Solomons Campaign,* p. 300.
32. McGee, *The Solomons Campaign,* p. 297.
33. Dick Thill, interview.
34. Crenshaw, *South Pacific Destroyer,* p. 43.

Chapter 12

1. Letter, Capt. Richard Farwell to LCDR Arnold Lott, April 12, 1976.
2. Deck Log USS *Ward,* July 17, 1943.
3. *Ibid.* July 20, 1943.
4. Donovan, *PT-109,* p. 71–72.
5. Orville Ethier, interview.
6. Letter, Capt. Richard Farwell to LCDR Arnold Lott, April 12, 1976.
7. Deck log USS *Ward,* July 31, 1943.
8. McGee, *The Solomons Campaign,* p. 421.
9. Deck Log USS *Ward,* August 14, 1943.
10. Hoyt, *The Glory of the Solomons,* p. 173–181.
11. Deck Log USS *Ward,* August 19, 1943.
12. Dick Thill, interview.
13. Deck Log USS *Ward,* September 30, 1943.
14. McGee, *The Solomons Campaign,* p. 445–453.
15. Deck Log USS *Ward,* October 6, 1943.
16. Hoyt, *The Glory of the Solomons,* p. 206.
17. Deck Log USS *Ward,* October 26, 1943.
18. Letter, Capt. Richard Farwell to LCDR Arnold Lott, April 12, 1976.
19. Hoyt, *The Glory of the Solomons,* p. 212.
20. Letter, Capt. Richard Farwell to LCDR Arnold Lott, April 12, 1976.
21. Deck Log USS *Ward,* October 27, 1943.
22. Letter, Capt. Richard Farwell to LCDR Arnold Lott. April 12, 1976.
23. McGee, *The Solomons Campaign,* p. 493.
24. *Ibid.* p. 512.
25. Deck Log USS *Ward,* November 12, 1943.
26. McGee, *The Solomons Campaign,* p. 512–514.
27. Deck Log USS *Ward,* November 8, 1943.
28. Hoyt, *The Glory of the Solomons,* p. 280.
29. Deck Log USS *Ward,* December 3, 1943.
30. Will Lehner, interview.
31. Deck Log USS *Ward,* December 24, 1943.

Chapter 13

1. Morison, *Breaking the Bismarcks Barrier,* Vol. VI, p. 381–382.
2. Hoyt, *MacArthur's Navy,* p. 16.
3. Morison, *Breaking The Bismarcks Barrier,* Vol. VI p. 385.
4. *Ibid.* p. 386.
5. Deck Log USS *Ward,* December 27, 1943.
6. *Ibid.* December 29, 1943.

7. Letter, Capt. Richard Farwell to LCDR Arnold Lott, April 12, 1976.

8. Deck Log USS *Ward,* February 14, 1944.

9. Morison, *Breaking the Bismarcks Barrier,* Vol. VI, p. 414.

10. *Ibid.* p. 419.

11. Deck Log USS *Ward,* February 18, 1944.

12. *Ibid.*

13. *Ibid.* March 2, 1944.

14. Morison, *Breaking the Bismarcks Barrier,* Vol. VI, p. 423.

15. Deck Log USS *Ward,* March 17, 1944.

16. Dick Thill, interview.

17. Morison, *New Guinea & the Marianas,* Vol. VIII, p. 403–406.

18. Deck Log USS *Ward,* April 22–23, 1944.

19. Will Lehner, interview.

20. Morison, *New Guinea & the Marianas,* Vol. VIII, p. 104.

21. Deck Log USS *Ward,* May 25, 1944.

22. *Ibid.* June 1, 1944.

23. *Ibid.* July 20, 1944.

24. Morison, *New Guinea & the Marianas,* Vol. VIII, p. 143.

Chapter 14

1. Morison, *Leyte,* Vol. XII, p. 19–21.

2. *Ibid.* p. 22.

3. Deck Log USS *Ward,* September 10, 1944.

4. *Ibid.* September 19, 1944.

5. *The Western News,* Corvallis, Montana, April 19, 1945.

6. War Diary, USS *Ward,* September 21, 1944.

7. Guy Thompson, interview.

8. Morison, *Leyte,* Vol. XII, p. 13–15.

9. *Ibid.* p. 113 & 415–423.

10. Guy Thompson, interview.

11. Deck Log USS *Ward,* October 17, 1944.

12. Guy Thompson, interview.

13. Deck Log USS *Ward,* October 20, 1944.

14. *Ibid.*

15. Guy Thompson, interview.

16. Deck Log, USS *Ward,* October, 20, 1944.

17. Guy Thompson, interview.

18. War Diary USS *Ward,* November 1944.

19. Deck Log USS *Ward,* November 12, 1944.

Chapter 15

1. Guy Thompson, interview.

2. Letter, Capt. Richard Farwell to LCDR Arnold Lott, April 12, 1976.

3. Deck Log USS *Ward,* December 6, 1944.

4. Guy Thompson, interview.

5. War Diary USS *Ward,* December 1944.

6. Guy Thompson, interview.

7. Morison, *Leyte,* Vol. XII, p. 381.

8. Deck Log USS *Ward,* December 7, 1944.

9. *Ibid.*

10. Orville Ethier, interview.

11. Byron Baldwin, interview.

12. Action Report, USS *Ward,* December 7, 1944.

13. Guy Thompson, interview.

14. War Diary USS *Ward,* December 1944, p. 3.

15. Action Report, USS *Ward,* December 7, 1944.

16. *Ibid.*

17. Dorothy Hughes, interview.

18. Letter, Capt. Richard Farwell to LCDR Arnold Lott, April 12, 1976.

19. Orville Ethier, interview.

20. Ed Bukrey, interview.

21. Guy Thompson, interview.

22. Orville Ethier, interview.

23. Morison, *Leyte,* Vol. XII, p. 382.

24. War Diary USS *Ward,* December 1944, p. 12.

25. Guy Thompson, interview.

26. Letter, Capt. Richard Farwell to LCDR Arnold Lott, April 12, 1976.

27. Morison, *Leyte,* Vol. XII, p. 383.

28. Guy Thompson, interview.

Chapter 16

1. Morison, *Leyte,* Vol. XII, p. 383–384.

2. *Ibid.* p. 384.

3. Guy Thompson, interview.

4. Ed Bukrey, interview.

5. Don Pepin, interview.

6. Will Lehner, interview.

7. Guy Thompson, interview.

8. Kinderman, USS *Ward Fires First Shot WW II,* p. 47.

9. First Shot Naval Vets of St. Paul, files.

10. *Ibid.*

11. *Ibid.*

12. *Ibid.*

13. *Ibid.*

14. *Ibid.*

15. Ken Swedberg, interview.

16. *Ibid.*

17. Letter, Terry Kerby, Hawaii Undersea Research Lab, to author, September 1, 2004.

18. *Ibid.*

19. Will Lehner, interview.

20. Letter, Terry Kerby, Hawaii Undersea Research Lab, to author, September 1, 2004.

21. *Ibid.*

22. Kerby, *Discovery and Survey of WW II Japanese Type A Midget Submarine,* p. 4.

23. *Ibid.* p. 5.

24. *Ibid.* p. 6–21.

25. Will Lehner, interview.

26. Burlingame, *First to Die,* Honolulu Star-Bulletin, September 8, 2002.

27. *Ibid.*

Bibliography

Archive Reports

USS *Ward* Deck Logs: June 1918 to June 1922; January 1941 to December 1944

USS *Ward* War Diaries: December 1941; April 1943; December 1943 to December 1944

USS *Ward* Action Reports: December 7, 1941 (Sinking of Japanese sub); April 7, 1943 (Air Attack)

June 16, 1943 (Air Attack); April 22, 1944 (Aitape, New Guinea); April 23, 1944 (Aitape, New Guinea); May 27, 1944 (Biak Island); July 15, 1944 (Cape Sansapor); September 15, 1944 (Morotai, NEI); October 17, 1944 (Dinagat Island); November 12, 1944 (Air attacks); December 7, 1944 (Ormoc Bay landings)

USS *Ward* Muster Rolls January 1941 to December 1944

USS *Antares* Action Reports: December 7, 1941

USS *Scout* Action Report: December 7, 1944

Commanding Officer, USS *Ward* to Commander in Chief US Fleet, "Report On Attacks on Enemy Submarines of April 24/25, 1942," May 3, 1942

Commander, Destroyer Division Eighty to Commander 14th Naval District, "Participation by DesDiv 80 in Attack of December 7, 1941," Dec. 12, 1941

Commanding Officer, USS *Ward* to Commander, Destroyer Division Eighty, "Attacks on Submarines, December 7–17, 1941," December 23, 1941

Commanding Officer, USS *Antares* to Commander in Chief, US Fleet, "Report on Air Raid on Oahu, December 7, 1941," December 10, 1941

Commanding Officer, USS *Allen* to Commander Inshore Patrol, 14th Naval District, "Attack by USS *Ward* on Submarine on January 2, 1942," January 3, 1942

Radio Log, Bishop's Point Section Base, December 7, 1941

Various other ship's logs, reports, and histories, U.S Naval Historical Center and National Archives and Records Administration

Books

Adcock, Al. *WW II U.S. Landing Craft in Action.* Carrolton, Texas: Squadron/Signal Publications, 2003

Alden, John D. *Flush Decks and Four Pipes.* Annapolis: U.S. Naval Institute Press, 1965

Arroyo, Ernest. *Pearl Harbor.* New York: Michael Friedman, 2001

Bonner, Kermit H. *Final Voyages.* Paducah, Kentucky: Turner, 1996

Burlingame, Burl. *Advance Force Pearl Harbor.* Kailua, Hawaii: Pacific Monograph, 1992

Caras, Roger A. *Wings of Gold.* Philidelphia & New York: J. B. Lippincott, 1965

Clark, Curt. *The Famed Green Dragons. The Four Stack APDs.* Paducah, Kentucky: Turner, 1998

Cohen, Stan. *East Wind Rain.* Missoula, Montana: Pictorial Histories, 1981

Crenshaw, Russell Sydor Jr. *South Pacific Destroyer,* Annapolis, Maryland: Naval Institute Press, 1998

Dickey, LCDR John L II. *A Family Saga: Flush Deck Destroyers 1917–1955.* Waldoboro, Maine: Prints Charming, 1999

Donovan, Robert J., *PT-109.* New York: McGraw-Hill, 1961

Dictionary of American Naval Fighting Ships Vol. 1–9. Washington DC: U.S. Government Printing Office, 1959–1981

Falk, Stanley L. *Decision At Leyte.* New York: W.W. Norton, 1966

Friedman, Norman. *U.S. Destroyers — An Illustrated Design History.* Annapolis: U.S. Naval Institute Press, 1982

Griggs, William L. *Preludes to Victory: The Battle of Ormoc Bay in WW II*. Hillsborough, New Jersey: Atlantic Press, 1997

Hoyt, Edwin P. *MacArthur's Navy*. New York: Orion Books, 1989

_____. *The Glory of the Solomons*. New York: Stein and Day, 1983

Kinderman, Bernard J. and Kenneth C. Swedberg. *USS Ward Fires First Shot-WWII*. St. Paul, Minnesota: First Shot Naval Vets, 1983

Klobuchar, Dick. *Pearl Harbor: Awakening a Sleeping Giant*. Bloomington, Indiana: 1st Books Library, 2003

McGee, William L. *Bluejacket Odyssey 1942–1946*. Santa Barbara, California: BMC Publications, 1997

_____. *The Amphibians Are Coming*. Santa Barbara, California: BMC Publications, 2000

_____. *The Solomons Campaign 1942–1943*. Santa Barbara, California: BMC Publications, 2002

Morison, RAdm Samuel Eliot. *History of United States Naval Operations in World Ward II*. Boston: Little, Brown, 1947–1990

_____. Vol. III *Rising Sun in the Pacific 1931- April 1942*

_____. Vol. IV *Coral Sea, Midway & Submarine Actions May-August 1942*

_____. Vol. V *The Struggle for Guadalcanal August 1942- February 1943*

_____. Vol. VI *Breaking the Bismarcks Barrier. 22 July 1942–1 May 1944*

_____. Vol. VIII *New Guinea and the Marianas March 1944-August 1944*

_____. Vol. XII *Leyte June 1944-January 1945*

Prange, Gordon W. *December 7, 1941,* New York: Warner Books, 1988

Preston, Anthony. *Destroyers*. London: Bison Books Limited, 1977

Silverstone, Paul H. *U.S. Warships in World War II*. Garden City, New Jersey: Doubleday, 1965

Toland, John. *But Not in Shame, Vol. I*. New York: Random House, 1970

Watts, Anthony J. and Brian G. Gordon. *Imperial Japanese Navy*. Garden City, N.J.: Doubleday, 1971

Watts, Anthony J. *Japanese Warships of World War II*. Garden City, N.J.: Doubleday, 1966

Wilmott, H.P. with Tohmatsu Haruo and W. Spencer Johnson. *Pearl Harbor*. London and Cassell. 2001

Unpublished Studies

Hackler, Ken. *The First Shots in a Very Long War*. Eagle, Nebraska: 2003

Interviews with Ward *Crewmen and Families*

Service time on Ward *shown in parentheses, followed by date of primary interview.*

Baldwin, Byron, son of Baldwin, Russell, Lt. (jg), Tyler, Texas, (9/18/44 — 12/7/44), February 2004.

Ball, Robert, S2c, St. Paul, Minnesota, (1/29/41— 6/11/42), November 30, 2002.

Bukrey Edward, GM1c, Houston, Texas, (1/29/41/—12/7/44), November 2002.

Campion, Walter, TM2c, South St. Paul, Minnesota, (1/29/41— 2/23/43), November 2002.

Dyrda, Joseph, S1c, St. Paul, Minnesota, (1/29/41—12/12/42), September 7, 2004.

Entenmann, John, F3c, Avon, Minnesota, (1/29/41— 6/9/41), September 18, 2005.

Ethier, Orville, MM1c, St. Paul, Minnesota, (1/29/41—12/7/44), August 17, 2002.

Hajdu, Frank, S2c, Speedwell, Tennessee, (1/29/41—12/12/43), September 7, 2004.

Hughes, Dorothy, widow of Hughes, Frederick, S2c, Maui, (1/29/41—12/7/44), September 2004.

Heiberger, Gene, S2c, Bonito, Florida, (1/29/41—12/12/42), September 7, 2004.

Hultman, Gordon, TM3c, White Bear Lake, Minnesota, (1/29/41— 2/23/43), November 2002.

Hurley, Maurice, WT2c, Lakeland, Florida, (1/29/41—12/1/43), November 2002.

Lehner,Willett, SC1c, Stevens Point, Wisconsin, (1/29/41—12/7/44), November 14, 2002.

Merthan, John, F2c, St. Paul, Minnesota, (1/29/41— 8/19/42), November 9, 2002.

Mondo, Gust, GM3c, White Bear Lake, Minnesota (1/29/41—12/2/41), September 2004.

Morgan, James, son of Morgan, David, WT1c, (1/29/41— 2/23/43), Imperial Beach, California, February 2004.

Nolde, Raymond, SF1c, St. Paul, Minnesota, (1/29/41—12/7/44), November 2002.

Peick, Jack, GM3c, Sun City, Arizona, (1/29/41—1/11/43),November 2002.

Pepin, Donald, SM2c, St. Paul, Minnesota, (1/29/41—12/7/44), September 28, 2002.

Pfaff, Kenneth, RM3c, St. Paul, Minnesota, (1/29/41— 4/23/42), August 12, 2004.

Reetz, Russell, MM2c, St. Paul, Minnesota, (1/29/41— 5/28/43), September 28, 2002.

Swedberg, Kenneth , WT2c, St. Paul, Minnesota, (1/29/41— 2/23/43), June 12, 2003.

Thill, Richard , SC2c, St. Paul, Minnesota, (1/29/41— 5/20/44), November 9, 2002.

Thompson, Guy, Ens., Tucson, Arizona, (9/28/44 — 12/7/44), 2004–2005
Zechman, Edward, WT3c, Stillwater, Minnesota, (11/8/41—12/1/43), November 2002.

Other Sources

First Shot Naval Vets of St. Paul organization
Minnesota Historical Society
Hawaii Undersea Research Lab (HURL), National Oceanic and
Atmospheric Administration, at the University of Hawaii, reports/letters
United States Coast Guard
History Channel, *Hotel Street*
St. Paul Dispatch
Honolulu Star-Bulletin
The "Four Stacker," APD Veterans Newsletter
Naval historians Ken Hackler and Tracy White
Letter, Captain Richard E. Farwell, USNR (ret.) to LCDR Arnold S. Lott,
USN (ret.), April 12, 1976.
Discovery Productions and Network Projects, *The Atlantic and the World,* 1992

Index

Numbers in **_bold italics_** indicate photographs.

Aaron Ward, USS (DD-483) 145, 149, 151; sunk 151
Achilles, USS (ARL-41) 200
Adhara, USS (AK-71) 145, 146
Aitape 182, 183; landings 183, 184
Alcibiades, SS 185
Algorab, USS (AK-25) 153
Allen, USS (DD-66): air attack on Pearl Harbor 95; Pearl Harbor patrol 56, 57–58, 60, 61, 100, 117–118, 120
Almandite, USS (PY-24) 129
Aludra, USS (AK-72) 156; sunk 157
Amagiri, IJN 161
Andrews, Ens. Frank 53, 116
Antares, USS (AKS-3): air attack 93; *Ward's* attack on midget sub 75, 74–80, 84, 90
Anthony, USS (DD-515) 179, 180
Arethusa, USS (IX-135) 200
Argonne, USS (AG-31) 99
Ariadne, HMS 193, 197
Arizona, USS (BB-39) 57, 58; sunk 90, 95, 98, 99
Arizona Memorial/Visitor Center 233
Astoria, USS (CA-34) 130
Augusta, USS (CA-31) 64
Australia, HMAS 193
Aylwin, USS (DD-355) 94
Azores Islands 31, 32

Babelthaup Island 198
Bainbridge, USS (DD-1) 13
Bainbridge class destroyers 13–14
Baldwin, Lt. Russell 202, **_203,_** 209, 214, 218
Ball, Robert 42, 43, 105, 113, 127
Ballantine, Robert 158
Ballard, Raymond 145
Ballard, Robert 225, 226, 227
Baltimore, USS (CA-3) 57, 62, 119, 120
Barbers Point Radio Station 88
Bates, Lt. John 33, 34
Bath Iron Works 16
Beale, USS (DD-374) 177

Beazley, Arlo 158
Behme, William 199
Benge, Charles 184
Bennett, Louis 158
Bennett, USS (DD-473) 178, 179
Benson, Lt. Lloyd 131, 135, 178, **_181_**
Bethlehem Steel 16
Bevelaqua, Peter 209, 214
Biak Island 185, 189, 191; landings 185–186
Bisbee, USS (PF-46) 197
Bismarck 226
Black Cat Café 111
Bloch, Adm. Claude 89
Bloch Arena 113, 114
Blue, USS (DD-387) 94
Bobolink, USS (AM-20) 165
Boggs, USS (DD-136) 33, 35
Boise, USS (CL-47) 185, 193
Bougainville Island 150, 152, 158, 162, 163, 165, 166, 178, 218; landings 169–170
Braine, USS (DD-630) 179, 180
Breese, USS (DD-122) 30, 33
Bremerton Naval Yard 131, 132, 136, 137; *Ward* converted to APD 133–135, 138–140
Bridge, USS (AF-1) 51
Bronx Bungalow 111
Brooks, USS (APD-10) 174, 176
Brownson, USS (DD-518) 176
Buchanen, USS (DD-261) 30
Bukrey, Edward **_186;_** leave 135–137; Leyte 197, 213, 215, 218; liberty 109, **_110,_** 112; post-war 225; reserve training 42, 43, 44, 48, 49
Burke, Adm. Arleigh 160

Cache, USS (AO-67) 157
Caldwell class destroyers 15, 16
California, USS (BB-44) 58, 84, 98, 99, 134, 135
Campion, Walter 42, 45, 47, 77, 109, 138, 218
Cape Gloucester 174, 175; landings 176–177

Cape Sansapor 189, 192
Carney, Ens. John B. 213
Cassin, USS (DD-43) 15
Cassin, USS (DD-372) 99
Cassin class destroyers 14
Celeno, USS (AK-76) 156
Centaurus, USS (AKA-17) 184
CG-400 90
Chandeleur, USS (AV-10) 178
Charleston Naval Yard 16
Chavalier, USS (DD-451) 162
Chavalier, USS (DD-805) 219
Chepachet, USS (AO-78) 196
Chew, USS (DD-106): attack on Pearl Harbor 94, 95; Pearl Harbor patrol 56, 57, 58, 60, 62, 64, 65, 69, 98, 101, 120; South Pacific 145
Chikoskia, USS (AO-54) 181
Choiseul Island 166, 168
Christopherson, Ens. Carl 36
Citizen Patriot Award 224
Civilian deaths, Honolulu 94
Claxton, USS (DD-140) 35
Clemson class destroyers 16
Cockatoo, USS (AMc-8) 56
Coggins, Ens. Clyde 36
Colhoun, USS (APD-2), sunk 134
Condor, USS (AMc-14) 56, **_69,_** 74; midget sighting 69, 70, 71–72
Constitution, USS 21
Converse, USS (DD-509) 164
Conway, USS (DD-507) 168
Cooper, Lt. Charles, Md. 167, 202
Coral Sea, Battle of 121, 127, 172
Corry, USS (DD-463) 162, 163, 167
Craven, USS (DD-382) 161
Crescent City, USS (AP-40) 199
Crosby, USS (DD-164/APD-17) 30, 31, 32, 33; Leyte campaign 191, 193, 197, 198; New Guinea 173, 174, 176, 177, 178, 182, 185, 187, 188, 189; Ormoc Bay 210, 214, 216, 217, 218; Solomon Islands 153, 156, 159,

164–166, 168, 169, 180;
trans–Atlantic flight 31, 32
Crossbill, USS (AMc-9) 56, 69, 74
Cumberland, USS 21
Cummings, USS (DD-365) 54,
65, 85, 94
Curtiss, USS (AV-1) 145
Cushing, USS (TB-1): first US
torpedo Boat 13
Cuttlefish, USS (SS-171) 59

Dale, USS (DD-353) 94
Daniels, Ernest 58
Davis, Com. Milton 22, 29, 30,
33, 34
Day Star 145
Decatur, USS (DD-5), first US
destroyer 13
Deimos, USS (AK-78) 156; sunk
157
Delphy, USS (DD-261) 30
Dennebrink, Lt. Francis 36
Dent, USS (DD-116/APD-9) 30;
New Guinea campaign 173,
182; South Pacific 156, 162,
164, 166, 169, 173
depth charge attacks on:
December 7, 1941 87, 88, 93,
94, 96; December 1941 97, 98,
100, 102, 103; midget sub on
December 7 81, 82, 83; 1942
117, 119, 121–122, 129;
1943/1944 144, 201
depth charges 14, 26, 50
DeRosia, George 219
Destroyer Divisions (DesDiv):
DesDiv 5 30; DesDiv 12 33;
DesDiv 14 30; DesDiv 17 35;
DesDiv 18 30, 33, 34; DesDiv
42 130; DesDiv 80 56, 120, 126,
129, 131
Dickerson, USS (APD-21) 178,
179, 180, 182, 184
Dickinson, Lt. Clarence 98
Dinagat Island 197, 198
Dionisopoulis, Panagiotis 80
Dixie, USS (AD-14) 152, 153, 180
Dobbin, USS (AD-3) 184, 187, 193
Domogall, Ambrose 76, 77, 127
Dorsey, USS (DD-117) 30
Doughty, Lt. Hartwell 53, 62, 71,
127, 129; attack on midget sub
76, *84*, 86; reserve training 39,
47, 48
Downes, USS (DD-375) 99
Drayton, USS (DD-366) 177
Dubuque, USS (PG-17) 40
Duchin, Paul, drowning 198–
199, 213
Dunlap, USS (DD-384) 161
Duval, William 126, *186*

Earle, Capt. John 88, 89
Eaton, USS (DD-510) 166, 169
Ebusu Maru No.2 86, 87

Egeria, USS (ARL-8) 200
Eichenberger, USS (DE-202) 202
Ekblad, Kenneth 137, 138
Ellet, USS (DD-398) 157, 158
embargo of Japan 38, 62, 66, 67
Emirau Island 180, 181
Entenmann, John 218
Enterprise, USS (CV-6) 64, 90,
97, 98, 102, 117; friendly fire
incident 95
Epping Forrest, USS (LSD-4) 182
Erskine Phelps, USS 149, 151, 153
Espiritu Santo: in New Guinea
campaign 177, 179; in Solomons
campaign 145, 151, 152, 153,
156, 157, 165
Etamin, USS (AK-93) 184
Ethier, Orville 9, 62, 63, 120, 151,
186; leave 136; liberty 108, 111,
112, 114, 172; Ormoc Bay 209,
213, 214, 215; Pearl Harbor
attack 77, 92, 93; post-war 218,
219, 225; reserve training 42,
43, 44, 46

Fahrenholt, USS (DD-491) 152,
153, 164
Fanning, USS (DD-385) 15
Farragut, Com. David 17
Farragut, USS (DD-348) 94
Farwell, Ens. Richard 62; land-
ings in 1943 143, 146, 167, 168;
New Guinea 178, 199; Ormoc
Bay 204, 205, 207, 210, 212–
216, 217, 219; post-war 223
Fenton, Clarence 49, 81, 112,
135, *186*, 211, 215
Fiji Islands 144
Fink, Alfred *186*, 210
First Shot Naval Vets of St. Paul:
activities 220–224; formed 219
Flanagan, Harold 46, 80, 112
Fletcher, USS (DD-445) 145, 146,
148, 165
flush deckers 15, 17
Flusser, USS (DD-368) 177
Foote, USS (DD-511) 164
Ford Island 54, 55, 57, 95, 101
47th Naval Reserve Division 53,
124, 127, 140, 143, 149, 171, 179,
181, 185, 218; activation 45;
training 39–47; post-war 218–
220
48th Naval Reserve Division 39,
43
four-pipers 15
four-stackers 15, 38, 133, 134
14th Naval District 63, 86, 88, 89
Fowler, Lt. (jg) Irv 138
Fratto, Frank 53, *186*, 213
French Frigate Shoals 120
Fritzham, Peter 58
Fullam, USS (DD-374) 178, 179
Fuller, USS (AP-14) 148
Furuno, Lt. Com. Shigemi 74

Gamble, USS (DD-123/DM-15)
30, 33, 145
Gearin, Howard 76, 112, *186*
George Clymer 148
Gerner, Louis 78
Gill, John 218
Gilmer, USS (APD-11) 174, 176
Goepner, Ens. Oscar 53, 127,
129; attack on midget sub 70,
76, 81, *84*, 85; reassigned 131
Gorman, Robert 57
Grannis, Com. Laurence 74, 76,
93
Green Islands 178, 179
Grefe, Ens. Theodore 48
Gregory, USS (APD-3) 134
Gridley, USS (DD-92) 32
Gridley, USS (DD-380) 157, 158,
161
Griep, William 49, *186*
Gruenning, Daniel 80, 105
Guadalcanal 64, 130, 133, 134,
142, 145; advance base 145–151,
153–158, 161–165, 169–171, 174,
177–178, 180, 203
Guantanamo Bay, Cuba 29, 30
Guardfish, USS (SS-217) 165
Guest, USS (DD-472) 178, 179
Gwin, USS (DD-433) 153; sunk
159

Hajdu, Frank 42, 83, 218
Halford, USS (DD-480) 178, 179
Halibut, USS (SS-232) 129
Halmahera Island 191, 192
Halsey, Adm. William: at Pearl
Harbor 90, 95, 98; sinking of
I-70 98; South Pacific 162, 168,
174, 178
Hamilton, USS (DDE-141/DMS-
18) 35, 36, 183
Hampton Roads, Virginia 29
Harmon, USS (DE-678) 177
Harris, Buckner 58
Harris, Harrold 112, 136, *186*
Harrison, Lt. H.A. 36
Harry Lee, USS (AP-17) 184
Havock, HMS, first torpedo boat
destroyer 13
Hawaii Island 12, 52, 60
Hawaii Undersea Research Labo-
ratory (HURL) 226, 227; dis-
covery of midget sub 228, 229
Hayes, Todd 213
Haynie, Ens. Donald 48, 53
Hebel, Lt. Francis 95
Heiberger, Gene 52, 213
Helena, USS (CL-50) 150; sunk
159
Helm, USS (DD-388) 90, 93, 94,
101
Henley, USS (DD-391) 94
Henry T. Allen, USS (AP-30) 184
Herbert, USS (APD-22) 189, 191;
Leyte 193, 199; New Guinea

185, 188, 189; saves *Ward* crewman 198–199
Hercules, USS (AK-41) 199
Hilo, Hawaii 60, 114, 128
Hiro-o, Ens. Akira 74
Hollandia/Humboldt Bay 183, 184, 185, 186, 188, 189, 217, 218; Leyte landings 193, 194, 196, 199, 201, 202, 214; Morotai 191, 193
Holley, Irvin **186**
Holloway, Chuck 228
Homonhan Islamd 198
Honolulu, USS (CL-48) 150
Hood, HMS 58
Hopewell, USS (DD-681) 182
Hopkins, USS (DMS-13) 147, 154
Hornet, USS (CV-8) 119
Hotel Street 111
Howorth, USS (DD-592) 199, 203
Hudson, USS (DD-475) 178, 179
Hueffmeier, Gordon 58
Hughes, Fred **186**, 212, 213
Hughes, USS (DD-410) 204
Hultman, Gordon 42, 44, 46, 83, 121, 136
Humphreys, USS (APD-12) 174, 176
Hurley, Maurice 42, 83, 92, 112, 171, 218, 221
Hutchins, USS (DD-476) 176, 177

I-7 102
I-9 120
I-15 120
I-16 73, 74, 98
I-18 73, 98
I-19 117, 120
I-20 73, 74, 98
I-22 73, 74
I-24 72, 73, 74, 98, 101, 233
I-69 98
I-70 98, 100
Idaho, USS (BB-42) 57
Inagaki, Petty Officer Kiyoshi 74
Inshore Patrol Command 56
Ionia 32
Iron Bottom Sound 142, 149, 150, 153, 155, 157, 160, 162; air raid of April 7, 1943 150–152; air raid of June 16, 1943 155–156
Iwasa, Lt. Naoji 74

Jacob Jones, USS (DD-61), sinking 15
James Baker Francis, SS 177
Jamestown, USS 21
Jankowski, Leo 58
Jenkins, USS (DD-447) 164
Jig Turner 145, 146
John Penn, USS (AP-51) 162
John Rogers, USS (DD-574) 184
Jones, Donald 218

Ka'imikao-o-kanaloa **227**, 231

Kalk, USS (DD-611) 184
Kalvaitus, Al 228
Kaminski, Lt. Com. Harold 88, 89, 90
Kanawha, USS (AO-1) 149; sunk 151
Kane, Lt. (jg) T.P. 34
Kane, USS (APD-18) 182, 184
Kankakee, USS (AO-39) 177
Katayama, Petty Officer Yoshio 74
Kauai Island 114, 126
Kelley, Dr. Christopher 227, 228
Kenmore, USS (AK-221) 157
Kennedy, Lt. jg. John F. 151, 160, 161
Kennison, USS (DD-138) 35
Keosanqua, USS (ATO-38) 74, 85, 90
Kerby, Terry **226**–230
Kilty, USS (DD-137/APD-15) 35; Cape Gloucester 176, 177; Leyte 193, 197, 200; Morotai 191, 192, 200; New Guinea 173, 174, 181, 182, 185, 188, 189; Solomons 158, 159, 160, 162, 164, 166, 168, 169, 178, 180
Kimmel, Adm. Husband 89
Kinderman, Bernard **109**, **222**
Kinimbla, HMAS 184, 187
Knapp, Russell 81
Kolombangara Island 159, 161, 162, 163
Kotaagoeng, SS 157
Kurtz, Lt. Marcus 36

Laettner, Arnold 214
Lamberton, USS (DD-119) 33
Lamson, USS (DD-367) 176, 217
Lang, USS (DD-399) 159, 197
Lansdowne, USS (DD-386) 164
Lardner, USS (DD-487) 164
Lassen, USS (AO-3) 157
Latch, Karl 80, 137
Laub, USS (DD-263) 31, 32
Lavellette, USS (DD-448) 165, 182, 203
LeClair, Giles **186**
Lehner, Willett 59, **186**; December 7, 1941 71, 77, 90; Leyte 199, 208, 213, 215, 217; liberty 112, **115**, 172, 190; New Guinea 175, 202; post-war 217, 218, **224**, 225, 226; reserve training 42, 44, 45, 52; ship's cook 59, 123, 126, 128, 130; South Pacific 150, 156, 179; visit to midget sub 230, 231
Lemely, Lt. Fredrick 135, 143; Leyte, 193, 199, **207**; New Guinea 185, 187, 189; South Pacific, 146, 149, 150, 160, 173, **181**
Leopard, USS (IX-12) 187

Lexington, USS (CV-2) 102, 117, 121
Leyte Island 201, 217; Allied plans 193–196, 203–204; landings 197–198, 200, 204–205; Ormoc Bay 203–205
Liberty 107–115
Libra, USS (AK-53) 153
Liddle, USS (APD-60) 216, 217
Lightning, HMS, first torpedo boat 12
Litchfield, USS (DD-336) 69, 96, 129
Little, USS (APD-4), sunk 134
Liverpool, HMS 60
Lombardi, Daniel 49, 132
Long, USS (DMS-12) 103
Long Island, USS (CVE-1) 143–145
Lorentz, Lt. W.J. 35, 36
Louisville, USS (CA-28) 104
Lovsted, James **186**
LST-70 169
LST-167 164
LST-181 191
LST-207 169
LST-334 164, 169
LST-339 161, 169, 170
LST-340 154, 156
LST-341 154, 169, 170
LST-343 154
LST-353 156, 160, 161, 169, 170
LST-354 169, 170
LST-390 65, 169
LST-395 154,163, 169, 170
LST-396 154, 163
LST-397 154, 163, 169
LST-398 154, 156, 159
LST-399 167
LST-446 165, 169
LST-448 164, 165; sunk
LST-449 164, 165, 169; John F. Kennedy arrival 151–152
LST-459 191
LST-460 164, 165, 166
LST-464 217
LST-467 191
LST-472 164, 169, 191
LST-477 169
LST-485 164
LST-488 163, 164, 169, 170
LST-660 200
LST-706 200
LST-748 200
Ludlow, USS (DD-112) 30
Lunstead, Jake 213
Luppis, Com. Guiseppe 12
Luzon Island 194
Lyman Beecher 145

MacArthur, Gen. Douglas: Allied planning 174, 175, 183, 185, 187, 189; Philippine campaign 194, 203
MacDonough, USS (DD-351) 36

Mahan, Dennis 58
Mahan, USS (DD-364) 177, 205, 206; sunk 216, 217
Manley, USS (APD-1) 134
Mare Island shipyard 50, 51, 130, 132; destroyer construction (1918) 16–17; *Ward* built 18–20, 22, 26, 34, 35
Maritime Self-Defense Force Academy 101, 233
Maryland, USS (BB-46) 99, 105
Maskeawitcz, William 81, 82
Maui Island 57, 59, 60, 114, 126
Mauna Loa, USS (AE-8) 218
Maury, USS (DD-401) 158, 161
Mayrant, USS (DD-31) 30
McCalla, USS (DD-488) 164
McKean, USS (APD-5): Solomons 158, 159, 162, 164, 165, 166, 167, 168, 169, 170, 171
Menominee, USS (ATF-73) 179
Merthan, John 112, 128, 129; attack on Pearl Harbor 103–104; *Condor* sighting 69–72; inside Pearl Harbor 88, **89**; midget sub crews 72–74, **83**; midget submarines 100–101, **229, 230, 232**; plans for Pearl Harbor 67–68; sighting by USS *Ward* 74–76; USS *Ward* attack 76–84
Mindanao Island 194, 195
Minoora, HMAS 184
Minter, Henry 128
Mississippi, USS (BB-41) 57
Moa, HMNZS 151
Mohican, USS 17
Molokai Island 62, 114, 126
Monaghan,USS (DD-354) 88, 90, 93, 94, 101; sinks midget 88
Mondo, Gust 43
Monodock, USS 17
Monongahela, SS (AO-42) 155
Monterey, SS 218
Montgomery, USS (DD-121/DM-17) 33, 102, 119
Morgan, David 54, 92, 93, 114, 138, 218
Moroney, J.T 17, 18, 19, 20, 52
Morotai Island 189, 191, 192, 200
Mount McKinley, USS (AGC-7) 204, 218
Mrozak, Edward 42, **109**, 112
Mugford, USS (DD-389) 176

Nadeau, Tom 42, 92, 112
Nashville, USS (CL-43) 185, 193
Nathaniel Currier 157
National Museum of the Pacific 225, 233
Nautilus, USS (SS-168) 131
Naval Appropriations Act 15
Naval Emergency Fund of 1917 15
NC flying boats 31, 32

Nevada, USS (BB-36) 23, 57, 99
New Britain Island 166, 174–176
New Georgia Island 148, 158–162, 165
New Guinea Island 62, 66, 121, 152, 158, 172, 173, 174, 175; amphibious operations 176, 177, 182–190, 191–193
New Ireland Island 180
New Senator Hotel 111
New York harbor 29, 30, 31
Newman, USS (DE-205) 202
Newport R.I. Naval Base 29, 31, 32
Nicholas, USS (DD-449) 162, 165
Nicholson, USS (DD-52) 15
Nimitz, Adm. Chester 127, 129, 162, 174
Ninth Naval Reserve District 39, 40
Noa, USS (APD-24) 174, 176, 178, 180, 181, 182, 184
Noble Sidney 77
Nolde, Raymond 42, 43, 81, 109, 110, 135, 213
Norfolk Naval Shipyard 16, 29, 30, 33
North Platte Canteen 46
Noumea 115, 148, 154, 155, 157, 171, 172, 179; town 154
Number 3 gun 127, 135, 213, 220; attack on midget sub 78–81, **82**, 83, 84; dedication of 220–221; maintenance of 221; relocation to Minnesota 220

O'Bannon, USS (DD-450) 150, 156, 157, 162
O'Brien, USS (DD-725) 130; rescues *Ward* crew 210, 213, 214; sinks USS *Ward* 215
O'Brien class destroyers 14
Oglala, USS (ARC-1) 98
Oklahoma, USS (BB-37) 23, 98, 104
Operation I 149, 150, 152
Ormoc (Bay) 201, 203, 214; landings 204–205; sinking of USS *Ward* 209, 214–216
Ormsby, USS (APA-49) 184
Ort, Anthony 80, 149
Osterhaus, USS (DE-164) 218
Outerbridge, Lt. William 64–65, 66; air attack 90–92, 93–94, 96; attack on midget sub 76–82, 84, 85, 86, 87; *Condor* incident 70, 71, 72, 73; December 1941 97, 99, 100, 101, 103, 106; Navy Cross **85**, 97; Ormoc Bay 214, 215, 216; post-war **219**, 222, 223; reassigned from *Ward* 130; at war in 1942 116, 117, 119, 121, 122

Pacific Restaurant 111

Paducah, USS (PG-18) 40, 41, 42, 43, 44, 45
Palau Islands 199
Palmer, USS (DD-161) 30, 31, 33
Panay, USS (PR-5), sunk 37
Patapsco, USS (AOG-1) 153
Patterson, USS (DD-36) 30
Patterson, USS (DD-392) 94, 164
Paulding class destroyers 14
Pawnee, USS (ATF-74) 170
Paynter, Howard **186**, 213
PBY-14–1 76, 80–81
PCE-897 219
Pearl, Gerald 77
Pearl Harbor 12, 23, 50, 54, 55, 57, 59, 60, 61, 63, 67, 68, 99, 109, 111, 112, 113, 114, 116, 119, 120, 1211, 126, 127, 129, 132, 134, 140–158, 179, 185, 216; air attack 90, 91, 92; attack on midget sub 76–83; *Condor* sighting 70, 71–72; facilities 54, 55; friendly fire incident 95–96; inner harbor patrol 56, 57, 58, 61, 62, 65, 69, 70, 97–106; naval battle, inside of 88; post-war 220, 223, 226, 233; second bombing of 120–121
Peick, Jack 42, 43, 80, 112, 135
Penetrante, Manuel 124
Pennsylvania, USS (BB-38) 57, 95, 99, 105
Pepin, Donald **186**; attack on midget sub 77; liberty 110, 111, 112, 172; Ormoc Bay 209, 213, 215, 218; reserve training 42–43
Perkins, Lyle 218
Perry, USS (DMS-17) 183
Pfaff, Kenneth 43, 52, 111, 112, 113
Phelps, USS (DD-360) 94
Phenning, Fred 63, 218
Philippine Islands 55, 62, 66, 106; Allied plans 174, 185, 189, 195, 203; landings 196, 197
Phillip, USS (DD-498) 163, 166, 169
Phoenix, USS (CL-46) 185, 193
Pisces IV 227, 228, 229
Pisces V 226, 227, 228, 229
Platt, Ens. Louis 70, 127
Pompano, USS (SS-181) 61
Pringle, USS (DD-477) 162, 166
PT-109 160, 161
Purvis Bay: anchorage in Solomons 159, 160, 161, 163–165, 167, 168, 169, 171, 173, 178, 179, 180, 181; *Ward*'s home in 1943 142, 146, 148, 155
Pyro, USS (AE-1) 184

Quie, Gov. Albert 223

Rabaul 166, 167, 170, 175, 176, 178, 180, 187

Radford, USS (DD-120) 33
Radford, USS (DD-446) 164
Railsback, Lt. Edward 198
Ralph Talbot, USS (DD-390) 94, 164, 165
Ramsay, USS (DD-124/DM-16) 33, 98, 100
Ramsey, USS 39
Raubig, Herbert 76, 78, 179
Reedbird, USS (AMc-30) 56
Reetz, Russell 135, 218; attack on Pearl Harbor 71, 77, 90, 92; Ballard expedition 225, 226; leave 137; liberty *103*, 111, 112, 113, 114; reserve training 42, 43
Reid, USS (DD-369) 177, 184
Reliance, USS (WPD-150) 57
Reno, Lt. Charles J. 34
Renshaw, USS (DD-499) 169, 179
Reserve Fleet 34, 37, 38, 48
Ritz 111
Riverside Tavern 112
RO-34 150
RO-103 157
Robert F. Hand 184
Robin, USS (AM-3) 143
Rocky Mount, USS (AGC-3) 202
Rowe, Lt. Hilary 53
Royal Hawaiian Hotel 109, 110
Russell Islands: amphibious operations 171, 179; supply runs to 147–149, 158

Sacramento, USS (PG-19) 40
Saginaw, USS 17
St. Louis, USS (CL-49) 150, 178
Sakamaki, Ens. Kazuo 74, 225
Salomoni, USS (AO-26) 196
Salt Lake City, USS (CA-25) 143, 218
Sampson class destroyers 14
Sands, USS (APD-13) 147, 148, 149, 174, 176
Santa Cruz, SS 178
Sasaki, Naokichi 74
Saufley, USS (DD-465) 165, 169
Saunter, USS (AM-295) 205, 210
Savannah, USS (CL-42) 126, 218
SC-760, USS 165
SC-761, USS 164
SC-773, USS 161
Schley, USS (APD-14): conversion to APD 135, 138, 140; inner harbor patrol 54, 56, 587, 59, 60, 61, 120, 129, 131, 132; Leyte 191, 192, 193, 197, 198, 199, 202; New Guinea 182, 184, 285, 187, 189; South Pacific 145, 153, 156
Schmitt, Carol 112
Scholtes, William 84, 181
Schroeder, Ens, Clifford Jr. 140
Scott, Lt. Edgar 192, 193
Scout, USS (AM-296) 205, 210, 214, 217

second bombing of Pearl Harbor 120, 121
Seeadler Harbor 187, 196
Self-propelled torpedo, invented 12
Selfridge, USS (DD-357) 164
Service Hotel 112
Shackelford, Rachel 228, 229
Shaw, USS (DD-68) 15
Shaw, USS (DD-373) 99, 176
Shoho IJN 121
Shropshire, HMAS 193
Signourney, USS (DD-643) 169, 171
Skylark, USS (AM-63) 156, 157
Smith, USS (DD-678) 64, 177, 204
Smith class destroyers 14
Smithsonian Institute 220
Smorowski, Wilfred 58
Snead, James 158, 214
Solace, USS (AH-5) 63
Sonoma, USS (ATO-12) 58
sound screens 126
South Dakota, USS (BB-57) 64
Southard, USS (DMS-12) 164
Spratt, James 137, *186*
Stack, USS (DD-406) 159
Stembel, USS (DD-644) 182
Sterrett, USS (DD-407) 148, 149, 152
Stewart, Lt. Norman 199
Stoddertt, USS (DD-302) 36
Strapp, Joseph 150
Stringham, USS (APD-6) 173, 177; New Britain landings 173, 174, 179; Solomons campaign 159, 160, 162, 164, 165, 166, 169, 178, 179, 180
Struble, RAdm. Arthur 204, 214
Suluuan Island 198
Swanson, USS (DD-443) 184
Swedberg, Kenneth 54, 99, 129, 143, 218; liberty 110, 112, *113*; Pearl Harbor 71, 83, 91, 92, 93, 94; post-war 223, *224*, 225; reserve training 42, 45, 46, 49
Sydney, Australia 108, 154, 179; liberty 115, 172–173, 174, 189–190

Talbot, USS (APD-7) 179, 180, 181, 182; Solomons landings 162, 164, 166, 169, 170, 171
Taney, USS (WPG-37) 56, 61, 98
Tanner, Ens. William 76, 80, 89
Taylor, USS (DD-468) 152, 162, 165
Tennessee, USS (BB-43) 99, 105
Terry, USS (DD-513) 179, 180
Thatcher, USS (DD-162) 30, 31, 33
Thill, Richard 63, 138, 144, 181, *224*, 225; attack on midget sub 77, 83, 87; liberty 110, *111*, 112,

114; reserve training, 39, 42, 43, 44, 45, 46, 47; ship's cook, 124, 126, 128, 218
Thirty-One Knot Burke 160
Thomas Freeborn, USS 22
Thompson, Ens. Guy 193, 196, 202, 218–219; Dinagat landing 197–198, 199; Ormoc Bay 205, *206*, 209, 210, 214, 217
Thousand Tonners 14
Thresher, USS (SS-200) 96
Thurmond, Rudolph 187
Tido, John 84
Tiger, USS (WPC-152) 56, 87, 90, 94
Tin Roof 113, 114
Titanic 225, 226
Tomich, Peter, Medal of Honor 99
torpedo boat developments 12–13
Tower, Com. John 32
Trans-Atlantic flight 31–32
Transport Division 12 (Trans-Div12) 166, 169, 170, 174, 176, 178
Transport Division 22 (Trans-Div22) 140, 145; New Guinea, 174, 178, 188, 191, 193, 196; Solomons, 158, 159, 160, 166, 169, 170
Treasury Islands 166, 167
Trepassy Bay, N.F. 31, 32
Trever, USS (DMW-16) 154
Trimmer, Judson 129
Le Triomphant 61
Triton, USS (SS-201) 119
Trotter, Jesse *206*
Tucker class destroyers 14
Tulagi 146, 147, 148, 149, 153, 155, 157; air raid of April 7, 1943 150, 151; supply base 158, 160, 161, 163, 165
Tulsa, USS (CA-129) 172
Tumleo Island 183, 184
Twitty, Jack 116
Two Ocean Naval Expansion Act 38

Units, ground: 1st Inf. Reg. 188; 1st Mar. Parachute Reg. 164, 165, 168; 1st Mar. Raider Reg. 152; 4th Mar. Raider Bat. 164; 4th Mar. Reg. 180; 5th Mar. Reg. 176; 6th Ranger Bat. 193, 196, 198; 7th Marine Reg. 173; 8th New Zealand Brigade Group 166; 19th Mar. Reg. 169; 21st Inf. Reg. 196; 21st Mar. Reg. 169, 170, 176; 25th Medical Bat. 159; 27th Inf. Reg. 166; 27th Reg. Combat Team 160; 30th New Zealand Bat. 178; 33rd Construction Bat. 179; 35th New Zealand Bat. 178;

36th New Zealand Bat. 166; 37th New Zealand Bat. 164; 75th Construction Bat. 169; 77th Inf. Div. 203; 97th Field Artillery Bat. 154; 103rd Anti-Aircraft Bat. 149; 124th Inf. Reg. 191, 192; 126th Reg. Combat team 177; 127th Reg. Combat Team 184; 161st Inf. Reg. 159; 163rd Reg. Combat Team 182; 169th Inf. Reg. 148, 149; 186th Inf. Reg., 185
Utah, USS (AG-16) 98, 99, 100
Uyeda, Warrant Officer Sadamu 74

Vallejo, California 17, 18, 20, 23
Vella Lavella Island 162; forward base on 168, 178; landings on 162, 163, 164, 165
Villalobos, USS (IX-145) 193
Vireo, USS (ATO-144) 188
Virgo, USS (AKA-20) 184
Vitus Bering 153

Wadsworth, USS (DD-516) 179
Waikiki Beach 110, 111, 114
Walke, USS (DD-723) 206
Walker, USS (DD-163) 31
war warning message 63
Ward, Dorothy Hall 20
Ward, Com. James Harmon 20–22
Ward, USS (DD-139, 1918–1922 career): authorization 16; building 18–20, 22–23, 24–25; commanding officers 240–241; commissioning 22–23; crew accommodations 28; decommissioning 36; first crew 25; initial armament 26, 235, 236; launching 20; Panama Canal transit 28, *33;* President Wilson Review 34; Provisioning 24–25; reserve fleet *35,* 36; sea

trials 26, *27;* trans–Atlantic flight 31–32
Ward, USS (DD-139, 1941–1942 career): air attack on Dec. 7, 1941 90–93; armament 52–53, 235, 236; attack on midget sub 74–83; *Condor* incident 69–70; conversion to APD 71–72; discipline 130–13; drills 59; first crew 53; galley 124; leave (1943) 135–138; meals 123–126; reactivation (1941) 38; recommissioning 48–50; sampan incident 86–87; sea trials 49–50; ship's roster 243–253; voyage to Pearl Harbor 51–54
Ward, USS (APD-16, 1943–1944): air raid of April 7, 1943 150–152; air raid of June 16, 1943 155–156; amphibious landings, list of 237; armament 139; citations 238; crossing the equator 144; Dinagat Island landing 197–198; John F. Kennedy incident 160; kamikaze attacks 200–201, 206–208; landing craft 138–139; liberty in Sydney 172–173, 189–190; only fatality 198–199; Ormoc Bay landing 204–205; sinking 214–215; Solomons landings 158–171
Warren, USS (APA-53) 199
Warspite, HMS 61
Wasatch, USS (AGC-9) 192
Waters, USS (APD-8): New Guinea 178, 179, 180; Solomons campaign 158–160, 162–166, 169, 180
Weltevreden 153
Wendt, Arnold 209
West Virginia, USS (BB-48) 57, 99, 104, 112
Westrailia, HMAS 184
Whitehead, torpedo inventor 12

Whitney, USS (AD-4) 157, 178
Wickes, USS (DD-75) 16
Wickes class destroyers 16, 19, 123
Wilkinson, Lt. Com. Robert 130, 135
William Howell, SS 177
Wilmette, USS (IX-29) 40
Wilmingtton, USS (PG-8) 40, 41
Wilson, President Woodrow 34
Windsor, USS (APA-55) 184, 199
Winooski, USS (AO-38) 196
Winter, Lyle 63
Wo Fats 111
Wollerman, Colin 228
Wood, Lt. Hunter 48, 53, 64, 114; CO of USS *Smith* 64
Woodward, William 145
Woodworth, USS (DD-460) 164, 180

Yamamoto, Adm. Isoruku 67, 68, 73, 150, 152, 153; death 152, 153
Yarrow boilers 16
YMCA, Honolulu 109, 111, 112
YMS-119 172
YNG-17 69
YO-21 121
YO-167 147
Yokoyama, Masaji 74
Yokoyama, Shigenori 74
Yorktown, USS (CV-5) 119, 121, 127
YP-514 156
YP-518 156

Zane, USS (DMS-14) 116
Zeal, USS (AM-131) 178
Zeilen, USS (APA-3) 184
Zechmann, Edward 42, 84, 92, 112, 171
Zechmann, Robert 92, 112